Fierce Ambition

ALSO BY JENNET CONANT

*The Great Secret: The Classified World War II
Disaster That Launched the War on Cancer*

Man of the Hour: James B. Conant, Warrior Scientist

A Covert Affair: Julia and Paul Child in the OSS

*The Irregulars: Roald Dahl and the British
Spy Ring in Wartime Washington*

*109 East Palace: Robert Oppenheimer
and the Secret City of Los Alamos*

*Tuxedo Park: A Wall Street Tycoon and the Secret Palace
of Science That Changed the Course of World War II*

Fierce Ambition

✳✳✳✳✳✳✳✳✳✳✳✳✳✳✳

THE LIFE AND LEGEND
OF WAR CORRESPONDENT
MAGGIE HIGGINS

✳✳✳✳✳✳✳✳✳✳✳✳✳✳✳

Jennet Conant

100

W. W. NORTON & COMPANY
Celebrating a Century of Independent Publishing

For information about permission to reproduce selections from this book, write to
Permissions, W. W. Norton & Company, Inc., 500 Fifth Avenue, New York, NY 10110

For information about special discounts for bulk purchases, please contact
W. W. Norton Special Sales at specialsales@wwnorton.com or 800-233-4830

Manufacturing by Lake Book Manufacturing
Book design by Beth Steidle
Production manager: Julia Druskin

ISBN 978-0-393-88212-4

W. W. Norton & Company, Inc., 500 Fifth Avenue, New York, N.Y. 10110
www.wwnorton.com

W. W. Norton & Company Ltd., 15 Carlisle Street, London W1D 3BS

1 2 3 4 5 6 7 8 9 0

For Kay,
with gratitude

I wouldn't be here if there were no trouble.
Trouble is news. And gathering it is my job.

—Marguerite Higgins

CONTENTS

✳✳✳✳✳✳✳✳✳

Fierce Ambition

Prologue

We did all kinds of crazy things that I never would
have done by myself. But you know, you don't
want to be shown up by a beautiful young lady.

—Peter Furst, *Stars and Stripes* correspondent

ON SUNDAY, APRIL 29, 1945, MARGUERITE HIGGINS WAS AT THE
Third Infantry Division command post outside Augsburg, in southern
Germany, trying to figure out a way to get to Dachau. Less than twenty
miles of unsecured road separated her from the infamous concentration
camp, which was about to be freed by American forces. Maggie intended
to be there when the tanks rolled in.

A twenty-four-year-old unknown cub reporter with the *New York
Herald Tribune*, she had teamed up a few weeks earlier with Sergeant
Peter Furst, a combat-seasoned correspondent with the army newspaper,
Stars and Stripes. Furst's chief attraction was that he was in the possession of a jeep, which meant he could take her where she wanted to go
without some military minder ordering her to the rear. Hitchhiking a
ride with the young soldier reporter, she had covered the Third as it tore
through Bavaria in pursuit of the fleeing enemy, capturing the Nazi cit-
adel at Nuremberg after a furious house-to-house siege, followed by the
astonishing bloodless capitulation of Augsburg. The latter was orchestrated, in part, by Furst, who had called ahead to the Burgermeister and
warned him that resistance was futile. When a German emissary later
brought word that the Burgermeister, with the help of the local anti-Nazi

underground, was prepared to hand over the city to the Americans, Augsburg fell without a fight on April 28. Delighted at the outcome, the two correspondents congratulated themselves for their part in such thrilling wartime exploits as "taking cities by telephone."

Early the next morning, Maggie, all smiles, had tried to persuade the commander of the Third Division, Maj. Gen. John Wilson "Iron Mike" O'Daniel, to fly her to Dachau in a spotter plane. She might as well have asked for the moon. A tough-talking soldier of the old school, he told her bluntly that it was a good way to get killed. What was left of the Wehrmacht, the armed forces of Nazi Germany, was in their sector. The XV Corps, the Seventh Army's major tactical unit, was moving south with the mission of taking Munich, and it had three of its infantry divisions—the Forty-Fifth, the Forty-Second, and the Third—in line. O'Daniel's orders were to push to Munich, where the enemy might be preparing to make a last, desperate stand. The other two infantry divisions were targeted to pass through the Dachau area, but the concentration camp was not his military objective.

Undeterred, Maggie put the proposition to Furst: "Let's drive to Dachau."

He looked at her and decided—it was worth the risk. Many of the neighboring villages were draped with white flags. In the prevailing mood of surrender, he thought the odds were pretty good that they could make it across the enemy-held territory in one piece. The tricky part was that no one seemed to know the exact location of the camp, just that it was in or near the town. But Furst could see Maggie was ready and eager, and he did not want to let her down. Then the driver of a half-track armored vehicle, who had overheard them discussing their plans, offered to lead the way ahead of the troops. They set off immediately, racing ahead of the Forty-Second (Rainbow) and Forty-Fifth (Thunderbird) Divisions, hoping to be the first reporters on the scene.

The liberation of Dachau would be front-page news. For Maggie, it would also be a huge scoop—a chance to break the biggest story of her career in the waning days of the conflict. The Third Reich was almost finished. Hitler's soldiers were in headlong retreat. She was running out of war and out of time. She had been tipped off that the Americans would be closing in on Dachau that day. But the military situation was fluid, and the rapid and confused advance, also spearheaded by two combat commands from the Twentieth Armored Division, encountered more resistance than expected. No one was more surprised than Maggie to discover that a battle for a neighboring village was not yet over, and instead of converging on the camp with their triumphant troops, she and Furst were staging an ad hoc liberation operation of their own.

While Dachau was no great distance on the map, it turned out to be an interminable, white-knuckle drive. Maggie felt very exposed in their open jeep with *Stars and Stripes* stenciled in large letters on the front, a fluttering American flag on the side announcing their allegiance. She held her breath as they rolled past group after group of heavily armed Wehrmacht soldiers bearing rifles, pistols, and grenades.

The bedraggled infantrymen seemed to know the war was all but over and willingly offered up their guns, piling them into the back of the jeep until it was full. Even after the soldiers were disarmed, Maggie's sense of danger did not abate. She had not been in the field long enough to feel comfortable around so many weapons. Dressed in a bulky German Army jacket and fatigues to disguise the fact that she was a woman, her blond curls tucked into a fur-lined hat with ear flaps, she was less afraid of being shot than that one of the grenades rattling around the back of the vehicle would explode.

When they reached the quaint, cobblestoned town of Dachau, they stopped to reconnoiter. They could hear the sound of artillery fire in the north, where at least one of the American divisions was still engaged. The local townspeople were friendly, however, and some even cheered them on. The civilians they questioned told them that white flags had been spotted flying from buildings on the southern edge of the camp. Encouraged, they decided to head in that direction. A quick end run around the fighting and they would be there.

While passing through town, they encountered five U.S. Army jeeps belonging to Brig. Gen. Henning Linden, the stocky, fifty-three-year-old assistant commander of the Forty-Second Division, and his men. Linden had orders to take a small reconnaissance group and secure the concentration camp. His instructions were to keep the inmates contained and "frozen in place" until medical help arrived and the necessary relief supplies could be brought in by support columns. With his party was a sixth jeep bearing two Belgian journalists, accompanied by two former French prisoners of war who knew how to get to Dachau and offered to serve as guides.

Maggie and Furst joined the caravan and fell in behind the lead jeep, where Linden's aide-de-camp, Lt. William Cowling, acted as scout. With the assistance of the French POWs, they had no difficulty finding their way. By the time they approached the outer edge of the camp that afternoon, the tanks of the Forty-Fifth Division had already arrived at the western end and were moving in.

As the sprawling Dachau complex came into view, Maggie could see it included dozens of administrative and factory buildings, barracks, officer quarters, and training grounds. She scanned the horizon, searching for any sign of the barbed-wire enclosure where the prisoners were kept. It was the most segregated and secure part of the camp, a separate walled-off compound ringed by guard towers, electrified fencing, and along the western side, a canal that functioned as a moat.

Unlike Linden and his men, Maggie had some idea of what lay ahead. At the time, most American soldiers knew almost nothing about the concentration camps beyond the rumors of terrible conditions and mistreatment—rumors many, including Maggie herself, had tended to discount as exaggerated wartime propaganda about the enemy. But as one of the first reporters inside Buchenwald, which she had toured shortly after it was liberated on April 11, she had seen firsthand that all the tales about the Nazis' extreme brutality were true. Her story about the unimaginable horror at Buchenwald had helped to reveal to the world the reality of the concentration camps as a cold-blooded operation designed to degrade, torture, and exterminate untold thousands of inmates. Now she was intent on being the reporter who broke the news of the Nazi atrocities at Dachau as well.

From what she and Furst had gathered at headquarters, it was going to be grim. One of the oldest concentration camps in Germany, Dachau was established in 1933 to hold upwards of five thousand political prisoners who had voiced opposition to Adolf Hitler's regime. But the numbers had quickly swelled as the Nazis began rounding up Jews, Jehovah's Witnesses, and homosexuals, as well as ever-increasing numbers of foreign nationals from occupied territories, so that the inmate population soon far exceeded the camp's maximum capacity. With Germany on the brink of collapse, the conditions in the camp had steadily deteriorated, with the situation becoming desperate in recent months. There were rumors that the food and water had run out some days ago, and the prisoners, who had staged a revolt, were trying to hang on until help arrived. Maggie steeled herself for the depths of human misery they would encounter.

As they drew nearer, she was hit by the smell. It was the gut-churning stench of decay. Outside the perimeter of the Dachau complex, on a railroad siding that led into the camp, was a long, stationary train consisting of some forty boxcars. Dead bodies spilled out of the open doors and gondola cars. Men, women, and children had been packed in like cattle and left to die of hunger, thirst, and disease in the locked carriages. The grotesque cadavers, with their distorted features, bony arms and legs protruding at odd angles from ragged blue-and-gray-striped prison uniforms, told of the agony of their final journey. Alongside the tracks there were mounds of corpses, the rotting remains of those who had been hauled out and shot. They had been piled in heaps, waiting to be carted away and buried or burned in the crematorium. Trash, excrement, and scraps of clothing littered the ground. Sickened by the sight, she bent double and retched.

General Linden gave the order to press on. They turned right and drove up the wide avenue that led to the arched main entrance of Dachau, topped by a large wreathed swastika and imposing stone eagle. They made their way deeper into the camp, where they encountered a small reception party. Waving a makeshift flag of truce—a white sheet tied to a broomstick—was the acting commandant of the camp, Lt. Heinrich Wicker, accompanied by his aide and by a Swiss civilian, Victor Maurer, a member of the International Red Cross. Wicker, a strapping young officer who was smartly attired in his helmet and uniform, saluted with a

"Heil Hitler," clicked his heels, and stated that he was ready to turn over the camp and all of its prisoners. His stiff, formal demeanor, and arrogant expression, so outraged Maggie that she slapped him.

Furst offered to act as interpreter. Born and raised in Germany, he had fled with his family after the Nazi regime began its persecution of Jews and later emigrated to the U.S. As the American soldiers and reporters gathered around the acting commandant in a semicircle, Wicker explained that he had been put in charge only the previous day, and that most of the garrison—members of the SS, or *Schutzstaffel*, Hitler's elite guard—had absconded. Only a small contingent remained behind—about fifty soldiers—to man the machine-gun placements in the guard towers. Furst told Wicker that General Linden would accept the official surrender of the camp on behalf of the American Army.

While the terms were being negotiated, Furst asked the acting commandant to assign someone to take him and his colleague directly to the inmate enclosure. Maggie, hovering on the periphery, was close enough to hear the conversation but not so close as to attract notice. She knew that Furst, wary of the high-voltage fencing, had requested an escort as a precaution because he had no intention of trying to open the prison gates himself.

Just then they heard the sputter of a machine gun coming from somewhere on their left flank. Everyone dove for cover. Furst thought that they were being fired on by the SS guards. As soon as the shooting stopped, he and Maggie took off in a hurry in their jeep, with Cowling and one of his MPs perched on the hood. A German prisoner served as their escort. Everything happened so fast that no one agrees on exactly what took place next, and over the decades it has been the subject of varyingly self-serving accounts from all involved.* According to Maggie and Furst, a group of SS guards suddenly appeared beneath one of the concrete watchtowers. Looking up, the reporters saw that the observation platform was crammed with more sentries, rifles at the ready. There was no point in trying to run.

With a show of false bravado, Maggie called out to them in German:

---

* For more about the Dachau liberation controversy, see the endnotes.

"Kommen Sie hier" (Come here). "They obediently came toward us," she recalled, "hands in the air." Then another group of a dozen or more guards descended from the tower. A total of twenty SS guards approached and forfeited their weapons. Cowling had the men remanded into custody.

The lieutenant and the two journalists then got back in the jeep, and with their German escort in tow, they crossed a small concrete bridge over the canal that bordered the enclosure. Directly in their path, a man lay dead—a bullet through his head. The German prisoner dismounted and shoved the body aside. They proceeded straight to the two-story *jourhaus*, or entrance building, that served as the main guard post of the compound, and without delay went through the heavy wrought-iron gate emblazoned with the Nazi slogan "Arbeit Macht Frei."

"There was not a soul in the yard when the gate was opened," Maggie wrote in the *Herald Tribune*. "But the minute the two of us entered a jangled barrage of 'Are you Americans?' in about sixteen languages came from the barracks 200 yards from the gate. An affirmative nod caused pandemonium. Tattered, emaciated men, weeping, yelling and shouting 'Long live America!' swept toward the gate in a mob. Those who could not walk limped or crawled."

In the wild outpouring of joy that followed, the prisoners sprinted toward her, running, falling, tripping, getting up and rushing forward again. One flung his arms around her in an enthusiastic embrace that lifted her off her feet. Another enveloped Furst in a huge bear hug. The ecstatic inmates picked up their liberators and tossed them in the air, hoisting them from shoulder to shoulder and parading them around the camp, too excited to detect a soprano voice of protest rising above their raucous cheers. The atmosphere of hysteria produced unbelievable strength in men who looked too weak to stand, and Maggie was quickly overwhelmed by the welcoming stampede. One man, who had his arms around her neck and was kissing her effusively, heard her cry out that she could not breathe. He hastily disengaged, and fended off the others.

"Mon Dieu, mon Dieu, c'est une femme!" he exclaimed in French. "Pardon, madame." A Catholic priest, and a deputy of August Cardinal Hlond, Primate of Poland, he was deeply chagrined by his mistake. Once

Maggie had wriggled out of the priest's embrace, off came the goggles and helmet. "Golden locks fell down, and a pert made-up face was revealed," recalled Nerin Gun, a Turkish reporter who was one of the internees in the yard. "The officer was a woman, a war correspondent, Marguerite Higgins of the *New York Herald Tribune*."

After half an hour of being tossed around by the delirious throng, the rattled and badly bruised reporters were relieved to see the American soldiers at the gate. When General Linden spotted Maggie in a crush of prisoners, all of them clamoring to tell her their name and nationality, he bellowed, "What the hell are you doing in there? Don't you know the place is raging with typhus. Come here!"

There were thirty-three thousand half-starved, lice-infested, traumatized prisoners incarcerated at Dachau, many ill with typhoid. The barracks were filled with the sick and dying. Linden had to keep the POWs locked up until the medics arrived. If the prisoners got out and spread the epidemic throughout the countryside, it would be a disaster. Inside the compound, tensions were running high. The prisoners were working themselves into a fever pitch at the prospect of their imminent liberation. A crowd by the fence was on the verge of rioting after being told they could not leave because of the quarantine edict.

When Maggie approached the gate, Linden reached through the grillwork and grabbed her by the collar, shaking her hard in an effort to knock some sense into her. At that moment, a sea of inmates surged forward, flattening her against the gate and winding her for several seconds until she managed to extricate herself with the help of Cowling, who had entered the yard ahead of her.

"God dammit to hell!" she swore, her initial astonishment giving way to anger as she twisted loose. Finding her voice, she shouted at Linden at the top of her lungs, giving vent to all the pent-up fear and anguish of the past few hours. "Lay off. Let go of me. I've had my typhus shots. I'm in here doing my job."

She went back to work, determined to interview as many of the prisoners as she could. She had been told that some of the greatest brains of Europe had spent more than eleven years interred at Dachau. She was not going to leave until she learned the fate of several important political and religious hostages—Léon Blum, the last premier of France; Kurt von Schuschnigg, the former chancellor of Austria; Prince Leopold of Prussia; and Martin Niemöller, a prominent anti-Nazi Lutheran pastor. If they were found alive and rescued, it would make headlines around the globe.

Recognizing that the situation was fraught with danger, Linden directed his men to remove the reporters and to restore order in the enclosure area, which was now filled with thousands of shoving, screaming prisoners. Hundreds had climbed onto the roofs of the barracks. Some were frantically trying to break out via the *jourhaus* building, and the windows and doors had been burst open and people poured through.

By now, soldiers of the Forty-Fifth Division, Lieutenant Colonel Felix Sparks's Third Battalion of the 157th Infantry Regiment, had reached the *jourhaus* gate. Sparks's task force, which also had orders to secure the camp, had been busy clearing buildings and capturing small clusters of German troops. The shots the reporters had assumed were fired by the SS probably came from Sparks's platoon, which had fought its way from the other side of the Dachau complex. The shots could also have come from the coal yard, where several of Sparks's men, enraged by what they had seen at the death train, opened fire on a large group of captured SS guards, killing at least seventeen, and wounding as many as seventy-five.

By the time Sparks got control of his men and made his way to the *jourhaus* gate, the prisoners had worked themselves into a frenzy. In response to the growing violence in the compound, Sparks ordered his men to fire their weapons in the air to quell the bedlam. Over the next hour, soldiers of the Forty-Second and Forty-Fifth managed to push all the prisoners back inside the enclosure, seal it off, and install their own armed guards.

Once the crowd had quieted down, Linden agreed to allow the journalists to see the rest of the camp. Even as darkness fell, and Furst urged that it was time to go, Maggie kept on reporting. She kept searching for the special prisoners until an inmate told her they had been evacuated days earlier. When at last she and Furst departed, it was late and the roads were clogged by convoys. At midnight, when the RCA transmitter shut down, they were still miles away from the press center.

She had cut it too close and missed her deadline. It would be another sixteen hours before she could file again. She spent the night dozing fitfully by the side of the autobahn, cursing the stubbornness that had resulted in a rookie error. However, the next morning, instead of heading straight back to the press center, she could not resist taking a slight detour to Munich, less than ten miles away, to watch the fabled Bavarian city, where Hitler rose to power, fall to the Seventh Army.

The *Herald Tribune* ran two front-page stories, datelined April 29 (delayed) and April 30, both carrying Marguerite Higgins's byline. The stories, written in a hurry, did neither event justice. Still, her stark eyewitness account of the liberation of Dachau was the exclusive of a lifetime, and it made her a star overnight. The other journalists who were there that day also wrote personal stories for their respective publications, but none was as dramatic as Maggie's. She had cast herself as a prime player in one of the most momentous episodes of the war, relegating to the accompanying soldiers and their nameless officers only minor walk-on roles, ensuring her own place in history.

Furst's vivid portrayal of her jubilant reception at Dachau was the stuff of legend. In his dispatch for the *Stars and Stripes*, he described how Higgins, a pretty, blonde war correspondent, was the first person to announce to the inmates that they were free: "She shouted the glad tidings in German, French and English to the prisoners, who crowded around her with tears streaming down their worn and bearded faces." He wrote that the men, most little more than walking skeletons, fell to their knees in gratitude, grasping her hands and kissing the dusty ground at her feet "in one of the maddest and most heart-rending liberation scenes of the war."

A few days later, Furst learned he was being called back to the Rome bureau. He and Maggie went their separate ways. Their journalistic partnership, and road romance, were short-lived. But emboldened by his fearless approach, a brand of courage she adopted as her own, Maggie had succeeded in establishing her reputation as a nervy and relentless reporter who, as her editor put it, "covered the news with a singlemindedness and determination . . . that brooked no interference." In only eight weeks at the front, she had reeled off an amazing string of page-one stories and made her byline known to the newspaper's hundreds of thousands of readers in Europe and the U.S. The *Tribune* would take to trumpeting the daring exploits of their "girl correspondent" behind enemy lines, establishing a practice that, for better or worse, would become a hallmark of her career. From then on, the mere fact of Maggie's presence in the combat zone would be almost as newsworthy as the events she covered.

To cap it all off, she and Furst were awarded campaign ribbons for outstanding service with the armed forces under difficult conditions. Maggie later learned the recommendation was made by her erstwhile foe, General Linden. During the worst chaos at the camp, when several prisoners flung themselves against the fence in an attempt to get out and were instantly electrocuted, she rose to the occasion and helped to alert the inmates to the danger. Taking over the loudspeaker system, she warned of the lethal current and urged calm until Furst and another officer found someone to flip the master switch and cut the power.

Within twenty-four hours of Dachau's liberation, Hitler was dead. A little more than a week later the war in Europe was over. On May 8, the night of Germany's total surrender, Maggie attended a victory party at a magnificent castle near Salzburg, where Joachim von Ribbentrop, Hitler's foreign minister, had once hosted important guests. Schloss Klessheim was now the palatial headquarters of the Third Division, and O'Daniel had invited all his regimental and battalion commanders, plus the half dozen correspondents who had been covering them, to celebrate the end of the war.

At exactly one minute after midnight, they all went out on the balcony and watched as the artillery guns fired into the black sky. For nearly half an hour, red and blue flares and tracer bullets flashed in a patriotic display, and the percussive guns echoed across the valley, while the surrounding mountains roared and shook with the noise. High above in the Obersalzberg, outside the remote village of Berchtesgaden with its toy-like houses, was the Berghof, Adolf Hitler's beloved alpine retreat. And far above, clinging to a rocky outcrop, was the famous Eagle's Nest, his spectacular mountain aerie, said to be a fiftieth-birthday present from his inner circle. Days earlier, O'Daniel had superseded his orders and sent the Seventh Infantry Regiment to capture Berchtesgaden so that his men would have the honor of taking the Nazi prize. An hour before the Americans arrived, Hitler's SS bodyguards had set fire to the Berghof. All that was left, Maggie wrote, was a "gaunt blazing ruin."

The day after they took the Nazi stronghold, she toured the smoldering remains of Hitler's once-lavish home, with its cavernous living room and grand marble staircase now blackened by flame. The enormous picture window was missing, chunks of melted glass on the sill. The bombproof cellars, which survived intact, contained great stores of food, liquor, linen, china, and silver—the latter engraved with the monogram AH—used for elaborate dinners. The Nazis, with their mania for tunnels, had honeycombed the hillside with underground bunkers. Some were fitted out as apartments, stuffed with paintings, books, records, photographs, and odd bits of personal memorabilia, which the GIs were busy pilfering as souvenirs. Bypassing the loot, Maggie ran the chalet's majordomo to ground and got the lowdown on the Führer's private life and mistress, Eva Braun. It was another fabulous scoop.

For Maggie, it was a night of mixed emotions. Since the start of the conflict, she had only one ambition—to be a war correspondent. She had worked her way up at the paper from a lowly stringer to city reporter, paying her dues and proving that she was as good as the boys. After the Normandy landings, she had begged to be sent abroad, knowing it was the last best chance to make her name. In mid-March, she had left the Paris bureau for the front lines in Germany, an untested reporter whose editors still maintained that the combat zone was "no place for a woman." Now it was May 8, V-E Day, and the war that had been raging for five years had come to an end. The Big Show was over. There would be no more battles to write about, no conquered cities to cover, no screaming headlines underlined in red. The soldiers she had interviewed earlier that day on the spacious, tree-shaded castle grounds had greeted the news of the armistice with deep relief, but for Maggie it was a disappointing anticlimax.

As she stood there on the balcony in Salzburg watching the fireworks, it struck her that she was probably the only one there who was not happy at the prospect of going home. Unless she could find another war to cover, the journalistic glory that she had just achieved, and so fiercely coveted, would soon fade. Peace was the last thing she wanted.

1

✳ ✳ ✳ ✳ ✳ ✳ ✳ ✳

Freak

Good candidates for the job are rare. They
are usually freaks who have landed head
first at their goal either by opportunity,
hard work or luck—most often luck.

—Ishbel Ross, *Ladies of the Press*

MAGGIE HIGGINS GREW UP IN A MIDDLE-CLASS FAMILY IN AN
ordinary middle-class neighborhood in Oakland, California, a city, she
recalled with scorn, "noted for neither character nor excitement."

Her craving for the latter was cultivated from an early age by her
father, who spoon-fed her tales of his thrilling escapades as a World War I
ambulance driver—he joined a field-service unit attached to the French
army—and later as a flier. Irresistibly drawn to the action, Lawrence Daniel Higgins abandoned his studies at the University of California to cross
the Atlantic to help fight for the Allied cause. When America entered the
war in 1917, he answered the call for pilots "to darken the skies over Germany," and after completing his flight training with the Lafayette Escadrille, a legendary squadron composed largely of American volunteers,
he was commissioned a second lieutenant in the U.S. Army Air Service.
He was a tall, strikingly handsome Irishman whose early manhood was
marked by astonishing risk and adventure, an unparalleled experience
during which he served alongside men of honor and purpose, bonded with

them at the front, and felt his life and work were imbued with "the human closeness and magnificence of character that danger sometimes provokes."

Like many of his generation, he never got over it. After the war, he could not settle down. Civilian life seemed meaningless. Nothing Larry tried his hand at could ever match the intensity of his time in France. In her father's telling and retelling of his exploits as a flying ace, Maggie perceived his dismay at the "flabby routine" of their suburban existence. Through some strange twist of fate, the dashing young aviator and his lovely French wife, Marguerite, whom he had chanced upon in the Paris metro during an air raid, had ended up marooned in a drab little house on Chabot Court, a new residential tract on the unfashionable side of Oakland. They lived on a dead-end street, surrounded by matching two-story stucco bungalows with "neat little rows of lawns and neat little rows of people," Maggie wrote, with the limited horizons imposed by geography and the genteel poverty that was their lot.

Years later, some of her family members and childhood friends would take exception to the uncharitable description of the sleepy cul-de-sac that appeared in her memoir, protesting that Chabot Court was a perfectly respectable if modest neighborhood. It was populated by young, upwardly mobile couples who were attracted by the opportunities in Oakland, a fast-expanding city that was home to numerous thriving manufacturing industries. But this was lost on Maggie, who shared Larry's dreams of adventure in far-off lands and saw Chabot Court only through his disappointed eyes.

Growing up, Maggie adored her father and absorbed his unhappiness, his loneliness, and his longing for the tumult, camaraderie, and derring-do of his youth. Larry was a great talker. She listened with wonder to his heart-pounding yarns, the daring maneuvers and close brushes with death. She pored over the many photographs of him in uniform—lovingly framed and on display—leaning against a tilting, rickety-looking biplane. She admired the campaign ribbons and wings on his chest, the Sam Browne belt that wrapped around the shoulder and trim waist of his tunic, and the breeches tucked into high leather boots. He had commanded the skies in his Sopwith Camel, had performed amazing feats, and she burned with pride in him and basked in the light of his reflected glory.

To Maggie, her father seemed every bit as gallant and brave as the famous pilot Charles Lindbergh, to whom everyone said he bore more than a passing resemblance. Like "Lucky Lindy" he, too, had once returned to a hero's welcome. "And so THE WAR became to me the whole complex of things that made my father's eyes shine with emotion," Maggie wrote, "and his Irish spirit escape the humdrum as he talked of the days on the Marne, of the Rhine, of the flights on the line, and of Paris. Always of Paris."

In assessing her lifelong affinity for faraway places, she didn't need to look any further than the romantic tales she heard of her parents' early married days. After the armistice of 1918, the newlyweds sailed to the Orient, where her father had secured a job as an assistant freight manager with the Pacific Mail Steamship Company. The decision to go abroad was motivated less by the lure of travel than by Larry's realization that it would be impossible to continue his studies at the Sorbonne and support a French war bride. But that did not prevent Maggie from being enchanted by their picturesque account of life in colonial Hong Kong, then a bustling British port town, the harbor filled with sampans and majestic junks with billowing sails like storybook pirate ships. In her imagination, it was a mysterious, multifaceted jewel of a city, as sparkling as Oakland was dull.

It was where Maggie—known as "Gri" to her family—was born on September 3, 1920. Her doting parents retained a Chinese amah, or nursemaid, as was the custom, and so it was that her first words were in Cantonese. In baby photos, she looks like an exquisite porcelain doll, with her mother's fine features, corn-silk hair, and huge sapphire eyes. When as a six-month-old infant she was stricken with malaria, her worried parents whisked her to Dalat, a mountain resort in what was then French Indochina (later Vietnam) to recover, advised by the doctor that the cool, clear air would work its cure.

Later, it would seem prophetic to Maggie of her life's tempestuous course that the family patriarch had met a tragic end in that same part of the world, dooming his heirs to an uncertain fate. Her maternal grand-father, Count Georges de Godard, an aristocratic young officer with the French colonial forces, had died in Indochina in the 1890s after being wounded and contracting a tropical fever. Her mother had been born in scandalous circumstances to the count, who had offended his titled clan by marrying the fetching Marguerite Piguet, whom he had plucked from peasant stock. Only months after the count's demise, his young widow died from injuries sustained in a hunting accident. Rejected by the de Godards, the couple's three children—Marguerite and her two older sisters, Genevieve and Juliette—were left penniless and placed in an orphanage. By all accounts, their impoverished Piguet relations came to the rescue. Their maternal grandmother went back to work as a postmis-tress in Lyon, France, and saw to the upbringing of the girls. But Indo-china remained forever a tragic land in the family lore.

The Higgins family's Hong Kong odyssey was not nearly as eventful, nor did it last long. Although they could afford to live in relative luxury on Larry's salary, the overcrowding, sanitation problems, and growing unrest made it an unsuitable place to raise a child. Recurrent strikes and anti-imperialist protests threatened the shipping trade. In the fall of 1923, Larry booked their return passage to the U.S., and to California, where he had lived before the war.

Looking back, Maggie wrote that it must have been difficult for her parents to be suddenly transplanted to the dreary Oakland suburb that was so removed from the colorful expatriate life they had enjoyed. Her father, a feisty redheaded Irish charmer with undeniable presence, was soon accepted, despite a tendency to drink too much, and occasional dis-plays of temper, as on the day he became so enraged at his daughter that he chased her down the street while clad only in his shorts. Although he suffered from black moods, and there was never a time he did not view the world through a vale of tears—and predict approaching doom—Larry was immensely likable. He was a striver, with a steadying sense of discipline and direction. He had made it the hard way, working his way up from running the local Piggly Wiggly grocery store to managing the Oakland branch of the Bank of Italy, which served San Francisco's large immigrant community. Even though money was tight, he presented himself as a man with prospects. People naturally took to him and gave him the benefit of the doubt.

Her mother was a different story. She looked nothing like her American counterparts, with her platinum updo, high heels, and chic clothes copied from the pages of *Vogue*. She was just eighteen when she got married, and was younger, thinner, and sexier. Being Latin and less inhibited, she compensated for the lack of excitement in life at Chabot Court by inventing crises of her own. As Maggie put it, "She was possessed of the Frenchwoman's love of *le grande drame*." Outbreaks of weeping, bursts of gaiety, tipsy solo tangos in the living room, serial flirtations, and fainting spells were all part of her repertoire.

During the Depression, when money was short and life especially boring, the fainting spells became more frequent. Maggie could spot one coming on from across the room. Once her mother collapsed in the midst of a cocktail party, bringing a half dozen concerned guests to their knees, all of them hysterically chafing her hands and bleating in alarm. Maggie simply got up, excused herself, and walked out of the room. She despised her mother's phony act—would forever despise phoniness of any kind—and refused to play along. She just headed for the kitchen to fetch the bottle of ammonia and a wet cloth. But afterward, her calm exit was the subject of talk. To the good folk of Chabot Court, she seemed an odd, cold sort of child.

In truth, she was mortified, but Maggie would have done anything rather than give the tut-tutting local gossips the satisfaction of seeing her squirm. She was embarrassed by her parents' behavior—their noisy quarrels and bouts of drinking—and the odious conjecture it elicited. As she would bitterly recall, people were only too happy to have an excuse for "feeling superior to those who broke from the norm."

Any child newly arrived in America has an overwhelming desire for conformity, especially when it comes to family. Maggie yearned to fit in. Unfortunately, to their Oakland neighbors, her parents were an exhilaratingly exotic and endlessly diverting pair. Her mother filled the house with mementos of their sojourns in France and the Far East—watercolor prints, bright silk rugs, and carved jade figurines—which guaranteed people would regard her, like the decor, as different, foreign, and quaint. "I'd never seen anyone like her," said Jean Craig, a childhood friend who grew up on the same street and attended mass at the same Catholic church. "They were a strange, glamorous family, unlike any I'd ever known—or ever would know."

Maggie was conscious of her bizarre background, what she took to calling her "Irish-French-Hong-Kong-heritage." Her attempts to blend in were frustrated by the fact that she spent the better part of the next few years in France with her aunts, who were like second mothers to her. Maggie divided her time between her Tante Genevieve's vineyard at Prissé near Mâcon, and her Tante Juliette's home at Bornel-sur-Seine, outside Paris. Because Marguerite wanted to "start her education off right," Maggie began her schooling in France alongside her cousins. By the time she returned to the U.S. for good in 1927, she was bilingual and so far ahead of the other children that she skipped two grades.

To make matters worse, conversation chez Higgins tended to be a mixture of her mother's classic French, her father's soldier patois, and her own slightly accented English, with the occasional Chinese expression thrown in. When excited, Maggie never quite knew what was going to come out of her mouth. It was many years before she felt entirely comfortable speaking English. Despite her best efforts, even decades later she would still catch herself slipping in some Gallic idiom leftover from her youth. Always a slow writer, who labored over her style and sentence construction, she envied those who, from the cradle, effortlessly acquired the rhythm and flow of their native tongue.

When she first came to Chabot Court, Maggie felt like an outsider. She was teased mercilessly by the kids on the block, who mocked her broken English and ran after her chanting insults: "Dirty Chinamen! Dirty Chinamen! You were born in China." Furious and humiliated, Maggie would flee home to her father in tears. Larry, who was indifferent to convention but never to cowardice, taught her to never run from trouble. It was a matter of principle. He would turn her around and send her back outside to face her tormenters. Larry wanted her to have grit, and to always be able to stand on her own two feet. "From the time she was little," he told an interviewer, "I tried to make her realize that she need never fear anything or any individual." Though still smarting, Maggie did as she was told. Above all, she wanted to please her father.

Larry was convinced his daughter was special and took charge of preparing Maggie for the big future that awaited her. If he sometimes indulged her, it was because he saw in her qualities of his own. Her acumen and enormous vigor matched his, along with a ferocious inner drive. A reckless streak was in evidence early. When the kids on Chabot Court were all learning to ride their bicycles, Maggie was the first to try with no hands. She was also the first to master the perilous trick of riding with her feet on the handlebars, coasting round and round the circular drive in front of her house wearing a triumphant "Look at me" grin. If anyone tried to race her, she approached hair-raising speeds. She was always good for a dare. "She led in exploits where we would often be cowering in the background," recalled a neighborhood playmate.

Larry Higgins felt his daughter was not so much competitive as she was perfectionist—focused on achieving her own self-imposed goals. "There was only one place for Marguerite, and that was the top, regardless of what she was doing," he said. "But it was strictly for her own satisfaction, not to beat somebody else out."

Her father helped her map a course of high achievement and instilled in her a confidence in her own judgment and a combative stance toward the naysayers in life. They spent hours together, happily engaged in any kind of activity that took them outdoors, from hiking and horseback riding to fishing and swimming. Like him, she was tall and slender, with a coltish physique that suggested both delicacy and strength. She became a wild tomboy, diving fearlessly into the crashing surf, looking back only to catch a glimpse of his nodded approval. If imprudence led her to go too far, and she found herself flailing against the tide, he expected her to extract herself and know better the next time. No whining or whimpering was allowed. Maggie rose to every challenge he put to her, eager to be a contender. Years later, she would write of a similarly close father-daughter relationship, "She preferred his company, and he in turn realized that a child so independent-minded and strong-willed needed a firm guiding hand."

Larry also imparted his enthusiasm for news of armed conflict around the globe, and together they followed the reports of the Japanese invasion of Manchuria in 1931 and, two years later, the accounts of Hitler's coup in Germany. When the Spanish Civil War erupted in 1936, the writer Ernest Hemingway chronicled the fighting, and his dispatches were not to be missed. Maggie devoured Hemingway's novels. She promised herself that if there was another war, she would be there, if only to find out for herself "what force cuts so deeply into the hearts of men."

As a brooding adolescent, she once angrily confronted her father about the discrepancy between his sentimental view of war and Hemingway's much darker vision, especially the sense of futility and loss described in the opening pages of *A Farewell to Arms*. It seemed to her that aviators were able to remain comfortably above the fray—unless they were shot down and plunged to their death—and knew nothing of the pain and suffering endured by the common fighting man. But this was just one of their running battles. "They used to fight like cats and dogs," recalled a family member. "They both felt so intensely about everything, and they both had an opinion on every subject, and they never agreed on anything, but liked each other a great deal."

Maggie would always recollect her father with affection, but even in her carefully edited selection of childhood memories, her mother emerges as a stern, demanding figure. Like her husband, Marguerite was ambitious for their beautiful daughter, but a life of deprivation had robbed her of any illusions, so that her role in the family was that of critic and constant prod. She knew all too well that beauty could be ephemeral. It needed to be polished and carefully molded into something of lasting value. From the beginning, she was determined her child would have the best possible training—the best education, the best music lessons, the best dance classes. Maggie shone with potential. She was a star. With the right opportunities, and that face, she would go far. At various stages in her daughter's development, Marguerite was convinced she had produced a prima ballerina, a concert violinist, and a first-rate scholar.

Larry and Marguerite gave their only child every advantage their precarious finances would allow. Then, in 1928, Larry lost his job when the Bank of Italy merged with the Bank of America and many of the employees were laid off. It was a cataclysmic event Maggie would always remember as the "worst moment" of her life. It knocked the foundations out from under her world, and the awful repercussions left her with a permanent sense of vulnerability, so that she never again felt entirely safe and secure. A few months later, the stock-market crash wiped out what remained of their savings. Larry eventually found another position with a brokerage firm, but people had little left to invest and business was slow.

During the bleak Depression years, the Higgins family, like so many, was forced to economize. Accustomed to sacrifice, Marguerite found a way to supplement their income so her daughter would not have to do without. She began by tutoring the neighborhood children in French to pay for Maggie's ballet class as well as her violin and piano lessons. Then Marguerite took a job as a French teacher at the Anna Head School, an exclusive girls' academy, where she arranged for her daughter to be enrolled as a hardship case with the tuition fee waived.

In January of 1930, a few months before her tenth birthday, Maggie entered the sixth grade at the Anna Head School. Named for its founder, a legendary progressive educator, the school was located near the Berkeley campus of Head's alma mater, the University of California, where she was among the first women graduates. One of the finest college-preparatory programs in the Bay Area, the school attracted the daughters of California's best families. Maggie was never allowed to forget how fortunate she was to be afforded such a rare opportunity, and she struggled valiantly to prove herself worthy. Her mother expected her to "justify her free education" with long hours of study and academic excellence. "Every time my report card showed a B instead of straight As, I risked the loss of the scholarship," she recalled. "More important, any such flirtation with the second-rate meant a real humdinger of a crisis at home."

Her memories of those years are underpinned by a lingering resentment at the relentless pressure to perform. As soon as she completed her homework, Maggie was expected to put in four to five hours of daily practice on the violin, a routine rigidly enforced until the day she graduated. As a teenager, there were times when the oppressive grind became too much, and she found release in little fits of rebellion. Usually this took the form of some harmless mischief or practical joke. These minor acts of insurrection resulted in poor marks for deportment, the only bad grades she received in high school.

There were few such lapses in her self-imposed discipline. The need to earn her keep had been drilled into her early, pushing her to ever-greater efforts to succeed and inspiring even greater anxiety about whether she was good enough, had done enough, or had truly given it her all. The strain, she later noted, was hardly conducive to what psychologists would consider a "stable personality, or what is known as serenity."

The tensions at home, and the perpetual nagging worry about money, magnified her self-doubt. At night, Maggie struggled to shut out her parents' escalating quarrels, the progress of which she could monitor from her bedroom by her father's thundering French, "which would become louder and more incomprehensible in proportion to his outrage." In order to function, she turned inward. Gradually she developed a kind of "numbness." A form of control, and self-defense, it allowed her to disengage from the domestic storms and concentrate on her studies.

Her sensitivity to being a scholarship student at a school attended by some of the richest girls in California only accentuated her feelings of inadequacy, of always being the odd one out. She saw herself as a "financial misfit" among the likes of Diana Dollar, of the Dollar Steamship Line family, and Phyllis Head, of the Hills Bros. coffee empire, who flouted their wealth and lived in sprawling mansions nestled in Oakland's foothills. Mercifully, Anna Head had a uniform—a no-nonsense gray pleated skirt and white blouse designed by the tennis player Helen Wills Moody, an alumna. In school, at least, she did not have to try to keep up with her posh classmates, with their stylish clothes and weekend shopping expeditions to San Francisco's gilded emporiums.

Since she could not live up to their splendid standards, Maggie found other ways to shine. She excelled at sports, compelled by her competitive instinct and hunger for victory. Anna Head placed a premium on athletics: it boasted the most lavishly equipped gymnasium of any girls' academy on the West Coast and had the first women's basketball team in the country. Winning was Maggie's route to acceptance and success. She went on to become a star athlete. Her school records show she channeled her prodigious energy into every kind of activity and contest: junior-year captain of the basketball team; senior-year captain of the swim team; hockey, volleyball, and baseball teams; tennis; president of the Athletic Association; Girl Reserves; Life-Saving Corps. A picture of the champion field-hockey team shows Maggie in the center of a row of smiling girls, all brandishing their sticks. Her expression is portentous, resolute. Hips forward, head cocked provocatively, she stares down the camera.

Maggie graduated at the top of her class. Although an honor student, her prizes were all for prowess on the field. At her June commencement, looking almost ethereal in a long white dress, her hair a crown of spun gold, she collected the Athletic Pin. At sixteen, the only sign she gave of any literary aspirations was revealed in a yearbook entry: her stated goal in the "Horoscope" section was to become a drama critic; for the "Probable End" that every student was asked to imagine, she settled for court reporter. Journalism was not yet the focus of her ambition, but Maggie had already begun to mull the possibility that working for a newspaper might be a viable career. At the very least, it was a job that might get her out of Oakland.

She later lamented that her "bookworm status" prevented her from having much of a social life, but her classmates recall that she was well liked, had a friendly, outgoing personality, and was regarded very much as a leader. They remember a slender blonde with an enviable figure, big blue eyes like saucers, and a whispery voice. She was not the prettiest girl in her year, though she was very pretty. But there was something about Maggie—a singular air of self-assurance that made her stand out. It was a quality that made her seem equal to every occasion, and up for anything.

She was accorded the slightly awed respect of one who was seen as more experienced—or, at least, more in the know—when it came to boys than most girls their age. Apart from a few chaperoned dances, the only members of the opposite sex any of them spent time with were the boys from the neighborhood. Maggie had her pick of the motley crew. "It was pretty rough on us girls unless she decided she didn't like a boy," recalled a friend. "They were all so crazy about her we wouldn't have had a chance."

Some school friends theorized that because Mrs. Higgins was French, and not bound by the same strict Anglo-Saxon morality that governed their mothers' every waking thought, she had more advanced ideas on sex. How else to explain Maggie's impish urge to shock? She did not shy away from the intimate or the indiscreet. Once, during a weekend outing with the YWCA, she scandalized her peers in the middle of a midnight gab session by suddenly asking who among them had "gone the limit." Anne Duhring was struck absolutely dumb by the boldness of her question. Such things were not openly discussed. Maggie thoroughly enjoyed their discomfort. But for all her apparent sophistication, her blasé attitude, Duhring thought Maggie was probably just as naive as the rest of them, "though she sometimes came out with what we thought were very worldly ideas."

In the fall of 1937, Maggie enrolled in the University of California at Berkeley. To her great relief, she had been awarded a scholarship that would help defray the cost and leave her with enough money to cover her dormitory fees. A number of Anna Head graduates would be in the incoming freshman class, and the most pressing question facing the group was which sorority to pledge. Maggie and her friends spent the summer debating the pros and cons of each house, meticulously planning their wardrobes for rush week, and nervously anticipating the round of alumnae receptions, luncheons, and teas during which the girls and their mothers would be carefully vetted. Newspaper clippings neatly pasted in her scrapbook record the giddy succession of parties that autumn, held in a sweltering heat wave. Maggie's set aspired to Alpha Phi, which, while not at the pinnacle of the social order, was only a rung or two below.

To her infinite regret, Maggie did not make the cut. She was not recruited by Alpha Phi, where her friends delightedly pledged. She was blackballed. She professed not to care but privately, Maggie was disconsolate. She hid her hurt at the bitchy speculation about the reasons for her ostracism—it might have been her family's Catholicism, her mother's pronounced French accent, or their small house on the wrong side of Oakland. In any event, the thin-lipped committee had concluded the Higgins family did not quite rate. It was Maggie's first public failure, and it stung. Phoebe True, a friend who pledged Alpha Phi, observed that while Maggie prided herself on her individualism, she "desperately wanted to be part of the 'in' crowd."

While her old companions became caught up in the social whirl, Maggie quietly went her own way. She made a show of going through the motions for the first year, then drifted from the scene. The whole tedious and trivial pageant had lost its charm for her. If the ultimate goal of sorority life was to meet the right fraternity boy, there was more than one way to win at that game. She plunged into the campus social life with an almost vengeful spirit. Soon all the boys were after her. She quickly earned a reputation as a "party girl," according to Billy Jones, a fellow member of the class of '41: "She tended to have a good time all the time. She didn't seem very serious-minded."

One thing she was serious about, however, was trying out for the college paper, the *Daily Californian*, which was one of the best student-edited publications in the country and wielded considerable influence. Editorial-board appointments were highly sought after. Freshmen were relegated to gofer jobs and proofreading and were expected to work their way up the ranks. Competition was stiff, and frequent staff cuts designed to weed out the slackers kept them on their toes.

Maggie surprised her friends by being very keen from the start. She worked herself ragged. Her first byline—an interview with the illustrious English novelist W. Somerset Maugham—was so gratifying she made up her mind to become a journalist and, "without fail, a career woman." She devoted so much time and energy to working on the paper that she paid little attention to her appearance, often turning up to meals in wrinkled clothes, her blond curls askew. One day, Jean Craig bumped into her emerging from the basement offices of the *Daily Cal* at full speed "wearing one blue sock and one white, with apparently no knowledge of her attire."

The newspaper and its select hierarchy became all-consuming for her. Anne Duhring, who also hoped for a reporter slot, was struck by Maggie's almost desperate need to prove herself. She studied the older students whose efforts made it into print with a kind of feral envy, as though her very survival depended on it. Edmund Antrobus, who worked on the *Daily Cal* and later became a war correspondent, admired her burning desire to improve and recalled her being so intent on honing her writing skills that she asked a mutual friend for advice. Others, who were initially flattered by her interest, grew wary, and learned not to leave notes on their desk. Maggie, some said, had a habit of biting the hand that mentored her.

In June of her freshman year, Maggie got a summer job at Yosemite National Park. She would be waiting tables in the dining room at Camp Curry, which would allow her to spend several months in the mountains while still earning enough to pay her college expenses. When Jean Kelly, a high school friend who was in her class at Berkeley, learned she would also be working at Yosemite, the two girls began excitedly making plans, when Kelly's mother overheard an offhand comment that changed her mind about letting her daughter go. In the course of propounding her latest theory on the merits of unmarried sex, Maggie had argued that their time away presented an ideal opportunity to gain some invaluable experience, asserting in a tone of irrefutable logic, "You wouldn't buy a horse without riding him?"

Kelly's mother did not approve. She informed Jean that Maggie was perhaps a bit too mature, and it might be better if she did not accompany her to Yosemite. When Jean saw her friend again that August, there was no doubt Maggie had enjoyed "a very equestrian summer: She had discovered Bertrand Russell and was an advocate of free love."

By her sophomore year, Maggie was experimenting with new ideas, and testing the limits of her newfound freedom. She did just enough to maintain the grade point average required by her scholarship, played the violin in the orchestra, participated in the Little Theatre plays, and still found time for a hectic romantic life. She openly flaunted her sexual liaisons, picked up and discarded boyfriends at a dizzying pace, and brazenly thumbed her nose at middle-class propriety. In an era of chaperoned parties and strict curfews, Maggie broke all the rules. Her flagrant disregard of the sorority-house sign-out system and general lack of decorum raised eyebrows, and brought her before the university's judicial committee for violating the code of conduct for women.

Unconcerned, she penned a series of spirited letters to the editor of the *Daily Cal* suggesting it was time Berkeley coeds considered broadening their outlook, and announcing her interest in carving out a role for herself unconstrained by the gender limitations placed on previous generations. In one wickedly sardonic missive, she made fun of the boys who fretted that the "Household Science" majors were less interested in getting an education than in "looking for a husband." While that might be the case, Maggie taunted, the UC Berkeley boys had no reason to hide, as they were hardly marriage material. She advised the "poor little fellows to stop quivering in their boots for fear some girl will scoop them up."

Her budding feminism was not ideological as much as an innate attitude: she simply did not believe that men were better at anything than she was, and she did not want the fact that she was a woman to mean that she would be treated any differently. The suggestion that she might be in college pursuing anything other than a degree infuriated her.

The male students quickly learned not to be taken in by her sweet appearance. At first glance, she had the face of an angel, but she was earning a reputation on campus as something of a hellion. Her old circle of friends was not sure what to make of this new rambunctious, spiky side to Maggie. While they regarded it as just another phase, it was, nonetheless, disquieting. Raised to believe that women could not be too careful, and that a large part of their future married life would be determined by their present associations, they were alarmed by the change in her behavior. She was moving too far, too fast. "We were a very protected, conservative, 'properly-raised and properly-conducted' bunch of young ladies," explained Marjorie Barker, who was in the same pledge group at Gamma Phi Beta. "She had what we considered to be a very liberal viewpoint on dating and politics." Today, no one would give her conduct a second thought, she added, but back then, Maggie was "years ahead of her time."

Under the influence of a series of left-wing beaux, Maggie began flirting with campus politics. Inspired by the idealistic spirit of Franklin Roosevelt's New Deal, she was among an increasing number of students in the thirties who were concerned about the social injustice, unemployment, and hardship endured by so many during the Depression. She was animated by a sincere belief that her generation could forge a better society. The economic panacea envisaged by socialism made enough of an impact on her that she wrote a long essay in which she argued fervently that the abolition of poverty would "do away with thievery and greed."

Her conscience had been aroused, in part, by two brilliant and charismatic Berkeley professors: Haakon Chevalier, who taught French literature and was one of the most liberal and outspoken members of the predominantly conservative faculty; and Stanley Moore, a handsome young teaching assistant in the philosophy department, who was active in the student movement.

Tall and blond, with the chiseled features of a Greek god, Chevalier was the Pied Piper of radical Berkeley campus politics. He and his wealthy wife gave large parties at their spectacular hilltop home, which became the informal center of left-wing college society, not to mention the local Communist Party. He mixed with highbrow luminaries, from the physicist Robert Oppenheimer to the playwright Lillian Hellman, as well as assorted intellectuals, artists, poets, and actors. Maggie frequented his political salon, read the books he loaned her on Hobbes, Rousseau, and Hegel, and listened to him preach about labor unions and civil rights. Chevalier thought she showed great promise and considered her to be one of the bright lights on campus.

To Maggie, the twenty-four-year-old Moore was an especially intriguing figure. She first encountered him the fall of her freshman year, when he led her philosophy section. He had received his BA from Berkeley in 1935, was elected to Phi Beta Kappa, spent a year at Harvard immersed in philosophy, and then returned to the University of California to continue his graduate studies, teach, and work on his doctorate. Descended from a wealthy, prominent San Francisco family, with the lanky good looks of a matinee idol, he was someone her mother would have considered a good catch. He was also an avowed Marxist and a member of the Young Communist League.

Moore believed that in a time of upheaval and engagement around the world, he and his fellow students needed to take a stand. "Fascism and communism seemed the main combatants," he recalled of his youthful ardor, "and the positions in between seemed rather pale by comparison." Maggie was captivated by him. Her friends thought Stanley Moore and his politics were "pretty far out." One pal could not resist remarking that Maggie's interest in the cause extended "only to those meetings where the men are."

In the fall of 1939, Maggie became increasingly caught up in the strident anti-fascist debates and emotionally charged anti-war protests that rocked Berkeley's campus. On September 1, German troops marched into Poland. Two days later, Britain and France, both allies of the invaded nation, fulfilled their vow to declare war rather than allow further German expansion. Stunned by the disastrous turn of events, some political leaders were insisting that only American intervention could save Europe from Nazi domination. A bitter dispute erupted on campus between the isolationists and interventionists, and Maggie was in the middle of it. She reacted against the increasing hysteria of Allied sympathizers like her parents, and sided with the peace lovers. Committed to the idea that another war would solve nothing, she campaigned vigorously against mandatory conscription and handed out pacifist leaflets.

As the news from Europe worsened, she and the other reporters on the *Daily Cal* scrambled to cover the political unrest on campus and abroad. The student publication challenged the establishment and frequently tussled with the administration. Their reporting took on a new importance. "It was very tense," recalled James Pool, a classmate and senior editor on the paper. "We were teetering on the edge of war. We were under a lot of pressure."

Maggie scored her first big feature in February 1940 in a special two-part article on the rumblings of revolution in Mexico. The stories were based on her observations of the country, where, during the three-week Christmas break, she had gone on vacation accompanied by no less than the paper's roguish managing editor, Raney Reid. In "Mexico: No Bed of Roses," Maggie reported, "There are no elections as we conceive of them in the United States. The GOVERNMENT candidate always wins, no matter who is the people's choice." It was a coup for a junior, but it was Maggie's repeated use of the royal "we" in the piece that confounded her colleagues: Was this the editorial "we," or was she brazenly telegraphing her latest conquest?

Raney Reid was smitten. Rumors spread that he had proposed. What few people knew was that Maggie had come back from their holiday jaunt to Mexico pregnant. Only nineteen, she was adamant that she did not want to get married. And she did not want a baby. After a tense family council, the decision was made that Larry would drive her to Phoenix, Arizona, where there were reliable, if illegal, abortion clinics. Predictably, her mother was beside herself. It was difficult to tell what bothered Marguerite more—the church's moral strictures, the social embarrassment, or the risks associated with the medical procedure. Maggie put up a brave front. Her predicament was hardly unique. Gossip columns often hinted at the Hollywood starlets who frequented Arizona clinics, registering under assumed names and recovering in nearby motels.

She returned to college chastened, but unbowed. There is no record of her pain or regret, save a confession to a close friend years later that she had undergone one too many terminations in her youth. Maggie did not allow herself to dwell on past mistakes. With characteristic fortitude and determination, she moved forward. She would not indulge in self-pity. "What's done is done," she would always say, never one to agonize once she had settled on a course of action.

The loss of innocence had been violently swift. She had thought she was ready for everything life could throw at her, but she did not emerge from the experience unscathed in body or spirit. Her anger sustained her. Anger at her ignorance, and at the implied shame of her ordeal. Her rebellion against her parents' "petit bourgeois" values now took a new form. She threw herself into the radical student movement, giving vent to all her rage and frustration. She began hanging out with members of the Young Communist League. Then she latched onto Fred Vast, a journalism student who wrote for the *People's Daily World*, the official Communist Party newspaper, who convinced her to take part in their campus rallies.

Despite her high-pitched little girl's voice, Maggie discovered an aptitude for public speaking. She joined in the student demonstrations against the coming war in Europe and the peacetime draft. She had her father's flair for bombast, and she liked being the main attraction. On September 3, 1940, several of her former Anna Head classmates were astounded at the sight of Maggie giving a fiery speech "practically on a soapbox" at Sather Gate on Telegraph Hill, surrounded by other dissenters. Directly attacking university president Robert Gordon Sproul for his announcement that he would not tolerate student opposition to the national defense effort, she insisted on their right to freedom of speech. "There is much talk about it being unpatriotic to oppose conscription," she declared. "I think it's unpatriotic to threaten to expel students because they oppose conscription."

Some members of the contentious crowd of spectators booed. A few fraternity men hurled rotten tomatoes. Maggie, slim and erect, her face pinched with embarrassment, remained defiant. Her sorority sisters were appalled to see one of their own making such a spectacle of herself. They took it as proof that she had morphed into a "pink communist type." When the incident made the local papers, Maggie was chastised by a covey of sorority-house officers for giving their chapter a bad name. After that, she severed all ties with Gamma Phi Beta, though by then the antipathy was mutual. Maggie followed up with an unapologetic column in the *Daily Cal* stating that the frat boys had ended up with ketchup on their faces because their "tomato-throwing faux pas" had resulted in far more publicity for the radicals' cause.

Her father, a died-in-the-wool Republican, was a grim-faced witness to the melee at Sather Gate. A firm proponent of military preparedness, Larry believed war was inevitable and was itching to find a way to get back into uniform. On that morning, however, he had put his prejudices aside and come to campus to support his daughter. Even though he hated her socialist politics, and did not agree with a single word she uttered, he admired her passionate certainty. She had the courage of her convictions. Before he left, he dropped a dollar in the hat that was being passed around the crowd of onlookers.

Her childhood mandate to redeem herself through work drove Maggie to new extremes on the *Daily Cal.* She cranked out editorials against the conscription bill, and continued to advocate for members of her sex, creating a column entitled "What About the Women?" Tackling the problem of bias at the battlefront, she wrote that the sudden appearance of Swedish women war correspondents—"blonde, beautiful, and efficient"—had reportedly had a destabilizing effect upon the men, as "the scramble for their favor broke up the fraternal congeniality." Fortunately, she observed with trademark acidity, the news-gathering blondes managed to establish themselves, peace was restored, and "the war within a war was over."

Despite her best efforts, Maggie did not cover herself with glory at the *Daily Cal.* There were no complaints about her work, just her methods. She had returned from a summer job at the *Tahoe Tatler* with a swelled head and an expanded appetite for bylines. Greedy for recognition, she ignored the paper's carefully contrived rotation system and repeatedly blundered into the upperclassmen's beats. "Time and again, it seemed that her single-minded pursuit of a story blinded her to the territorial assignments of her fellow reporters," recalled Duhring. "There would be cries for her scalp, and she would be scolded, and repentant, and it would quiet down until the next time."

In the clannish, meritocratic fiefdom of a student paper, Maggie's behavior smacked of self-interest. She was too obviously ambitious and only out for herself. Eventually, her colleagues' annoyance crystallized into dislike. "She was seen as a demure-faced barracuda," said Duhring.

In her senior year, Maggie earned one of the prestigious staff appointments to the *Daily Cal.* She was named one of five associate editors and presided over the night shift one day a week. She had a new column, "The Ins and Outs," which was chiefly concerned with foreign affairs. But she had not endeared herself to her colleagues and was beaten out for the job of managing editor, which for the first time in the publication's history went to a woman. As a sign of the changing times, the outgoing staff awarded four major positions to coeds who were regarded as capable and constructive, and who had devoted hours of their time to helping the younger students. Maggie was always brushing off the newbies and complaining that she was too busy. In short, she was not a team player.

When the new masthead was announced, Maggie was crushed. Her colleagues' rejection took her by surprise. She had been so absorbed in her own problems that she had not seen it coming. As usual, she feigned indifference, concealing her bruised feelings behind the brash, arrogant front she wore like armor. She had coveted the distinction of running the *Daily Cal*, which she believed would be "the practical proof of her worth." She had worked so hard, only to come away empty handed. Possibly as a salve to her ego, in the spring she was named rewrite editor, a position that was apparently created for her and was eliminated after she left.

In her final semester, Maggie maintained only a tenuous connection to the paper. Sullen and aloof, she gave her colleagues a wide berth. She came in just once a week to turn in her column and serve her shift as night editor, leaving at dawn with dark circles under her eyes. Duhring hardly recognized her old friend. Maggie had become so involved with left-wing campus politics that she had let herself go. Gone were the dainty shirtwaist dresses of her Anna Head days, replaced by the sloppy attire of the militant minority. She looked tired and somewhat unkempt, her hair badly in need of a comb. They scarcely spoke.

By May, Maggie was exhausted. She developed mononucleosis and missed her graduation exercises. She spent a miserable week confined to her bed, contemplating her future. Her mother, always the pragmatist, had advised her to major in French, a useful skill. Maggie had acceded to her wishes, but the last thing she wanted was to become a teacher. Although she was anxious about finding a job, her family's financial situation had improved in recent years. Her father, who had been made a partner in the investment firm of Wilson, Johnson & Higgins in 1937, urged her to think beyond just earning a living to what she truly wanted to do.

For Maggie, fresh out of college and ready to strike out on her own, a career in journalism "symbolized the epitome of excitement and adventure." Unfortunately, the newspaper business was still struggling to recover from the Depression and jobs were scarce. Making it onto a big-time city paper seemed as "improbable as becoming a Broadway star overnight."

With her father's encouragement, however, she decided to try to find a summer internship on a local Bay Area paper. Maggie drove to one small-town publication after another, lugging a bulging scrapbook with all her college clippings. She finally found work on the Vallejo *Times-Herald*, a ten-thousand-circulation daily in a tiny town just south of San Francisco. Her initial enthusiasm faded, however, when her start in the profession turned into three long, dull months of processing classified ads. She persevered, and hung around the assignment desk after hours in hopes of being sent out. "She was eager as a sophomore halfback," recalled the managing editor, Will Stevens, who eventually gave her a chance to do a few stories.

At the end of the summer, after being turned away by a succession of editors who expressed a clear preference for hiring copy boys, and regarded copy girls with undisguised suspicion, she decided to extend her search to the East Coast. She had saved enough money for an airline ticket. An uncle she had never met lived in Long Island, and her father had arranged for her to stay there while she tried her luck in New York. Maggie gave herself one year to land a position on a metropolitan newspaper.

As she prepared for her "last-chance job hunt," she rapidly set about reinventing herself. Whatever the truth of her fractious apprenticeship on the *Daily Cal*, Maggie rewrote her résumé and with typical brio gave herself a promotion. A decade later, she would still glibly refer to the "dubious merit of having edited a college newspaper." She also began to appreciate for the first time the advantages of her cosmopolitan background and language skills, especially when it came to convincing a big-city editor that she was a woman of the world. Far better to be Marguerite Higgins from Hong Kong and France than plain old Maggie from Oakland.

But she never got over the outsider status she had so badly wanted to shed. The experience was still raw enough that when she wrote her 1955 autobiography, *News Is a Singular Thing*, she had not forgotten or forgiven the social slights and snubs that made her early years a misery. "That is the penalty you pay for being different," she wrote of the hard lesson learned in childhood. "The sin of uniqueness frequently makes those who have it the target of legend and vicious comment. It also causes some of the human race to treat you as a freak."

2

✳ ✳ ✳ ✳ ✳ ✳ ✳ ✳

Hustling

She was not the best writer in the class, but
she had a go-for-broke attitude that made
up for her sometimes shaggy sentences.

—John Chamberlain, A *Life with the Printed Word*

IN THE MYTH ACCORDING TO MAGGIE HIGGINS, SHE ARRIVED IN
New York in the autumn of 1941 with only a suitcase, seven dollars,
and her fierce ambition. She wasted no time getting down to business.
On emerging from Grand Central Station, she promptly asked a Times
Square newsdealer for directions to the nearest metropolitan paper, and
he pointed up to an old-fashioned, utilitarian-looking building with a tall,
narrow facade on West Forty-First Street. "It was just an accident," she
wrote later, that the powerful and venerable *New York Herald Tribune*,
home to the renowned female columnist Dorothy Thompson, "happened
to be the first object of my effort."

The next piece of good fortune on that hot August afternoon was
due not to luck but to pure moxie. Her unsuccessful tour of West Coast
newspapers had taught her that every managing editor's first line of
defense was the receptionist, a merciless breed to be avoided at all cost.
In the lobby, as plain and unassuming as the facade, she ascertained that
the *Tribune*'s editorial offices were located on the fifth floor. When she
got off the elevator, Maggie fell in with the group of chatting reporters
who strode purposefully by the front desk. Moving with the herd, she

managed to elude the receptionist and walked straight into the gigantic, bustling city room. The enormity of the brightly lit room, with its rows and rows of reporters' desks, and chaotic atmosphere produced by the clicking of the teletype machine and loud clatter of typewriters, was overwhelming. She had to quell a momentary surge of panic. If it had not been for her meager funds, she might not have been bold enough to continue on.

Feeling self-conscious in the all-male preserve, she approached a stout, bulldoggish fellow with a cocky attitude who fit every preconceived notion she had of the hard-bitten newspaperman. "Where is the city editor?" she asked, uneasily aware that if she was escorted out the door past the rows of staring eyes, it would be the most humiliatingly public rebuff of her life. She smiled tentatively and added, "And by the way, what's his name?"

The clamorous city room is the heart of any newspaper. At its beating center is the city desk, which was presided over at the *Herald Tribune* by no less fearsome and demanding an editor than Lessing L. Engelking. A tall, gangling Texan known for his short attention span and volcanic temper, "Engel," as he liked to be called, inspired feelings in his staff of city reporters and rewrite men that ranged from mild apprehension to outright terror. His tirades made even the grizzled veterans' blood run cold. He had little patience for the college boys on his payroll and kept them penned in the back of the newsroom until he bellowed a summons. He had even less use for women reporters. Fortunately, Maggie had not the faintest idea of any of this as she blurted out her reason for being there, and then in a rush gave him the whys, whens, and wherefores of her past experience and future ambitions.

With her round, virtuous face, big blue eyes, and skinny frame outfitted in a brand-new gabardine suit, Maggie, at twenty, looked more like a bashful teenager. She later supposed it was her youth and "misleading air of fragility" that bought her Engel's forbearance, and a few minutes of his time. Instead of throwing her out for barging into his newsroom, he politely listened to her tales of working for the Vallejo *Times-Herald* and leafed through her scrapbook of clippings. He seemed genuinely amused that she had wandered in off the street and did not know a single soul in the newspaper world.

But Engel did not pass out jobs like bouquets. He expected his new recruits to earn them and then sweat each and every day to keep them. "You know, kid," he drawled, not bothering to remove the unlit cigar jammed in the corner of his mouth. "You really must be crazy to leave a perfectly good state like California to try to crack a newspaper town as tough as New York." Then he added, as much to himself as to her, that with the draft taking so many of his staff he might be forced to fill some of the vacancies with women.

"Come back in a month," he told her offhandedly. "There may be an opening."

Clutching that slender reed, Maggie made up her mind to stay in New York. Frustrated by the job search, she decided at the eleventh hour to apply to the Columbia University Graduate School of Journalism, known as the J-School. Advised by the secretary in the admissions office that it was too late to apply for the upcoming academic year, Maggie refused to be put off. She removed her hat and coat, plopped down at one of the wooden desks, and would not budge until some compromise could be found. She finally persuaded the dean of the J-School to allow her to submit a last-minute application that would put her name on the waiting list for one of the eleven places allotted to women. She ignored his warning that it would be impossible to collect all the supporting documents in the four days left before the deadline. Scarcely had he finished speaking when she was out the door and racing to a phone.

Damning the expense, she placed an urgent long-distance call to her father. At her insistence, Larry dropped everything and ran around Oakland procuring her transcripts and five letters of recommendation—the rumor that he woke a former professor at 2 a.m. begging his forgiveness may be only a slight exaggeration—and had them telegraphed to the registrar's office. Maggie dashed off an application essay that was typically forthright and direct. In touting her abilities, she wrote that she was a fast learner, had an insatiable curiosity, and got "a tremendous kick out of the need to be mentally wide-awake which newspaper work calls for." She had been assured that Columbia provided an intensive course in the tools of the trade, making it easier to break into the industry. "In other words," she concluded, "it is the most satisfactory and trustworthy steppingstone to the kind of career I want."

She got the last of the paperwork in just ahead of the dean's deadline. Then she kept her fingers crossed. Only days before the fall term was set to begin, she was notified that a student had withdrawn. She was officially a member of the class of '42. The hoped-for scholarship money did not materialize, so her father footed the bill for her tuition. Maggie made up the difference by working for the university public relations department.

She applied herself to mastering her new craft with the same furious energy that had won her admittance. "Sorry if you think me a negligent correspondent," she wrote her parents that fall, "but from 7 in the morning until 10 or 11 in the evening I am either in class or attending a political meeting." Her grades were good, having progressed from a B+ to an A average, and she was already scoping out the various academic prizes awarded to the top students at the end of the year. "The professors comment that my work is 'professional but slaphappy,'" she added jauntily, "so there you are!"

She was not as lighthearted as her letters home suggested. In truth, she was often miserable that first winter in New York. She was broke, depressed by the array of talent personified by her forty Columbia classmates, and riddled with insecurity about her failure to find any kind of newspaper work. It was beginning to feel like she was attempting the impossible. "The odds were enormous," agreed Flora Lewis, another smart, attractive Californian who would go on to forge a parallel career as a newspaper correspondent.

In Maggie, Lewis saw someone who had her eye on the main chance. She was openly competitive and always sought the inside track. She would try to outreport, outwrite, and outdo anyone and everyone. Once, when the class was assigned to write an editorial on a specific topic, Maggie went straight to the library and checked out every relevant book and journal pertaining to the subject. Many of her peers thought her behavior was selfish and indefensible. Yet when people would start complaining about

Maggie and her "dirty tricks," Lewis was more sympathetic. There were so many barriers to women entering what was historically a man's field, it was hardly surprising Maggie would resort to some devious shortcuts.

Most editors regarded them as "paper dolls," dilettantes who were only dabbling in journalism, their careers just something to fool around with before finding a husband. Their male competitors saw them as a nuisance and just wanted them out of the way. "Even women were against you," recalled Lewis. "They could be so cruel in such subtle ways." "Ambition" was still a dirty word. Being too aggressive was frowned upon. Many of their sister scribes were content to steer clear of breaking news and work the calmer by-waters of society and fashion, where they enjoyed better hours and the approval of the chauvinists on the paper. "Maggie didn't know that game," added Lewis. "She was earnest and played for keeps."

John Chamberlain, a *Life* magazine writer who taught at the J-School, recognized the same drive in Higgins early on. Just before the Japanese attack on Pearl Harbor, he asked the class to write a compact 750-word article assessing the prospects for peace in the Far East. Maggie turned in a twenty-page paper. Chamberlain's first thought was, "This young woman will never make it in a city room." He started to give her a zero when his eye caught on an interesting aspect of Asian history that he knew nothing about. Interested, he read on. In the end, he gave her high marks for her exhaustive research, even though she had violated one of the basic requirements of journalism—"terseness."

In a class of bright, self-directed students, it was Maggie, the determined beauty, who made the most vivid impression. "She knew right where she was going," recalled Chamberlain. "Some of her Columbia classmates thought that she was arrogant. They used to quote her prediction that she would 'one day be as well-known in the newspaper world as the columnist Dorothy Thompson,' who was then at the height of her fame as a pundit." On Maggie's part, he noted wryly, it was "not mere bravado. It was a statement of desire matched by a unique quality of iron in her will."

Maggie credited her fear of second best with propelling her to the front of the pack. Restless and impatient by nature, she had a tendency to "get down on herself, to take things too hard." She had been on an emotional rollercoaster since the August day when Engel had muttered his few words of encouragement, and with each passing month she had to struggle to buck herself up and hold firm to the belief everything would work out. The anxiety that gnawed away at her that whole year at Columbia was "a great driving force."

She had been sick with envy upon learning that an older, more experienced student, Murray Morgan, had secured the position of campus correspondent for the *Herald Tribune*. The first in the class to have a real job, he was the object of universal admiration and awe. He was also a nice, clean-cut boy from the West Coast with a deft mind and ready wit, and Maggie cultivated him as a friend. Then, early one February morning, Morgan intercepted her in the hall and told her he had accepted a position at *Time*, and had recommended her as his replacement at the *Trib*. On seeing her flush with excitement, he warned her not to get her hopes up. Engelking had told him in no uncertain terms that he "didn't want to hire a woman reporter."

The unfairness of it all was more than she could bear. Maggie rushed down to the *Herald Tribune*'s Forty-First Street offices, hell-bent on getting there before any of her male classmates learned of the opening. Breathless and somewhat agitated by the time she reached Engel, she confronted him about the vacancy and his stated objection to employing a woman. "But I had to try," she barreled on. "I know I could do a good job for you." She talked him into giving her a shot. The big Texan had hired dozens of ambitious apprentices in his fifteen years at the *Trib*, the last three of which he had been in charge of the city desk. He could see that Maggie was "intensely competitive," he said later, and had "more zeal and fire than most."

Chamberlain watched with grudging admiration as she edged out the young men on the make in her Columbia class. "She made the first step in her career by beating the boys to the city room of the Herald Tribune," he observed, musing that even the formidable Engel "couldn't resist Maggie's combination of little-girl appeal and uninhibited nerve."

Once she had snagged the job as campus stringer for the *Tribune*,

Maggie was determined to parlay it into a permanent position. The country was at war, and with the exodus of men for service—even her forty-seven-year-old father had rejoined the air force—she could sense the opportunity was there for the taking. She pulled all kinds of stunts to get stories for the paper, crashing private parties and worming her way past security guards, police cordons, and picket lines. She scored an exclusive view of a wealthy tycoon's wedding reception by borrowing a housekeeper's uniform and sneaking into the ballroom via the service elevator after being unceremoniously ejected from the passenger lift.

Money was a powerful motivating force. The *Trib* paid its stringers according to the number of column inches printed—the length of the copy was originally measured in string—and she was soon filing story after story, and supplementing her income by as much as $175 to $250 dollars a month.

She poured her heart and soul into working for the paper, concentrating on it to the exclusion of everything else. Nothing else mattered, and she made no secret of it, paying scant attention to either her classes or her classmates. From her point of view, she was too busy to bother making friends. But on campus, she came off as "cold to women," recalled a fellow student, Julia Edwards, still spiteful four decades later, when she quipped that Higgins had the "face of a Barbie doll and the mannerisms one might expect from the little girl who owned it."

As a rule, Maggie never had much time for her female contemporaries. She was too aware of their jealousy and, for her own part, too grudging of the few opportunities available to their sex to make much of an effort to be agreeable. She regarded the top rung of male reporters as her real peers, and worthy of her respect and friendship. Flora Lewis was an exception. Maggie tried in vain to convince her to share an apartment in Greenwich Village. Lewis preferred living close to campus. But to Maggie, the Village was adventurous and bohemian. So it meant getting up earlier to get to class. "What's an hour's extra sleep?" she urged.

In the spring, Maggie got her way and moved to the Village. She and an old college friend, Roberta "Mackie" MacDonald, a gifted illustrator who had already published several cartoons in *The New Yorker*, had found a four-and-a-half-room apartment in a run-down Greek Revival town-house at 305 West Eleventh Street. It was cheap and full of charm, she informed her parents, with antique furnishings that lent it "an air of dig-nity and aristocracy." A framed photograph of her father, Captain Law-rence Higgins, in his new uniform, adorned the mantelpiece in the living room. "Stanley gave us his phonograph and records," she added, "and we are considering renting a piano, so you see that we will live with proper artistic accessories."

The "Stanley" who kept cropping up in her letters home was the same Stanley Moore whom she had met at Berkeley. During her college years, she had kept up a flirtatious acquaintance with the handsome teaching assistant. He had received his PhD in 1940 and then left to take up a two-year appointment as a lecturer at Harvard. The following summer, she had bumped into him on a Berkeley street corner, and when she told him of her plans to go to New York they had arranged to get together. Shortly after her arrival in the city, they met for drinks and discovered a strong mutual attraction. As neither felt constrained by what they considered to be inane, outdated rules of propriety, they immediately became lovers.

"Now, about Stanley," Maggie wrote with evident pride in her new beau, who was six years her senior, and to her mind entirely suitable no matter what anyone back home had to say about it. "You people seem to be very much afraid that I am in the clutches of some senile old gentleman so here are some facts to set your minds at ease." She went on to describe his appearance—"tall, black-haired and Irish"—and to provide a glowing account of his character, education, and pedigree. "Stanley's family are the Piedmont Stanley Moores," she continued, complacent at her swift entrée into the upper classes. "His father was one of California's most famous lawyers."

Anticipating her father's dismay at Stanley's leftist leanings, Maggie had prepared an argument in defense of her future partner:

> He is radical, and I'm afraid, incurably so. We do not agree
> politically except on such general principles as: The best
> world is one where both Negro and Jew and Rockefeller

and Roosevelt have a chance at enough to eat, a chance at assimilating the culture and art and happiness or at least a fair share of them—a chance you don't get when working 10 hours a day for $12 a week.

I don't think Stanley's radicalism will ever hurt him, for he will always be able to rely on money which he is scheduled to inherit, and furthermore he is too brilliant in my opinion, to be discarded by society because of his political beliefs.

In truth, she had reason for concern. Unlike most young men of his age and background, Stanley had not applied for a military commission because he was worried that he might be disqualified. Even a cursory investigation into his past would probably have revealed his communist sympathies. A patriot, he was more than ready to put politics aside to defeat global fascism, but he had to wait on the whims of the local draft board. He was finally called up in June and, like her father, would be joining the air corps.

She went on to assure her parents that although they seemed an unlikely pair, Stanley was good for her. He had a keen intelligence and quick sense of humor. They had a shared passion for truth, and a strong allergy to cant in all its various forms. "Though he, like Daddy, has a tendency to bark and be sarcastic," she noted. "Then I hate him. But he says, I'm to 'give him the blast' when he tries to squelch what I have to say with irreverent quips."

Instinctively, Maggie understood that she would need to fight to protect her identity. She could not allow her own ideas and individuality to be subsumed by her opinionated, and sometimes overbearing, lover, who liked to split hairs and throw scholarly book references at her. But she was confident she could hold her own in the relationship. Maggie was sure that in time, she could bend him to her will. For all his "advanced notions," she sensed that beneath the surface Stanley was "quite a sentimentalist," and more conventional than he cared to admit. "The point is, we agree not to win an argument, but to arrive at the truth," she continued, trying to convince herself as much as her parents. "And, surprisingly enough, he really trys [*sic*]—so you see, human nature, or at least habits, can be changed."

On May 29, 1942, just days ahead of her Columbia graduation, a jubilant Maggie wrote to announce that she had achieved her life's ambition: "I am only the second woman ever to be hired as a straight news reporter on the New York *Herald Tribune* (circulation 400,000)—unless I make some dreadful mistake between now and next week."

Women were still such a novelty in the city room in 1942 that Maggie could have counted them on one hand, though the honor of being the second hired rightfully belonged to Ishbel Ross, a pioneering reporter who joined the paper in 1919 and quit after fifteen years to write novels. The first was the stalwart Emma Bugbee, who befriended Maggie when she first arrived and who had been pounding away at her typewriter since before World War I. For years, she was the only female reporter on the *Trib*, which had suited her fine because it meant she was always in demand, especially after Eleanor Roosevelt banned men from her press conferences. Bugbee, who had outlasted scores of reporters and several city editors, might have been a role model, except that Maggie did not want to be pigeonholed as a woman covering women.

Her first official day on the job would be Saturday, June 6. Her hours would be 1 p.m. to 9 p.m., five days a week. Money, as always, was first and foremost in her mind. Promotion to the regular staff meant she would take a pay cut, as she had been an especially industrious stringer. When she was put on the payroll, her starting salary would be $25 a week. Fortunately, she had just sold an article to *This Week*, the *Trib*'s Sunday magazine. Even though it was only a short piece, it netted her $100. Freelance work was lucrative, and she had already pitched a half dozen new story ideas. With fixed expenses of $65 a month, her finances were in "excellent shape."

She told her parents not to worry about the expense of coming to New York for her Columbia commencement as she would not be able to participate. Instead, she would be covering the ceremony for the paper, her biggest story to date. She would be graduating with honors, though was disappointed that she had failed to snag one of the three $1,500 Pulitzer Traveling Fellowships. But she had not given up her dream of going abroad. "I am still determined to become a foreign correspondent," she wrote, adding that she planned to enroll in some language courses in the fall. Spanish and Russian lessons to begin with, and perhaps basic Chinese.

A few weeks later, she dropped a quick line to say all was going well. "It is a splendid feeling to be on the staff of the New York *Herald Tribune*," she wrote. "I'm now equipped with the coveted police-card and have a press card. So you see my dreams have come true—I'm really 'of the press' now."

To her disgust, her first assignment was a weather story—the bane of every rookie's existence. At a loss for a way to liven up a run-of-the-mill piece on the oppressive June heat wave, she elected at the last minute to write about Rosita, a South American jaguar at the Central Park Zoo, who was suffering from sunstroke. The poor creature had to be hosed down by a fire truck. "Meanest cat in the world," she quoted the zookeeper saying. "You ought to see her now. Docile as you please, lying there with an ice pack bandaged onto her head!"

It was a clever angle, and it showed she had an ear for a quote. The ice pack was a nice touch. The *Trib*, always a patsy for an animal story, even ran an exclusive photo. Engel had not been expecting much when he handed her a batch of clippings on beach-attendance figures, thermometer readings, and traffic fatalities.

In those early probationary months, her round dimpled face became a source of despair. Even though she was quite tall, at almost five foot eight, whatever air of authority she might have had was undermined by her cherubic countenance. On one of her first important assignments, she was mortified when the famed elder statesman Bernard M. Baruch turned to her in the middle of a press conference and asked, "What high school do you represent, Miss Higgins?" Aware of all the amused glances, Maggie suffered "an agony of embarrassment." She was still immature and unsure enough to prickle with shame at being thought of as a kid. Hating the hot flush that stained her cheeks, and revealed her emotional vulnerability, she resolved to develop a tough outer shell.

To test her mettle, Engel sent her to interview James Caesar Petrillo, the powerful head of the American Federation of Musicians, who was in the midst of tense union negotiations. Two days earlier, Petrillo had pulled his dance bands from the network radio programs in an effort to pressure the broadcast companies into increasing their wages and royalty payments. To Engel's surprise, Maggie got in to see the iron-fisted labor czar, who had been playing hard to get with the press. She had tracked Petrillo down at his hotel, obtained his room number, and promptly at nine in the morning knocked on his door. Still clad in his silk pajamas and bathrobe, Petrillo let her in only because she claimed to be the maid. She managed to cajole him into giving her an interview, he said later, because she "looked like his daughter."

Maggie scored another page-one exclusive that fall using a similar ploy. Hearing that Madame Chiang Kai-Shek, the wife of China's Nationalist leader, had checked into Columbia-Presbyterian Medical Center as a private patient and was refusing all interviews, it seemed a good time to pay a sympathy call. Maggie waited in the hall outside Madame Chiang's room and, when the opportunity presented itself, picked up a medicine tray and followed a nurse in.

The boys in the city room took notice. Being sent out on the trail of elusive quarry—usually a fruitless errand—was part of the hazing process. It was a way of showing the new kid the ropes. Higgins had done well. She had a deceptively diffident look that she clearly knew how to use to her advantage. She was still a cub reporter, but she was resourceful.

Maggie did not, however, distinguish herself for producing clean and clear prose. The doubts raised by copyeditors about her work were legion. Some wondered whether she had even a nodding acquaintance with the English language. She seemed incapable of writing a simple declarative sentence. Her copy pages were littered with cross-outs and scribbled revisions, revealing the painstaking effort that went into every composition.

M. C. "Inky" Blackman, a short, gray-haired rewrite man, straightened out her mangled sentences in the early days. Higgins was never his idea of a graceful writer, but she always came back with something worth the effort of repairing. "Smoothing her stories did not require a great deal of effort because they were seldom of the type that lent themselves to what we thought of as the *Trib* treatment," he explained. "They were usually straightaway stories that she had obtained . . . where other reporters had failed, or an old story with a new slant that had been overlooked by her competitors." The *Trib* was full of wordsmiths, Blackman added, but a really good reporter was a rarity. "Writers can be taught," he asserted, "but reporters are born that way."

Known as "a newspaperman's newspaper," the *Trib* expected every member of staff to be able to deliver the distinctive style and flavor that supposedly made it the paper of choice of "a literate Tammany boss, a college president, and the more brainy taxicab drivers." Engel wanted his paper to be the best-written, best-edited newspaper in the country. Above all, he insisted that it be a more *writerly* newspaper than its chief competitor, the *New York Times*. The secret to the paper's superiority was that it had the best copyeditors in the business. They applied the final polish, the finesse that could turn an ordinary piece of reportage into a masterpiece.

There was no place to hide in the garishly lit city room. The city desk, where Engel was enthroned, was at the center of the floor so he could survey his entire kingdom and quickly spot and place every reporter within its hierarchy. "The city editor," noted Edwin Lanham, who once sat at his elbow, "was a man who had acquired the malevolence of the perfectionist and wore it like a robe of office." Engel was flanked on one side by the horseshoe-shaped copy desk, close enough to be within shouting distance during deadline periods, where he quickly passed each page after close scrutiny. Nearby were the rows of rewrite men. The railed-off reporters' desks were lined up against the far wall, with some of the paper's most famous names—Homer Bigart, John J. "Tex" O'Reilly, John G. Rogers, and Peter Kihss—at the front, the reliable shoe-leather types occupying the middle ground, and greenhorns like Maggie somewhere in the hinterlands.

A cub reporter who kept up a run of good stories was destined to move closer to the city desk, while one whose work was repeatedly spiked might wind up banished to obituaries or the caboose, the last news section of the Sunday paper. The next level to aim for was "district work," night-shift reporting that usually involved crime, fire, or some other unforeseen disaster. Those who showed a sure touch would progress to the rewrite desk, then on to features. As young reporters grew in confidence, the game became one of getting a story by the copydesk as unmolested as possible, and then landing it in the most desirable real estate in the paper, which was close to the front and above the fold.

City reporters were never done hustling—searching for the next scoop, the next tantalizing lead that would keep their copy prominently placed and satisfy the insatiable demand of their editors. You were either seen as a comer, on the way to greatness, or you did not have what it takes, and would be relegated to the nameless ranks of poorly paid hacks who toiled for lesser publications. Reporters with proven ability could pursue stardom by winning prestigious national or foreign postings. Staffers learned to read the daily paper like a scorecard, gauging who was up and who was down by watching the key variables—the assignment, the "play" or placement of stories, and the byline. In the eternal competition of the newsroom, everyone always knew exactly where they stood in relation to everyone else.

Engel, hailed by his disciples as "the greatest school of journalism ever invented," nurtured Maggie's talent. A demanding and challenging editor, he was as unsparing of her as he was of the young men on his staff. He might make her rewrite a lead a dozen times. If she misspelled a word or bungled an official's name or title, he saw red. Readers needed to know exactly who they were getting their news from, and nothing riled Engel more than slipshod attribution. Maggie was so terrified of making a mistake that she obsessively checked and rechecked her facts, a habit that remained with her for the rest of her life.

She still managed to rack up her share of blunders. There was the first dread-inducing occasion when she heard him boom—"Miss Higgins, please come here!"—and she made the interminable walk to the city desk, her face white and hands trembling. Engel gave her a withering look and growled something about her lead containing a "complete non sequitur." As she had no idea what he was talking about, she could only mumble an apology and ask meekly, "What's a non sequitur?" When he pointed out that the second line of her story did not logically follow the first, she saw that he was right and hastily corrected it.

Even though Engel could be an absolute bastard at times, he taught her to trust her instincts and to be self-reliant. "He was not the kind to whom one could say, when handed an assignment, 'How shall I go about this?'" she recalled drily. When Maggie refused to wilt under his glare, she began to earn a modicum of respect. She realized he was the kind of bully you had to stand up to or risk being tyrannized. Once she became accustomed to his intermittent rages, when he yelled and ripped out telephones in anger, she discovered he had a compassionate side and came to believe that underneath the gruff exterior was a fine person.

Thanks to his constant criticism, she gradually began to turn out decent prose. But she was always more interested in finding things out than framing a lead. She had a knack for bright quotations and "color," the small details that bring a story to life. A good digger, she could unearth fresh material in well-trodden avenues and collect quantities of scattered intelligence about any subject she was sent out to investigate. As one office watcher noted, she had the qualities every editor likes in his young champions, "cyclonic energy and an uncontainable need to prove her worth anew every day."

The promise of seeing her name in print kept her hopping. As time went on, she began to get better assignments. In September, a series on the opening of a naval training school at Smith College in Northampton, Massachusetts, showed her gift for observation, and brought her the first of three bylines. "The Berkshire foothills echoed today for the first time in history to the tramp of feminine feet in military march," she wrote, after watching the WAVES (Women Appointed for Volunteer Emergency Service) being drilled on the lawn outside their dormitory. "The newness of their regulation low-heeled black oxfords was summed up in the remark of one of the junior officers, who said, 'We'll creak today and groan tomorrow.'"

No sooner had she returned from Northampton than her editor gave her a front-page story. From a stern taskmaster like Engel, it was more gratifying than any compliment. Even from her remote section of the city room, she could feel her stock rise. Maggie was exultant. She had tasted success, and it sent her emotions soaring. Her chronic insecurity craved reinforcement, and this was a feeling of pure unadulterated joy like none she had experienced. Her work, published overnight, brought immediate satisfaction—however fleeting. She loved the speed and visibility of newsprint, even though the story would be forgotten in twenty-four hours. "So right now your young daughter is feeling quite cocky about her professional achievements," she wrote her parents that night, still elated. "I will include the clippings so you can see for yourselves."

She was so enamored of her new job it was hard to feel properly sad about Stanley. He had left for Florida after a four-day visit in July, "his farewell before going into the Army," she told her parents. He would be temporarily based at the Miami Beach Training Center in Florida, which for all practical purposes was "a million miles away." For the most part, he seemed happy with enlisted life and hoped to go overseas soon. "And I don't blame him," she added, "for I should like to also." A few weeks later, she reported that she had received a collect telephone call from Stanley that weekend and thought he "sounded a bit lonesome and less self-sufficient than usual." He wrote to her nearly every day and pressed her to marry him.

The procession to the altar was quick, as it was for so many wartime couples, mistaking sexual tension and longing for true affection. Maggie and Stanley flew separately to California for the hastily arranged wedding, held on the evening of November 20 at St. Clement's Episcopal Church in Berkeley. Her mother was disappointed that it was not a Catholic ceremony. Moreover, Maggie had dispensed with most of the silly trappings, so that the simple seven o'clock service was witnessed only by immediate family and a few close friends. Instead of the de rigueur white satin gown, the bride wore a green wool afternoon dress with gold accents at the bodice and a small brown felt hat with a veil. Her only concession to tradition was a corsage of snowy orchids. Larry Higgins, resplendent in his new captain's uniform and looking ten pounds lighter and a decade younger than he had before reenlisting, gave his daughter away.

After receiving their guests informally in the lobby of the church, the newlyweds left for a brief honeymoon in Carmel. Then Maggie returned to New York alone, and Stanley to Kelly Field, Texas, to complete his training.

In January 1943, Stanley was transferred to a wartime training program at Harvard Business School. At the end of a six-week course, he was made a private first class. While awaiting his orders, he was based in Connecticut and came to New York every weekend to see her at the small basement apartment they had rented at 28 Jones Street. It was cramped, dark, and depressing—not a promising start. Before leaving for England in August, Stanley took her to Nantucket for a long weekend. They spent a few bittersweet days going for leisurely walks along the cobblestoned streets and enjoying lazy picnics on the beach. Then he was gone.

It was all over and done with in the blink of an eye. Except for the ring on her finger, it seemed rather unreal. Their relationship, built on borrowed time, felt a bit hasty and ill-considered now that all she had to remind herself of him were his letters, and even those were few and far between. The companionship of work colleagues helped to fill the void and push away her doubts. It boosted her morale to have someone to take her to dinner, but that was not without its own complications. As the weeks blurred into months, there were times when Maggie found it hard to remember that she was married. Especially when, with each passing day, she was more fully alive to the romance and fascination of her chosen profession.

3

✳✳✳✳✳✳✳✳

Tricks of the Trade

Was it feminism, then, to use her beauty
in such a fashion—or a travesty on the
goal of emancipation for her sex?

—Richard Kluger, *The Paper*

A WEEK AFTER HER MARRIAGE, MAGGIE WAS BACK AT WORK. ASIDE
from the fact that Stanley was away, she was enjoying herself immensely.
"My life is unusually pleasant," she wrote her parents. "I privately think
that I have the best job in all New York." She was rarely lonesome. No
weeping war bride, she went out almost every night. It was the great time
of "cocktails-for-freedom" parties and patriotic hangovers. With Russia
an American ally, she followed the fashion and switched from gin to
vodka martinis.

Her letters home were filled with descriptions of lively dinners and
late-night escapades. She and her new downtown friends frequented Café
Society, a speakeasy on Sheridan Square. No ordinary urban watering
hole, Café Society was the first racially integrated nightclub in New York,
and a favorite of the Village's liberal elite. Known as "the wrong place for
the Right people"—a jab at sanctimonious conservatives—it was famous
for promoting Black jazz musicians from Billie Holiday and Lena Horne
to Big Joe Turner. On one night, Maggie and Mackie were squired by
Henry and George Simon, younger siblings of the founder of the publishing firm Simon & Schuster who were music critics for the tabloid *PM*.

(Mackie and Henry Simon would soon marry.) The place was packed with celebrities, and, as the brothers were reviewing one of the new acts, she wrote, "the whole evening was on the house."

In the summer of 1943, Haakon Chevalier moved to New York to work for the Office of War Information and took an apartment nearby on Jane Street. (By this time, Chevalier was already a person of interest to the FBI because of his close association with Oppenheimer, and his frequent visits to Higgins's apartment would fill dozens of pages in her burgeoning FBI file.) Through him, Maggie met all sorts of left-wing artists and writers, including the wildly precocious Viola Ilma, a New York socialite and former actress. At the age of twenty-two, Ilma had founded a radical magazine, *Modern Youth*, and she followed up a year later with a book calling for generational change. By the time Maggie encountered her, Ilma had moved on to social work and had launched the Youth Morale Corps to help ex-cons who were entering the armed services. Maggie found her fascinating. Hers was a mixed-up life of prisons during the weekdays and yachts on the weekends, of dealing with delinquents and coaxing wealthy philanthropists like Doris Duke to sponsor a subway vagrant who wanted to be an air force pilot.

A raven-haired beauty with high cheekbones and a sleek pageboy cut, Ilma had twice ended up in marriages to communists. The first, to an ascetic intellectual who wanted to save her, and the second to a butcher and the manager of the local Amalgamated Meat Cutters Union, whom she had met while trying to find work for her parolees. With her husband of less than sixty days now in the army, Ilma apparently considered herself as good as single. She had a duplex apartment on East Eleventh Street that was too large for her, and she invited Maggie to move in and share the rent. "This was the beginning of a gay wartime friendship," recalled Ilma. "There was no competition between Higgie and me as sometimes is the case with roommates. We saw men through different eyes—she for the story, I for funds. They never had both."

Besides absent spouses, they had another thing in common, according to Ilma: "We were sloppy." In defiance of their buttoned-up era, they could not be bothered about their appearance, and on their days off traipsed about in trench coats, flats, and no hats. If they wore anything on their heads, they were of the firm conviction that it had to be a beret. After rent and food, they spent all their money on records and books. Ilma got a kick out of her high-spirited housemate, who was "incredibly girlish" and always good for a laugh.

"Higgie looked like Alice in Wonderland with her long golden hair covering her shoulders," she recalled. "She was crazy about ballet. Often on a Saturday afternoon she would put on her ballet slippers and dance to her favorite record, 'Gaité Parisienne.' Many was the time, too, she would get into the 'fifth position' at a party (she really was a good dancer), twirl around, and make one helluva leap into some lucky guy's lap."

Ilma regularly joined Maggie and her pals at the *Trib* hangout on West Fortieth Street, formerly known as the Artists and Writers Restaurant, affectionately called Bleeck's (pronounced "Blake's"), after its proprietor. The decor was dark English tavern, the bartenders Irish, the food vaguely German, and the crowd—mostly drunken newspapermen, two and three deep by late afternoon—was rowdy. "Drink is the curse of the *Tribune*," the old adage went, "and sex the bane of the *Times*."

The *Trib*'s patrician owner, Ogden Reid, was the bar's leading customer. Bald, genial, and easygoing, "Oggie," as he liked to be called, often stopped in for rounds with his employees, imbibing scotch after scotch until he almost fell down. But he always picked up the tab, which bought him a lot of goodwill. It also contributed to the paper's rambunctious fraternity atmosphere. Earl Ubell, a longtime science writer, described the staff in the 1940s as "a lot of rah-rah boys and Texans and good ol' Southerners."

Maggie's gang was composed of a handful of top reporters and rewrite men—Inky Blackman, Bob Bird, Sy Friedman, Bill Glascow, Les Midgley, and John Watson. The latter, an alcoholic Irish charmer like her father, was over forty, married, and past his prime, his considerable gifts eroded by the bottle. He was clearly infatuated with the pretty but messy blonde who followed him around the newsroom asking for help, copy papers flying everywhere, her fingernails broken from typing, a pencil stuck into her disheveled mass of gold curls. Ilma realized it the night

Watson, wearing a soppy grin, raised a glass to them in a fond salute, though he had eyes only for her roommate: "You are both ambitious and unconventional, with gaiety approaching abandon; you are in love with life, you are warmhearted." Maggie ended up in Watson's lap. Inevitably, they became an item.

Despite all the armchair critics—and the city room was full of them—it would be hard to say who was using whom. Watson was beloved by his colleagues for his sensitive mind, revered for his pristine prose and ability to improve any piece of copy. Maggie wanted to soak up all the knowledge and skill he had at his ink-stained fingertips. She longed for the kind of respect he effortlessly commanded from his peers. There was also a certain safety in knowing he had her back. Being a part of his blue-pencil brigade provided some protection against the treachery of the city room. He, in turn, was drawn to her youth, desire, and frank admiration. How nice to have an adoring acolyte who hung on your every word and then took you home at night. No one thought the affair would last, including them. But it led to a lot of poisonous gossip and gave her a reputation she did not deserve.

It was a time when nice girls were expected to say no. Maggie's willingness to stray outside the bonds of marriage branded her as a hussy. Men were congratulated for their office conquests, but women always wound up being judged for them. There is a reason that newsrooms are generally known as the "snake pit."

Watson's drinking buddies looked nervously over their shoulders at Maggie, fearing that when she dropped him, he would lose his battle with drink. They cast her as a cold, scheming vixen, double-crossing the poor sap on her relentless climb to the top. When the relationship ran its course, and she was spotted with a young buck from the newsroom, Watson's pals cast aspersions on her character, honor, and professional conduct. It never occurred to anyone to accuse him of robbing the cradle.

Back then, every paper had its share of burned-out newsmen who had been put out to pasture and spent their days spewing bile about their replacements and stoking the rumor mill. When it came to women, they tended to talk in crude terms and tired clichés, like locker-room habitués.

When it came to Maggie, they "derided her babyish face and unmistakably adult body and claimed that she selected most if not all her bedmates for intensely practical purposes, to add to her power or promote her career." They spread rumors of one-night stands and speculated about "whether she was intimate with more than one man at a time or took them up and discarded them seriatim."

In *The Paper*, his doorstop history of the *New York Herald Tribune*, Richard Kluger, a former literary editor, described the intense animosity Maggie aroused in some quarters of the city room, where her foes were united in the sentiment that she exploited her feminine charms to get ahead. "Few men could wield their sexuality so strategically," he asserted. "Her aggressiveness became office legend, replete with charges that she stepped on those who got in her way, snatched off desirable assignments, arranged to phone in the legwork of others as if it was her own when out on team assignment, and otherwise comported herself with a competitiveness bordering on the pathological." Quite a performance for a still-wet-behind-the-ears twenty-three-year-old.

Of course, it has been said that all reporters are pathological, or at least deluded to some degree. They spend their days scrambling over one another to get stories, often employing sneaky and disreputable means to do so, all the while protesting that theirs is a noble profession. As the *New Yorker* writer Janet Malcolm once observed, journalists are masters of seduction, "preying on people's vanity, ignorance, or loneliness, gaining their trust and betraying them without remorse." Age and gender are of little consequence. Appearances can be deceiving—a handsome face is no guarantee of gentlemanly behavior. One thing is certain, the cutthroat competition breeds a certain meanness. Territorial, tribal, and obsessed with the old rules and unwritten codes of their world, reporters are always most savage when attacking other reporters.

Kluger, a career newspaper man, knew all the tricks of the trade. In cataloging Maggie's many crimes and misdemeanors, he set out to indict her coy femininity, what he called her "manipulativeness." She had a way of stealing the limelight—as well as stories, interviews, and sources—that left her male peers sputtering with rage. Naturally, real newspapermen, for whom camaraderie is sacred, would never behave in such a fashion. This was the view of Carl Levin, a tried-and-true *Trib* man who had risen from copy boy to correspondent, and who was still nursing a grudge after Maggie grabbed the main story on a joint assignment and left him with only a sidebar. "Men didn't do that to other men," Levin complained.

Even as late as 1986, when *The Paper* was published, it was apparently acceptable to run a demeaning anonymous quote about Maggie from a city room colleague saying, "She had to learn how to write—we all broke her in, some in more ways than one." That colleague was Robert Shaplen, who was involved with her for about a year until she dumped him, though he maintained it was because he left to cover the war in the Pacific for *Newsweek*. While he considered her to be opportunistic, he stopped short of implying she slept with him as a means to an end, telling Kluger, "Hell, she just liked to get laid."

While many resented Maggie's rapid climb, there were those who respected her, too. "[She] blew through the city room like a whirlwind," recalled Alden Whitman, a *Trib* colleague. "She was a scruffy, immensely good-looking blonde, with bright blue eyes and a freckled face that was often smudged black with carbon copy; she was 22 years old, brash and brassy, with her little girl's voice projecting an innocence she did not possess."

Whitman had heard the rumors that she would do anything to get a story, meaning she was generous with her sexual favors and stingy about sharing credit. "In what was then a virtually all-male preserve, she played the part of girl reporter with ferocity," he acknowledged. But the way her affairs were exaggerated out of all proportion—both then and later—was "unfair," in his opinion. "Maggie's conduct was no better and no worse than that of her male counterparts."

Margaret Parton, who joined the *Tribune* in 1943, was familiar with the office intrigue. Higgins was one of the most "thorough and concentrated reporters" she had ever met, and she thought those who would add the word "unscrupulous" were just jealous. By her own admission, Parton, plain and chubby, posed no threat to her male colleagues. Her arrival did not make the copy boys swoon or disrupt the equanimity of the city room. Moreover, she made a conscious decision not to draw attention to herself, and took whatever assignments came her way without fuss. As a consequence, she never felt particularly discriminated against, except in the event of fast-breaking news events—fires, floods, murders, and riots.

Yet these were the big stories that the ace reporters lived for, and that offered fledglings an opportunity to prove what they were capable of in the mad approach of deadline. "On these occasions," she conceded, "excited editors completely forgot there were women on the staff, but this happened rarely and we accepted it with philosophic amusement as part of nature's law."

Before going to work at the *Herald Tribune*, Parton had acquainted herself with the general policy for "professional" female behavior put forth in Stanley Walker's book *City Editor*, an invaluable guide to the paper by one of its own. Walker believed female journalists should never sit on desks, use foul language, or engage in office entanglements. Parton tried to heed his cautions. "For newspaper men are old-fashioned romantics," she observed. "If a woman *must* work on a paper, they want her to work like a man but to remain a 'lady.' "

Maggie was less tolerant of the double standard. She had a low boiling point for the daily indignities of being a woman, such as being turned away from lunch at the Oak Room at the Plaza because she might distract from the dealmaking, or being told she could not cross the threshold of the Century Association, another bastion of male bonding. If she was sharp elbowed at times, it was because she was denied the chummy barroom confidences of Wall Street traders and politicians. Excluded from so many of the places where men could meet and talk, cultivate sources, and catch up on the latest scuttlebutt, she had to create opportunities of her own. Since it was not a level playing field, she saw no reason to play fair.

She was not oblivious to the city-room sniping but shrugged it off. If it occasionally got under her skin, she hardened herself to the office scolds. It only made her that much more determined to do whatever was necessary to achieve her goals. "The anti-Higgins group maintained she used her feminine wiles in unsportsmanlike ways in pursuit of a story," recalled Ilma. "She inclined to scoff at this manifestation of masculine envy. It never slowed her up or changed her *modus operandi*."

Long before, Maggie had decided that "chips on male shoulders were among the occupational hazards that women reporters should be prepared to take in their stride." In a January 1943 diary entry, she brought a gimlet-eyed clarity to her assessment of the traditional prejudices of her profession:

> *In the New York newspaper world, the female minority seems to be the favorite verbal target of the male majority. From what I heard tonight at Chumley's [a Village bar] a woman reporter is "temperamental" if she objects to five night assignments in a row. But a man who objects to five night assignments in a row is "standing up for his rights." A woman who gets a scoop by sticking by an assignment after the others go back to their offices is "tricky." Further, she "takes unfair advantage." A man who stays on an assignment after all the other reporters go back to their offices is "a go-getter." And if ever there is a controversy between a woman reporter and a male colleague on the same paper or a woman reporter and an editor, the woman is sure to be at fault because every newspaperman knows "women are hard to get along with," et cetera.*

But now that she had her foot in the door, Maggie was not about to be dislodged. She loved the rough-and-tumble of the city room and wanted to be in the thick of it. She was not fazed by the razzing of her male colleagues. She did not mind the newsroom wisecracking, or even the baser barroom stuff at Bleeck's, when they started in with the drunken leering and winking back-and-forth. She never turned away embarrassed or offended. She just sat there with a little one-sided smile on her face, half shy and half superior, studying the jokers until they started to fidget and redden and finally drifted away. She reveled in the late-night bull sessions, picking up the slang and immersing herself in the tough, earthy ethos of the trade. More than anything, she wanted to be regarded as one of the boys.

The problem with Maggie, according to Judith Crist (née Klein), who came to the city room via the women's pages and went on to become a noted writer and film critic, was that she was too beguiling. It was not that she flaunted her attributes or went in for alluring clothing; it was simply that her sex appeal was impossible to ignore. "She had a sort of movie-star prettiness, almost like a cross between Betty Grable's and Marilyn Monroe's, with a super figure," Crist remembered. "She looked taller than she was because she was so slender."

The tabloids had a long tradition of employing glamour girls—the media magnate William Randolph Hearst believed that a little pulchritude could work wonders—and although it was a proven formula, it was not the *Tribune's* philosophy. Back then, there was a clear division between the respectable and the sensational press. A serious newspaper, it was thought, needed sober, sensible-looking reporters. Maggie did not fit the mold.

Crist, who was two years younger and several rungs below her, recalled Maggie as "all drive." Around the office, she found her to be "warm, pleasant, and very attractive." Like Parton, Crist suspected "the rampant stories of her horrifying competitiveness had their origins from men who had hoped Maggie would look with favor on them and didn't."

Not that Higgins was above doing some underhanded things to get a scoop. The story of her "hogging the phonebooth" on deadline—to prevent anyone, including reporters from her own paper, from calling in their copy—had the ring of truth. But that was par for the course. "She was a *very good newswoman*," Crist said with added emphasis, "but because she was a woman and good-looking, there was a suspicion of promiscuity." The office always buzzed with unseemly tales of closed-door meetings. "Hell," Crist added, "I'm sure any number of people in the city room thought I must have been banging the editors to get the stories I did."

As the war went on, more women joined the staff. While there were never more than a handful in the city room, the *Tribune* had a number of senior women in key positions, and they made their presence felt, more so than on any other metropolitan paper. Most were on the business side or in special departments, such as the influential Dorothy Thompson, whose hugely successful thrice-weekly "On the Record" column was introduced in 1936; the sagacious books editor, Irita Van Doren; *This Week* editor Marie Meloney, the brains behind the *Trib*'s highly regarded Sunday magazine; and the popular food writer Clementine Paddleford, who helped start the paper's domestic-science institute and test kitchen. The newly installed editor of the women's page, Dorothy Dunbar Bromley, a prominent feminist, was hired to expand the society section and turn it into something more substantive, part of a larger effort to attract women and suburban readers and help transform the stodgy old *Tribune* into a more modern paper.

All this was done at the impetus of Helen Rogers Reid, the tiny, dynamic, forward-looking wife of the paper's president and publisher, Ogden Reid. Her rise from small-town Wisconsin girl to New York aristocrat was, Maggie knew, "a saga in itself." After graduating from Barnard College, Helen served as social secretary to the majestic Elisabeth Mills Reid in New York, and then in London when her husband, Whitelaw Reid, was appointed ambassador at the Court of St. James's. In 1911, Helen married the Reid scion, editor apparent of the most prominent and most respectable right-wing newspaper in America.

While Ogden learned the family business, Helen devoted herself to their three children—Whitelaw, Ogden Jr., and a daughter, Elisabeth, who died in childhood—and to her true passion, women's suffrage. In 1918, after the vote was won, she decided to help revitalize the ailing *Tribune*, which was in financial difficulties. She started in the advertising department and immediately showed a genius for selling, increasing sales, and bringing in new accounts at an astounding rate. Three months later she was made head of the department, and for more than twenty years she was listed on the masthead as vice president.

A small figure, regal and chic, Helen Rogers Reid—"H.R.R." was how she signed her memos to the editor—was a potent force at the paper, as well as in New York's social and civic life. "Queen Helen," as the *Saturday Evening Post* anointed her in an adulatory 1944 profile, was "hostess to the famous, mistress of an old fortune, a high-powered sales executive with sandpaper resistance, [and] one of America's remarkable women."

In recent years, Mrs. Reid had quietly taken over the reins from her husband, who had made a slow descent into alcoholism, and she had established herself as a formidable publishing executive in her own right. Maggie often glimpsed her at five o'clock in the afternoon, just as the city room was beginning to hum, when she strode past the reporters' desks on her way to the office of the managing editor, George A. Cornish. By that hour, as everyone knew, Ogden Reid had taken up his position at the bar at Bleeck's, usually accompanied by Geoffrey Parsons, the chief editorial writer, who treated it as an extension of the office.

Within the building, no one doubted that Mrs. Reid was in charge. While she rarely interfered with editorial matters, or passed judgment on an individual story, she took a keen interest in anything that would affect the paper's base and revenue, whether it was buying a big syndicate feature or bringing in a top columnist such as Walter Lippmann. Filled with a sense of dynastic pride, she treated the staff as members of her extended newspaper family and became personally involved in the smallest decisions about their fate. She had given women an even chance throughout the organization, and Maggie could only hope that her enlightened attitude would extend to foreign assignments.

By the spring of 1944, the idea of going abroad had become an obsession. While Maggie was stuck covering local news in New York, she was missing all the action overseas. In the meantime, her husband had been promoted to captain and was stationed at an Allied shuttle-bombing base in Russia. Her father, who was now with the Office of Strategic Services (OSS), had been sent to England and was planning secret operations all over the continent. Her mother's entire family—two aunts, uncles, and several young cousins—were all in harm's way in German-occupied France, their safety and whereabouts unknown.

In June, following the Normandy invasion and the Allies' big push on the continent, a large group of male reporters from the city room departed for Europe. The word was that victory was within sight. Even though she knew it was impertinent to ask for a sought-after overseas post after scarcely two years on the paper, Maggie insisted on adding her name to the list of those under consideration. She spoke up, loudly and often, about her desire to cover the conflict. "I was so violently intent on going to the wars that there was no time or emotion left over for humility or self-doubt," she wrote. "Getting overseas was something I felt too strongly about to be prepared to stand politely in line and wait my turn."

She waged a tireless, unremitting campaign to be sent abroad. She badgered her city editors until they were sick of the sight of her. Although they dismissed the idea out of hand—she was far too green—Maggie persevered. She had heard through the grapevine that Sonia Tomara, a Russian émigré who had distinguished herself in the Paris bureau early in the war, had asked the *Tribune* to send her back but had met with the usual objections to lady war correspondents. Forty-five years old and fluent in four languages, Tomara, with Mrs. Reid's support, finally overcame the foreign editor's resistance, and in August 1942 she was one of the first women to receive full accreditation as a war correspondent.

When Tomara was approved, women were still such an anomaly that there were no ready-made uniforms available. At the time, civilian and enlisted journalists were assimilated into the army at the rank of captain and required to wear uniforms. The Army War College had only just gotten around to outfitting women that spring, when *Life* arranged for their celebrated photojournalist Margaret Bourke-White to be accredited to the U.S. Air Force, with the Pentagon getting first dibs on her pictures. Bourke-White served as both consultant and model for the army's first official women correspondents' uniform. It followed the basic pattern of a gold-buttoned officer's jacket, shirt, and slacks—standard khaki for every day, dress "pinks" (really gray) for special occasions—except that it included two skirts. In a hurry to leave, Tomara had her military ensemble run up by a tailor.

While Maggie lacked Tomara's robust résumé, she knew her fluent French was an argument in her favor. To boost her chances, she enrolled in a crash course in German at a Berlitz language school, attending classes in the evenings. She played the practice records late into the night, repeating the phrases over and over again until her roommate complained. "She put in hours and hours of study," recalled Ilma. "The guttural din, I was certain, would arouse the suspicions of our neighbors that we had a Nazi hidden in the apartment."

In the meantime, Maggie made the most of her assignments, hoping to score points with her superiors. She earned a mention in an interoffice memorandum—a sure sign a reporter's star was ascendant—with another page-one story on Madame Chiang Kai-Shek. China's captivating first lady was in the midst of a public relations tour of the U.S. in a last-ditch effort to drum up support for her husband's faltering Nationalist regime. Assigned to cover what looked like an unpromising chicken dinner at the Waldorf, Maggie managed to wangle her way into an A-list event being hosted later that evening by *Time-Life* publisher Henry Luce, at which Mme. Chiang was to meet with twelve Republican governors and an assortment of New York luminaries.

As the meeting was closed to the press, the other reporters left after collecting a transcript of Mme. Chiang's planned remarks. Maggie stayed just in case. The Secret Service questioned her, but she sweet-talked her way past the gray suits. Following the dinner, she intercepted Luce and asked if she could tag along for the private tête-à-tête with the governors. He demurred, explaining that he could not admit her without granting access to her colleagues. "But all the other reporters have gone," she beseeched him. "It would be just one more person. Just me."

That "just me" spoke volumes about her resolve and earned her a reputation as a tenacious and enterprising reporter. Her colleagues had never seen anything like it. As *Newsweek* would later observe of the breathtaking audacity that won Maggie the Mme. Chiang exclusive, "Into the very masculine world of journalism she carried her intense ego-centrism and combined it with a frightening determination and a strong-men-will-melt smile which, when used in tandem, held her to the bitter end of every story."

She proved she could handle the pace and pressure of the toughest assignments with her harrowing account of the Ringling Bros. and Barnum & Bailey Circus fire in Hartford, Connecticut, on July 6, 1944. Under normal circumstances, she would never have been trusted with such an important breaking story, but by the time the first call came in around 3 p.m., most of the reporters had already been sent out on assignment. In the meantime, the big top was ablaze. Of the thousands who had flocked to see the afternoon performance, it was estimated that more than a hundred, many of them children, had been trapped inside, and in the confusion were burned, suffocated, or trampled to death. Engel dispatched the only man left in the city room, Ted Laymon, telling him to grab the first train out of Grand Central for Hartford. As Laymon waited impatiently for it to leave, he caught sight of Higgins "running down the length of the depot, blond hair flying." The moment she leaped aboard, the train started to move.

They arrived at a scene of nightmarish proportions. All that was left of the tent was a smoking pile of canvas and charred seats. Bedraggled circus performers, still in their tights and spangles, were assisting the firemen. Police officers, some of them weeping openly, carried out the small bodies of burned children. No one knew how the fire had started, but it was theorized that a dropped cigarette had ignited a tiny flame that turned into a devouring curtain of fire, racing through nineteen tons of canvas in the main tent in "less than ten minutes." Maggie had gotten that staggering detail from the survivors. "If she hasn't talked to all the 6,000 or so who weren't killed, she will before morning," Engel hollered at rewrite, which was putting together the running from her dictated notes.

Maggie worked the story, reporting nonstop and phoning in voluminous eyewitness accounts to the city desk, until 4 a.m. First thing the next morning, she was at city hall demanding answers. How could the fire have spread so quickly? How could it have claimed so many lives? The final death toll was at least 168 killed and more than 700 injured. According to the *Tribune*'s exclusive report, the tragic fire, the worst in circus history, had been fueled by the waterproof coating on the tent, a highly flammable solution of paraffin wax and gasoline. By the end of the day, warrants charging manslaughter were issued for five circus officials.

Both Maggie and Ted Laymon were commended for their efforts. The two of them had competed against six *Times* men for material vital to the story. No other paper had the waterproofing angle, which explained the stunning swiftness of the blaze. Covering a major disaster was a rite of passage, and she had passed the test with flying colors. Laymon thought she had performed well on deadline, remaining calm and unruffled.

She had helped to marshal the facts and refused to be put off by lies and excuses. At one point, he remembered a harassed Hartford city official griping, "Where did you get that girl? She's so aggressive."

Laymon had to laugh. "That was Maggie all right, not afraid of anything or anyone," he said. "She could be pushy as hell, but there was never anything small or spiteful about her. She was quick to congratulate others on good work and was ready with compliments or commiseration."

Maggie renewed her bid for an overseas assignment. This time, she decided to go over the heads of her editors and appeal directly to the boss, Mrs. Reid. She picked the right publisher at the right time. "The *Herald Tribune* was an especially good place for women just then," recalled Tania Long, then a correspondent in the paper's London bureau. "Mrs. Reid liked to promote up-and-coming women journalists and Marguerite was lucky in having her support and sympathy as she was, in my view, very inexperienced and naïve."

But Helen Reid recognized the raw ambition in Maggie. It was a quality she looked for in her female employees. In her view, not enough women pushed against the boundaries of convention and "projected their imaginations" toward positions generally thought to be beyond their reach. Maggie was nothing if not aspirational. She wanted to seize control and shape her own destiny, not wait around to see if chance would shine on her. In Reid's opinion, she had displayed "drive and ingenuity" beginning with almost her first assignment on the paper. If she had stepped out of line and tramped on some male toes along the way, so be it.

At that very moment, the *Tribune* was busy making a play for women readers. A saleswoman at heart, Helen Reid was eager to encourage their patronage—especially since women did 80 percent of the nation's buying—and she believed they wanted to see more stories with a woman's byline. Another woman war correspondent might be just the thing.

A month later, on a sultry August afternoon, the paper's mild-mannered managing editor, George Cornish, called Maggie into his office and announced, "You are all set for overseas."

4

✳ ✳ ✳ ✳ ✳ ✳ ✳ ✳

Latecomer

I cannot tell you how she was like or different
from other women reporters—only how she
was like or different from all reporters, men
and women. She was like the best of them in
most respects and differed from the best only in
that she was more aggressively competitive.

—Walter B. Kerr, *Tribune* foreign correspondent

SHE ALMOST MISSED THE BOAT. AFTER WAITING ANXIOUSLY FOR
seven long weeks for the War Department to push through her accreditation as a war correspondent, Maggie was late for her midnight departure on the *Queen Mary*. The huge luxury liner had been retrofitted as a
troopship, dubbed the "G.I. shuttle," and now ferried thousands of men
across the U-boat-infested Atlantic to Great Britain twice a month, its
superior speed making the hazardous journey in just five days. On the
chilly November night of the sailing, a small group of veteran reporters
were assembled on deck when the vessel paused by one of the lightships in
New York Harbor, and the pilot ladder was lowered over the side. When
it was raised, they were amazed to see a slim young woman in army uniform clinging to the side ropes, her helmet slipped back to reveal a tousled
mane of blond curls.

Maggie's theatrical leave-taking would later strike some of her colleagues as typical of the headline-grabbing style she would inaugurate in

the months to come. As the story goes, Janet Flanner, the silver-haired fifty-two-year-old doyenne of foreign correspondents in France, whose signature pieces appeared in *The New Yorker* under the pen name Genêt, regaled friends with a droll account of the tardy *Tribune* ingenue's appearance: "She looked so sweet and innocent, I immediately thought of Goldilocks and wanted to protect her. If I'd known then what I know now, I'd have thrown her overboard." But like so many of the best-known tales about Maggie, it was apocryphal. Flanner was not on the *Queen Mary*— she had flown to London earlier that month—though that has not prevented the anecdote from being reprinted in virtually every account of Higgins's life. With Maggie, observed a colleague, "people often believed the myth rather than the reality."

It is fair to say that she was not exactly welcomed with open arms by the war-weary correspondents in bombed-out, blacked-out London. Many of them were refugees from the Paris *Herald*, the European subsidiary of the *New York Herald Tribune*, who had been forced to abandon the paper's operations there when the city fell to the Germans in the spring of 1940. They had endured three bleak, cold English winters, a diet of C rations and powdered eggs, and regular, remorseless Luftwaffe assaults. They all looked worn out and run-down in their shabby olive drab. Maggie's newness, by contrast, was all too apparent, announced by her dewy skin and shiny hair, and the stateside correctness of her pristine uniform and freshly issued correspondent's patch, its yellow lettering still bright against the green felt.

Her arrival in the closing days of 1944 coincided with the beefing up of the *Tribune*'s London bureau. Behind all the activity was the "whispered certainty" that the Allies would soon smash the German defenses and the war would finally end. The London bureau chief was Geoffrey Parsons Jr., the cheerful bon vivant son of the paper's chief editorial writer, who had been sent over to report on D-Day and was now in charge of a dozen or more correspondents covering the European war. Their temporary offices in the Fleet Street building of the *Daily Telegraph* were bulging with new people, most of whom were just back from the front or, like Maggie, en route to somewhere else. Jack Tait and John Durston were among the first of the reinforcements, followed by Richard Tobin, Herbert Clark, Joseph Driscoll, Tex O'Reilly, and Homer Bigart. The foreign editor, Joe Barnes, came over from New York to help direct traffic.

Maggie joined them at the Savoy, where most of the foreign correspondents were holed up. A bastion of Art Deco elegance, the storied hotel was favored by wealthy Londoners, who retreated to the relative luxury of its subterranean air-raid shelters during the Blitz. The bureau staff enjoyed the comfort of the feather beds and drank in the famed American Bar. But it was not as cushy a berth as it sounded. On one occasion a bomb struck the Thames Embankment nearby, shattering the hotel's windows, and the *Trib*'s James "Don" Minifie was struck by flying glass and lost an eye. As Eric Hawkins, the displaced managing editor of the Paris edition, recalled, "The lavish appointments, such as steam-heated towel dryers and enormous bathtubs, failed to compensate for the paucity of other amenities such as food."

If Maggie was late to the war, she was in plenty of time to experience the shuddering dread of the Luftwaffe's nightly visitations. After a brief lull, the Germans resumed their attacks on London that fall, terrorizing the city with a new bombing offensive. While most of the big newspaper buildings on Fleet Street remained intact, everywhere she looked there were piles of bricks and debris. On November 10, shortly after she arrived, Prime Minister Winston Churchill informed Parliament, and the world, that the Germans were again laying siege to England, this time with new long-range V-2 rockets.

Over the next few weeks, the *Tribune* gave prominence to her tightly written, descriptive accounts of the Allied air forces' destruction of vital enemy targets, the disintegrating German officer corps, and the chaos caused by the tens of thousands of German civilians fleeing ahead of the advancing Red Army. The Nazi propaganda machine tried to keep up their troops' morale by promising victory in the New Year. "The Berlin Radio," she reported, "predicted tonight in a broadcast that 'with another month of rockets nothing will be left of London.'"

She scored her first page-one story by picking up on the rumor that the War Department had instructed Clare Boothe Luce, the famously tart-tongued representative of Connecticut and member of the House Military Affairs Committee, to "keep quiet" during her tour of the European war theater. Disappointed by the controversial playwright's uncharacteristically low profile, she noted, "The English reporters who have not had an opportunity to interview Mrs. Luce seem the most put out."

It was an exciting time. Maggie loved the tension in the air, the lightning pace of events. She worked long hours, attended military briefings, and rushed each night to the Ministry of Information news center, housed in a huge London University building on Russell Square. The press center provided space and communications facilities, and offered immediate access to official news and handouts from SHAEF (Gen. Dwight D. Eisenhower's Supreme Headquarters Allied Expeditionary Force). She had to learn the frustrating task of collecting and transmitting news, and what she could and could not get past the military censors. She tried to hide how little she knew, but she was on unfamiliar ground and filled with uncertainty.

A beginner in the London bureau, she once again found her appearance to be more of a hindrance than a help. "As a foreign correspondent," she wrote later, "my biggest disadvantage in being both young and a woman was the resulting tendency of male officials to associate the combination of femininity and blond hair with either dumbness or slyness, or both." The cabinet ministers and military spokesmen consistently tried to brush her off with the "run-along-now-little-girl-I'm-a-busy-man" line, leaving her fuming and always on the back foot. "[They] seemed to consider that a bona fide foreign correspondent had to smoke a pipe (showing thoughtfulness and a sense of balance), ask long-winded questions (displaying scholarliness), and drop names." As this clubby, old-boy approach was not available to her, she often had to resort to rudeness to get questions answered.

Maggie had been in London only a short time when Charles Bernard, who had just joined the staff of United Press (UP), ran into her at the Ministry of Information, where they both had desks. Despite her obvious youth, she was doing a good job of covering the air war and helping produce the nightly main leads on the war that would make headlines in the *Trib* the next day. "She was beautiful enough to have made her mark in Hollywood, but in a news conference or at the typewriter she was a no-nonsense, let's get the job done reporter and writer," he recalled. Of course, she fell prey to the usual rumors. "There were suggestions that her looks got her into places and to see the right people easier than it was for others of her colleagues less endowed. But if so, she also had all the qualifications to meet the requirements of her assignment."

John MacVane, an NBC broadcast journalist who had won acclaim for his coverage of the Battle of Britain alongside Edward R. Murrow of CBS, was also impressed by the willowy blonde with the backbone of steel. He remembered her as one of the few newspaperwomen whose ability the men flattered by resorting to the same dirty tricks to beat her that they employed against each other. "Male reporters knew that she was just as able to scoop them or beat them to the news as any of the best of their brother men and acted accordingly," he said. MacVane described Maggie as a class act. "She never used her sex to further her professional career," he added, "something not possible to say about all women correspondents."

By the time the excitement of being part of the London bureau wore off, and her desire to be at the front rekindled, Maggie heard that she would be part of the large contingent moving to the newly reopened Paris office. She was delighted. She could not wait to savor the thrill of filing from the city of her dreams. The Allied armies had liberated the French capital in August of 1944, but it was several months before the presses in the *Trib*'s old six-story building on rue de Berri were ready to roll. The first issue of the new European edition of the *Herald Tribune* appeared on December 22, 1944. Its four pages were filled with grim accounts of the Battle of the Bulge, a surprise attack by the German army that resulted in one of the bloodiest battles of the war in the frozen Ardennes Forest.

Maggie spent an unhappy Christmas in London with Stanley. Earlier that fall, he had been transferred from Russia to headquarters of the U.S. Air Forces in Europe, located near Hampton Court, a half-hour drive from London. The initial bliss of being reunited quickly faded as they realized they had become different people during the year apart. After they moved from her room at the Savoy into a small flat, they argued incessantly. Stanley discovered to his dismay that as far as his bride was concerned, the paper came first. She did not eat or sleep until her story was finished, sitting in the freezing kitchen pounding away on her portable typewriter until all hours of the night. She was always late, broke dates, and could not be bothered with even the smallest domestic chores. It was like being with someone who was not really there.

Even in the short time they spent together, it was apparent they had little in common. Maggie, who in the first bloom of love had embraced his communist beliefs, had moderated her college radicalism to suit the tastes of the Republican *Tribune*. With the advent of war, her surging patriotism had replaced any concerns she once had for the proletariat. In her mind, fascism trumped capitalism on the list of evils that needed to be eradicated. She was still fond of Stanley, she wrote to her old friend Jean Craig, but they no longer seemed aligned, either politically or personally.

Looking back, Maggie thought that what she felt for him had been "admiration and affection but not love." Her liaison with John Watson, another mentor turned suitor, had taught her the difference. She had learned much from the affair and left it behind wiser and without regret. For all her defiant individualism at Berkeley, she had badly wanted the seal of approval and success conferred by a good marriage. It was what she had been raised to believe all young women aspired to—betrothal to a fine young man from a substantial family. A child of the Depression, she had never really gotten over her father's financial ruin and the awful penny-pinching years. Stanley represented security, what she had yearned for most during her Oakland adolescence. But almost as soon as she tied the knot, she felt constrained by it.

She had done a lot of growing up since her trip down the aisle. Her sense of self had blossomed in Stanley's absence, and she had forged an exciting, independent life. She was now recognized as Marguerite Higgins of the *Herald Tribune* and she would not trade her byline for the title of Mrs. Moore, let alone her career for the banal occupation of wifehood. Intensely aware of the opportunity this tumultuous moment in time presented, she saw the chance not just to report the news but to cover history and make her mark on the world. Years later, she recalled how it felt to be in the grip of such a compelling profession. "My ideas and personality had been subjected almost constantly to the direct and intense pressure of great events," she wrote. "Under those circumstances life can change you very fast."

It was almost a relief when Stanley moved headquarters again, this time to Saint-Germain on the outskirts of Paris. Maggie, no longer the pliable girl she had been when they first met, held out little hope for the marriage. Her father, who was also in Paris, met with his son-in-law, and then crossed the channel to console his daughter, offering advice and a shoulder to cry on. Worried about the stigma of divorce, Maggie's parents persuaded her to give the relationship another chance. But it was not to be, and they parted badly. An old Berkeley pal who was in town recalled Stanley's bitter disappointment. His darling girl had been warped by ambition, altered beyond recognition by her coarse profession. She was wedded to the job, not to him.

Maggie had no time to dwell on her personal troubles. Used to compartmentalizing her problems, she disciplined her mind to focus no further ahead than the next day, the next deadline. The urgency of the news made it easy to sweep aside all other concerns. She kept her head down and became even more consumed with her work. If she was going to sacrifice her marriage for the sake of her career, then she would damn well make it count. She would become a star correspondent. She would make it to the very top of her profession, and the paper's masthead, one day taking her place as a national pundit alongside Dorothy Thompson. She had always had high expectations of herself, as a student and as an athlete, harnessing her immense energies to achieve whatever goal she set herself. Now, more than ever, Maggie was driven to succeed. She moved forward with one single purpose—to make a name for herself before the war was over.

In addition to her regular bylined pieces for the *Tribune*, she sought out freelance assignments that would allow her to showcase her writing and reportorial skills. In February 1945, the first of a series of articles by her on young women in war-torn Europe began appearing in *Mademoiselle*. The editors touted their new foreign correspondent—"just turned twenty-four, with the training and international background that is exactly right for us"—in a fine introduction, accompanied by a large, flattering photograph.

She devoted her first column to the valiant young women in the French Forces of the Interior (FFI), members of the Resistance movement who continued to fight the Germans after the military collapse of their country. On a personal note, Maggie revealed that writing about the Resistance was "more than just another assignment," as it brought long-awaited news of her missing French relations. She learned that her young cousin Jacques Tomachot had been a leader of the Maquis, the guerilla bands that hid in the mountains, attacked the enemy, and aided downed airmen and escaping Jews. He was now fighting with the French army. His mother, her aunt Genevieve, had died on her farm in the South of France after the Germans had refused her medical aid. Thankfully, her other aunt, two uncles, and assorted cousins were all safe.

By injecting herself into the story, Maggie was breaking with a basic tenet of newspapering that a journalist should be a dispassionate narrator. At the time, *Trib* reporters avoided the first person, which was considered an unseemly form of navel-gazing, not to mention self-promotion. Maggie had no such scruples. Dramatizing her own life was second nature to her. Writing for *Mademoiselle* allowed her to highlight the novelty of her adventures as a woman correspondent doing what was once a man's job in the war. She sought fame—personal and professional—and welcomed the chance to pose as a glamorous role model in the pages of a glossy magazine.

She was counting the days until she went to Paris when she got sick. A viral infection landed her in the hospital and left her with a lingering case of jaundice. The London damp, months of hard work, and emotional distress caused by the breakdown of her marriage had sapped her reserves. Ralph McGill, editor of the *Atlanta Constitution*, remembered accompanying Wilbur Forrest, the associate editor of the *Tribune*, to see Maggie in the infirmary. "It was my first introduction to her," he recalled. "Lying there in the hospital bed, wearing a candy-striped flannel nightgown against the cold of the room, she looked like a tiny young girl." Forrest told him that at full strength she was a real dynamo and expected to go far. "No one who ever met Marguerite Higgins could forget her," McGill added, "or wish to."

5

✳ ✳ ✳ ✳ ✳ ✳ ✳ ✳

Early Maneuvers

She didn't need to sleep with anyone to get
a story. She would just bat her baby-blue
eyes at them and that would be enough.

—Russell Hill, *Tribune* foreign correspondent

BY THE TIME SHE MADE IT TO PARIS IN LATE FEBRUARY, MAGGIE FELT
behind and out of place again. The collapse of her marriage had shaken
her confidence, and she felt very alone and inadequate when she walked
into the Hotel Scribe, a faded tourist establishment in the Opera district that had been designated the new headquarters of the Allied press.
The Scribe housed hundreds of correspondents from all over the world,
as well as several hundred military censors and public relations officers,
and served as the SHAEF transmission center for news of the Allied war
effort. A Western Union office had been installed, along with Press Wireless, telegraphic machines, and radio studios.

On that wintry night, the hotel lobby was "as clamorous and bustling as a wartime railway station," Maggie recalled. "Helmets, musette
bags, mud-caked typewriters, bedrolls were strewn about waiting to be
claimed by correspondents going or coming from the front." Many of
the reporters milling around sported the brass insignia bearing the title
"War Correspondent," which meant they had been there since the North
Africa campaign or, at the very least, the cross-Channel invasion, and she
enviously noted the combat badges that indicated which force they had

accompanied. She instantly regretted the new red-velvet mittens poking out of one pocket of her uniform. They had been a gift from her parents, along with a small leather case holding a half dozen of her favorite records. Acutely aware of her "status as a novice," she worried the frivolous accessories made her that much more conspicuous.

She was certainly conspicuous. Daniel De Luce, an AP reporter whose coverage of the partisan resistance to the Nazis in Yugoslavia won the 1944 Pulitzer, had no trouble recollecting his first glimpse of Higgins in the hotel's crowded lobby—"Young, blonde, and beautiful," he declared without hesitation.

Maggie was rescued from her embarrassment by the *Tribune*'s Russell Hill, a handsome, twenty-four-year-old reporter who had a sensitive face and the reputation of being something of a boy prodigy among foreign correspondents. He had seen some of the worst of the fighting and had the scars to prove it. Hill had only recently been released from the hospital after a jeep he was riding in on the way back from Aachen, Germany, hit a land mine. He was injured and his colleague, *The New Yorker*'s David Lardner, son of the novelist Ring Lardner, was killed, along with their driver. It was young Lardner's first and last combat assignment.

Slightly awed at finding herself in the company of a wounded hero, Maggie spent the next few hours in the Scribe's basement bar in a daze. While Hill pointed out some of the journalistic luminaries—the tall, prematurely gray Vincent "Jimmy" Sheean, the dean of foreign correspondents, and the portly Hemingway—who added to the hotel's ambience, she tried to adjust her image of these idols to the somewhat disappointing reality. She had difficulty reconciling their fame with their inconsequential appearance in the flesh. Even more disconcerting was that they all seemed to know one another on sight, and even the most celebrated among them was greeted with a studied nonchalance.

When she finally got to her room, Maggie pulled out her sporadically kept diary and at the top of a new page jotted down "1 Rue Scribe"—she had arrived!

In her own fantasies, there was no more deliciously romantic address. As inwardly excited as she was, however, she knew it would not do to carry on like a giddy schoolgirl. A quick study, she had noted the offhand, unimpressed demeanor of the hotel's war-weary regulars and aspired to the role. Since foreign correspondents like to talk about themselves more than any other subject, it was not hard to get the gist of their conversational style. Her ear for the vernacular is evident in the deadpan journal entry describing her meeting with the larger-than-life writer who had exerted such a profound influence on her generation of would-be reporters:

> *Hill introduced me to Hemingway tonight. Hemingway was sitting on the couch in the basement lobby of the Scribe near the correspondents' mess. Beside him was a girl whose close-cropped hair looks like Maria in For Whom the Bell Tolls. Hemingway is rather fat and has a beard. Nobody pays much attention to him. In fact, reporters around the Scribe seem to make a point of not paying special attention.*

For Maggie, the most satisfying part of the encounter was that Hemingway seemed to accept her as a full-fledged—"well, almost"—member of their mutual profession. Instead of the dismissive attitude she had come to expect, he inquired, "How's London?"

"Lousy," she replied. "I got jaundice there."

"Bad case?" he asked.

"I'm on a no-drinking routine," she explained, aiming for the frayed tone of one for whom being on the wagon was a hardship.

Hemingway did not seem to doubt her affinity for the bottle and merely remarked, "Well, you won't find much temptation in there." With evident disgust, he pointed to the dimly lit bar, which had been looted by the Nazi propagandists who had taken over the hotel during the occupation, and now provided only a sickly pale variety of rosé.

Maggie, delighted that the great man had bought her hard-boiled act, concluded her journal entry with a flourish: "I, war correspondent Marguerite Higgins, am a colleague of war correspondent Ernest Hemingway. How about that?"

While her exchange with Hemingway had lifted her spirits, the latter part of the evening with Hill, who was nominally her boss, had left her discomfited. He had sat her down and immediately launched into an explanation of why it was fortunate the *Trib* had sent her to Paris, and not a moment too soon. The bureau was understaffed and overwhelmed: Sonia Tomara, who covered French politics, had been sidelined with pneumonia; Tex O'Reilly, who handled most of the war news, had been called back to New York for several weeks; and Geoff Parsons, who had been doing the diplomatic stories and running the bureau, was busy courting French officials so they could get the new European edition off the ground.

Given how shorthanded they were, Hill continued, he would be taking over the lead military story and was counting on Maggie to pick up the slack. She would deal with all the foreign news as well as French domestic politics. Seeing her blanch at this, he asked with a frown, "You do speak French, don't you?"

Maggie nodded in the affirmative, too shy to admit that she might be in over her head. Once again, it seemed, she was faced with the choice of learning fast or failing spectacularly. What Hill had just outlined sounded like a very tall order.

Even more earnest than she was, he studied her with concern: "Don't you think you can do it?" She assured him that she could. Of course, she could. What she did not let on was that she was "terribly, terribly scared."

Pressure brought out the best in Maggie. Her competitive instincts kicked in and she buckled down to work. The Paris bureau was a madhouse, with reporters rushing in and out at all hours and the phones ringing off the hook. There was so much breaking news that the established correspondents had enough on their plates without going out in search of stories. They were not lazy so much as resting on their laurels. Having no laurels, Maggie did the only thing she knew how to do—she became a city reporter let loose in post-liberation Paris.

Each day, she assigned herself the task of scouring all the French dailies, as well as the Agence France-Presse, the French wire service. When he had time, Hill gave her tips on who to talk to and tried to steer her in the right direction. Maggie, fearful of displaying her ignorance, opted to cover the waterfront. She requested interviews of every major government official, met with the top American military brass, and even paid a call on the American ambassador, Jefferson Caffrey, so he could fill her in on his national agenda. Along the way, she found angles and slants that were going unreported and submitted a steady stream of copy.

Her greenness was less of a handicap than it might have been because she had a facility for the language and brought fresh eyes to events her colleagues were tired of covering. In those first weeks in Paris, she worked around the clock, churning out two to three stories a day, and filing up to three thousand words a night. She covered the pronouncements of General Charles de Gaulle, chief of the French Provisional Government; the return of Marshal Phillipe Petain, who had presided over the puppet Vichy regime that cooperated with Hitler; and the trials of the accused traitors and Vichy collaborators who now stood charged with crimes against the state. She chronicled the difficulties of daily existence, and the dire food shortages and health problems plaguing the city that was "still on a semi-starvation basis as spring rolled around."

Desperate to prove herself, she kept up a frantic level of activity. In the process, Maggie irritated some of the bureau veterans, who thought she wasted a lot of time and energy because of her inability to be selective. But her exuberant hustling had its benefits. Because her byline appeared almost daily in the European edition of the *Tribune*, as well as in the New York paper, she was able to quickly establish her reputation with the local Allied officials and SHAEF staff. The sheer volume of her output meant that she occasionally hit the mark. She landed several front-page stories, some of them with international repercussions. "This attracted attention," she noted, "and, like most people, I like attention."

Paris was a joy after the drab austerity of London. She loved strolling along the wide boulevards and peering into the elegant shop windows. The city was full of lively little bars and cafés where the reporters could congregate and drink. In the carnival atmosphere of the Scribe, where everyone hung out for fear of missing something, she was caught up in the whirl of cocktail parties, dinners, and evening poker games. Walter Kerr, who had taken leave from the *Trib* to join the army, met Maggie when he stopped by the hotel's pressroom to say a quick hello to his old pals Parsons and Sheean. "When the three of us headed to dinner, Geoff invited Marguerite along," Kerr recalled. "I thought she was a very pretty girl, bright, interested in everything, with a good sense of humor."

Maggie never lacked for company. The Scribe was a hotbed of temporary liaisons, and it was teeming with solicitous men eager to make her acquaintance. Its residents lived in a suspended fantasy of the here and now, warding off intimations of mortality by pretending only the present mattered and they had no personal ties or obligations that extended beyond the front door. "Those wartime and immediate post-war years were really wild," explained Hill. "Nobody was bound by conventional restraints. Reporters were sleeping around, with women reporters as well as with other women. . . . Most of them had girlfriends, some of them living-in on a more or less permanent basis."

This cozy arrangement had been going on for nearly a year when the first wife arrived. She was Tex O'Reilly's better half, unexpectedly at the Scribe front desk and demanding to be let into her husband's room. But the army, which had commandeered the hotel, had its rules: "I'm sorry, Madam," she was told, "wives are not permitted here." The ensuing fracas gave O'Reilly enough time to allow the *jeune femme* who had been sharing his bed to make an unobtrusive exit. And it was hardly a secret that Hemingway, who was married to the *Collier's* correspondent Martha Gellhorn, had been shacking up with *Time's* Mary Welsh, who was estranged from her husband, an Australian reporter named Noel Monks. Similar tales of wartime assignations, some more ribald than others, were a dime a dozen.

Rumors swirled about what Maggie got up to after hours. If she sought comfort in a colleague's warm embrace, or just wanted a bit of fun, Hill considered it nobody's business. "Marguerite liked sex and she slept with a lot of people," he stated matter-of-factly. "But she didn't consider herself promiscuous. Once she said: 'I don't see how V. can be sleeping with two men at the same time?' 'Don't you really?' I asked, looking at her very hard. She had the grace to blush."

Hill never doubted that her work took precedence over any affairs of the heart. "I shared many intimate moments with her," he added, "but there was always the feeling that love was not the important thing to her." She courted fame more ardently than she ever did men.

Maggie had no intention of having her head turned. Nor did she plan to fall for one of the time-honored traps of the foreign correspondent—becoming so ensconced in her swell digs that she forgot what she had come to do in the first place. "When the war moved on from Paris, it left behind in press headquarters at the Hotel Scribe a lot of correspondents who felt there was nothing to be said for following armies going at full tilt," observed the Australian journalist Phillip Knightley. They could pick up enough stories just by "plucking the sleeves of soldiers on leave." Some were so glued to their barstools that they had to be prodded by their home offices to follow the troops as they pursued the fleeing Nazis. Not Maggie. Paris in springtime was lovely, but it was far from the battle lines, and a far cry from the excitement of war.

After seven weeks, she felt she had the bureau work under control. She began to get restless again. Fed up with tame assignments that kept her from the front, she pleaded to be allowed to do more. "The war," she wrote, "seemed so close, and yet—for me—so unattainable." The nearest she had come to any real adventure was when she almost made the group being convened for a parachute jump onto the Rhine River approaches. The correspondents had all drawn lots and Maggie had won. But Hill and Parsons would not hear of it. What if she jeopardized the mission? It was much too dangerous.

After they refused to let her go, Maggie sulked for days. Given half a chance, she was sure she could match any of the typewriter soldiers. She did not want any preferential treatment, just the chance to show what she could do. Her editors argued that no matter how rough and ready she claimed to be, SHAEF had banned female correspondents from the combat zone. Women had fought a mostly losing battle to be part of the first wave of correspondents who had mounted up for Normandy. There were 326 accredited American war correspondents, 38 of whom were female. SHAEF's directive permitted the latter to "go no further forward than women's services go," by which it meant the field hospitals with their nurse detachments. If the women correspondents violated the policy, they could be deported. Gellhorn reported from Omaha Beach, but as soon as it was discovered that she had made the crossing with the invasion armada as a stowaway on a hospital ship, she was stripped of all her credentials.

Col. Barney Oldfield, a public relations officer with the U.S. Air Force, understood that for reporters the war was the big story that would lead to a big career: "It was the lure of the front-page by-line and the established reputation for all time." He saw no reason not to give the gals a fair shot, but Oldfield did not make the regulations, he just enforced them. Although it continued to be a subject of debate, the army's view was that the presence of women was a distraction. As the Allied armies marched across France and on into Germany, Maggie watched one after another of her male colleagues depart for the forward press camps while she cooled her heels in Paris. Her frustration increased. She had to find a way to get closer to the action.

By March, she was miserable, sure the conflict would be over before she got within the sound of gunfire. Then she heard about an upcoming air force junket that might be her ticket to the front. Now that the Rhine had been crossed, the Allies were pouring into the industrial heart of Germany. The Ninth Air Force announced that it was going to fly a half dozen correspondents inside the Fatherland to inspect the damage inflicted by Allied aerial bombing. Among those who would be making the trip were Margaret Bourke-White of *Life*; Lee Miller, a former model turned photographer/correspondent for British *Vogue*; Rita Vanderwert of *Time-Life*; and Helen Kirkpatrick of the *Chicago Daily News*. Maggie immediately seized on their example as "excellent ammunition for those of my bosses who were still saying the front was no place for women." She stalked Hill and Parsons, arguing that this time, at least, they could not use her gender as a reason to disqualify her.

Unfortunately, Parsons had his own objections. He felt he had been stuck behind a desk too long, and wanted to ride along with the air force to see the fighting firsthand. Just when Maggie had resigned herself to being a war correspondent in name only, she caught a break. The night before Parsons was supposed to leave, he called to tell her he had been unavoidably detained. A crisis had developed on the European edition and he would have to stay and sort it out. If she was still determined to go to the front, he added, she could take his place.

Maggie was on the plane to Germany the next morning. The beauty of the air force junket was its mobility. In addition to their own C-47, the correspondents were provided with two jeeps, two public relations officers, and two sergeants—one responsible for communications, in this case a press teletype circuit, and another in charge of scrounging food and billets as they followed the advancing U.S. troops from city to city. They landed at Darmstadt, zigzagging around the bomb craters.

On March 17, Maggie filed her inaugural dispatch from the Western Front. She reported that for the first time in the war, Allied bombers would be taking off from airfields inside Germany, "made ready by aviation engineers in the face of shellfire, mud, and some of the worst weather conditions in years." She described the vast Allied air armadas hammering the Rhine's west bank, laying siege to Aachen, Cologne, and Jülich. More than fourteen thousand planes were taking part in the raids and providing continuous cover as the assault troops from the British Second Army and the U.S. Ninth Army landed. She filed story after story trumpeting their success in smashing Germany's defenses and establishing advanced outposts for their fighters to run bombing operations "in the heaviest air offensive in history."

After a week, she returned to her base at the Scribe for a few days to rest and regroup. She was ready to go again on April 1 when the Eighth Air Force advance unit took off for Frankfurt am Main. When they got there, the tanks were approaching the city, and a battle was underway at the crossing of the Main River. "Here roofs are a rarity," she reported after a jeep tour of the destruction, "and the thousands of heavy bombs have battered walls and buildings alike into rubble which, as it is cleared off the streets, forms piles two and three yards high."

The story was made to order, the prose pedestrian. But the quid pro quo implicit in their flying junket was that the air force provided transportation for the sightseer correspondents in return for a little favorable publicity, and Maggie was doing her part. A few days later, while she was stuck on a group jeep tour of yet another razed city, Helen Kirkpatrick made her own way to Schweinfurt, where the mayor had just committed suicide. It was part of a wave of suicides—what the Germans called *selbstmord*, or self-murder—sweeping the country as Nazi officials chose to end their lives rather than face defeat. Maggie had missed the story.

From the moment she arrived in Germany, she had looked around to see who else was making headlines, and it irked her when others seemed to outflank her. She came up short again at Torgau, near the Elbe, where the Soviet army, advancing from the east, and the American forces, marching from the west, were scheduled to meet for the first time. When she pulled up with a convoy of reporters, she spied Lee Miller and the *Life* photographer David Scherman, her lover, with whom she covered the war in tandem. They had already recorded the symbolic handshake and were about to drive away. Maggie griped to Scherman, "How is it that every time I arrive somewhere to cover a story, you and Lee Miller are just leaving?"

Even more vexing, Ann Stringer of UP got the print exclusive, filing the first dispatch on the historic link-up of Allied armies. Furious, Maggie realized that with so many journalists accompanying the liberating troops, the competition was intense. She would have to break free of her air force chaperones if she was to have any hope of distinguishing herself from the pack.

At dusk, the female members of the air force contingent, along with the colonel shepherding them, went in search of someplace to billet. On their first evening in Frankfurt, they drove to a residential area on the west bank of the Main River that had sustained only light bombing, where they proceeded to "requisition" an empty house. There was no running water or electricity. Forced to share a room that had four beds crammed together, the women made the best of it. When it was time to turn in, they agreed to keep the window open, all except for Maggie, that is. "A good part of the night was spent opening the window and Marguerite Higgins closing it," Kirkpatrick recalled with a chuckle. Although it may sound like a minor transgression—one of those "silly things you remember," as Helen put it—it was also a remarkable demonstration of egocentricity.

Not only did Maggie make little attempt to get along with her colleagues, most of whom were a decade her senior and far more accomplished, she blatantly ignored the unspoken pecking order among war correspondents that new arrivals defer to the old hands. At thirty-five, Kirkpatrick had earned her spurs the hard way. She had been reporting from Europe since the mid-thirties, finagling a job at the *London Sunday Times* after the *Herald Tribune* refused to send her abroad, and then joining the staff of the *Chicago Daily News* with the outbreak of war. To a veteran like her, Maggie seemed like a bad-mannered spaniel, wholly unconcerned with the norms that governed how a reporter should behave in the field, though whether this was out of innocence or arrogance was hard to say.

The neatly coiffed Kirkpatrick, who was regarded as the epitome of the seasoned professional, was not alone in taking a dislike to the willful little "minx," as she called Higgins. As they moved from city to city over the next few weeks, the women took a dim view of Maggie's lack of fastidiousness, courtesy, and consideration for others. She seemed to have a tin ear for the social nuances that allowed people to rub along together in trying circumstances. Even the fact that she flouted the dress code and wore sneakers instead of boots with her khakis was a point of contention.

Many of the women correspondents whose paths Maggie crossed in the spring of 1945 were appalled at the way she had cannonballed into their midst, with her spitfire personality and impeccable timing, ready to walk off with the honors at the end of the war. The best-natured women in the world—and after so many years in the trenches they were anything but—were apt not to relish putting up with so much blonde ambition. The war theater inspired a certain solidarity and, out of necessity as much as choice, the correspondents worked together as friends and colleagues, or friendly competitors. It was immediately apparent, however, that the *Trib*'s gung-ho young recruit saw them all as rivals. The same qualities that had ensured Maggie's rapid rise—the driven personality, ferocious work ethic, and single-mindedness that bordered on ruthlessness—now worked against her, and she would not soon be forgiven.

Maggie did not have a minute to waste on pleasantries. Being part of the sisterhood of war correspondents did not interest her. All her charm went to winning over the officers and soldiers who could be pumped for information, scrounging lifts, and cajoling the air force press sergeants into giving her dispatches priority. Wes Gallagher, head of AP operations in Germany, kept close tabs on the competition, including Higgins. No fan of having women in the field, he would chew out any AP man who offered her, or any less beauteous reporter, a ride. "Get 'em the hell out of that jeep," he would bellow, growing apoplectic at the sight. "They're no buddies of yours—they're just trying to get on top of AP's best story of all time."

According to Gallagher, Maggie hit the ground running and was soon outstripping the "Rhine Maidens," the honorific term for the Western Front's three most respected women correspondents—Iris Carpenter of the *Boston Globe*, Lee Carson of the International News Service (INS), and Ann Stringer of UP. All three had been threatened repeatedly with disaccreditation for violating their travel orders. After the liberation of Paris, the army finally caved in to the trio's demands that women correspondents be permitted to stay in the press camps and attend the briefings, but it had reiterated the ban against their presence at the front. Still, it was a hard-won feminine victory and Maggie made the most of it. Noting their success in getting major stories without always adhering to the regulations, she went a step further. She ignored the rules altogether.

As the Allies raced across Germany, the military public relations officers began to ease their restrictions. As soon as they gave an inch, Maggie took a mile. She quickly learned that exceptions were made, and that she could count on some commanders to look the other way when she was out of bounds. "She was very competitive, giving no quarter nor asking any," recalled Gallagher. "In those days, women correspondents were either treated better in many instances by the military than the men because there were so few of them, or worse because they were women, but Maggie always seemed to come out well no matter what."

Her looks, blonde and kittenish, and uncanny ability to contrive opportunities and exclusives wherever she went, soon gave rise to complaints that she was trading on her sex—and trading favors for information—in a way the other women correspondents would never stoop to, or at least never so brazenly. But Maggie was not averse to using all the weapons in her female arsenal, even if it was a strategy her peers condemned. As Russell Hill, who probably knew her better than anyone, observed, "The reason she stirred-up controversy is that her colleagues felt she used unfair methods to achieve her ends. She herself took the view that women war correspondents were discriminated against, especially in war zones, and that if she used her sex appeal, she was merely righting the balance."

Andy Rooney, then a twenty-six-year-old correspondent with *Stars and Stripes*, did not care for her. "She was smart, attractive, and unquestionably a good reporter," he recalled. "She was also one of the few I ever knew who was widely disliked by a generally collegial group of reporters." At any given time, there were usually three or four women among the thirty or so war correspondents in the army press camps, and as far as he could tell they were all accepted without reservation as part of the group. "None except Higgins," he noted, "was ever accused of using sex for their professional advantage."

Higgins was seen as the archetypal seductress—no man was safe around her—but the typecasting ignored the inherent hardship of her profession. Most foreign correspondents, male or female, found the road lonely, and at times frightening, and looked for solace and companionship wherever they could find it. Many women ended up forming liaisons with reporters or officers they met during the war, and more than a few— Iris Carpenter, Tania Long, Judy Barden, Betty Gaskill, Shelley Mydans, and Mary Welsh —married them. As Julia Edwards, who reported for *Stars and Stripes*, observed, "The double standard was never more evident than in the fact that newsmen who cheated on their wives and children back home aroused no criticism."

Ironically, as far as the male war photographers were concerned, there was an even more notorious Maggie in their midst—namely, Margaret Bourke-White. An outrageous flirt, she was regarded as so unscrupulous in pursuit of exclusive pictures that she would stop at nothing to persuade a commanding officer to take her—and her hundreds of pounds of equipment and luggage—on his plane, earning her the label "the general's mattress." In her forties and twice divorced, Bourke-White was known to like men. Whenever she shared the CO's quarters, her biographer Vicki Goldberg noted, "the news spread faster than a military directive."

Probably better than most, Maggie understood that as successful women in a man's world, they would always be accused of using sex for advancement, whether it was true or not. She liked and admired Bourke-White, who had competed and excelled in a male-dominated profession. To some extent, Maggie modeled her career on that of the pioneering photographer, who had achieved world fame at an early age. She had read Bourke-White's acclaimed book about the Italian campaign, *They Called It "Purple Heart Valley,"* and emulated her lean, hard prose, as well as her none-too-deprecating descriptions of her own bravery. She also could not help noticing that the statuesque brunette somehow always managed to look well turned out in her tailored uniform. Neither the rigors of the field, nor the slander of her colleagues, diminished her defiant femininity. Not surprisingly, the two Maggies became friends.

The famed *Life* photographer Carl Mydans, who worked closely with both women, thought the barrage of criticism about their sex lives was just a way of diminishing their accomplishments, implying it was the only way they could get a leg up on their rivals. "[They] faced all kinds of problems because they were the real forerunners of women in journalism and they were blazing new trails," he recalled. "Their competitors would do anything to deter them. (Newsmen have no honor.) They dealt continually with resentment from almost all their peers. Both received all kinds of rebuffs from people who thought they couldn't and shouldn't be doing the job they'd decided they wanted to do, and, in fact, they were able to do very well."

The much bandied-about claim that they had "slept their way to the top" was payback for invading the war front, which the men considered their privileged domain. "Indeed, if you listened to all the stories about Marguerite, you could conclude that she slept with the entire U.S. Army," Mydans said. "It was the ultimate put-down for a woman. It wouldn't work in reverse—for example, a male reporter being accused of sleeping with a source—because that would actually be seen as complimentary, and it would not cause a man to lose face in the same way." The motivation behind the smear campaign "was fear," plain and simple. "The men were afraid the women would get the story or picture they didn't."

For her part, Martha Gellhorn was sufficiently rankled by the rampant sexism she encountered that in 1945 she and Virginia Cowles, a Hearst correspondent, cowrote a play entitled *Love Goes to Press*, satirizing the way the men viewed the women who covered the war. In one scene, a swaggering correspondent, an unmistakable caricature of Hemingway, warns his mate to be wary of predatory females: "Don't be deceived by Miss Mason. She and her pal Miss Jones sail around looking like *Vogue* illustrations and they get stories before you've even heard of them. Some of our colleagues have a low opinion of those girls just because of that little trait."

BLESSED WITH SEEMINGLY IMPERVIOUS self-belief, Maggie went her merry way. On the evening of April 11, she was back at the Scribe when she heard that a big story was about to break—Gen. George S. Patton's Third Army had just overrun Buchenwald, the first major concentration camp in Germany to be liberated by the Americans. The tip-off came from Capt. Gordon Fisher of the 312th Ferry Squadron, a hardy blond pilot from Wisconsin who had promised to give her a lift whenever she needed it. Sounding keyed up, he told her that his unit had been instructed to round up a group of reporters and bring them to the camp ASAP.

Early the next morning, Maggie—joined by Margaret Bourke-White, Lee Miller, and the *Time* writer Percy Knauth—boarded Fisher's cargo plane for the two-and-a-half-hour flight to the tiny town of Weimar. Word had gotten out and so many correspondents showed up at Orly Air Base that there was not enough room for them all to go. By then, the persecution of Jews was well known, but the rumors of death camps—of thousands of people being systematically gassed and incinerated— were so extreme that they seemed beyond belief. Like many of the reporters, Maggie was deeply skeptical of wartime-atrocity tales designed to rile up the troops. She, for

one, "wasn't going to fall for such stuff." Until she saw the camps for herself
and could investigate, she would reserve judgment. As a consequence, she
approached Buchenwald in "a mood of journalistic conservatism."

At the Weimar landing strip, they were anxiously awaited by Col.
Max Boyd, an air force information officer, who bundled them into command cars for the ten-mile drive to the camp. They arrived only hours
after Buchenwald had been liberated. On the way, Boyd told them that
approximately twenty thousand prisoners remained at the camp. According to what the Americans had been able to learn, some two thousand
victims were being killed every month. He tried to warn them that the
conditions were deplorable. Maggie thought she was prepared, that she
had seen enough battlefields to be inured to the cruelty and barbarism of
war. But nothing could have prepared her for what was there.

As soon as they passed through the iron gates of the main entrance,
her doubts evaporated. Her first, and most lasting, impression was the
terrible, cloying stench of death that lay heavily in the air. She and the
other reporters stood in the command car and stared in stunned silence
at the human wasteland. At first, it was difficult to take in the enormity
of the slaughter that had taken place. Her mind recoiled at the sight of
stacks of rigid bodies, unable to believe human beings were capable of
doing this to one another.

As her initial shock and revulsion receded, she set herself the task
of describing the scene before her, filling her notebook with the hideous
details. The dead and dying were everywhere. Thousands of men, women,
and children, left naked and uncovered, had been piled carelessly in cor-
ners and packed against the walls. She was struck by this final cruelty:
"The most awful testimonial to the utter degradation of the Nazi jailors
was the indignity to which their human victims were subjected even in
death." Many of the corpses were mutilated beyond recognition, missing
eyes and ears, the shaven heads bruised and bashed like overripe apples.
"As if to emphasize the horror," she wrote, "the frosty spring nights had
frozen into ghastly stalactites the trickles of blood and yellow bubbles
of mucus that oozed from the eyes and noses of the many who had been
bludgeoned or otherwise tortured to death."

There was no time to process the macabre sight. Appalled, she blocked out everything, numbing her emotions the way she always had in times of crisis in order to function. She had to compartmentalize her feelings, putting aside her condemnation and disgust for later. She compared her mindset to that of a surgeon operating on a patient, or a military leader ordering his men into danger. "At Buchenwald," she recalled, "all my energies were focused on obtaining the pertinent facts against the Nazis in the shortest possible time; for in light of the importance of the story and the vast number of facts to accumulate, I had an uncomfortable early deadline."

Working quickly and methodically, Maggie set about documenting the dead and acquiring testimonials from the living. She began by questioning and cross-questioning the stronger-looking inmates with an almost clinical detachment, her manner brusque, even challenging. After interviewing a number of survivors, she realized her hard-charging approach was uncalled for and softened her tone. She later castigated herself for her insensitivity, recalling the "relentless persistence" of her questions with shame. Her focus had been so intense she had omitted any show of compassion. In retrospect, she thought that the victims of Buchenwald must have found her adherence to journalistic rigor both baffling and callous.

A French prisoner took her to see the crematorium where the Nazis incinerated the bodies of the dead. When he told her that some of the guards had put victims in the ovens while they were still alive, Maggie demanded to know if he had seen it with his own eyes. When he explained that he had heard the story from a fellow prisoner, she insisted on immediately interviewing the sole surviving witness. They located the English-speaking Pole, a hero of the Warsaw uprising, who had an excellent memory. He not only confirmed the story, he provided the names of the victims, and the names of the guards, as well as approximate dates.

The young American pilot, who had tagged along out of curiosity, found it difficult to cope with the surreal scene as they walked on and on, through one torture chamber after another. Maggie and several of the other reporters had tied bandannas over their noses and mouths in an attempt to filter the choking pestilential fumes. But in the cellar beneath the crematorium, where men had been hung on hooks fixed to the wall, Fisher felt like he was suffocating. He could not stand it a second longer. "The stench of the place drove us to seek fresh air," he recalled. "We stumbled into daylight, over dried bones and below the gallows where the Nazis illustrated to their students how dull and common hanging could be."

When they finally returned to their car, they sat in morose silence, too distressed to say anything. "The reaction of Captain Fisher," Maggie noted later, "and nearly all was, 'I wouldn't have believed it if I hadn't seen it.'"

As they drove to the airstrip along the highway, she saw the good citizens of Weimar walking back to their houses. After touring Buchenwald early that morning, Patton was so incensed he ordered the town mayor to bring one thousand people to bear witness to the evidence of the Nazi crimes at the concentration camp. American officials wanted to ensure that German citizens were made to confront the Nazi atrocities so that what happened at Buchenwald could never be dismissed as wartime propaganda, and wiped away by people who preferred to forget.

Maggie's story, "Horror Comes Home," ran on the front page of the *Herald Tribune* on April 18, 1945. It was reprinted as a special editorial in the *Stars and Stripes* and appeared in hundreds of newspapers across the U.S., helping to increase awareness of the fiendish reality of the Nazi extermination camps. She gave an unvarnished account of what she saw and described the reactions of the weeping, protesting Weimar citizens as they were forced to trudge sixteen miles through "the vast arena of sadism and mass murder" that made the huge Buchenwald camp the vilest of the prisons yet liberated by the western Allied armies:

One thousand men and women of the town where the poet Goethe wrote Germany's greatest songs were marched past the heaps of rigid, naked bodies of people who, through starvation, beatings, and incredible torture, had died in such great numbers that the Gestapo had not had the opportunity to dispose of them before the Americans swept in. At the crematorium, where some 200 prisoners were disposed of daily, several women fainted at the sight of the half-burnt humans still in the ovens. Others attempted to put their hands over their eyes to block out the gruesome sight. A military authority forbade this, and ordered them to look, telling them: "You must find the courage to face the things for which you are responsible."

The next day, Maggie and Percy Knauth returned to Buchenwald for a memorial service in honor of more than fifty-three thousand political prisoners who had died at the hands of the Nazis. In the gathering twilight, they watched the long lines of liberated prisoners slowly shuffle into the meeting grounds, most still dressed in their striped prison garb, and stand at attention in neat rows. They stood silent as statues, mourning their murdered comrades. Then they swore an oath to keep fighting until the last guilty person had been judged by a tribunal of nations, until the absolute destruction of Nazism had been achieved. Under a black flag of mourning, they also paid tribute to America's fallen leader. Earlier that day, a radio report had delivered the news that President Roosevelt had died of a massive cerebral hemorrhage. Learning of it that way, while they were at the death camp, it was almost too much for Maggie to take in.

As the ceremony was coming to an end, a wild-eyed American soldier rushed up to them and, tugging at Knauth's elbow, urged him to hurry if he "really wanted to see something." She trailed them to the entrance of the camp. In one of the adjacent cellblocks, two dozen GIs were taking turns beating up six German youths they had found cowering in the woods. They had summarily sentenced them as members of the SS and were in the process of meting out their own punishment. Afraid the violence would escalate, Knauth went off in search of help. Within minutes, he returned with a second lieutenant who bawled out the soldiers and separated them from their helpless captives. It turned out the German youths, all teenagers, had been drafted only days earlier into forced-labor gangs to help dig trenches. Disaster had been averted, but just barely. The sight of her own forces taking instant retribution shook Maggie to the core.

Her view of the world changed irrevocably that day. There was something about the brutality exhibited by the American troops that shattered "some very smug, very black-and-white notions" she had about the nature of war, a romanticized image of the army nurtured by her father, and even some of her fundamental convictions about the distribution of good and evil between the Allied and Axis sides.

In some ways, of course, the GIs' response was understandable. They had seen too much death that day and their anger had spilled over. They had acted like a mob rather than a military unit. "The difference between what our GIs had done and the calculated brutalities of the Nazis was a very important matter of degree," she reflected later. "But not until Buchenwald did I begin to comprehend, in terms of my own experience, how this matter of degree is directly related to the difference between totalitarian police states and democratic forms of government."

Maggie left Buchenwald with a new sense of mission. She came away with an expanded understanding of her role as a reporter, and the importance of the press as a check on the excesses of the military, the government, and fanatical demagogues. Her anger at all the death and suffering she had witnessed became her personal battle cry, her calling. She felt it was her duty as a journalist to expose such terrible abuses and to hold the villains accountable. One of the prisoners, a woman who had been a lawyer before she was arrested, had told her that it would take "constant vigilance" to make sure that Hitler's monstrous Third Reich never happened again. Her words resonated so powerfully with Maggie that she quoted them at length in a subsequent dispatch. She decided then and there that she would keep a constant watch on authoritarianism and injustice around the world. She would keep the vigil.

There was a new tone to her articles, an undercurrent of gravity and moral responsibility. Traveling in the wake of the Twelfth Armored Division in Bavaria, she remarked on the civilians' "blithe disregard for consistency" as they hastily hauled down the swastikas from their homes and town halls and greeted the American troops with smiling faces. The Germans showed an infuriating inability to confront the truth about Hitler and the concentration camps. Sounding more like a columnist than a journalist, Maggie ended one article that April with a rousing diatribe that channeled Dorothy Thompson. "Many of the people are ripe for guidance by the Allied authorities, and the great pity is that our psychological warfare people are not on hand," she wrote. "As far as this correspondent can see the most important thing is to let these people know how the world feels toward the Nazis and why."

She spent weeks chasing the big running story of the moment, the hunt for the Nazis still in hiding. Living on adrenaline, she filed dispatch after dispatch, working nonstop. She got close to the counterintelligence corps, trading tips with them and sometimes being invited along on raids. She covered the capture of many of the top officials in the Third Reich: Hermann Göring, the commander in chief of the Luftwaffe, "stony-faced and grave" in his sky-blue uniform as he spoke to correspondents in the garden of the house where he was being held; Robert Ley, the Nazi labor leader, who was wearing "rumpled white pajamas beneath a shoddy overcoat" when he was picked up in Schleching; and Julius Streicher, the virulently anti-Semitic publisher of the newspaper *Der Stürmer*, "manacled and silent," and placed under a twenty-four-hour watch to prevent an exit similar to that which deprived the Allies of their prize war criminal, the Gestapo chief Heinrich Himmler, who swallowed a cyanide pill after being detained.

The closing days of the war were thrilling for Maggie. Weary correspondents who had spent months slogging through the mud, foraging for stories at the front, watched her clean up as town after town fell and the Third Reich quickly came unraveled. The final phases produced some spectacular headlines. She reported the discovery of the secret library of Dr. Alfred Rosenberg, author of the Nazi racial theory, in a cellar five stories below the sixteenth-century Lichtenfels Castle; the seizure of an enormous haul of art treasures, valued at more than $2 billion, found in seven different hideouts, from mountain tunnels and castle vaults to Göring's leather-lined luxury train; and the fantastic trek of five hundred thousand Wehrmacht troops, tired and frightened, from the mountains of Austria to Munich to await discharge.

She also managed to write a lengthy piece for *Mademoiselle*, "Finale in the West," recapping her adventures with Peter Furst. In recounting the final surrender of Munich, Maggie left out how they had returned to the Bavarian capital after filing their Dachau stories. They drove through the crowd-filled streets, this time dodging flowers instead of bullets as civilians cheered and waved and pounded on their jeep with joy. Searching for a place to stay that night, they stumbled on a magnificent pinewood mansion that belonged to Hermann Giesler, a leading Nazi architect. After they ascertained that no was living there, the reporters promptly made themselves at home. "We lived it up for two days," said Furst. "We had a beautiful bath. His wine cellar was stocked with champagne. It was quite wonderful."

Afterward, Furst went back to Rome and Maggie to Salzburg. He was not surprised by the way she took off, with hardly a backward glance. She was always honest and unabashed about putting her career before any personal attachments. Furst, who was all of twenty-two, had been amazed when she had cheerfully confided that she had slept with the *Tribune*'s foreign editor to clinch the overseas assignment. But he knew what she was like and liked her anyway.

His most enduring memory of Maggie was when they were caught in a traffic jam on the autobahn after the battle for Frankfurt. Army trucks, tanks, jeeps, and command cars had all slowed to a standstill. In the distance, they could see an officer angrily gesticulating with his arms and barking orders—it was Patton directing traffic. When he spotted them, he came striding over and demanded, "What are you bastards doing in a closed jeep?"

Army rules demanded that all jeeps had to have their tops down. That day, however, a surprise snowstorm had blanketed the countryside and Maggie had raised the soft top in an attempt to stay warm. She was wearing her favorite furry hat, a Russian helmet liner, and Patton, a stickler for the dress code, ordered a colonel to have them cited for that infraction as well. Furst tried to explain and stammered, "Hold on, this is a lady you are talking to . . ."

Maggie just smiled sweetly at Patton and said, "General, you are out of uniform, too." He was wearing a helmet with four stars on it, but his promotion to full general was not yet official and would not be announced until the following week. Whereupon Patton uttered his favorite epithet and waved them on.

6

✳✳✳✳✳✳✳✳✳

Uncharted Terrain

When I first met her, in uniform in Germany,
I thought her attractive, but rather plain.
An untidy woman with a shiny rather pallid
face. It was her brain that attracted me, and
her keenness on the job of newsgathering,
and a basic wistfulness and humility.

—George Millar, *Daily Express* correspondent

AFTER THE PROLONGED TENSION OF WAR, THE SUDDEN RELEASE
was disorienting. Maggie felt no sense of elation, just the emotional let-
down that follows a period of great exhilaration. She had mobilized all her
resources to cover the war and now felt a bit lost. Peace felt like uncharted
terrain, new and unknown. "Four months without a break in Germany
with its ruined, silent cities, its empty stores, and the vacant, bewildered
people, was too long," she wrote. "It was hard to judge the news. The lack
of newspapers left one completely confused about what was happening
in the rest of the world." Rudderless, and unsure what to do next, she
decided to go back to Paris for a while and try to get her bearings.

Before she left the Third Army's palatial headquarters in Salzburg,
she "liberated" a German Auto Union sportscar that had once belonged
to von Ribbentrop, which she had painted the regulation olive drab with
all the proper army insignia. It was not the only thing she took with her.
She had also acquired a new traveling companion, the British journalist

George Millar of the *London Daily Express*. As she confessed in her memoir, it was a *coup de foudre* that came out of nowhere and swept her off her feet, nearly taking her byline off the front page: "I might have interrupted my newspaper career in the summer of 1945 by marrying George Reid Millar, D.S.O., M.C. [Distinguished Service Order, Military Cross], a hero of the Maquis, a talented writer, and the most beautiful man I ever met."

To be fair, Millar had that effect on people. The scion of two wealthy Scottish families, he was every bit the bonny Prince Charming—rosy of lip and cheek, with wide-set blue eyes and lashings of thick blond hair—and outrageously attractive. A quiet, self-mocking modesty did not quite hide the steely self-confidence. There was something so compellingly seductive about him, and at the same time so intensely solitary and mysterious, that he cast a spell on men and women alike. If most war correspondents felt that by virtue of their frontline work they also belonged to a kind of military elite, "Golden Millar," as his friends called him, was regarded as a first-ranker in both worlds.

He had won acclaim covering the Battle of France in 1940 for the *Express* before quitting journalism for action. He enlisted in the Rifle Brigade of the British Army, fought in North Africa, and was wounded, captured, and interred in various POW camps. After two escape attempts, he jumped a moving train in Germany and spent months relying on his wits to survive behind enemy lines before making his way back to England. He was decorated, initiated into the Secret Operations Executive (SOE), trained as an agent, and dropped into occupied France just before D-Day to help the Maquis establish a sabotage unit. By the autumn of 1944, Millar had been missing so long that most of his former colleagues had given him up for dead.

The CBS radio correspondent Eric Sevareid, his best friend in Paris in the early days of the war, was so astonished when Millar reappeared in Besançon after it was liberated by the Americans that his description of seeing him again is arresting:

> Here, suddenly, he was striding toward me, more radiantly alive than ever, his incredibly beautiful face blooming like that of a

young girl in love. He was dressed immaculately in the uniform of a British captain, his square shoulders squarer and more soldier than before, and his bearing, his whole being conveyed an impression of personal triumph, of a happy self-mastery that was carried with delight.

Maggie's pulse also quickened at her first glimpse of Millar. It was at a press conference at Schloss Klessheim, only months after he had returned to reporting for the *Express*. Although nearly thirty-five years old, he was bronzed and bleached by the sun, and wearing the knee-length khaki shorts and open-collared shirt favored by British officers in warm weather, so she took him for a lad in his twenties. "This annoyed him," she recalled. "For despite all his accomplishments, he was almost as sensitive as I about not being taken seriously." She was perceptive enough to realize that he hated his pretty-boy looks, and it drove him to seek out hazardous escapades that would dispel once and for all any suggestion of "girlish softness." Like her, he courted danger. They both had a need to prove themselves, to push themselves to extremes—to place themselves literally *in extremis*. It made them a volatile, combustible pair.

At first, Maggie agreed to give Millar a ride only because he worked for a British paper and was not a direct competitor. Neither was looking for romance, but the relief of victory, sense of success, and glorious spring days were intoxicating. They entered easily into a lusty camaraderie, alternately flirting and sparring and making love against the storybook landscape of Austria. After V-E Day, Europe opened up like a flower in sunshine to meandering correspondents no longer under the constant threat of deadlines. Maggie and Millar made their way leisurely to Paris. They wandered around the lush countryside, through fertile fields planted with vines and fruit trees, gorging themselves on fresh peaches and plums, tender green asparagus, artichokes, and lettuce.

Maggie had been detached from her emotions for so long that when she finally let her guard down, she fell head over heels in love. Happiness made her foolish and childlike. Millar was a decade older, a decorated war hero, and she was enthralled by him. In her eyes, he was a true adventurer, "unaccepting of the humdrum and the ordinary, never allowing himself to be trapped by the routine of life." He had trained as an architect at Cambridge University, worked as a merchant seaman, and explored the mountains and monasteries of northern Spain on a donkey. Unlike her, he had grown up with money among Britain's cosseted aristocracy and enjoyed a sybaritic youth as a member of what was referred to in the society columns as the "international set." He could handle a horse, ride to hounds, and fly a plane; he could even rumba. He knew all about champagne and fine wines, could order expertly from a French menu, and treated her to the first real gourmet meal of her life.

Millar had already written a book, dashed off during a month's leave, recounting his experiences with the French Resistance. Entitled *Maquis*, it had been rushed into print and became a bestseller. On the eve of its publication, Millar was awarded the DSO. De Gaulle was sufficiently impressed to award him the Legion d'Honneur and the Croix de Guerre. Millar was almost finished with a second memoir based on his life on the run in wartime Europe. He planned to call it *Horned Pigeon*—an obscure reference to a bird wounded in flight—because the beautiful redheaded woman with whom he had eloped a few years earlier, and whose memory had sustained him throughout his ordeal, had not waited for him and was living with somebody else. A less narcissistic personality might have appreciated the irony in the fact that the woman who had been unfaithful to her first husband to be with him had now betrayed a second. Maggie interpreted this melodrama to mean that he was at a loose end, and available.

Millar introduced her to things that had previously been beyond her ken, and she began to daydream about a future in which they roamed the globe together: "We would sail to Byzantium, navigate the Amazon, float down the Nile. We would climb the pyramids in the stealthy silence of the desert nights. We would interview the great and the poor of the world. We would expose the corrupt and champion the true. And be magically in love." The cringing sophomoric tone is indicative of just how young she was, and how impressionable. She thought their romance was written in the stars and would last forever. She failed to notice that there was something tortured about him, something wayward and, beneath the suave exterior, a little ruthless.

She was so besotted that she wrote unreservedly of her latest liaison in the pages of *Mademoiselle*, gushing about how she and Millar had just passed "an idyllic two days in this lovely valley, where the Wolfgangsee—a lake as blue as forget-me-nots—lies hidden in the towering Tyrolean mountains." After they went skinny-dipping, they were arrested by two American MPs who thought they were spying on King Leopold III of Belgium, whom the Nazis had kept under house arrest in a nearby villa. Millar managed to get them released after he convinced the authorities that they were unaware of the royal family's whereabouts.

Taking a break from hard news, they went in search of colorful stories and characters. The valley was full of fugitives. It was Millar and a friend, an English photographer, who tracked down Hitler's butler in his secret hideout in the Alps, though it was Maggie who got all the credit. Arthur Kannenberg claimed to be living in fear because he "knew too much about the Fuhrer's private life." He confirmed Hitler's long love affair with Eva Braun, a former Munich shopgirl. He described her as a sensuous blonde who dressed and perfumed lavishly, and puffed incessantly on cigarettes despite smoking being strictly verboten in the Nazi leader's house. The butler painted a strange picture of his employer of fifteen years, whom he still revered, describing Hitler's obsessive neatness, fondness for flowers, and frequent tantrums.

Kannenberg, who insisted on bringing out his accordion, told them that one of the Führer's favorite tunes was Walt Disney's "Who's Afraid of the Big, Bad Wolf?" To Maggie's delight, dozens of news outlets gave her story a ride. *Newsweek* reprinted her scoop under the headline, "What Long Teeth, Adolf," and congratulated Higgins for ferreting out the butler in his bolt-hole. It was another feather in her cap.

By the time they reached Paris, the city that had lain somnolent and shuttered over that bitter cold winter was slowly coming to life. But it was not the "Gay Paris" of old. The end of the war, the cause of so much rejoicing back in the States had brought sorrow to scores of French women who feared they might never see their husbands again. Maggie wrote movingly of the forlorn groups of wives who stood for hours outside Gare d'Orsay waiting in vain for news. "The only notification of widowhood will, for most, be the continued absence of their men," she wrote. "For the furnaces of Dachau, Buchenwald and Auschwitz did their work well."

Millar introduced her to a White Russian princess who had helped hide him from the Germans after his escape. Her family was dead, the fortune long gone. She lived in a large apartment near the Tuileries that she shared with a family of cats. During the occupation, she had concealed more than a half dozen American and British pilots, all fliers who had been downed in France. Millar only stayed one night. Unable to stand the smell of the cats, he opted for a hotel and the "risk of capture." Maggie listened spellbound to their stories of donning disguises and staying one step ahead of the Gestapo. She wrote about the memorable afternoon in her next column for *Mademoiselle*, where Millar had begun to feature rather prominently.

Everyone at the Scribe knew about their affair. Maggie was obviously mad about him. "He was certainly her one big love," said Hill. "She didn't make any secret about it to her friends." Maggie viewed her first marriage, to Moore, as ancient history. She had seen Stanley in Paris earlier that April, and they had signed a separation agreement. By then, there was no rancor between them. She had agreed to relinquish his surname—not that she had ever used it—and any claim to money or property. They had decided to seek a French divorce, but the legal bureaucracy proved too complicated. Instead, Moore worked out the details in friendly consultation with her father and filed the divorce papers on his return to California.

Maggie did not reproach herself for the relationship's untimely end. She did not allow herself to think in terms of failure. No one was to blame. "My marriage had been a wartime thing," she wrote in her memoir, "and had gone the way of many marriages built on a seven-day honeymoon, followed by many years of separation."

In hindsight, she realized that her concept of love had evolved with age and experience. If love, as she now defined it, meant needing someone so much that it was painful to be without him, then she had never felt that for Stanley. "I don't think I ever needed my first husband at all," she reflected, "because there was never time or occasion for the need to develop." When she compared her feelings for the two men, she realized Millar was her first true passion. "I discovered love," she wrote, "and the kind of need for another of which I had not imagined I was capable." If her first attempt at matrimony had proved disappointing, it did not dim her enthusiasm for the institution. She was sure she and Millar were meant to be.

At the time, many of Maggie's contemporaries were leaving the profession to get married and start a family, returning to more traditional prewar roles. Iris Carpenter was engaged to a colonel she had met in Germany and was sailing to America. Sonia Tomara resigned from the *Trib* to begin planning a future with her husband-to-be, Judge William Clark, whom she had met in Algiers. "You can't be married and be a correspondent," she explained. "It takes all your time and all your soul and," she added with finality, "all your attention." But Maggie was convinced her partnership with Millar would allow them to flourish both in their careers and as a couple. "For a while," she wrote of that period, "I thought I could have my journalism and George too."

There was plenty to do at the Paris bureau, where there had been a flurry of departures and staff changes, leaving them shorthanded as ever. Maggie spent the hottest weeks of the summer covering Marshal Petain's trial for high treason, which was by turns a historical inquiry, high-stakes political theater, and legal drama. Day after day, she sat in the small, crowded courtroom in the Palais de Justice watching as the white-haired, waxen-faced former Vichy leader and hero of Verdun was accused by former colleagues of betraying his country and "selling out" to the Germans.

The exhausting trial ended at 4 a.m. on August 15. Petain was found guilty of collaborating with the Germans and sentenced to death. Five days later, de Gaulle, who himself had been condemned to death by the Vichy government, commuted Petain's sentence to life imprisonment. Maggie reported that most Parisians seemed satisfied with the outcome: "The solution, it is felt, imposes the nation's full censure on Petain, but saves the country from sending before a firing squad a man who is nearly ninety."

Long before the trial was finished Millar had left. Living in her clut-
tered room at the Scribe among the hungover press corps had tried his
patience. He had done his time on Fleet Street and was fed up with newspapers and newspapermen. Tabloids were anathema to him. Moody and
irritable, he had been quick to denigrate her work and would go off on long
rants about how journalism was an "inconsequential and tawdry trade."

Misconstruing the cause of his restlessness, Maggie would take his
attacks personally and lash out in return. They goaded each other into stupid arguments. She filled her diary with his gibes. "How I would hate to
introduce you to my mother," he taunted. "She would be so pleased at the
prospect of my marrying a rich American and that is something I couldn't
stand." Every time he began a sentence with "You Americans," she felt her
Irish hackles rise. "In our relationship," she recalled, "George was temper-
amental, sensitive, and on occasion utterly impossible, and so was I."

Finally, Millar declared he had had enough of living in the seedy press
center, but the friend's place he had planned to rent was too filthy. House-
hunting gave Maggie reason to hope the relationship might become permanent, so when Millar abruptly packed his bags for London it came
as something of a shock. "If it had been an apartment overlooking the
Seine," he told her, "I think I would have stayed." She did not believe him,
but she was so tired of the dreaded scenes she let him go without a fight.

For a few days, she almost enjoyed the respite from the emotional
storms. As the anger wore off, however, she began to miss him. Then a
wire came from Millar saying that he had decided to stay in London.
Maggie was stunned. No one had ever broken off with her before; she had
always been the one to leave. She realized, too late, that she was devas-
tated. She begged him to come back, by phone and then in person, flying
to London to plead with him to reconsider. In the process, she humbled
herself in ways that were harder to recover from than the fact of his leaving. Maggie wrote about the wrenching sense of loss she felt when she
realized the relationship was over:

> As everyone learns sooner or later, it is one of life's tricks that you
> become most certain of your desire for something when you are

most sure that you cannot have it. I had told George many, many times, and with complete conviction, "I don't ever want to see you again." But secretly my heart believed the enchantment would endure. And that things would be again as they had been on the long golden afternoons in Bavaria, or on the clamorous mornings in the Paris flower markets, or even as in Harry's American Bar.

Looking back on the whole sorry business years later, Millar conceded it was not his finest hour, but he never misled her into thinking marriage was a possibility. He could not have done so because at the time he loved another woman, who was waiting for him in London, and he fully intended to marry her as soon as they could both obtain divorces. Millar's estranged wife, Annette Stockwell, had left him while he was in captivity, and he had rebounded by running off with her friend, Isabel Beatriz "Bea" Paske-Smith, the Anglo-Spanish wife of a fellow officer, Charles Hardwell. It was all a bit of a mess. His dalliance with Maggie had just been one of those things. "The truth is that when we met," he wrote, "I was abnormal, strained by a too-exciting though much enjoyed war; in a condition of great tension; a shit."

Millar, who married Bea immediately on his return to England, persuaded himself that he and Maggie had parted amicably. Their brief relationship, though turbulent, had been based on genuine friendship and mutual respect. "I deeply admired her as a practicing journalist," he explained. "She was a beaver, tireless, conscientious, fearless, always thinking through and round her subject." He had absolutely no idea how hurt she was after he left until, more than three decades later, he was asked his opinion of the melancholy pages of her memoir. "I have read them with considerable anguish and have now destroyed them," he replied in a letter in 1981, admitting that he was appalled to discover that she had nursed a fantasy of happily-ever-after that had no basis in reality. However, he was gracious enough to add, "She has written it well, as one would expect, and on the whole there are few inaccuracies."

For months after they parted, Maggie was so "love-struck" she could not move on. When friends advised her to forget him, she refused, shaking her head at any suggestion Millar was one of those feckless rogues not worth the tears. She still thought he was a marvel. George would spend the rest of his days doing things that other people dreamed of but rarely had the courage to try. He had already planned his next adventure—sailing a cruising ketch across the Adriatic to the Greek Aegean. It pained her to discover that the *Express* was publishing a series on his travels with his new wife, under the headline "Voyage of the *Truant*."

Prone to self-romanticizing, Maggie decided that if she could not have Millar, she would at least cling to his vision of a life of adventure. She would go to all the places and do all the things that he had spoken of so rapturously while they were together, only now she would do it on her own. "I hoped that George's courage would give me courage," she reflected years later. "And in a way this did happen but not at all as I had expected."

In the meantime, there was only one remedy for her heartache and that was to keep busy. All she had was her work. It was the one thing she could do to restore her bruised pride and sense of self. "After George left," she wrote, "I turned to my work with all the need, intensity, and determination of an alcoholic turning to a bottle."

AS IT HAPPENED, in September the *Tribune* sent her to Germany to cover the Nuremberg trials of the Nazi war criminals, what promised to be a unique and historic reckoning of worldwide import. Maggie welcomed the challenge and the change of setting. Paris had lost its appeal.

Six hundred fifty correspondents from more than twenty nations converged on the old city of Nuremberg in advance of the trials, along with dozens of representatives from the major radio networks and newsreel associations. Elaborate press facilities were set up to accommodate the horde of reporters. They would be spending most of their time at the Palace of Justice, corralled in a large pressroom, where loudspeakers carried the court proceedings. Communications facilities were set up in an adjacent room so the reporters could file stories in a minimum amount of time. In the freshly painted courtroom, the four judges and their alternates sat at the far end of the room. Facing them across the aisle was the prisoners' box. At the opposite end, the correspondents sat behind the defense counsel in what was the equivalent of a large orchestra pit. The interpreters, court reporters, judges, and attorneys used mock scripts and rehearsed two hours a day for two full weeks before the trial opened on November 19.

The prisoners were being held in solitary confinement under heavy guard at the Nuremberg city jail. The defendants, forty high Nazi war leaders, would not be tried individually but in groups. It had been decided that even in evaluating those who played a role in creating the death camps, conducting experiments on unwilling subjects, and employing slave labor for the war effort, there were gradations of guilt. The first group of twenty-four to be indicted were members of the SS and high command of the German armed forces, and included such infamous names as Hermann Göring, Rudolf Hess, Joachim von Ribbentrop, Wilhelm Keitel, Hans Frank, Alfred Rosenberg, and Julius Streicher, among others.

The correspondents, who complained that they were not being treated nearly as well as the war criminals, were housed in the ramshackle Schloss Faber-Castell, a German version of a neo-Renaissance castle built by the noble Faber family, the famous pencil manufacturers. The Faber estate, located six miles from the courthouse in the suburb of Stein, included seven buildings in all, and could accommodate a hundred members of the press corps. The men were packed into the main castle, ten to a room, while the women were billeted at the dower house.

Maggie initially shared a small suite with Helen Kirkpatrick, until an alternative arrangement could be found. It was primitive dormitory-style living, and Janet Flanner, whose room was on the same floor with the Russian reporters, complained endlessly about the sanitary conditions. Despite all the discomforts, dinner in the capacious castle ballroom was enjoyable. A large bar was set up, where the ex–war correspondents found themselves reunited with old friends from various fronts, press camps, and bureaus across Europe. The room buzzed with conversation, news from the outside world, and, wherever three or more were gathered, gossip. So many familiar faces were there. Everyone said it felt like old times.

At the courthouse in the mornings, Maggie made a beeline for her pal Wes Gallagher. He was directing AP's coverage of the trials and had a handpicked team of six top-notch wire-service reporters. "As a correspondent for the *NYHT*, one of AP's most distinguished member newspapers, Marguerite would have the cooperation of any AP staffer anytime, anywhere," recalled De Luce, who was one of the crew. "We were all fond of her, anyway. She was a powerhouse of a reporter."

Maggie coaxed a guard into giving her a tour of the prison cells, where the once-powerful Nazi leaders, who had aspired to rule the world, were now reduced to "living in conditions equal to those of Sing Sing." Rosenberg, who originated the "Aryan" superman theory, paced the small exercise yard with military precision, "a look of blankness and utter resignation on his face." Göring "writes the longest and best letters, according to the Army censors. He speaks a good deal of his loneliness and how much he misses his family." In contrast, Julius Streicher, who had married his secretary, "writes only three or four lines in his weekly notes." She humanized the faceless evil of the accused by homing in on the details of their prison lives, describing how some of the men tried desperately to kiss their wives through the bars separating them, while others maintained the arrogant posture of military leaders. The officers made the greatest effort to look presentable for the trial, "like Keitel, with his blue field marshal's uniform with the red-stripe down the pants legs and visor hat, who has managed to stay the sharpest."

In December, she reported on a sensational secret speech by Heinrich Himmler, the SS chief, in which he instructed his generals to treat all foreign prisoners as "human animals" who could be starved and mistreated except when "needed as slaves." The shameful document, Maggie wrote, had a sobering effect on the twenty defendants in the dock:

> They had been brimming with good humor and were almost exultant after seeing a four-hour motion picture, made of captured German films, portraying the Nazis' rise to power.... Like a group of school children, the defendants would nudge each other when Der Fuhrer appeared on screen or when they themselves were shown, and then they would whisper to each other and volubly explain the circumstances.

They were no longer laughing, she noted, after the American prosecution team presented Himmler's speech at the beginning of its case as proof that "slave labor, persecution of the Jews, and the terror of murder and brute force were instruments of Nazi policy."

As the months passed, De Luce observed the painstaking research that went into Maggie's stories. She pored over the archives. Hundreds of thousands of captured enemy documents, records, and files were assembled for use in the prosecution's case against the Nazi war leaders. As the material was introduced into evidence, it was made available to the reporters. Appalled by the testimony, most of the reporters needed a break at the end of the long sessions, and some breathing space to digest what they had heard. Many headed straight for the bar. Maggie, De Luce recalled, "was always among the last to leave the courthouse pressroom at night. She dug into all the documentary evidence—there seemed like tons of it. Indefatigable."

Walter Cronkite, a thirty-year-old UP reporter, echoed De Luce's comments that Higgins owed her success to her tireless exertions, only his words conveyed something else. "She dug and dug—she left no stone—or person—unturned," he quipped, thinking to make a joke in the way men did when they talked about Higgins.

On reflection, he seemed to think better of that remark, explaining that much of the jealousy she inspired was because few reporters were willing to put in the same hours. "Maggie pursued her work with such singlemindedness that she didn't quite know how to turn off," he said. "She'd drink with the men but there would be very little in the way of relaxation. She'd keep replaying the stories, keep probing for information. You always thought there was the possibility of your being a source for her, not underhandedly but because she was still 'on.'"

She was not above using her charms to get information, but Cronkite saw nothing amiss in that. If she was really out to do a Mata Hari impersonation, he added, then she would have dressed to kill, but instead she usually looked "sort of thrown together," an attractive mess. "She could look beautiful at times, but she didn't groom herself, she had an absolute lack of interest in it."

Cronkite's boss, Clinton "Pat" Conger, the manager of UP's German operations, found it impossible to make light of her presence. Higgins at Nuremberg, he recalled, was "as competent and energetic as she was attractive, a dangerous combination in a competing correspondent."

At the height of the trials that winter—when the public's interest was at its peak, and their sources at their least forthcoming—Conger came up against a problem. "It developed that all three wire services were getting an unusual number of blivets from our respective headquarters about missing angles that appeared in Maggie's *Herald Trib* stories," he recalled. The wire services were expected to be ahead of the pack. Conger, whose superiors were growing more restive by the day, needed to find out how Maggie was consistently staying a step ahead of them. "I finally figured it out," he said. "Maggie was circulating amiably each evening, chatting with all the other correspondents, wheedling goodies from the reporters who were willing to help because they were not in direct competition with the *Trib*. As a result, she was able to come up with the best and most complete Nuremberg report every day."

Conger had a grudging admiration for her spirit, but he acknowledged that not everybody appreciated her swoop-and-scoop tactics. *Newsweek* correspondent Toni Howard, who had her eye on James P. O'Donnell, the magazine's eligible new Berlin bureau chief, took exception to the way Maggie fraternized with unsuspecting males and then filed their work as her own. The two women immediately squared off, and thereafter the hostilities commenced.

It would be hard to imagine a greater contrast in style and temperament than between Higgins and Howard. "Maggie," Conger recalled, "came off as the friendly girl-next-door back home, impish grin, rumpled field gear—wool shirt and pants, combat boots, one of those wool caps that Ernie Pyle used to favor perched on her head. In a word, wholesome and delightful." Then there was the tall, glamorous Toni Howard, with her brown eyes and jet-black hair: "She once came close to giving General Patton apoplexy when he ran across her in dark sunglasses, officer dress–green Ike jacket and slacks, long dark curls on her shoulders, and purple nail polish on her sandaled toes—topped off by an escorting Doberman

Pinscher." There was only one word for Toni Howard, he added: "Exotic." Rumors abounded as to Howard's simmering animosity toward Higgins, and they would eventually find expression in print.

In February 1946, Maggie learned that she was the recipient of the New York Newspaper Women's Club award for outstanding work as a foreign correspondent for her stories from Germany. The prize was fifty dollars in war bonds. From Berlin, she sent a cable that was read aloud to the gathering of her peers at the Cosmopolitan Club in New York: "I am honored if in somebody's considered opinion my dispatches have helped make a little sense out of the tangled situation that is Europe."

Her front-page habit had already made her a minor celebrity back home. Hal Johnson, a columnist for the *Berkeley Daily Gazette*, saluted her achievement. "It has only been a few years since women were able to step into newspapermen's shoes and fill them," he wrote in his long-running "So We're Told" column, describing how Higgins, a recent University of California graduate turned "super newsgathering girl," had rocketed to fame. He went on to tout her coverage of the historic Nuremberg war trials and Dachau exploits, even giving a nod to her military father, who was now with the OSS and doing secret intelligence work in North China. It was Maggie's first appearance in a gossip column. It would not be her last.

7

✳ ✳ ✳ ✳ ✳ ✳ ✳ ✳

Roving Correspondent

Whenever she showed up, we were all delighted
to be with her but always a bit fearful of what
exclusive stories she would dig up that would
earn us callbacks from our home offices.

—Charles Bernard, UP correspondent

ONCE IT BECAME CLEAR THAT THE COURT PROCEEDINGS WOULD
continue for months, Maggie began bouncing back and forth between
Nuremberg and Berlin. She went in with the first contingent of the
American military government in June of 1945, which was expected to
act as the new guardian of peace and stability in a region dominated by
the Soviets. This bit of luck, groused Conger, allowed her to develop "better than average sources" in the high command in Berlin, which gave her
an edge in reporting the next big story: the postwar future of Germany.

On her first chauffeured jeep tour of Berlin, Maggie drove through
empty avenues lined with hollowed-out buildings and scorched stone.
The city had not been flattened so much as gutted. The ruins were monu-
mental, endless, apocalyptic. The grand march route that led to the Brandenburg Gate, which she recognized from newsreel footage of the Nazi
victory parade after the fall of France, was now a debris-strewn obstacle
course that slowed their progress to a crawl. The scale of destruction was
so staggering it was hard to imagine how it could be rebuilt—or the shape

of things to come. "It has an atmosphere," Maggie wrote of Berlin, "that sets it apart from Germany's other ruined cities."

Here was the capital of the toppled Reich, the shattered heart of Hitler's empire. Now to all appearances the Russians were the masters. They had occupied the city for two months and had used the time to assert their authority. Fifth Guard units and tanks blocked streets, guarded barricades, and patrolled intersections. Over seventy thousand Russian soldiers had died in the Battle of Berlin, and the Red Army had exacted revenge on the city in the form of mass rapes and murder. The rampaging spree of violence and looting defied belief.

At Yalta, the Allied leaders had decided that conquered Germany would be divided into four zones—Russian, American, British, and French. The city of Berlin, though technically part of the Soviet zone, was itself divided into four zones, with the Russians taking the eastern part. In June, the four-power military authorities had assumed control, individually in their respective sectors, and jointly under the Allied Control Council, in what amounted to an unprecedented experiment in quadripartite rule. At their mercy was Berlin, a sprawling metropolis of 3.3 million people—the largest city between Paris and Moscow—now a tiny island in a communist sea.

Almost immediately, tensions flared. Maggie reported on the frequent clashes between the capitalist West and the communist East, which "did not bode well for Allied harmony." The unease she felt was shared by most of her fellow reporters and extended to all the ranks of the American forces. They still regarded the Germans as the enemy, but they had begun to worry that the Russians might be a lot like them, and the Allies' hard-won victory over Nazism was going to give way to another ruthless dictatorship.

In the lingering exultation at the war's end, millions of people around the world waited for details of Hitler's death in Berlin. The formal declaration came on May 1, when the Nazi-run Radio Hamburg announced that the Führer had fallen at his command post in the Reich Chancellery as the Red Army closed in on the city. His successor, President Karl Dönitz, then called on the German people to mourn their leader who had died "a hero's death" defending the capital. The next day, newspapers printed Hitler's obituary. Some called for skepticism, however, and like the *Tribune* ran accompanying editorials which urged caution about accepting Dönitz's version of Hitler's fate at face value. The source was unreliable and, in the absence of any physical proof, many remained unconvinced. Even after reports emerged of Hitler's suicide, the debate continued. All kinds of stories and theories proliferated. Allied officials began to realize that something had to be done to quash the martyrdom myths and provide confirmation that the evil man was really gone for good.

The Soviets, meanwhile, denounced the reports of Hitler's death as a "Fascist trick," a false narrative designed to distract from his escape. Given his mistrust of Nazi propaganda, Stalin was said to have a morbid obsession with finding the German leader's body. Special squads of Soviet intelligence officers combed the labyrinth of tunnels under the remains of the Chancellery searching for Hitler's corpse. The last thing Moscow wanted was for his subterranean tomb, now in East Berlin, to become a memorial and place of pilgrimage for Nazi fanatics.

That first postwar summer—the silly season for journalism—wild rumors abounded: Hitler had "fallen at his command post at the Reich Chancellery and was buried in the rubble" (Hamburg radio); he had collapsed, felled by a cerebral hemorrhage (as reported in Stockholm); or he had spent his last days as Himmler's prisoner. Others claimed he had a doppelgänger, and the dictator was in hiding, alive and well. It was fodder enough for conspiracy theorists, who maintained he was residing in Argentina with other high-ranking Nazi officials. Still others said he had been spotted in Spain. The sightings continued.

In July, Allied headquarters, in an attempt to end the outlandish speculation, released the statements of two eyewitnesses—Hitler's chauffeur, and one of his police sentries—who described the Führer's demise. They told a fantastic and ghastly tale: On April 30, Hitler, who had married his mistress two days earlier, was found dead together with Eva Braun on a sofa in his concrete-reinforced quarters beneath the Reich Chancellery. It was a suicide pact. He had shot himself, the Walther pistol at his feet; she had taken a cyanide pill. The witnesses saw a burial party carry the bodies to a shell crater outside the bunker, where they were doused with gasoline and burned. While this account was taken seriously, and confirmed much of what was known about Hitler's last days, it was not enough to put all the doubts to rest.

It was on a July evening almost exactly a year later when Maggie, acting on a tip, went down to the old Reichstag, where she had been told there was some unusual activity. The possibility that new evidence had been unearthed among the ashes was too tempting to pass up, even if she was not supposed to be in the Soviet sector. Skulking in the shadows, she caught sight of *Newsweek*'s Jim O'Donnell, who had written one of the first stories about the Hitlers' cremation. To her chagrin, she discovered he was acting on the same tip. Even more irritating, it turned out he had the same informant on his payroll.

Maggie admitted that she had been unable to locate the entrance to the stairway that led to the Führerbunker, Hitler's command post located twenty-eight feet belowground. In the process of searching for a way in, she had twice been turned away by Russian guards. O'Donnell was amused that the sentries seemed immune to her insistent charms. "When competing for something," he noted, "Maggie, the blond bombshell, seemed to have three elbows, but that had not helped her to gain access to the bunker."

Fully aware that his determined colleague was not going to quit and leave him to it, he suggested they join forces. Since he toiled for a weekly and she for a daily, they did not have to vie against each other and could share the spoils. Maggie agreed. Together, they went around to the old emergency exit, a square blockhouse with an unfinished pillbox tower, which appeared to be the only viable portal. They were spotted by four Soviet sentries flourishing submachine guns and chased all the way onto Wilhelmstrasse. A Russian officer told them to make themselves scarce, making his point, O'Donnell recalled, "with a drawn pistol."

They managed to sneak into the New Reich Chancellery, a long, narrow parliament building. It had been damaged in the bombing, but they made their way to the roof, where their shaky perch afforded them a view of the bunker and old Chancellery garden. In the moonless night, they could just make out the dark forms of people milling around. Suddenly, klieg lights illuminated the scene below. It looked like a movie set, complete with cameras and a dozen actors clad in deep purple uniforms. A handful of Russian officers were giving directions. At the sound of the clapper, the group filed back into the bunker. Then the lights went out.

Unsure what they had just seen, Maggie and O'Donnell stayed put. Twenty minutes later, the same group emerged and started filming again. This time, the reporters saw enough to surmise that what they were watching was a reenactment of the Führer's funeral. "Marguerite and I came to the conclusion that a Russian movie company was making a film documentary," O'Donnell recalled. "Soon, the whole mysterious troupe departed in trucks. A spooky feature, we thought; another Berlin midnight rendezvous and nothing more."

It turned out that they had stumbled onto a much bigger story, one O'Donnell would finally piece together three decades later in his bestselling book *The Bunker*. The actors in purple fatigues were a dozen captured members of the Reich Chancellery Group, the loyal German officers, adjutants, and bodyguards who had stuck by their leader. Soviet intelligence, which had found the remains of Hitler's charred body back in May 1945, had whisked the group of Nazi stalwarts out of Berlin and subjected them to months of interrogation. Tasked with compiling a complete historical record, the Russians had secretly brought the group back to Berlin in 1946 and made them reconstruct the bunker melodrama, step-by-step, in the original location. The German prisoners were back in Moscow in less than twenty-four hours and scattered among various Soviet camps for another decade.

That midnight rendezvous was the beginning of O'Donnell's long friendship with Maggie. They shared many more adventures, nocturnal and otherwise, but he never forgot the strange, stirring scene they witnessed that summer. When the time came to tell the whole story—half a lifetime later—he dedicated his book to her.

FOR A YOUNG REPORTER, it was a fascinating time to be in Berlin. It was a period of rumor, suspicion, and mounting distrust. Maggie enjoyed the excitement, "the zest of danger" and undercurrent of intrigue that were part of everyday life in the divided city. The Allied troops steadily moved in and took up their positions, the American military government setting up shop in the massive Kaiser Wilhelm Anthropological Institute. As the army presence grew, Berlin turned into a garrison town, raw and unruly. Drunken GIs brawled in the streets. The black market flourished, along with tawdry nightclubs and brothels.

Despite its outward grimness, Maggie thrived in the military enclave of the American zone. She spent more and more time assisting Russell Hill, who had been sent over from Paris to establish the new Berlin bureau. She dashed from the daily Allied Control Council meetings to press luncheons to gossip-filled embassy dinners, which in the case of the Russians were boisterous affairs that involved a river of vodka and ran into the wee hours. It was impossible to be bored. There were so many stories—political feuds, plots, defections, and espionage operations—that she scarcely had a moment to herself. When things were running high, and her assignments were of the first rank, she always felt at her best. "It left no time for introspective brooding," she noted, "and certainly no opportunity for loneliness."

One night, when the city still felt like an open frontier town, she and Hill ventured out to a Soviet officers' club. They invaded it with aplomb, returning to their own press camp loaded with tins of caviar, as well as $400 worth of reichsmarks that Hill obtained through the sale of his $20 watch to a Soviet captain. Two days later, Martha Gellhorn and Charles Collingwood of CBS were arrested by the Soviets and held seven hours for attempting to visit the same club.

Berlin was a dangerous and chaotic city, considered by most correspondents to be a hardship post. Hill admired Maggie's willingness to remain, despite the fact that riots, robberies, shootings, and abductions were so common they had become part of the daily file. But then, she had always scorned personal comfort. "Her success as a war correspondent was due in part to her courage," he recalled. "She would accept great personal risks in order to get a story." He never thought of her as a great writer—her normally slapdash approach to punctuation and grammar degenerated into cablese under pressure—but few were better at spot news. Covering Berlin meant hard work and great headlines, and she was born for it. "She was a great reporter," he said. "She was good at getting stories, and they were accurate."

Sometimes she was too good and the results raised suspicions. "She drove the competition up the wall," recalled Gallagher, especially after Maggie struck up a relationship with a handsome Russian interpreter named Igor, attached to American headquarters, who gave her the highlights of the Allied Control Council meetings only minutes after they were adjourned. Her access to secret intelligence led to a string of exclusives that created enough noise and comment to invite further scrutiny. When the council discovered the source of the leaks, the interpreter was canned, and embarrassed Soviet officials covered up the affair.

Maggie was reprimanded by the home office, but to the dismay of some of her peers, it was nothing more than a slap on the wrist. According to the grapevine, the problem was that Helen Reid regarded Maggie as her invention and reveled in her conspicuous success as a war correspondent. The *Tribune*'s proprietress had once aspired to a career in journalism, and she saw something of herself in the scrappy young Higgins, who was so full of energy, drive, and desire. Instead of reining her in, Mrs. Reid was grooming her fair-haired reporter for bigger things and promoting her at every turn.

In the meantime, Maggie's shenanigans continued to leave small eddies of turbulence behind her. She was a constant source of aggravation to Edwin Hartrich, the *Trib*'s chief correspondent in Germany, whose long, appraising pieces about the Allied occupation often ran alongside hers. On more than one occasion, she wrote about events in the American zone of Berlin, thereby scooping Hartrich. The accepted procedure would have been to pass on the information, but Maggie, who felt she owed no fealty to the senior man on the beat, did not like to share her material.

Even after being reminded not to stray beyond her carefully defined patch, she repeatedly overstepped the mark. "Marguerite evidently had some difficulty restraining herself from competing against her colleagues on the same paper," Kerr observed in the carefully chosen words of one who has been called on to adjudicate many such disputes. When Hartrich could not settle the matter with Maggie, Kerr was compelled to intervene: "I ordered her to stay out of his territory, which she did."

Forced to look elsewhere for stories, Maggie soon discovered the advantages of being a roving correspondent. Instead of being tethered to the bureau, she was free to go almost anywhere in search of news. As the ideological battle lines between the Americans and Russians hardened, the spread of communism in Eastern Europe became the hot story. Churchill, who had lost his office in the last election but not his ability to make headlines, gave a speech warning of the dark future ahead for the two hostile camps, proclaiming that an "iron curtain had descended across the continent." Suddenly the papers were full of questions about Russia's "sphere of influence" and the fate of the countries that fell into its net.

In the spring of 1946, Maggie traveled to Prague to interview Jan Masaryk, the popular Czechoslovakian foreign minister and the son of the founding father of the republic, to ask him whether he was worried about the upcoming election, and Allied fears that the Russians would try to impose a Communist regime on his country. Tall, gregarious, and highly intelligent, Masaryk had enormous personal charm. He walked with an easy, confident stride, his feet hardly seeming to touch the ground, "the kind of man," she wrote, "who could surely twirl a graceful waltz or skim nimbly through an intricate polka." He was full of optimism about the reemergence of Czechoslovakia as a sovereign state and its destiny "to serve as a bridge between the East and the West."

Maggie was not alone in succumbing to his magnetic personality and passionate commitment to his homeland. Masaryk confidently predicted Czechoslovakia would stand firm against the Soviet Communism that seemed to be winning favor all over Europe. "Here in our country," he assured her, "even the communists are Czechs first and communists second."

She believed him, complacent in her ignorance. She believed him despite the signs of a Soviet-style crackdown on the press, including her own unpleasant encounter with the Czech secret police. On her first morning in Prague, they had barged into her hotel room at 5 a.m.

demanding to see her passport, and had refused to leave until they had inspected all her papers. Masaryk had brushed the incident aside with a wave of the hand, calling it an "isolated mishap."

His buoyant hopes resulted in her dispatching unduly rosy stories about the situation in Czechoslovakia. It turned out to be a bad call. When the communists ended up winning control of the government, and began tightening their grip on the country, Maggie was bitterly disappointed. She should have known better than to think Moscow would ever allow a political moderate like Masaryk, a patriot first and foremost, to prevail.

In November, against the advice of her colleagues in Berlin—who assured her she would be "kidnapped, robbed or worse"—she drove off alone in below-zero weather through the Soviet-occupied hinterland to Warsaw to cover the Polish elections. At Yalta and Potsdam, Stalin had pledged to make provisions for "free and unfettered elections," and this was seen as an important test of Soviet intentions. For Maggie, it would be a measure of her maturity as a reporter and the soundness of her judgment. In Czechoslovakia, she had been guilty of wishful thinking. It was a mistake she could not afford to repeat.

As one of only a handful of American journalists present in Poland, she would be expected to judge the relative fairness of the proceedings. Unofficially, however, many diplomats and embassy experts were already warning that the election would be fixed. There were reports of violence and voter repression and, beyond that, accusations of calculated fraud orchestrated by the communists, who were running under the cover of the benign-sounding National Unity slate. Accustomed to straight news reporting, Maggie found it difficult to cut through all the half-truths and propaganda to get a clear picture of what was going on. "I was still very new to international diplomacy and particularly to communist theory and tactics," she recalled. "The facts were evident. It was the interpretation that counted. Were the police state incidents products of the government's inexperience as [some Poles] claimed, or carefully planned as our ambassador claimed?"

Her doubts were exacerbated when Polish officials, eager to placate the Russians, began assailing her as a biased servant of the "dirty capitalist press." At the same time, she and several other American reporters in Warsaw came under attack from liberal critics in New York, who accused them of being so partisan that they had lost all touch with reality. At one point, Ralph Ingersoll, a former general manager of Time Inc. and the founder of the leftist New York tabloid *PM*, wrote an editorial in his paper excoriating the *Herald Tribune*'s Marguerite Higgins and the *New York Times*'s Sydney Gruson for declaring war in print on the Polish government.

Maggie was mortified by the public criticism. Her anxiety was such that she reacted physically, her face and arms erupting in a flaming skin rash. With dogged determination, she set out to ascertain what was really happening in Poland. Over the next few weeks, together with a Polish translator, she traveled 750 miles around the frozen countryside, through snowbound villages and sooty industrial centers, and spoke to hundreds of citizens. The peasants, factory workers, intellectuals, and priests she interviewed were unanimous in asserting that the communists were using force to facilitate their rise to power. In a story detailing their accounts, she compared the present-day methods of political persuasion to those employed under Hitler. The headline read, "Poland's Police Ape Gestapo in Election Drive."

On January 1, 1947, she reported that the election to be held later that month would be "a mere formality." The National Unity Party's victory was ensured, contrived through a campaign of intimidation, mass arrests, and voter disenfranchisement. Once again, Maggie underestimated the remorseless efficiency of the police state. A young member of the opposition party who had dared to speak out was rearrested. "It was a terrible responsibility," she recalled. "I blamed myself for having been foolish enough to acquiesce to his demand for publicity."

Two days before the election, Ralph Ingersoll arrived in Warsaw with great fanfare. After a flying trip around the city as Poles voted, he cabled *PM* that the people he had canvassed had "nothing to complain of," and added in typical bellicose fashion, "The picture of wholly fraudulent, rigged elections given Americans before the facts is at best a misrepresentation of a complicated political situation and at worst malicious repetition of malicious untruths."

Master of the snide put-down, Ingersoll observed derisively that the intensity Maggie had brought to her reporting alarmed some of the local dignitaries: "The *Herald Tribune*'s star reporter moves so rapidly through life that the British Ambassador said seeing her always made his fingers itch. He wanted to run them through her hair to straighten it out for her, because, he claims, she has obviously been so breathless that she hasn't combed it since she got to Warsaw."

In the end, the divergent press accounts only added to the confusion about the outcome of the Polish election and intensified Maggie's frustration at the lack of a U.S. response. By the time she returned to the Berlin bureau, her disillusionment with the socialist ideals of her youth was complete. Having come of age politically in the thirties, she, like so many of her generation, had embraced the idea of government intervention into the economy in the hopes of doing away with mass unemployment. She had not understood then the extent to which communism and totalitarianism were inextricably intertwined. That was the painful lesson she learned as she watched the slow demise of free Poland.

A visit to the country eighteen months later confirmed her worst fears of what it meant to live under the Soviet thumb: "The volatile, individualist Poles, the brave Poles who had defied the Nazis when the odds were hopeless, who had kept their pride and spirit through centuries of partition, and who had clustered around my little Auto-Union and its American flag despite the hostile glare of the police, were now unmistakably a drab and regimented people."

Being a witness to the death of democracy in Czechoslovakia and Poland affected Maggie deeply, in part because she could not forgive herself for her initial naivete, which had led her to second-guess herself and undermine her own reporting. Her "bright hope" that the small, struggling European nations might be allowed to find some middle path between Western freedom and Eastern power had been extinguished. It made the final blow, when it came—the communist coup in Prague— that much harder to bear. Unable to face the murder of his country,

Masaryk jumped out of a window, or more likely was pushed. "His tragic death," she wrote, "perhaps more than any other single event, spelled out the doom of these hopes."

It left her feeling angry and helpless. She felt, as she had after Buchenwald and Dachau, that she had seen the victims of totalitarianism, and that she had a responsibility to warn the world. "She became as fiercely anti-communist as one can imagine," recalled Peter Lisagor, who knew her first when he was an editor for *Stars and Stripes* in London, and later in Paris, and was a close friend. "She objected to communism as totalitarianism in the worst sense. She could not abide the enslavement of any people. She bled for all of them."

Looming over everything was the possibility that the Russians might abandon their diplomatic attacks and political subversion for more direct methods. Beneath the daily tensions in Berlin was the all-too-real fear that any misunderstanding, miscalculation, or provocation might kindle a new crisis or military confrontation between the rival blocs. The dropping of the atom bomb and the Soviet invasion of Manchuria had forced Japan's surrender, ending a hot war and ushering in the Cold War. The era of wartime collaboration was over. All sides understood that they would have to forge a new, uncertain path forward. Berlin was the focal point of Anglo-American-Russian cooperation—on which hung the fate of the world. It was where the peace would be won or lost. And it was where Maggie Higgins wanted to be.

8

✳ ✳ ✳ ✳ ✳ ✳ ✳ ✳ ✳

Dateline—Berlin

A careless, unauthenticated story out of Berlin
might conceivably inflame millions to white
hot anger, and even if the story was disproved
a day later the first impression would remain.
I've seen Drew Middleton and Maggie Higgins
sit on a story for twenty-four hours because
although it seemed certain to stand up they
refused to put it on the cable until they were 100
percent satisfied that there wasn't a hole in it.

—Quentin Reynolds, *Collier's* correspondent

IN THE SPRING OF 1947, MAGGIE WAS NAMED THE *TRIBUNE'S* BERLIN
bureau chief at the tender age of twenty-six. She learned of the decision
during a brief visit to the paper's Forty-First Street offices in New York at
the end of two months' home leave. Of course, she wanted the job. She
had lobbied hard for it. She had persuaded her former boss, Russell Hill,
who was back in New York writing editorials, to go to bat for her. But at
the same time, it was unexpected.

For months, she had gone moodily about Berlin predicting she would
never get tapped for such a big post. "I was wearing a chip on my shoulder
about the unlikelihood of my paper's picking a female to run an established newspaper bureau," she recalled. It was a petulant attitude she
indulged in when she felt put-upon because it offered "great and com-

forting opportunities to fool oneself." It was easier to blame her gender than admit that she was still too green after only three years overseas, or face up to the fact that she might not be up to the challenge. Even after Hill's replacement departed and left her temporarily in charge, she was convinced it would never become permanent. When the appointment came through, she could hardly believe it.

Maggie considered the promotion to be acknowledgment of her "coming of age as a foreign correspondent." She had celebrated in New York with Hill, gaily taking him along on a shopping expedition for the new mink coat she could now afford on her $5,000-a-year salary. In the news business, the ascent from reporter to bureau chief was like the jump from a captain in the army to colonel. She hoped the impressive-sounding title would help mitigate against the chauvinism of the military officials, who still tried to sidestep her questions, and who let it be known that they had better things to do than be interrogated by "a little slip of a thing" like her.

One of the more demeaning episodes of her career had come at the hands of Lt. Gen. Walter Bedell "Beetle" Smith, Eisenhower's chief of staff, who at the last minute had barred her from an off-the-record dinner Ike was hosting for a group of Berlin correspondents during one of his early visits. Maggie, excited at the prospect of meeting the hero of the hour, had been mentally composing a bragging letter to her parents when she learned the invitation had been rescinded. After making some inquiries, she discovered Bedell Smith had decided to exclude her solely on the basis of her appearance, reportedly saying, "I'd never trust those baby blue eyes."

The casual dismissal rankled. Insulted at being vetoed because of her looks—and judged to be disingenuous, even deceitful—Maggie was tempted to march right up to him and demand an apology. Since making a scene would only confirm his worst suspicions about her sex, however, she decided to let it go. But she privately vowed to one day make him eat his words.

Barney Oldfield, the army press wrangler, thought the Beetle was just being careful. Bedell Smith, who was known to be the strong arm that swept all obstacles from Ike's path, probably viewed Higgins as an unnecessary risk—and with reason. Oldfield had been present when Eisenhower first laid eyes on Maggie at a press conference in Berlin: "She was sitting there all pert and attractive looking in the front row, and as I walked in with the General, he whispered, 'Either the war correspondents are getting better looking, or I have been too busy to have looked up at the right time.'"

It was not just the military that gave her a hard time. A friend had passed on the warning that her main competitor, Drew Middleton of the *New York Times*, had "solemnly assured all of Berlin that she would not last six months." As the new head of the *Times* bureau, he had let it be known around town that he was a little put out that the *Tribune* had not seen fit to send someone his own journalistic size to compete against. The thirty-five-year-old Middleton presided over a staff that included three other correspondents. Maggie, who was trying to run a one-woman bureau, was teased mercilessly about his patronizing attitude.

While she tried to laugh off his comments, she suffered the first of many "moments of inner panic." She knew that at this point she should not have any fears about her ability to do the job, but the truth was she was still plagued by doubts and attacks of acute anxiety. She worried that if she bungled a story or got a single fact wrong it would have dire consequences for her career. In her memoir, she wrote candidly about the inner turmoil that afflicted her:

> I felt that if I made the slightest mistake my new job might be taken away from me. I can't explain this continuing lack of self-confidence. But I'm not exaggerating it. Perhaps it was in part the feeling that I, as a woman, had been given exceptional responsibilities at an exceptionally early age and that therefore particular attention would be paid to my performance—good or bad.

Of course, it did not help that her rival at the *Times* was polished, personable, and extremely well informed. Middleton was a reporter's reporter. A sports writer who was drafted into combat coverage, he was known for his gift for turning out smooth, well-balanced copy at great speed. He had arrived in Berlin fresh off a two-year stint in Moscow, where his expertise on the Kremlin's sinister machinations gave him special standing. Middleton was so unflappable and all-knowing that his peers addressed him as "Professor" with only the barest trace of irony. In spite of herself, Maggie liked him. When not pontificating, he could be engaging and very jolly, and he was in great demand at dinner parties. She even liked his wife, Stevie, who was British, tiny, and beautiful.

Marooned in a hostile environment, the Berlin correspondents banded together to form a close-knit community, combining the basic goodwill and bitter feuds of any gathering of their number. The Press Club on Sven-Hedin Strasse, in the affluent suburb of Zehlendorf, became their hostelry away from home. Oldfield had purchased a large, dilapidated mansion, which had purportedly belonged to Hitler's finance minister, and used army funds to have the building refurbished as an official headquarters. Its rooms and nooks rattled from dusk to dawn with the sound of busy typewriters. After their stories were finally put to bed, and the pressure was off, they would repair to the bar, or to the billiard room, which boasted a genuine, and probably stolen, Corot painting on the wall. The club was the center of their social life, such that it was. Some nights there was music, usually jazz bands, and dancing for the reporters and their wives, desperate to fashion some kind of normal life in the desolate city.

During her first year in Berlin, Maggie had stayed at the club, but as a bureau chief she was entitled to her own house. Most of the better-paid correspondents and military officers lived in and around Zehlendorf, a leafy green oasis that had escaped the Allied bombings, and was within walking distance of the club. Maggie had been lucky to find a lovely little romantic hideaway at 7 Lima Strasse in Zehlendorf-West. It had been built for the Japanese mistress of a wealthy German chemical executive, and the architecture had a vaguely Oriental flavor. Floor-to-ceiling windows opened onto a terrace and back garden, with a green lawn that sloped down to a small lake surrounded by woods. Her rent, paid for by the *Tribune*, was $125 a month, and included the services of a wonderful Alsatian housekeeper and cook named Anna.

Like most foreign correspondents, she found herself enjoying a life of luxury in a country impoverished by years of war. Servants, lavish homes, expensive furnishings, and art could all be had for ludicrously small sums compared to what they would cost back home. In addition, virtually her entire existence was subsidized by the paper, allowing her to bank most of her paycheck. Given the temptations on offer on the Kaiserallee, the famous boutique-lined avenue once frequented by Eva Braun, it was impossible to resist the occasional shopping spree. Maggie treated herself to beautifully made dresses and evening bags, undoubtedly hoarded from the days when the wives of the Nazi elite demanded the finest couture from France. She splurged on satin drapes for her home, along with matching velvet-covered divans.

Along with the allied military leaders, who requisitioned the grandest residences for themselves, the journalists lived in princely fashion in their colonial outpost, playing tennis on the courts attached to the Press Club, swimming in the lakes, boating on the Wannsee, and holding regattas. A riding group had even been formed. "Only the sleekest horses fill the army of occupation stables," she noted. The social whirl, as each unit attempted to outdo the others, was equally extravagant. Tables groaned under the weight of sumptuous buffets. Maggie received invitations to as many as five and six functions a week, sometimes two a night. It was a heady time for a girl from Chabot Court. "Life in the American zone of occupation has a dreamlike quality," she told the readers of *Mademoiselle*. "And it is not a nightmare, but rather a fantasia."

Her new position as bureau chief also came with an expense account for "purpose parties," the main purpose of which was to wine and dine high-placed officials and extract information. The home office footed the bill with the expectation that alcohol, the traditional lubricant of diplomacy, would loosen tongues and provide indiscretions that would hit the pavement in New York the next day.

A key part of a bureau chief's duties was entertaining visiting VIPs from the paper, and Maggie quickly established herself as an expert hostess. She mastered the black-market economy and was adroit at procuring hard-to-find delicacies, bartering cartons of Blue Seal cigarettes for thick steaks, oysters, French champagne, and, of course, Russian caviar. As luck would have it, David Parsons—brother of Geoff Parsons Jr., editor of the European edition of the *Tribune*—was head of American Overseas Airlines in Berlin and always ready to be helpful. More than one of his pilots stepped off a plane at Tempelhof airport carrying a package for Maggie. Most importantly, or strategically, she kept a well-stocked bar. She taught Anna how to make excellent martinis, and they were always ready, ice cold on a tray, when her guests arrived.

When Joseph Alsop, a top columnist for the *Tribune*, came to Berlin in March of 1948, Maggie hosted a formal dinner in his honor. She invited fourteen British, French, and German government and military dignitaries to provide a cross section of opinion about the growing frostiness between the East and West. Unfortunately, she missed the party.

That same afternoon, the Soviet marshal Vasily Sokolovsky had stalked out of a session of the Allied Control Council, at which the entire Soviet delegation, down to lowliest clerk, rose and left the chamber. It was impossible to know if the Russian walkout was just the latest attempt to aggravate the Western powers, or if the rift signaled the end of four-power rule in Germany. Maggie ended up working the story until well past midnight. When she got home, she discovered that her inebriated guests, who were heatedly debating whether the division of Germany was now inevitable, had held dinner for her. They did not finish until after 2 a.m.

Her unpredictable schedule wreaked havoc with her personal life. A relationship with a charming political-affairs officer fizzled when she was forced to decline his invitations night after night as news continued to break. When her exasperated suitor finally reached her by phone one evening, she tried to explain that there was simply no way she could see him. She had to stay and finish her story and then send off an early version for the European edition in Paris. He broke things off with her, saying angrily, "That's ridiculous. It's just an excuse."

At that moment, Maggie did not care. She was more interested in chasing stories than men. She could not be bothered with playing the conventional dating game. "I was proving something to myself about myself and my capacity to meet a big challenge," she recalled. "I should have disliked me if I failed. In that case, no amount of love from someone else could have helped."

Compounding the difficulties of her job was the fact that she was a slow writer, a result of her perfectionism and dread of making errors. Since it could take her twice the time to accomplish the same thing as other correspondents, she made up for it by putting in twelve, fourteen, and often eighteen hours a day, week in and week out, month after month. The relentless grind left little time for anything, or anyone, else. She was not unaware of an unhealthy single-mindedness, or even solipsism, but it was a basic part of her makeup and she made a virtue of it. "In order to compete I just had to stick at it longer," she wrote in her memoir of the practice-makes-perfect creed that had been inculcated in her from childhood. "In retrospect, I can see that a one-track preoccupied personality can be very wearing and in many ways unattractive. But even in retrospect I'm convinced that was the price I had to pay."

Her old friend Jim O'Donnell thought it cost her dearly, that beneath the bold, sometimes sassy facade, Maggie was as tightly strung as a whippet. She was a bundle of nerves, always on edge, always frantic to find out what other reporters had so she could add their information to her dispatches. Many an evening, they would be relaxing with a group of friends over a nightcap at the Press Club bar when Maggie would spot a newsman striding swiftly out of the room. She would toss back her drink and bolt for the door, following after him to see if he was onto something she had missed.

O'Donnell recognized the demons that drove her. Maggie never chose the easy path. She did things the hard way. Perhaps because he had the same obstinate, obsessive streak, he was inclined to cut her more slack than the others. He made a deal with her: on some occasions, he would give her a story with the understanding that it would not appear in the *Trib* until after *Newsweek*'s Wednesday publication date, and in return she would share rumors, insights, and anecdotes she had gleaned from her reporting. For a while, their teamwork paid dividends, and they regularly beat their respective adversaries, the *New York Times* and *Time*.

One Saturday afternoon, finishing early, O'Donnell filed a piece for the magazine that had the potential to be quite newsworthy. The Roman Catholic bishop of Berlin, Konrad Cardinal von Preysing, known as a fearless critic of the Nazis, was planning to break his silence on what the repressive communist regime was doing to his city. O'Donnell, who had a copy of the bishop's upcoming sermon, planned to give the story to Maggie, but knowing her to be an inveterate poacher, he decided to hold it back for a bit.

That same evening, he and his new wife, Toni Howard, gave a party and Maggie was invited. While he was busy playing bartender, his secretary rushed over and whispered that she had seen Higgins in his office perusing the papers on his desk. O'Donnell assured her there was no cause for concern, but he decided to teach Maggie the snoop a lesson. When he went to find her, she had joined the others. "What are you going to beat *Time* with this week, Jim?" she asked innocently when she saw him. "Anything special?"

"No, nothing special," he replied blandly.

During dinner, Maggie began to fidget and look at her watch. At quarter to eight, she jumped up and announced she had to leave. She returned an hour later looking inordinately pleased with herself. O'Donnell, knowing that her deadline had passed, and confident that she had already taken the bait, sprang his trap. He told her that he had planned to cap off the evening by giving her a tip about the cardinal's upcoming sermon, but unfortunately it had been called off at the last minute. The color drained from Maggie's face. Then she dashed from the room.

To make sure it was a lesson she would not soon forget, O'Donnell then called Middleton and gave him the story instead. Maggie called the *Trib*'s news desk in New York and got her article pulled, but the page had to be remade—a costly and time-consuming chore—and production was not happy about it. When the very same piece appeared in the early edition of the *Times* with Middleton's byline, her editors were apoplectic: "WHAT'S GOING ON THERE? ARE YOU DRINKING?" the cable read.

Maggie's comeuppance was the talk of the press community. Many enjoyed seeing her disgraced as a result of her own mischief. O'Donnell did not hold it against her. He tended to view their competition as a friendly game. He got a kick out of some of the crazy stunts she pulled to beat him, even though it drove his wife mad when he reacted with the I-told-you-so delight of a racetrack tout watching his horse nose out in front.

Not long after the Cardinal Preysing fiasco, when faced with her insistent pleas, O'Donnell relented and allowed Maggie to accompany him on a trip to the Ruhr valley. Before they left, he made her swear that she would not pull another fast one. Maggie, her face a picture of contrition, promised to behave. O'Donnell had arranged to tour the British sector of the Ruhr, the vast industrial region, where the coal and steel workers were threatening to strike due to the dire food shortages. The reporters visited a local hospital, where they were shocked to learn that the miners were so weak from malnutrition that 220 men had died in the past forty-eight hours.

At the end of the day, O'Donnell and Maggie returned to their lodgings and made plans to meet for a drink. After she failed to turn up, and there was still no sign of her by dinner, he could guess what she was up to. When she finally appeared at 9 p.m., he confronted her. She sheepishly admitted that she had cabled the news of the starving miners to her paper. Before he could berate her, Maggie argued in her defense that she could not in good conscience have sat on the story a moment longer. "Can you imagine how many people might die between now and Wednesday?" she asked, full of self-righteous indignation.

There was merit in her argument—*Newsweek* would not close for several more days and the situation in the Ruhr required urgent attention. O'Donnell was even a little ashamed of himself for being so fixated on his own deadline that he had lost sight of what really mattered. But he was not taken in by her holier-than-thou act. Maggie was incorrigible. Being first, not saving lives, had always been her priority. It was just a happy coincidence that the miners would benefit from her scoop. She would run roughshod over anyone who got in the way of her and a story. Afterward, she might apologize and try to make amends. Then she would go right out and do it again.

She was so committed to succeeding that she was incapable of restraining herself. Some of her colleagues were aghast at the lengths she would go to in order to prevent other publications from getting an exclusive. "She was ruthless," said Sonia Tomara, who still freelanced for the *Tribune*. "She would take anybody's story and run it as her own."

Tomara fairly bristled with contempt for her former colleague, despite acknowledging that Maggie had been "rather nice" in allowing Sonia and her husband to stay at the Zehlendorf house while they looked for a place of their own. Her animosity may have had something to do with the *Trib*'s refusal to hire her back now that they had Higgins in situ. "After all I had quit," she said. "The paper didn't want to have two people in Berlin. And she [Maggie] was on very good terms with Gen. Clay."

Lt. Gen. Lucius D. Clay, the American military governor for Germany, and commander in chief of the U.S. forces in Europe, was the top man in Berlin that tense spring of 1948. For months, Clay had been valiantly trying to keep the relations between the occupiers from falling apart. Maggie had been covering his negotiations with the Russians since the beginning and succeeded in ingratiating herself as one of the trusted chroniclers at his regular press conferences, quoting Clay as promising that as long as he was in charge in Germany, "American forces will not abandon Berlin."

As the crisis deepened, and they were thrown together at all hours of the day and night, they developed a feeling of solidarity and mutual respect. Maggie shared his crusading spirit and workaholic habits—they both lived on coffee and cigarettes. As a southerner, Clay's personal code of chivalry made it difficult for him to deflect probing questions from female journalists, and, according to his biographer Jean Edward Smith, "he rather liked Miss Higgins."

In the weeks following the Soviet walkout, the situation in Berlin quickly deteriorated. The U.S., Britain, and France announced they were merging the western zones of Germany economically, and introducing a new currency, in preparation for creating a federal republic there. They would resist any Soviet attempt to push them out. In an attempt to pressure the Western leaders to reverse course, Stalin began to take steps to curb the movement of people and supplies into the city, and to restrict traffic on the autobahn between Berlin and the West. With frictions alarmingly high, Maggie reported that the guards were doubled on the American and British military trains departing from Berlin. The train commanders were instructed to refuse to allow any Russian inspectors to board. The Soviets immediately retaliated by halting the trains at the border. No food or freight was coming in or out.

On April 1, General Clay gave the order to begin flying enough food to sustain its military garrisons in Berlin for forty-five days. "The United States began today to supply by air its 10,000 nationals in Berlin," Maggie reported. "It is part of a plan to block the Soviet move to exert control over traffic between Berlin and west Germany." The first lumbering C-47 Skytrains had begun landing at Tempelhof, which was under U.S. control. "The American experiment," she wrote, "was being watched with interest by the Western Allies for indications whether their nationals in Berlin could be supplied by air if the Russians should cut off Berlin completely by land."

On the tenth day, the Soviets allowed a military freight train through without attempting to board it, signaling an easing of the restrictions. But around Berlin, tensions worsened. The "baby blockade," as it came to be known, had heightened everyone's awareness of the city's vulnerability. A steady exodus of civilians began. In the silent beer halls and battered streets, she detected the first stirrings of fear. A showdown seemed inevitable.

Disputes over the impending currency reform became a flash point. The Allies decided to assert their power, and on June 18 announced they were issuing a separate new currency for the whole of western Germany, and then extended it to their occupation zones in Berlin. For the Soviets, the introduction of the deutsche mark signaled the West's determination to create an independent German state, and it effectively made the break final.

Marshal Sokolovsky, commander of the Soviet zone, denounced the move as "completing the split of Germany." The same day, he imposed a land blockade around Berlin, sealing off the frontiers of the western zones by ordering a halt to all road, rail, and canal traffic. Within days, the Soviets cut off all supplies to the American, British, and French sectors of the city, leaving two and a half million citizens and Allied troops without food, coal, and other basic necessities.

Berliners awoke on June 24 to find themselves under a full Soviet blockade. Stalin had invoked the weapon of mass starvation, and his intention was clear: either the Western Allies changed their policies, or they would be forced out of Berlin.

Clay was committed to staying. "As far as we are concerned, they cannot drive us out by any means short of war," he declared. He did not believe Stalin would try to seize the city by force and risk a direct military confrontation, which might provoke the U.S. to make use of its monopoly on the atomic bomb. At the same time, Clay felt that if the U.S. and its allies withdrew from Berlin, allowing all its citizens and industry to be swallowed up by a new East German state, it would irreparably weaken their position in Europe. If they wanted to hold the line against communism, they had to stand firm.

The West responded with a counterblockade, stopping all rail traffic into East Germany. Clay, who was unusually forthcoming with the correspondents, believed he could take an armored convoy down the autobahn to force their way through the blockade. He thought the Soviets were bluffing and argued that a dramatic show of strength might halt their aggressive posturing without a fight. But Washington urged caution, fearing the situation could escalate into a third world war. President Harry Truman was running for election, and he knew the American people would never support going to war with the Soviet Union just to defend Berlin, the capital of a country they had defeated only three years earlier.

On June 26, Clay authorized the start of a huge airlift to supply Berlin, the crucial Western outpost—and all-important symbol of democracy—inside the communist East. By taking to the skies, the U.S. could reach the isolated city without firing a shot or challenging the Soviets on the ground. Operation Vittles, as the air force called it, began its delivery service with eighty C-47s flying two daily round trips from West Germany into Tempelhof and Gatow, Berlin's second airfield, run by the Royal Air Force (RAF). The British joined the effort with Operation Plainfare, cobbling together a transport fleet of Dakotas and Yorks.

The morning after the blockade began, Clay worried aloud that it was "absolutely impossible" to supply the city by air power alone. But days later, upon learning that a group of large four-motor C-54 Douglas Skymasters would be made available from bases all over the world, he changed his tune. "I may be the craziest man in history," Clay told Maggie. "But I'm going to try the experiment of feeding this city by air."

At the end of the first weekend of the complete blockade, her story about the unprecedented aerial operation to support Berlin not only made the front page of her paper, it was the first of many to appear simultaneously on the front page of the *Washington Post*, which had purchased the Herald-Tribune News Service to extend its overseas coverage. The international stir created by the dramatic East-West standoff meant the eyes of the world were on Berlin. The biggest story since the war was unfolding in her bailiwick.

By July, Clay had assembled a fleet of fifty C-54 Skymasters, each hauling 9 tons of supplies and capable of making three round trips daily between Frankfurt and Berlin. The RAF announced it would bring in ten giant Sunderland flying-boats to supplement the lift, hauling 60 tons of cargo daily. Week by week, the tonnage rose. But it was still not enough to sustain the city. The minimum required to stave off the impending food crisis was 4,500 tons a day.

During the first month of the operation, there were only seven days when the weather was good enough to allow the transports to fly. The Allied forces were confronted with pelting rain and rolling, pea-soup fogs that normally would have kept flights grounded. Bringing heavily loaded planes into Berlin with a two-hundred-foot ceiling took guts and expert guidance. For the airlift to succeed, more pilots would have to be trained to rely on instruments, the runways lengthened, and new concrete landing strips built to withstand the constant pounding.

Maggie continued to file detailed reports, packed with facts and figures that illustrated the mind-boggling complexity of the airlift. Her focus on the nuts-and-bolts mechanics of the operation, and its daily successes and failures, meant she avoided falling into the hammy, sentimental style that characterized much of the flag-waving coverage. But she never lost faith in the Allies' capacity to prevail. Although Soviet propaganda ridiculed the airlift as an impossible enterprise, she reported that the attempts to frighten the local population into capitulating had failed. One street-corner sage opined that if the Allies had no problem delivering bombs, they could surely deliver potatoes.

West Berlin was plunged into darkness when the Soviets cut the power lines to the plants in their zone. With electricity limited to only a few hours a day, Maggie grew accustomed to working by candlelight. Food and fuel were strictly rationed. When she ran through the meager allocation of gas for her car, she borrowed jeeps from the correspondents' pool. She solved the problem of how to cover the large, sprawling city by building a network of sources in the other zones of occupation. An Australian pal, and occasional lover, Wilfred "Peter" Burchett of the *London Daily Express*, provided regular updates from the British side, and she kept him posted on developments in the American sector. She made a similar arrangement with a French reporter.

Faced with a perpetual, ongoing crisis, the *Times* and other large bureaus could stagger their shifts to accommodate the twenty-four-hour news cycle, whereas Maggie had to cope on her own. By the end of the first summer of the blockade, she was just managing to keep pace, with the help of an extremely able and attractive thirty-year-old secretary named Ellen Lentz, who was half American and half German. On her first day, Lentz explained that she would be late the next morning because her husband, a German POW who had just returned from Russia, had committed suicide by throwing himself under a train. She asked for no sympathy, only the time off to make funeral arrangements. Lentz turned out to be a remarkable individual, and a brilliant hire. Maggie added a second assistant, Suzanne Schumann, and the two women helped her ride herd over a team of German stringers and paid informants, running what amounted to a little industry of tipsters out of her living room.

Maggie drove her staff hard, but was no harder on them than she was on herself. As she reported in a gritty exposé in the *Saturday Evening*

Post, "The Night Raiders of Berlin," the Soviets routinely harassed Western journalists, civilians, and soldiers, using the preferred communist tactics of intimidation, arrest, and kidnapping, making it the "tensest city in a tense world." She knew firsthand the risks involved in covering the political strife. That fall, she and five other correspondents were detained for eight hours during a communist riot at Berlin City Hall. Another time, Lentz was rounded up with a group of UP reporters and held overnight in jail. One of Maggie's stringers, Dieter Friede, did not fare as well: he was lured into the Soviet zone, accused of espionage, and sentenced to ten years' hard labor. After he disappeared, Maggie lodged protest after protest, and asked the American military government to intercede on his behalf, but the Soviet authorities denied any knowledge of his whereabouts.

Ever present was the fear of impending conflict—that at any moment Russian troops might march into the Western sectors. "Clay felt that iron-nerved defiance of the Russians was the key to holding our position in Berlin," she recalled, "and the press cooperated by downplaying our own fears. But the apprehension was painfully real."

Collier's correspondent Quentin Reynolds, newly arrived to cover the blockade, described the conditions in Berlin as taut as a "coiled snake." The Russians were making veiled threats. Everyone was waiting for the incident that would trigger a shooting war. After sounding out the knowledgeable "first team" of reporters at the Press Club, including Higgins, Middleton, and John Scott of *Time*, among others, he found Maggie to be the coolest customer. Following a sobering discussion about the possibility of a full-scale Soviet attack, Reynolds asked if she was worried about what would happen if the fighting broke out on her doorstep.

"It might not be pleasant," she said. Then she shrugged her shoulders, and her eyes lit up. "But it would be the biggest story in the world, and we'd have a front seat."

Watching her leave, Middleton just shook his head. "That gal doesn't scare easily," he told Reynolds. "I think she has ice water in her veins."

Given all the real problems she had to contend with, Maggie found it that much more galling when she still lost out on a story merely because

she was a woman. At the height of the airlift, she was invited to an important dinner at the home of Ambassador Robert D. Murphy, Clay's political adviser. She had looked forward to speaking to him, along with several
Washington officials, only to find they were seated next to Middleton at
the opposite end of the table. As soon as the plates were cleared, the men
went off to the library for brandy and cigars. Maggie had to settle for
the wives. Middleton got the scoop on that occasion, but she eventually
found a way to even the score.

Under constant pressure, she became more and more of an independent operator, pitting herself against the Press Club gang. She developed
a "me against them" mentality that drove her to new extremes, and to
repeatedly violate the reporter's taboo against pickpocketing one's colleagues. (If only because there is always hell to pay.) When word spread
that she had embarked on an affair with Ed Morrow, a big, brawny *Times*
correspondent—who happened to be Middleton's assistant—it struck
many as foul play. Spying may not have been her main objective, but when
Middleton discovered what was going on he had Morrow transferred.

Everyone just assumed that Maggie had an ulterior motive. That she
must be taking advantage of the infatuated *Times* man, even though they
were both young, and single, and enjoyed each other's company. It might
simply have been that Morrow, who had fought in the Spanish Civil War
against the Nazi-supported Nationalist faction, possessed "great personal
courage," as she once observed, and it was comforting to have him by her
side at night. It was Morrow, after all, who rushed to her aid at 1 a.m.
after she fired his Luger, kept under her pillow, at a jackbooted stranger
trying to pry open one of her windows. The next day, the German police
captured the perpetrator, who they claimed was a Soviet agent. After
that, Maggie defied the no-weapons rule for correspondents by carrying
a small pearl-handled automatic in her purse. "The pistol," she later told a
friend, "looked damn silly."

The London-born correspondent Judy Barden thought that Maggie
got a bum rap. During those fraught times, Barden was seeing the *Chicago
Daily News* reporter David Nichol—whom she would go on to marry—
and they often worked as a team. It was safer than braving Berlin's mean

streets alone. "If you mention any man who had anything going for him at all, you can be certain Marguerite had some kind of association with him," she said. "But why not? I've never understood why people got so annoyed about it. God knows there were enough disadvantages to being a woman in a so-called man's world." If both parties got something out of the relationship, she asked in her clipped British accent, "whose was the advantage?"

Still, many of Higgins's colleagues came to believe that she was unprepared for the supervisory role of bureau chief and emotionally ill-equipped for so much responsibility. The Press Club echoed with complaints about her pettiness, outbursts of temper, and childish refusal to accept being beaten by a competitor. Reporters are a surly lot, especially on deadline, but the way Maggie stewed and carried on was out of all proportion to the regular ups and downs of daily journalism. She later admitted that she could not help overreacting to any scoop by another Berlin correspondent, responding each time as though it were a "personal disaster."

Things came to a head in September when she was injured in a massive riot of more than 250,000 anticommunist protesters in Platz der Republik, a huge square flanked on one side by the Reichstag building and on the other by the towering Brandenburg Gate, which marked the boundary between the British and Russian occupation zones. Standing at what they thought was a prudent distance, Maggie and a group of reporters watched the outpouring of anger at the ongoing blockade. When a group of German youths climbed atop the gate and tore down the red flag, Soviet military police and guards armed with submachine guns suddenly materialized. "The Soviet soldiers formed a semi-circle and fired into the crowd," Maggie reported. "This correspondent heard at least three shots fired."

The angry mob turned on the soldiers with stones and jeers. The correspondents tried to run for safety, but found themselves caught in the middle of the melee. As bullets spattered around them, and several people crumpled, the crowd panicked. The vast throng surged forward. Maggie was hurled to the ground and trampled, lacerating her arms and legs on the rough stones and broken glass. The injuries were not serious, and she ignored the scrapes and bruises and carried on reporting, covering the days of demonstrations that followed. But within a month, the eczema that always flared when she was under stress began to spread and turned into ugly running welts. By mid-November it had developed into a severe infection. After taking one look at her, the doctor ordered her into the hospital for a month of bed rest.

The first few days she spent in the Swiss clinic were heaven. Her editors had told her to take all the time she needed to recuperate. Although she felt guilty about abandoning her post, Maggie was confident that her assistants would be able to manage the workload. Stephen White, the *Tribune* European correspondent who was keeping her seat warm, should have no problem. All he had to do was take the information her team assembled and run it through the typewriter.

Then, in early December, a call came from a friend who was ostensibly checking on the state of her health. At the end of the polite inquiries, he asked, "Are you planning to come back to Berlin?"

"Of course," she answered, suddenly wary. "Why?"

"Because," he said, "I've just been talking to White. He showed me a letter he had written to your editors suggesting that you be transferred back to Paris." When Maggie, mute with astonishment, failed to respond, he continued awkwardly, "I gathered he thinks the job is too much for you. That you're overeager and made things rougher than necessary for yourself. Anyway, he thinks you're overtired and would like Paris."

Alarmed, Maggie sprang into action. Rage, and a growing sense of trepidation that White was plotting to supplant her, girded her for battle. The only thing she could do was to rush back to Berlin and defend her domain. She rang for her Swiss doctor. Realizing that short of tying her to the bed there was no way to keep her in the hospital, he reluctantly agreed to discharge her. She was back in Berlin the next day, a black cloud over her head. Rather than raise a ruckus with the home office, she decided to feign ignorance of his letter. She reclaimed her office, resumed her duties, and coolly informed White she would be taking over the bureau file. Immediately.

A short, smug man who took a dour view of most of his colleagues, and of Higgins in particular, White was astonished and irked by her abrupt return. There had been no need to cut her convalescence short. A champion bridge player with a precise, logical mind, White prided himself on always being a couple of moves ahead of everyone else. But he badly misjudged Maggie. He had no idea how ferociously she was prepared to fight to keep the Berlin job.

Before he left, White told her to her face that he thought there was "something adolescent" about her off-the-scale competitiveness and stubborn refusal to work more closely with her colleagues. What he told the editors in New York was that Maggie was "very aggressive and hard-working, but ignorant." She tried to compensate for what she did not know by constantly pumping all colleagues and associates for information until it became obvious that she was using them, inevitably poisoning the well. She needed to be transferred out of Germany, preferably back to Paris, where she might safely be allowed to cover fashion. "Maggie treated all reporters as enemies, even the one or two she slept with to my knowledge," White said. "She was a dangerous, venomous bitch."

Once again, Helen Reid turned a deaf ear to her staff's complaints and moved to protect her protégé. When later asked about Maggie's tenure as bureau chief, her eldest son, Whitelaw "Whitie" Reid, who became editor and vice president of the *Herald Tribune* on his father's death in 1947, recalled that his mother had only good things to say: "Marguerite did a very competent job in Berlin. She covered the news with a kind of singlemindedness and determination. These were the characteristics," he emphasized, "that I think contributed to her success."

To Maggie's immense relief, her sudden return to Berlin brought no comment from her editors other than that they were glad to hear she was back, if somewhat amazed by her speedy recovery. She heard no more about it until Geoff Parsons made a casual reference to the episode during a visit to Berlin. He told her that he had recently seen Middleton in Paris, and her *Times* rival had mentioned that he thought Steve White was better suited to be bureau chief. "Yes indeed," Parsons said with a twinkle. "Middleton thinks White is far less intense, more cooperative, shall we say."

When Maggie asked how Parsons had replied, he said, "Noncommittal." He added, however, that he did drop a line to the New York office to the effect that she must be doing an awfully good job if Middleton was so eager to be rid of her. Maggie took it as a compliment, even though she knew it cut both ways.

9

✳ ✳ ✳ ✳ ✳ ✳ ✳ ✳ ✳

Poison Pens

In the bars and boudoirs of occupied Germany
she cheated the newspapermen who confided
in her and lied to the love-hungry soldiers who
were her lovers. Beautiful and unscrupulous, she
enjoyed a passionate holiday among the ruins.

—Toni Howard, *Shriek with Pleasure*

BY JANUARY 1949, IT WAS CLEAR THE SOVIET BLOCKADE HAD BOO-
meranged, and the West had no intention of abandoning Berlin. Winter,
Stalin's last hope, had failed to stop the airlift. Despite the rain and snow
and intercepting Soviet fighters, the around-the-clock deliveries of food
and coal continued. The thin line of Allied planes coming in and taking
off at three-minute intervals was ensuring the city would survive. As the
evidence mounted that this vital lifeline could be maintained, the embattled population of Berlin began to breathe a little easier.

Living under the long shadow of the blockade fostered a strong feeling of esprit de corps in their small foreign outpost in Zehlendorf. Night
after night, Maggie collected reporters, officers, and government officials
for candlelit dinners at her home, drowning out the drone of engines
overhead by turning up the volume on the music. She had purchased the
latest-model phonograph, even if the sound wobbled a bit as a result of
the erratic current produced by her small generator. As the atmosphere of
urgency began to pass, and the Soviets signaled a willingness to reach a

settlement, everyone became almost giddy with relief. The whole colony was in a festive mood. The drinking and dancing often went until dawn.

Maj. Gen. William Evens Hall, Clay's director of intelligence for the European Command, had made a point of keeping his distance from Maggie and her soirees. "I steered shy of her for at least a year," he recalled, attributing his reserve to the obvious conflict of interest. "I was in intelligence, and the intelligence business and the newspaper business are not the most compatible in the world." Hall and Higgins were not the most compatible either, but that did not stop them from getting together.

At forty-one, Hall was a big, broad-shouldered, soft-spoken air force officer who, during his highly decorated career as a pursuit pilot, was unquestionably brave and, as the youngest general in the army when he was promoted at age thirty-five, already a rising star. An Oklahoma boy, he was an outstanding athlete, captain of the track team his first year at West Point and earning an All-American honorable mention as one of the best football centers ever produced by the academy. Clay had been an instructor back then, and Hall's biggest fan. During the war, Hall served under General of the Army H. H. "Hap" Arnold, was chief of the U.S. mission to Bulgaria, and later appointed deputy commander of the Fifteenth Air Force in Italy.

A glowing 1943 *Washington Post* profile touted the ruggedly handsome flier as tailor-made for enlistment posters and described his meteoric rise to deputy chief of the air staff with an office in the Pentagon. "Heads turn in the wake of this tall, lean officer," the reporter raved. "He is a dynamic young leader of a young man's game. Forthright, jaunty, but not cocky, the general's Western simplicity stands him in good personality stead." He was also married to the former Helen Callaway, and the father of four, his family tucked away in a Virginia suburb.

But Billy Hall always had an eye for the ladies, and there was no missing the lissome blonde who cut a neat figure around the Berlin Press Club and coming and going from division headquarters. He had never met Higgins, but he had spoken to her on the phone. Hall was in charge of the Berlin end of the airlift, and she was always pestering his staff with questions. Whenever possible, he took her calls himself, though he never said much. One day in early March, she rang about an incident she had just witnessed: an American cargo plane approaching Tempelhof had been strafed by Soviet fighters. She wanted to know if there would be any consequences. "Nothing for now," he said smoothly. "You're the one breaking the news to me."

By chance, they met for the first time that evening at a cocktail party at the home of Ambassador Murphy. Hall, who was used to seeing Higgins in rumpled work clothes, was knocked out by her appearance. "She was a beautiful girl," he recalled. "And when she got all dressed up, she was something to see." She radiated vitality, and captivated him with her effortless charm and infectious gaiety. Marguerite—he always called her by her full name—was "a lot of fun," he said, and with rare praise for a woman in a man's world, "and a good drinker."

They spent the next few hours dancing and laughing and talking about everything but the airlift. At the end of the night, Maggie knew she had won him over. She asked a favor, with that perfect blend of flattery and flirtatiousness that was second nature to her, expressing an interest in riding in one of his giant transport planes ferrying supplies from Frankfurt to Berlin. Hall promised to see what he could do. But by then, he already knew that he would never be able to refuse this woman anything.

After that, they kept running into each other. "She and I were both hiring the same guys as informants," he said. "We operated in the same way—newspapers call them stringers, and we call them spies. I tried to steer clear of her business, but Berlin was a small community and I couldn't do it. And I just liked what I saw." He would take her with him to check out communist rallies in the Soviet occupation zone, Maggie riding on the back of his motorcycle, her arms wrapped tightly around his waist. Her reaction to him had been just as immediate. She found herself drawn to Hall's solidity and easy air of authority, which only enhanced his magnetism. He was cast from the same mold as her father, a dashing aviator with an outsize appetite for life, for drink, and for good times.

They became an item that spring. Suddenly, they were always together and a couple in the way that individuals a long way from home can become a public pair. Sonia Tomara recalled seeing the two turn up at receptions arm in arm, leaving no one in doubt about the nature of their relationship. During lulls in the airlift story, Dan De Luce and his new wife, Alma, played doubles with them on Hall's "mil-gov requisitioned tennis court." Of their spirited games against the two gifted athletes, he said, "I don't think we ever won." Drew and Stevie Middleton also played, and the matches could get competitive. "That was a good-natured rivalry," said Hall with a smile. "Everybody was very friendly."

In early May, Hall arranged for Maggie to ride on a transport plane carrying sacks of flour, rice, and dehydrated potatoes from Frankfurt to Berlin. She arrived on the tarmac dressed in slim trousers and a short-sleeved shirt, her blond curls loose and windblown. He thought she looked wonderful. She had that mischievous gleam in her eye. Raising the small typewriter in its flat metal case, she said she thought it was "the only luggage she would need."

Just to show off, Hall had decided to surprise Higgins by taking her up himself. Even though he had his back to her when she clambered into the cockpit, Maggie instantly recognized the large, leather-clad figure fiddling with the control panel. Beyond his helmet, she could see the long, sinuous scar that ran down one side of his face, the result of a crash when Hall was still in training. It would be the first—and last—time a general piloted one of the planes in the airlift.

At one minute past midnight on May 12, the blockade ended. Stalin, finally convinced that the highly visible spectacle of trying to starve Berliners was not achieving anything, reopened the land routes. Maggie did not get to write about the historic moment when the checkpoint barriers on the autobahn that had been lowered for ten months and twenty-three days finally lifted, and the first vehicle—as it happened, a carload of American newsmen—crossed into Berlin. The reporter covering the airlift's triumph for the *Tribune* was Stephen White. He had been asked to pinch-hit for a few weeks while the Berlin bureau was being reorganized.

Shortly after her solo flight with Hall, a telegram arrived from the home office. She was being summoned to New York for a meeting to discuss her new assignment—as special correspondent in the Tokyo bureau. Maggie was stunned. What could she possibly have done to deserve being banished to Japan, of all places? It was a country in which she had little interest and no expertise. The postwar news scene was so dormant that there was barely one story per week, and even then, it was buried so deep on the paper's inside pages no one would ever find it.

When she tried to explain her reluctance to leave Berlin for a relative backwater like Tokyo, the foreign editor, Walter Kerr, tried to sound upbeat. He suggested her experience with occupation rule would give her an excellent slant for a series comparing postwar Germany and Japan. Maggie was not buying it. She begged to be allowed to remain in Berlin. Kerr told her the decision had been made at the top of the masthead: she was going whether she liked it or not.

It did not help Maggie's cause that her budding romance with the married Hall had become the subject of comment and concern. He had a very big job in Berlin, and a large family back home. She was known for casual flings, but this dalliance threatened to jeopardize not only a sensitive military mission but a high-ranking officer's promising career. When talk of their affair reached Helen Reid's ears, she was not happy. As a rule, Mrs. Reid did not like extramarital entanglements, which Margaret Parton had the misfortune to learn when she fell in love with a married British official during the war and was promptly shipped to Japan. The *Tribune*'s queen bee was progressive, but as the wife of the paper's owner, she still advocated the traditional values of marriage and family. After making a few discreet inquiries, she decided Maggie had crossed the line. In the cloistered, incestuous foreign-press community of Berlin, where everyone knew everyone else's business, she had become a liability.

Correspondents have no say in where they are sent. They hang their hat where they are told, and if they do not like it, they are free to seek employment elsewhere. Maggie could not imagine looking for another job. Working for the *Tribune* meant everything to her. Part of this was loyalty to her alma mater, and part was that she doubted any other newspaper would offer her the same opportunity to write about international affairs. But she was miserable at the prospect of leaving Berlin. "I tried to put on a cheerful front," she wrote, "but my upper lip was not quite as stiff as I wanted it to be."

Hall was also being transferred. General Clay left Berlin on May 15. A half million Berliners lined the streets and cheered in gratitude. With his departure, the Allied military administration of Germany ended and its officials dispersed. In November, Hall was reassigned to the Pentagon as deputy director of legislation and liaison, Office of the Secretary of the U.S. Air Force. It meant he would be back in Washington, and back with his wife.

When they said their goodbyes at the airport in Berlin, it felt like a definite farewell. They had known each other only a few months. He had a bankrupt marriage, but what serviceman could not say the same after years of separation? Divorce, for a man with four young children, was not possible. Nevertheless, she kept up a passionate correspondence with her lover, hoping against hope that they would find a way to be together.

When Maggie returned to New York in February of 1950, she heard that Steve White was telling everyone that he had gotten her kicked out of Berlin—and out of Europe altogether. Even more damaging was the allegation that she used sex to obtain stories. Hal Boyle of AP, who worked alongside Higgins in Berlin, dined out on stories of how he and the other correspondents would be banging their heads on the wall trying to get tight-lipped military officials to talk when in she would walk and crook her little finger. In short order, Maggie would be supping with the general, then flying away the next morning with her scoop. Inevitably, a lot of the boys believed she "offered more than lowered lashes to get the story."

According to the watercooler calculus, if she slept with one general, she probably slept with them all. True or not, the charge stuck. It would set her apart from her female colleagues for the rest of her life and even decades later would taint her legacy. As Carl Levin put it bluntly, "I always thought it was unfair that she advanced on her back."

Meanwhile, Maggie was in for another nasty surprise. That spring, Toni Howard, formerly of *Newsweek*, published a thinly veiled novel about a seductive female foreign correspondent who would "do anything to scoop a headline." Entitled *Shriek with Pleasure*, and featuring a voluptuous news nymph on the cover, the thirty-five-cent paperback managed to be both salacious and censorious. "This is, frankly, a sensational

novel," begins the jacket blurb, teasing "the frenzied affairs of a woman correspondent."

Howard's vapid and conniving heroine, Carla MacMurphy, a trench-coated cross between Becky Sharp and Scarlett O'Hara, is as amorous as she is thoroughly amoral. In a typical passage, a group of male correspondents discuss her pillow-talk exclusives:

> "She seems to do all right as a reporter. I'll say this for her, she really works."

"Yeah," said Jones, "she works everybody. She's the gal that broke D-day, you know. Got it from some colonel she was sleeping with then, a G-2 at SHAEF. Poor bastard got busted for a security leak. As for our Carla. She was severely disciplined by having her copy double-censored for the next four days. Tough break for the kid, wasn't it, after so much hard night work!"

Because of its shocking content, and straight-from-the-front authenticity, the novel was widely, if not favorably, reviewed. "Carla has learned how to mix duty with pleasure profitably wherever her assignments take her," noted the *New York Times* critic Richard McLaughlin, in a review bearing the headline "Boudoir Blitzkrieg." But he had to wonder at the prowling reporter's improbable number of conquests: "Her lovers are a weird lot—as dense as she is cunning. Picked from the wire service men, Army public relations and intelligence personnel, they are enraptured with monotonous rapidity."

The novelist Patricia Highsmith, writing in the *Saturday Review of Literature*, found the amount of time the fictional heroine spent sleeping around more than a little disturbing: "Indeed, her hoppings in and out of beds, if totaled up throughout the 275 pages, might get some kind of sexoliterary record for the year." Not surprisingly, the book sold well, except in Germany, where it was banned by the army.

Howard, who had long resented Maggie's close working relationship with her husband, Jim O'Donnell, never admitted her protagonist was based on Higgins. She was cagey in interviews about the inspiration for Carla. Later, after the book was panned by critics for its vindictive tone, she tried to maintain that Carla was a composite figure. But Ruth Montgomery, who got to know both women while covering the Berlin airlift for the *New York Daily News*, clearly recalled that when Howard presented her with a copy of her novel, she acknowledged that it was based on Higgins. Montgomery, a Washington-based columnist syndicated by Hearst and UPI to two hundred newspapers, was nobody's fool. Realizing the book's raciness would attract readers, she warned Maggie and Bill Hall what they were in for and loaned them the book.

Among journalists, there was little doubt that Howard's heartless femme fatale with a knack for combining business and bed was modeled on Maggie. Russell Hill did not think much of Howard's attempt at literary assassination, and derided the book as "a biased fictionalized account of Marguerite." But for a while it was all anyone at Bleeck's could talk about. Male correspondents crawled out of the woodwork claiming to have had a one-night stand with Higgins, even if they had been thousands of miles away at the time.

Dog-eared copies of Howard's roman à clef quickly made the rounds of the *Tribune*'s city room and distant bureaus. "Correspondents, who deplore gossip, are among the most confirmed gossips in the world," observed Keyes Beech, who was the *Chicago Daily News* bureau chief in Tokyo when Maggie was posted there in May of 1950.

The coincidence of her arrival, he explained, simultaneous with the publication of a steamy novel about a man-eating woman correspondent, no less one written by another woman correspondent, was bound to set tongues wagging: "Since the locale of this bitchy little story was postwar Berlin, and Higgins had just come from Berlin, since the heroine was Irish and Higgins was unmistakably an Irish name, and since the story ended with the unrepentant heroine aboard an airplane bound for

Tokyo, it was natural that Higgins' arrival in Tokyo aroused more than ordinary interest."

Maggie realized that her reputation had preceded her by the averted gazes and awkward silences with which she was greeted by her new colleagues. The conversational hush was most pronounced around the correspondents' wives, who cut her dead. "According to some Tokyo circles, this sort of 'forever Nellie Bly' was supposed to be I!" she recalled, referring to Elizabeth Cochrane Seaman, aka Nellie Bly, the notorious headline-chasing tabloid stunt girl of Joseph Pulitzer's turn-of-the-century *New York World*. Bly was a pretty, petite reporter whose meek appearance fooled many an unwitting man. She invented a new form of first-person investigative reporting—posing as a lunatic, a beggar, and a factory hand to expose the underside of society—and her undercover exploits made her the front-page star of her day.

Maggie had sought fame, not infamy, but was resigned to the fact that she had little say in the matter. Her one consolation was that she was in good company. Clare Boothe Luce, whom she had interviewed on several occasions and come to admire, had also been the subject of a scathing roman à clef. *A Time to Be Born*, written by Dawn Powell, and published in 1940, and then republished again and again, portrayed the exquisite writer turned politician as a status-hungry social climber, consummate liar, and schemer. It seemed to Maggie that it was the fate of successful women to be maligned by envious peers wielding poison pens.

Not all the women in Tokyo took against her. Helen Lambert, a bright, attractive brunette who was married to AP correspondent Tom Lambert, discounted all the talk and invited Maggie out to lunch. An accomplished San Francisco lawyer who moved to Japan in 1945 to join her husband, Helen had served as prosecutor in the Tokyo war crimes tribunal. She knew all too well what it was like to be a professional woman surrounded by worried wives and wary men. The two hit it off at once and became friends for life.

If Maggie was bothered by the gossip, she did not let on. She dismissed it in her memoir as a minor tempest, noting breezily that there had been "such a spate of books about lady journalists that the in-the-know groups are having a rough time deciding which real-life newswoman fits which fictional work." And there were worse things in the world than being confused with the dazzling Mrs. Luce. But she acknowledged that it was the first time she "consciously experienced the phenomenon of being the subject of a legend." Burdened with neither shame nor remorse, she told herself it did not matter. This, too, would pass. The Carla sobriquet would soon be replaced by others as she scaled new heights in her field.

She was also confident that her relationship with Hall would soon become official, which would help repair her tarnished image. He had flown to Oakland to see her off, pledged his love, and asked her father for her hand in marriage. At a farewell garden party at her home at Chabot Court, which Hall attended, Maggie's mother confided to guests that the public announcement of their engagement would have to wait until his divorce was final.

For all the controversy that attended her time in Berlin, Maggie had no regrets. She had achieved her goal of becoming bureau chief. She had covered America's first victory in the Cold War. She had filed hundreds of stories under the Berlin dateline, to the envy of her peers. Her opinions carried weight, and she had been asked to pen a chapter for a book about the historic events, *This Is Germany*, along with some of the most renowned correspondents in Europe.

Journalists had played a crucial role in shaping public perceptions of the stalemate with Stalin, as well as the strong leadership of General Clay and the other heroes of the airlift, who refused to be bullied by an evil dictator. It was a time when reporters were still partisan for the American cause, and she took great pride in her contribution. "Despite the grim moments," she later wrote, "I look back on Berlin as one of the happiest periods of my life."

10

✳ ✳ ✳ ✳ ✳ ✳ ✳ ✳

Scoop Trouble

A fatherly general took me aside, told me
we were about to be encircled by the enemy,
and suggested that I get "Miss Higgins out
of here." "The front," he said gravely, "is no
place for a woman." I told him I couldn't agree
more but that it was all right for Higgins.

—Keyes Beech, *Tokyo and Points East*

WHEN MAGGIE SWANNED INTO THE TOKYO PRESS CLUB AT NUM-
ber 1 Shimbun ("newspaper") Alley in early May, there was no disguising
the look of dismay on her face. Housed in an old, five-story, red-brick
restaurant building, the club had been redone in the bad taste then
thought of as "Western style," replete with hideous stained-glass windows, ornate moldings, fake fireplaces, and dark, oversize furniture. The
whole placed was suffused in a permanent gloom and was, even in spring,
uncomfortably humid.

When the club was founded in 1945, women were not allowed
upstairs, until a correspondent's wife put her foot down and space was
allotted on the third floor. Maggie's billet consisted of a sparsely furnished cubicle, with a small window and a high, narrow hospital bed. She
had to share the communal ladies' bathroom down the hall, which she
soon discovered was filled most mornings with Japanese call girls who
had spent the night with various correspondents. On the street floor was

a dim lounge with little red tables, and a long, gleaming bar that was never unoccupied, and which made it necessary to slap down the press-club wolves when returning late at night. It was quite a comedown from her home in Zehlendorf.

Her unconcealed nostalgia for Berlin did not make her popular with the Tokyo press corps. "Higgins found the Far East assignment about as exciting as a duck pond," recalled Keyes Beech, who did not much care for her attitude.

Tall, lanky, with a receding hairline and an urbane manner that masked a withering wit, the thirty-seven-year-old Tennessean had shipped out to Asia in 1943 as a marine combat correspondent and completed two tours in the South Pacific. After a brief stint stateside, he returned as a foreign correspondent for the *Chicago Daily News*. Beech had filed some of the finest dispatches describing the raising of the flag over Iwo Jima, and by the almost unanimous agreement of colleagues was one of the bravest pencil men around. He was utterly scornful of the blonde *Herald Tribune* import on arrival, who had hardly unpacked her suitcase before she started picking the brains of every male correspondent in sight.

Beech, who had shared an office with her easygoing predecessor, was looking for a new place to park his typewriter when Higgins announced she was leaving. She had been in Tokyo for only a few weeks. While most of the correspondents were doing stories on Japan's creeping economic recovery, it had come to her attention that South Korea, only a short four-hour flight away, and technically part of her beat, was about to hold highly contested national elections. There had been outbreaks of violence, border clashes, and all the usual forms of communist intimidation. It seemed much more her cup of tea.

Like Germany, Korea had been divided after the war. The arbitrary geographic demarcation line was the 38th parallel, with Russia occupying the half of the country that was to the north, and the U.S. the southern half. Despite both sides' support for national unity, the country became increasingly polarized between the two power blocs. The parallel soon turned into a permanent border bristling with machine guns and barbed wire. In 1948, the United Nations called for free elections, but the Soviets refused and instead helped to install a communist regime under Kim Il Sung in North Korea. Amid mounting pressure from its neighbors, the struggling American-sponsored democracy in South Korea, presided over by Syngman Rhee, a seventy-five-year-old Methodist minister, Harvard and Princeton educated, was attempting to hold independent elections.

On May 28, Maggie filed from Kaesong, which was being subjected to periodic mortar fire from guerillas as part of an ongoing campaign of terror to undermine Rhee's government: "This unpublicized mountain town on the 38th parallel of latitude," she asserted, "today rivals Berlin as a valiant model of how a people determined to be free fight a hot part of the cold war." The fall of China to the People's Army of Communist Mao Zedong in late 1949 had further exacerbated tensions in the region, as had the Sino-Soviet Treaty of Friendship, Alliance and Mutual Assistance, which was signed in February 1950. Although the communist guerillas' artillery shells missed hitting any important targets, she added ominously, "they were intended as a warning of things to come."

The storm signals reported by Higgins and others went unheeded by Washington. The Pentagon believed that the North Korean People's Army (NKPA) might make occasional raids, but the skirmishes would remain localized. The communist world was too weak to pose a serious threat. The disinterest in Korea was due, at least in part, to the confident predictions of Gen. Douglas A. MacArthur, the Allied Supreme Commander, whom Eisenhower had appointed as leader of the occupation forces in Japan. On June 21, Maggie, back in Tokyo, wrote that after meetings with America's visiting defense chiefs, MacArthur expressed the belief that there would be no war in Asia "for at least ten years," and that a communist attack upon Japan would not merit a major commitment of American troops.

Maggie could not help but be awed by MacArthur, a demigod to fans like her father and a considerable swath of the American public. "Very, very impressive," she wrote in a letter home after her first audience in his imposing office in the Dai Ichi building. "He has the most brilliant and encompassing views of the military and world affairs that I've ever encountered. I found him straightforward, charming, and far from pompous." The veteran Tokyo correspondents regarded the Napoleonic general as a supreme egoist and would-be dictator, but the patriot in Maggie could not understand the "press hostility" to such a legendary figure. She flattered herself that she had gotten off to a "good start" with MacArthur because he had liked her articles, rather than Beech's sneering suggestion that the seventy-year-old general had a soft spot for the fairer sex.

Sunday, June 25, promised to be a quiet, lazy day, devoted to errands. When Maggie wandered down to breakfast, she was startled to find her colleagues reeling from the still scanty but shocking news that following an artillery barrage North Korean troops had crossed the 38th parallel. "The Red invasion of South Korea," she wrote, "exploded in Tokyo like a delayed-action bomb. The first reports of the dawn attack were nonchalantly received by the duty officer in the Dai Ichi building. He didn't even bother to wake General MacArthur and tell him."

By 9:30 a.m., Kaesong had been captured. The bulletins poured in all morning. NKPA tanks were rolling down the Uijeongbu corridor toward the South Korean capital of Seoul. The swift attack had caught Rhee's fledgling army completely by surprise. Outnumbered and outmatched, the South Korean forces were already retreating in confusion. South Korea, the last noncommunist outpost in North Asia, was crumbling.

The correspondents scrambled to find transportation to Korea. None was available. Since it was a surprise attack, the army had not anticipated the need. At least the lines to Korea still worked, and they did what they could to report the opening battles by phone. By the next day, the club, which had been half empty, was a madhouse. "Like Dalmations running after firetrucks," recalled *Time*'s young Tokyo correspondent Frank Gibney, "the big names of journalism started flying in."

Maggie, who liked nothing better than to "land running for a story," as one colleague put it, was raring to go. She phoned Bill Hall to tell him she was on her way to the front. From then on, Hall bought a copy of the *Herald Tribune* each morning. It was the only way he could keep up with where she was, and make sure she was still alive.

On June 27, Maggie was milling around Haneda Airport, which

was crammed with reporters, when she a heard that a C-54 was headed to Kimpo Field in South Korea. It was one of the last evacuation planes being sent in to pick up the American civilians fleeing Seoul. The pilot said that if anyone was crazy enough to want to hitch a ride, it was all right with him. Maggie scrambled aboard, along with three other reporters: Keyes Beech; Burton Crane of the *Times*, an old Japan hand; and Frank Gibney, who looked like a Boy Scout with round wire-rim glasses.

At the last minute, Gibney tried to dissuade her from going along, insisting Korea was "no place for a woman." She chose to ignore him over the roar of the engines. "For me, getting to Korea was more than just a story," Maggie recalled. "It was a personal crusade. I felt that my position as a correspondent was at stake. Here I represented one of the world's most noted newspapers as its correspondent in the area. I could not let the fact that I was a woman jeopardize my newspaper's coverage of the war. Failure to reach the front would undermine all my arguments that I was entitled to the same breaks as any man."

They flew into the heart of the war zone under jet-fighter cover. When they reached Kimpo, they swooped in low enough to make out clusters of people below frantically waving sheets and pillow cases, a sign the airport was still in friendly hands. The pilot brought the plane in for a landing, but kept the engines running in case he needed to take off fast. Just off the runway, two bullet-ridden planes were burning.

The four correspondents made their way through the terminal to the deserted parking area. Everywhere there were signs of the chaotic retreat. Half-open suitcases spilled their contents on the ground. The Americans had abandoned their big shiny automobiles in their haste. Many of the cars had been left unlocked, the keys still in the ignition. Maggie helped herself to a new Studebaker. Beech picked out a Dodge, and Gibney and Crane grabbed a jeep. It was early evening, and just beginning to rain. To the sound of machine guns chattering in the distance, their odd little convoy set out for Seoul.

The road to the city was jammed with refugees. There were hundreds of Korean women with babies bound to their backs, bundles on their heads. Military trucks, camouflaged with branches lumbered by.

South Korean soldiers in vehicles and on horseback sped by in both directions. The sight of so many people on the run was both moving and terrifying.

In Seoul, they drew up at the gray-stone headquarters of the Korean Military Advisory Group (KMAG), home to the five hundred officers and men left behind to train the inexperienced South Korean army when American forces were withdrawn the previous summer. They had all cleared out that morning, but sixty men had returned that afternoon on orders from General MacArthur. The correspondents located Lt. Col. W. H. Sterling Wright, a handsome cavalryman, who was acting head of the American advisory force. He told them he had received a message from Gen. J. Lawton Collins, chief of staff of the U.S. Army, announcing the arrival of an American survey team charged with seeing what action needed to be taken to save Korea. It stated: "Be of good cheer. Momentous events are pending."

The word "momentous" was the first hint the correspondents had that America might be entering the war in Korea. Until then, the official U.S. position had been that the Republic of Korea (ROK) Army would be able to handle the North Korean incursion. Maggie and her three colleagues, the only journalists still in Seoul, had a "world scoop"—the beat that is the dream of every newspaper reporter. If only they could find a way to file their stories.

After a midnight briefing, Wright insisted that Maggie spend the night at his house in the KMAG compound. The three male correspondents were billeted with one of his deputies. She did not like being separated from her colleagues, and a strong sense of foreboding caused her to lie down fully clothed. It seemed like she had hardly closed her eyes before Wright's aide burst in. "Get up!" he shouted. "The communists have broken through—we have to get out!"

They piled into separate jeeps and drove at speed toward the Han River Bridge, the only escape route out of the city. As they raced through the dark streets in a heavy rain, they could hear gunfire all around them. An explosion split the sky and the horizon was lit by a sickly orange flame. "My God, there goes the bridge," the young lieutenant at the wheel said.

With the bridge impassable, the Han River now lay between them and safety in the South.

They had no choice but to turn around and go back to KMAG headquarters. Colonel Wright announced that, one way or another, they would find an alternate route. He quickly assembled a convoy of sixty jeeps, trucks, and weapons carriers, and they headed back out into the night. For hours, they searched in vain for a railroad bridge that spanned the river. Although they could encounter the enemy at any moment, Maggie's thoughts kept straying to her three colleagues. She had been told they had made it across the bridge before the panicking South Koreans prematurely blew it up. Her concern for her own welfare was nothing compared to her fear that her competitors were "safe and smug" in Suwon, and already filing their stories.

While they were waiting by the side of the road for a report from a scouting party, Colonel Wright noticed her dejected expression. "What's the matter, kid," he asked, "afraid you won't get your story out?" When she nodded glumly, he told her to stick by the radio truck. If they could establish communications, they might be able to get her dispatch out if she kept it short. Maggie immediately pulled out her typewriter and put it on the front of the jeep, and banged out a story, ignoring the chaos around her. She never got the chance to send it.

By daybreak, it became clear the only hope of not being captured was to leave their vehicles behind and get across the river as quickly as possible. The black waters of the Han were teeming with people. The South Korean troops were fleeing in droves, chucking their weapons as they went. Masses of refugees and soldiers were piling into small rowboats and rafts, swamping the tiny vessels. Some soldiers were shooting at the boatmen to try to force them to come pick them up. It was only by holding back the crush of people at gunpoint that the KMAG party got across the river, all the while harassed by steady rifle fire.

Then they headed south on foot. Maggie, dressed in the navy skirt and flowered blouse she had worn to work the previous morning in Tokyo, and carrying her five-pound typewriter, hiked fourteen miles through rice paddies and over a mountain trail toward Suwon. Conscious of being the only woman in the military detachment, she was determined not to slow them down. Fortunately, she had always been a good hiker, and she had worn flat shoes. After four hours, a jeep full of South Korean soldiers showed up. Maggie and a KMAG officer flagged it down, and they rode in the back for the final leg of the journey.

At Suwon, she learned that Beech, Crane, and Gibney had only narrowly escaped death. Their jeep was twenty-five yards from the blast that demolished the bridge. They were protected from the explosion by a truck filled with soldiers, all of whom died. Their jeep had rolled over and flying glass from the windshield had raked the faces of Crane and Gibney. Beech, who was unhurt, led his bleeding colleagues from the wreckage. The trio eventually got their jeep righted and across the river. Maggie finally found them looking somewhat worse for wear. Crane and Gibney had blood-soaked undershirts tied around their heads. Happy as she was to see them, she was even happier upon learning that they had not managed to file their stories yet.

Beech remembered their reunion differently. Maggie gave the three of them a stony look that said that not only had they gone off and left her, they had compounded the betrayal by driving back and leaving her to walk. But he knew what really pissed her off was the sight of their bandages, and the fact that she had not been wounded at the Han Bridge with them. "Any story-making disaster that befalls other correspondents and inconsiderately omits Higgins," he later noted, "will have to reckon with her ire." She was also more than a little miffed at Gibney because he had lost the two dresses she had stuffed into his pack to lighten her load. She made up for it later, she told him, by sticking the *Trib* with the bill for a pair of Paris gowns.

But they had been lucky. A French news-agency correspondent, as well as most of the staff of the French and British embassies, had been captured in the early morning hours. She and her comrades had gotten out by the skin of their teeth, and now they had a hell of a tale to tell. Maggie, Beech, and Crane flew to Itazuke Air Force Base in Japan, where they could file. Her bulletin from Seoul, Sunday, June 25, was the lead story in the *Herald Tribune*: "Korean Reds Open Attack on South Korea, War On."

Four days later, the *Trib* splashed her vivid eyewitness account on the front page in a four-column box, complete with a large photograph of their intrepid female war correspondent. The headline read, "Seoul's Fall: By a Reporter Who Escaped." The story had a spectacular lead, and included news of the first correspondent casualties:

> Suwon, Korea—Sixty United States Army officers and four newspaper correspondents escaped this morning by makeshift ferry across the Han River southward from Seoul after the South Korean Defense Ministry suddenly blew up all the bridges, trapping the Americans for hours in the isolated capital. . . .
>
> A bright red sheet of flame was seen by this correspondent as I was about to cross the bridge. The structure was ripped by the explosion, and two other correspondents who were closer to the dynamiting were injured. . . .

The *London News Chronicle* obtained special permission to reprint her copyrighted account of the fall of Seoul, and called Higgins "its" war correspondent, giving the *Tribune* a new customer for its wire service, and Maggie a new outlet for her stories. Of the seventy-seven foreign correspondents suddenly turned combat reporters, *Time* noted that Higgins, the only woman, was among the "few who got there first." The magazine ran a fetching studio portrait of the "winsome blonde" provided by the paper's publicity department. Wearing a bejeweled velvet hat, her hair pinned up, she appeared incongruously pretty, feminine, and fragile.

Back in Korea the next day, Maggie spotted MacArthur's famous four-engined plane, the *Bataan*, sitting on the Suwon airstrip. She learned the Supreme Commander had gone in person to survey the scene of the precipitous Han River retreat. The report he sent to Washington would determine the level of U.S. military support, and the all-important question as to whether ground troops would be necessary to repel the invading Red Army. She was kneeling by the side of the windy airstrip, pounding out a short piece about his inspection tour, when the general himself appeared. He was clad in his uniform of summer khakis, sunglasses, and trademark gold-braid-encrusted campaign hat, and carried a corncob pipe.

On seeing her, MacArthur, who still went in for old-fashioned gallantry, asked if she would like a lift back to Tokyo. Maggie, who in all likelihood had not pitched up by his plane by accident, gladly accepted. The *Bataan* offered the only means of flying back to her base of communications and getting her story out. Once onboard, she was given a chilly reception by "the palace guard," as she dubbed the heads of the four wire-service bureaus—Earnest Hoberecht of UP, Russ Brines of AP, Howard Handleman of INS, and Roy McCartney of Reuters—who thought they had MacArthur's plane, and the story of his inspection tour, all to themselves. They were even more enraged when she was invited to join the general in his private compartment.

Maggie reported that MacArthur's visit was a matter of strategic importance and assured both the South Korean troops and their American military advisers that the U.S. was not going to abandon the embattled nation. "News of MacArthur's presence spread like wildfire," she wrote, "and furnished proof that America is backing South Korea to the hilt."

The "palace guard" promptly pitched a fit. Unbeknownst to Maggie, they believed she had reported MacArthur's plans to bomb the enemy airfields north of the 38th parallel. They had all heard the general discussing the possibility with his aides but had agreed to hold back the information as a security measure. The irate news agency chiefs accused Higgins of breaking the embargo. Her alleged breach provoked INS and UP to issue a formal request for military censorship in the battle area. The contretemps made the press section of *Newsweek*, which described the thirty-year-old Higgins as having "talked her way" into MacArthur's cabin to obtain what she thought was a "first-class scoop." The magazine ran a photograph of a helmeted Higgins in her army uniform, with her Hermes Baby typewriter on her lap, accompanied by the caption "Scoop Trouble."

Incensed, Maggie rebutted the charges in a letter to the editor, which *Newsweek* ran in its entirety and entitled "Miss Higgins Speaks." She asserted that the magazine's story was full of "untrue statements" that she was belatedly obliged to correct. MacArthur never revealed his bombing plans on the plane, so she never leaked anything, and in fact had it from "quite a different source." Moreover, since she had been reporting "almost continuously at the front," she had no way of knowing about any headquarters directive concerning "a security blackout."

And because there is nothing a reporter relishes more than fact-checking the work of a fellow reporter, she got in several more whacks for good measure:

> I wish to make the point that my so-called "scoop trouble" did not involve any breach of agreement to which I was a party.
>
> Point No. 2: I was invited by MacArthur on the plane trip, through no request of my own.
>
> Point No. 3: I am 29, not 30.

Afterward, she wrote to MacArthur about the furor, and expressed the hope that by offering her a ride on his plane he had not exposed himself to too much wrath from the press corps. MacArthur responded in courtly fashion: "Pay no attention to what your jealous male colleagues say about you. I know them better than you do and they have been harassing me for more than four and a half years."

But the objections to her presence in Korea continued. In its letters section, *Newsweek* ran a response, "A Corporal Speaks," written by Paul Hershey, an army public-information officer with the Seventh Division. He had two points to add to Higgins's list:

> Point No. 4: Women should not be allowed at the front unless it is absolutely imperative—and then armed with firearms, not typewriters.
>
> Point No. 5: Even as a member of the Fourth estate, she cannot change her biology.

Newsweek could not resist running a cartoon lampooning the herd of male war correspondents that had descended on Korea, including a single lady correspondent, shown gazing into a handheld mirror and applying lipstick. On her helmet the number 30 had been crossed out and replaced with 29, which the caption explained was a reference to Higgins's "strenuous objections" to the magazine's erroneous claim about her age.

Women war correspondents were still a rarity, and *Newsweek*'s editors clearly felt the fuss kicked up by the pretty, pugnacious Higgins made for good copy. All the attention being accorded her frontline activities, along with all the photographs of her attractive profile, had thrust her into the spotlight. It also had the unfortunate consequence of making her a target of much of the continuing hostility toward women at the front, a development the *Chicago Tribune*'s Walter Simmons described as "about as popular as fleas."

The veteran INS correspondent Bob Considine, known for his syndicated column, "On the Line," observed that in Korea, which was seen as a particularly brutal war, the few female reporters were resented more than ever by their male colleagues. "Their bravery was annoying or embarrassing, especially the abundance of that commodity possessed by Marguerite Higgins," he wrote. "From the beginning of the fighting, she made many men correspondents solemnly agree that it's damned unnerving to be huddling in a hole, frightened, and look up long enough to see a good-looking babe moving up closer to the fighting."

ON JUNE 30, MAGGIE started back to Suwon. She felt impelled to return to the action, more worried about missing a story than her own safety. As their unarmed C-54 cargo transport rumbled off the runway in Seoul, both passengers and crew were "in a fine state of nerves." Yak fighters had been strafing the tiny Suwon airstrip. Only the day before, a plane had been shot down. If they got hit, the big 155 mm shells they were carrying would finish them. As they approached Puson Bay, she felt "a rush of fear—a trapped ball of breath that was pressing against my heart." Even after they bumped to a landing, breaking hard to avoid the charred fuselage at the end of the runway, it was hard to exhale, her lungs tight with apprehension.

No sooner had she stepped onto the airstrip than she was accosted by a dour army colonel who told her that she would have to leave. "He was the nervous, officious type that the Army seems to have a talent for producing," she recalled. " 'You'll have to go back, young lady,' he said. 'You can't stay here. There may be trouble.' "

Maggie, who was growing tired of this sort of unsolicited concern for her welfare, trotted out her stock answer: "I wouldn't be here if there were no trouble. Trouble is news, and the gathering of news is my job."

Just then, she saw Colonel Wright's aide, the young officer who had been her companion on the long trek out of Seoul. Certain that he would take her side, she called out, "Hey, lieutenant, how about a ride back to headquarters?" Seeing him smile and nod in recognition, she hopped in his jeep and they took off before the colonel could say another word.

At the Suwon command post, she found Keyes Beech, Tom Lambert of AP, Roy McCartney of Reuters, and Gordon Walker of the *Christian Science Monitor* huddled in one of the unoccupied huts. The atmosphere was tense. The KMAG reinforcements were talking in low voices. There seemed to be some vague intelligence that North Koreans had been seen in the vicinity. Beech assured her that he was still in possession of his trusty stolen jeep, and he had reserved a place for her in it in case they needed to leave in a hurry. At that moment, she was more grateful than she could say. She hoped it meant that she had an ally among the male correspondents.

Late that night, she felt someone shake her awake. A voice in the dark said, "Get to the war room fast. We may need to pull out." Maggie, who had been dozing on a blanket on the floor, heard the sudden scrape of doors opening and the thump of running feet. She grabbed her typewriter and musette bag. In the hall, she heard muffled shouts that they were surrounded. Hurrying toward the lighted war room with the other reporters, she almost collided with a colonel who was trying to get out.

A furious sergeant said to Beech, "Those sons of bitches are trying to save their own hides—there are planes coming, but the brass won't talk. They're afraid there won't be room for everybody." A rumor that the officers were trying to escape without the rest of them swept through the camp. "From then on," she recalled, "every mess sergeant, jeep driver, code clerk, and correspondent had just one idea—to get hold of every and any vehicle."

Someone shouted, "The Reds are down the road!" There were more shouts, more contradictory reports. A major informed them that they were preparing to defend the airstrip. Before leaving, the correspondents and some fifty young soldiers armed themselves with carbines. The sum total of Maggie's experience with a rifle was one afternoon on a range. In a torrential downpour, she and her companions piled into their jeep and followed the hastily formed convoy of trucks carrying the bazooka and rifle teams. After the initial panic subsided, however, they heard the road south was open. It seemed they were not surrounded after all. They headed toward Taejon, hoping that this time the army had good information. After a seventy-mile, all-night drive in an open jeep, they rolled into the provisional capital at 6 a.m., exhausted and drenched to the skin. Most of the way they had led the rearguard convoy.

Beech was disgusted by the disorderly retreat. "It is most unusual for war correspondents to lead military convoys," he noted with the pungent cynicism that often got him into trouble. "But this is a most unusual war."

In an empty government building, they found Brig. Gen. John H. Church, the senior American officer in Korea, sitting by himself at a long felt-covered table. As it turned out, there had been no need for haste. The green South Korean troops were easily spooked. Their defensive line had buckled the previous evening, and two thousand North Korean soldiers had crossed the Han River. However, the enemy was moving at something less than blitzkrieg speed and was still miles from Suwon. There had been a series of miscommunications, and costly mistakes.

Church, a spare, sharp-featured man, regarded the four bedraggled correspondents solemnly and said, "You may be interested to know that two companies of American troops were airlifted into southern Korea this morning."

Maggie, who was shaking like a wet puppy, her gabardine skirt dripping a pool of water onto the rug, was unconvinced. A veteran of two retreats in one week, she asked, "Don't you think it's too late?"

"Certainly not," Church said confidently. After blaming the mistakes on the South Koreans, and belittling their lack of backbone, he said things would change when the Americans arrived. While they had been in the field, the United Nations had voted to marshal their forces against the communist aggressors. After providing air and naval assistance, there could be no more halfway measures—the U.S. would have to commit everything they had to the fight. Their troops would be there in a matter of hours. And they would not stop until they had chased the invaders back over the border. "We will hurl back the North Koreans," he said.

"But suppose the Russkies intervene?" Beech inquired.

"We'll hurl them back, too," the general said.

The battle had been joined. The belief was the North Korean bandits could be stopped in their tracks. Higgins and Lambert, who were on deadline, rushed to file their stories. The problem was that at Taejon, the army had only one telephone line that could connect the correspondents to their Tokyo offices, which was how all news from Korea was transmitted to the world. By some miracle, Lambert got through to the AP bureau after only twenty minutes of trying. Then, as a favor, he asked the desk manager to also take his *Herald Tribune* colleague's story.

Maggie was only three paragraphs in when she was cut off. She could not believe it. She had not known the call would be limited to only a few minutes. It was the first time she had ever had to dictate a story off the top of her head and, rattled, she had left out many of the important facts. There was no *Tribune* Tokyo bureau for her to call back—she was the bureau. Frustrated and miserable, she rustled up a friend at the press club, who agreed to help her file. But by this time there was a line of correspondents waiting to read their stories over the phone. Maggie, bleary-eyed with fatigue, slashed the Suwon episode in half and compressed the rest into five or six paragraphs. She got her story out, but it was hastily conceived and disjointed.

She spoke for all the correspondents when she later wrote of the daily struggle they faced trying to file their dispatches with the paucity of communications equipment available. "Never once," she wrote, "have I been satisfied with the writing and organization of a single story. I know all of us in the beginning kept thinking, 'Well, next time maybe there will be more of a chance to think it through,' or, 'Next time I won't be so tired.'" But it never got any easier.

The Korean monsoon was still in full force two days later when Maggie and a jeepload of correspondents watched the two rifle companies of the Twenty-First Infantry Regiment, Twenty-Fourth Division, commanded by Lt. Col. Charles B. Smith, take up defensive positions on the outskirts of Taejon. Higgins, Lambert, McCartney, and Carl Mydans were on the front line as the raw, young American troops went into battle. NKPA tanks roared south across the distant fields. The bazooka teams, which had arrived only a few hours before, were ordered to attack.

Lying in a muddy graveyard foxhole, Maggie watched through her binoculars as the soldiers jumped out of the trucks and spread out along a nearby ridge. A tank turret rose into view above the foliage, and a belch of flame drew answering fire from the bazooka boys. A head poked up out of the grass, a young soldier looking to see if he had scored a hit. Flashes from enemy machine guns flicked the ground and she saw the soldier fall—Private Kenneth Shadrick of Skin Fork, West Virginia, had been struck in the chest.

It was Maggie who reported the first American casualty of the Korean War. "Death of the First Infantryman: Woman Reporter Sees the Battle," announced the *Tribune* headline. From the hole where she crouched, she watched the medics tenderly lift the nineteen-year-old's body, she wrote. "The lifeless form was shrouded in a blanket to keep the pelting rain off the young blond face. As the medics brought the body in, one young private said bitterly, 'What a place to die.'"

The American forces at Taejon were soon overrun by the NKPA. The enemy T-34 tanks, more than thirty by her count, advanced arrogantly, apparently unconcerned by the exploding shells, which seemed to bounce off them. Even when the Americans fired at point-blank range, their recoilless rifles and bazookas seemed to have little or no effect. Confusion reigned. The correspondents watched in horror as only an hour into the battle their bewildered troops suddenly began to pull back, moving toward them across the fields. "My God," said Mydans, a seasoned combat photographer, "they act as if the last inning in the ball game is over and it's time to go."

Isolated and dazed, the GIs were completely overwhelmed. Incredible as it seemed, their combat units had run out of ammo. Caught between the enemy tanks and infantry column, the inexperienced troops began to fall apart as a unit. Psychologically as unprepared as they were militarily, they had no idea of how to stand and fight. "The youngsters—most were under twenty—at first gazed at the tanks as if they were spectators in a newsreel," Maggie wrote. "[They] had been plucked so suddenly out of soft occupation life in Japan and plunged into battle. Most had had only routine basic training and were far from combat-ready. Only a small percentage had ever heard artillery fire before."

Many of the junior officers were as inexperienced as their men. Their commanders, who had earlier called the South Korean troops cowards, were now issuing their own humiliating orders for a "strategic withdrawal." By the end of their first day of ground action, approximately 150 men were killed, wounded, or reported missing.

In the days that followed, the pattern of defeat became painfully familiar. It was the beginning of what the correspondents called "the long retreat," Maggie wrote in a grimly effective magazine story, "The Terrible Days in Korea," for the *Saturday Evening Post*:

> Within minutes, the lesson of what happens when you underestimate the enemy played before us on the battleground north of the command post. It was a lesson learned in terms of lost battalions, abandoned wounded, and inadequate equipment. It was a lesson that destroyed the pre-battle myth that "These North Koreans will run when they come up against the Americans." . . .
>
> It began three continuous weeks at the front, in which I saw my countrymen take a vigorous mauling from a Soviet-directed raggedy-tag army that they had nicknamed "Gooks," and earmarked as a pushover. I was to report, firsthand, the price in lives and prestige paid by the Americans for being unprepared.

On Monday, July 17, in the midst of the battle of Taejon, Maggie received word that she had been ordered out of the Korean theater. It was "a blow," she recalled, "that rocked me as rudely as if it had been a bullet."

At first no one, including the officer who delivered the bad news, seemed to know the reason why. Everyone immediately jumped to the conclusion that she was being recalled by division brass on the grounds she had been "giving aid and comfort to the enemy" by referring to specific units, bases, or tactical maneuvers. While there was no formal censorship, the correspondents were expected to follow the guidelines, and avoid disclosing any information that might encroach on military security. Maggie did not know if she had somehow slipped up in one of her dispatches, or if her graphic portrayal of the beating their underequipped troops were taking had gotten her labeled a traitor. She believed it was necessary to tell the hard "bruising truth" about their troops' lack of preparation, but had the unfavorable reports gotten her recalled?

She soon learned her expulsion had to do not with the quality of her work but with the prevailing norms of the army. She was being thrown out of Korea on the orders of Lt. Gen. Walton Walker, the new commanding general of the U.S. Eighth Army, because she was female, and there were no facilities "for ladies" at the front. This was his way of delicately referring to the rudimentary conditions of an embattled army on the move, which included open-air urinals, uncovered latrine boxes, and communal showers and sleeping arrangements, to say nothing of the disease and filth that abounded in the country.

To Maggie, it was beyond absurd. "In Korea, nobody, including the Koreans, worries about powder rooms," she angrily vented in the *Saturday Evening Post*. "The nearest powder room is the nearest convenient bush." She had been going out on patrols at dawn, traveling a hundred miles to the front and back daily over horrendous roads, only to spend half the night wrestling with the bad connection to Tokyo. With sixty correspondents all dependent on the single army radio-telephone line, the only sleep she had gotten in recent weeks was on the tables in headquarters, where she stretched out while waiting for her turn. When it came to issues of comfort and convenience in this war, primitive "facilities" were the least of her problems.

Maggie called General Walker and pleaded not to be yanked out of Taejon. Unmoved, he told her to get out. She agreed to depart as soon as it was feasible. Desperate to remain, however, she appealed to MacArthur to personally intervene. She also sent an urgent cable to Helen Reid in New York to ask if there was anything the newspaper could do on her behalf.

In an effort to buy herself more time, Maggie dodged military officials, and hid out at the front. Maj. Gen. William Dean, the ruddy-faced, crew-cut commander of the Twenty-Fourth Infantry Division, sympathized with her plight. After so many weeks of covering the war, he saw no reason to give her the "bum's rush." In the succeeding days, a touching number of officers and soldiers told her they hoped the top brass would rescind the order.

But Gen. "Bulldog" Walker, as he was known, expected his orders to be obeyed. Removing Higgins was part of his larger plan to ban all women from Korea except for nurses, who would be confined to the rear. "This is just not the type of war where women ought to be running around the front lines," explained an army spokesman.

Under the headline "Army Orders Miss Higgins Out of Korea," the *Tribune* decried Maggie's removal and heaped praise on their reporter, "the only woman correspondent at the Korean front, who was one of the first on the scene when the fighting started." A defiant Maggie was quoted saying she had asked for a chance to argue her case in person: "I am going down to General Walker's headquarters to try to convince him that I, as a duly accredited correspondent, am here as a newspaper correspondent and not as a woman."

In the meantime, Helen Reid was working vigorously behind the scenes to have her reinstated. The *Tribune*'s influential publisher wired MacArthur in Tokyo an urgent plea to do right by Higgins, arguing her reporter had shown "personal strength and courage" both in Korea and in Europe:

[Walker's ban] will be a blow to profession which
has rated newspaper women on equal terms with
men. Also it will be severe blow to this newspaper
and to others which have been giving her dispatches
first page prominence. Would appreciate your help
in reconsidering decision. Greatly hope it can be
changed.

In a show of public support, the paper's young editor, Whitelaw Reid, issued a strongly worded response to the army order: "The *Herald Tribune* is shocked by news that Marguerite Higgins has been ordered out of Korea. She has been responsible for some of the best coverage of the war since the third day of the invasion. We believe the decision to order her out of Korea is wrong and unfair in view of the outstanding job of reporting she has done. Newspaper women are willing to assume the risks and in our opinion should not be discriminated against. We hope she will be allowed to continue her work."

Early on the morning of July 18, Maggie reached the Eighth Army's Taegu headquarters. Unfortunately, she was recognized by an army public relations officer, who told her he was escorting her out of the war zone, if he had to call the military police. "And you can write that down in your little notebook." She did.

Then she asked, "Am I under arrest?"

"Don't pull that stuff," he snapped. "I know your publicity tricks." She wrote that down, too. On the way to the train station, he further elaborated his views on women correspondents.

Robert "Bob" Miller of UP got wind of the story and recounted how the Eighth Army was in such a hurry to get Higgins out of the country that the public relations officer canceled her meeting with Walker and instead escorted her directly from the train to the airstrip, where he put her on a plane for Tokyo. Miller felt sorry for her, so he went to see her off. "Maggie was a very warm person, and a professional to the marrow of her bones," he said. "She claimed she was a victim of discrimination, and a justifiable claim it was. I had never seen Maggie cry," he added, recalling the hot tears of frustration rolling down her cheeks, "and I never saw her cry again."

Afterward, he always thought she avoided him out of embarrassment. "I don't think she ever forgave me for having seen her cry," he explained. "She wanted to be everything a male reporter was and, unfortunately, I had seen her, shall we say, naked in thought, and this was a weakness." He never told anyone of catching her in a vulnerable moment. "I've always thought that Maggie wouldn't particularly like people to know that she was a very, very human person."

As she left Korea, Maggie, who knew how to make a grand exit, declared, "I have been with the troops for three weeks and have been through some bitter retreats. I want to be with them when they start going back. I walked out of Seoul and I want to walk back in."

By the time she touched down in Tokyo late that night, she learned that MacArthur had personally countermanded the expulsion order. In an answering cablegram to Helen Reid, the Supreme Commander wrote:

ZEBRA ONE EIGHT ZERO BAN ON WOMEN
CORRESPONDENTS IN KOREA HAS BEEN LIFTED.
MARGUERITE HIGGINS IS HELD IN HIGHEST ESTEEM
BY EVERYONE. SIGNED MACARTHUR

The *Herald Tribune* front-paged MacArthur's statement and trumpeted Maggie's return. In an editorial that same day, the paper suggested that when the Eighth Army spokesman observed that Korea was not the type of war where women should be allowed, he did not go far enough, and he might have added that "it was not the type of war men should have to undergo either." When wars are fought, the editors continued, "it is essential that everyone play his or her part in them, and reporting a war honestly is as important as fighting it courageously."

Milking the situation, the following day the *Trib* ran a large photo of a triumphant Maggie in fatigues, grinning ear to ear as she prepared to climb into a jeep in Tokyo on her way back to Korea. She had every reason to smile—the editor in chief of Doubleday, Ken McCormick, had just offered her a large advance to write a book about her experience as the sole woman correspondent in Korea. At her suggestion, Carl Mydans would provide the pictures.

Higgins was a cause célèbre. She was herself page-one news. Her ouster and subsequent restoration had made headlines in newspapers and magazines across the country. Even the *New York Times* was forced to cover the controversy about its competitor, writing about her removal from and, twenty-four hours later, return to Korea, the headline announcing, "Miss Higgins Going Back."

Many prominent women journalists applauded Maggie's success, and letters poured in. Mary Hornaday, a pioneering political reporter for the *Christian Science Monitor*, who in her more than thirty years at the paper had served as the first chairwoman of Eleanor Roosevelt's White House press conferences and as president of the Overseas Press Club, wrote to thank Whitelaw Reid for taking a stand on the issue: "You have, and won," she crowed. "Congratulations!"

In a humorous postscript to the episode, the Soviet magazine, *New Times*, accused MacArthur of censoring war correspondents. The article was accompanied by a cartoon showing American soldiers frog-marching Higgins off the battlefield, under the heading, "The First Victory for MacArthur." The subhead read, "The enemy surrounded—one fountain pen seized." The *Tribune*, appreciating that their "non-deportable reporter" was now big news, ran with it: "Reds Call Reporters Bullied in Korea, Cartoon Shows Bayonets Turned on Miss Higgins."

Madison Avenue also recognized that Higgins was a hot commodity. Eager to cash in on all the publicity, the sales manager of Paillard, Ltd., wrote to ask her if they could use the photograph of her in uniform working at her Hermes Baby typewriter in an advertising campaign. Maggie happily supplied a testimonial, saying that as a combat reporter she found the Hermes "indispensable in front line coverage, and despite the rough treatment, exposure to soaking rains, jolting jeeps, dust and dirt, it never let me down." Paillard agreed to pay her $1,200, a fee more than eight times her weekly salary of $135.

Helen Reid, no slouch when it came to circulation and promotion, soon began running ads for the paper featuring the photo of Maggie in fatigues, along with the tagline, "The *Herald Tribune*'s recent Berlin and now Tokyo correspondent, who looks like a fashion model but lives on adventure, is back where she belongs—at the front."

11

✳ ✳ ✳ ✳ ✳ ✳ ✳ ✳ ✳

The Feud

The competition between Maggie and Homer was
a war on its own. And there was more competition
between those two than there was between the AP
and the United Press and The New York Times and
the Tribune. It was one of the greatest intramural
contests that we had ever seen and enjoyed.

—Robert Miller, UP

THE ARMY WAS NOT ALONE IN WANTING TO GET RID OF MAGGIE.
The Korean War was barely a week old when the *Herald Tribune* dispatched Homer Bigart to the front. He was a bona fide star, considered by
his peers to be the world's greatest living war correspondent. A legend in
his own time, the big, stocky six-footer had covered every kind of perilous
assignment from the bloody hill battles of Italy, and terrifying bombing
raids over Germany, to the savage fighting in the islands of the Pacific.
He had risked his life more times than anyone could count and won a
Pulitzer along the way. Now nearing forty-three, he was a little heavier
and a little grayer than the last time he saw action, but he did not need any
help from an impudent upstart like Higgins, who was untested in battle,
unsuited to the combat zone, and a known troublemaker.

From the moment he arrived, Bigart made it clear he had no intention of working with her. He told Maggie to return to Tokyo and run the
bureau, which was what she was supposed to be doing in the first place.

When she tried to argue that there was plenty of war for them both, and no need to banish her to the rear, he ordered her out of the theater. If she did not leave at once, he would "bring the house down on her." What he meant was he would have her fired. Then he cabled his editors in New York and told them he wanted her gone.

Bigart was a popular figure with a devoted following. Young correspondents in the field trailed after him, hung on his every word, and aped his writing style. He had a deceptively bumbling manner, due in part to his thick glasses and pronounced stutter, but he had long ago made a strength of his handicaps, disarming interview subjects with his helpless appearance and then extracting twice as much information as any other reporter. He had perfected his act to the point where longstanding colleagues could parody what they called the "Help Homer Club," but this did not stop him from conning admiring cubs into opening their notebooks and feeding him material, making sure a harmless old country rube like himself did not miss out on anything.

Maggie thought him anything but benign. In person, he was as blunt and uncompromising as his prose. After repeatedly threatening to have her fired, he turned on her friends, warning Mydans that if he continued to assist Higgins he would be responsible for the loss of her job. The forty-three-year-old war photographer, who worked in close partnership with his wife, Shelley, was one of the most fair-minded and empathetic souls around. Mydans's advice was to ignore Bigart's bluster and get back to work. "What is more important to you, Maggie," he asked, "the experience of covering the war in Korea or fears of losing your job?"

In a letter to the *Trib*'s managing editor, Bill Robinson, Maggie wrote that she had no problem with Bigart's being assigned to Korea. Given the growing scale and magnitude of the war, there was room for them both. However, she made it clear that she resented the insensitivity of the editors in New York in allowing him to stride in and order her back to Tokyo. She did not regard herself as in any way subordinate to Bigart. If anything, she took the view that he should have made the effort to work with her, the local correspondent. "It's all very boring and childish and generally sickening," she concluded.

Maggie stayed put. Without clear guidance from her editors, she carried on reporting, but she lived from day to day in fear that Bigart might have her not only exiled but axed from the paper altogether. She worried to her diary about the danger of going up against "the paper's senior military correspondent," especially given his "prestige" from years of reporting from the cannon's mouth.

Strung out from lack of sleep, and more jittery and emotional than usual, she let Bigart's undisguised antagonism get to her. Their turf battle was the talk of the press corps. She dreaded the fresh crop of look-what-Maggie's-done-lately tales that Mydans brought back after each trip to Tokyo. It was the last thing she needed on top of the Walker imbroglio. At one point, she turned to Jimmy Cannon, the *New York Post* sportswriter turned Korea columnist, for sympathy, only to have him respond, "If the Racing Form sent a horse to cover the war, he wouldn't be any more of an oddity than you are. That horse's activities would be the subject of all sorts of stories, and nobody would care how true they were so long as they were good stories."

No matter what she did, she couldn't win. The prospect was discouraging. She scribbled in her notebook before returning to the front, "Going forward in spite of Homer—heartsick."

Beech could see that Maggie was intimidated by her much-vaunted colleague. But in trying to bigfoot Higgins, Bigart did himself no favors. If there had been a question of her competence in covering the war, then no one would have questioned his right to send her packing. However, as Beech and the other Tokyo correspondents saw it, Higgins had jumped astride the story at the start and was riding it for all it was worth. Korea was part of her patch, and she had been filing from there since before the invasion. And the consensus was that she had been doing a damn good job. Now that the conflict had become a page-one story, she was being ordered to surrender it to the paper's famous ace, who had just flown in from New York. "There was, in this situation, an element of injustice," recalled Beech. "Thus a certain amount of sympathy was created for Higgins where none had existed before."

But it was sympathy without any illusions. When a *Time* editor cabled Gibney that Higgins looked so sweet and innocent in her photographs, and suggested she might be worthy of a feature, he cabled back: SHE'S AS INNOCENT AS A COBRA.

On July 6, stories by Bigart and Higgins appeared side by side on the front page of the *Herald Tribune* for the first time. He had the lead with a sweeping, wide-angled analysis of the rout suffered by the raw American troops in their first engagement with the NKPA. She matched his dispatch with her moving, closely observed account of the death of the young infantryman. Maggie could not surpass the majestic elegance of Bigart's prose, as he demonstrated a few days later in his tersely evocative four-thousand-word, hour-by-hour log of a day in a foxhole near Chonui. But she had a remarkable eye, an unerring instinct for drama, and the same penchant for putting herself in the thick of the action.

The editors of the *Herald Tribune* realized that the two competing correspondents each brought something unique to their work, and they brought out the best in each other. Together, they provided a one-two punch that outclassed everyone else's coverage of the war. Despite Bigart's howl of protest, the editors ruled that it was in the paper's interests to keep them both in Korea. Bigart would be the prime correspondent, responsible for the big picture. Higgins could stay and file all the color and sidebar pieces she could find. (Perhaps not surprisingly, the editors of the *Saturday Evening Post* struck the same bargain, assigning Bigart to do the "straight reporting job," while counting on Higgins to provide "a kind of lady-in-battle piece" that catered to the "female clientele.")

Maggie received a cabled vote of confidence from the paper's young editor, Whitie Reid, who cautioned her about her tendency toward risk-taking:

YOU HAVE SENT SUPERLATIVE STORIES STOP EVER
SINCE YOUR ARRIVAL TOKYO YOUR PIECES HAVE
BEEN AN ASSET GREATLY VALUED BY THE PAPER
STOP WE ALSO VALUE YOUR SKIN AND HOPE YOU
WILL USE DISCRETION IN TAKING CHANCES.

The following day, Bigart received a similar telegram. He got the message. From then on, he stopped trying to obstruct Maggie. Instead, he went about his business and pretended she was not there. He had absolutely nothing to do with her, though everyone knew he resented her proximity. He practically foamed at the mouth at the mention of her name. Correspondents for the same paper typically communicate with one another frequently, if only to avoid duplication of effort. Bigart would not deign to speak to her.

"Maggie intently went her own way, in her own way," recalled the photographer Max Desfor. "In fact, they went their separate ways. They avoided each other and pursued their own leads and means without talking to each other. A message from the home office, received by one, was not relayed to the other unless perhaps through a third party."

Bigart later admitted to being deeply aggrieved at the *Tribune*'s management for putting him in an untenable position, then playing them off each other and shamelessly exploiting the situation. To a journalist of his standing, it was undignified and embarrassing. Of his rivalry with Higgins, he said with his usual astringency, "It was less a clash of personalities than a simple tussle over turf."

For her part, Maggie had the sense to steer clear of her taciturn *Tribune* colleague. But after outmaneuvering the U.S. Army, she was not about to let Bigart get the better of her. As Beech observed, "The Higgins competitive instinct, a quality hardened and sharpened by childhood circumstance, was a fearsome thing."

Determined to show that she was more than Homer's equal, Maggie took off for Taegu in a borrowed jeep. At the Eighth Army compound, she found General Walker, who turned out to be a short, fat man of obstinate disposition. Although he remained convinced that the front was no place for a woman, he accepted MacArthur's decision. "Orders were orders," he said. She could be assured of "absolutely equal treatment." Walker, who disliked dealing with the press, told her the decision to remove her from Korea had been initiated by a public relations officer who had envisaged the nightmare that would ensue if anything happened to her pretty little neck. "The American public might never have forgiven me," he said, and asked if she could please avoid getting killed or captured on his watch.

While she was at field headquarters, the North Koreans were engaged in making a huge push on the west coast. They had already seized Chonju, and the communist troops in their mustard-colored tunics streamed down the main road south toward the strategic city of Taejon, an important communications center. Despite having suffered major losses, General Dean's weakened Twenty-Fourth Division prepared to try to defend Taejon with four thousand men.

On July 21, with Taejon encircled and many of his men slaughtered, Dean led the last remaining American troops in a desperate dash through the communist lines. After their convoy encountered a North Korean blockade, the Americans scattered, taking to the rice paddies. Dean was wounded, separated from his men, and reported "missing in action." (He survived in the mountains for thirty-six days before being captured and spent the rest of the war as a POW.) His besieged division was shattered. It was the worst American defeat of the war.

"We were sent over to do a delaying action and we were pretty much sacrificed to accomplish that mission," said Daniel Cretaro, then a twenty-year-old private and one of two hundred GIs who made the harrowing escape from Taejon. "There were a lot of guys killed, wounded, missing—a lot missing." He and the exhausted remnants of Dean's division joined what was left of the Thirty-Fourth Infantry Regiment. They were fighting simply to survive, taking in stragglers along the way. They headed west, and when they reached the high ground, the soldiers could see Taejon was on fire. Cretaro was startled to see Higgins, who was traveling with the Thirty-Fourth, scramble to the top of the hill.

Looking below at the smoldering ruins of the South Korean city, she said, "Well, the story's down there." Cretaro was struck by her sangfroid: "I thought it was odd that a female would get out of a deadly situation and think that she could go back into it."

Maggie did not flinch from telling the *Tribune*'s readers about the carnage in the Korean campaign. After enemy troops enveloped an aid station, they murdered all the American wounded, including a Catholic chaplain who had remained behind to administer last rites after urging his colleagues to leave. The massacre occurred after the litter patients had been carried across fields under sniper fire. In her dispatch, Maggie quoted a shocked officer with the Medical Service Corps: "The communist guerillas went after the patients with their rifles, shooting them in the side," Captain Lincoln Buttery said. "As I escaped over the hill, I saw the chaplain shot."

Throughout the rest of the month, the North Koreans continued to push the American and South Korean troops back into the southeastern corner of the country around the city of Pusan, a vital supply port. Maggie reported the brave resistance put up by their battered but still battling troops, who had fought a series of bloody rearguard actions, holding off the North Koreans while the Eighth Army established an effective defense around Pusan as they waited for reinforcements. When Bigart and the other correspondents went to cover the landing of the marines, she continued on her own, driving from Masan down the valley to Chindong-ni, where the Twenty-Seventh (Wolfhound) Regiment of the Twenty-Fifth Infantry Division had established its headquarters in an old schoolhouse under the brow of rolling green hills.

She wanted to interview the regiment's popular thirty-seven-year-old commander, Lieutenant Colonel John "Mike" Michaelis, onetime aide-de-camp to Eisenhower. He had won distinction early in his career as a member of General Maxwell Taylor's 101st Airborne force, which helped spearhead the Normandy invasion. A twice-wounded, much-decorated D-Day veteran, he was the glamour boy of the Eighth Army and attracted war correspondents like a magnet.

On meeting him, it was easy to see why. He was every inch the professional soldier—a lean, handsome, charismatic West Pointer, with the confident swagger of an ex-paratrooper. He was reputed to be an exemplary tough leader and brilliant tactician. While fending off platoon after platoon of North Korean tanks at Taegu, on the Pusan perimeter, in what became known as the "Battle of the Bowling Alley," he exhorted his men, "Remember, you're here to kill, and not to be killed." When Maggie encountered him, his unit had been fighting in the mountains for five straight days. Late that evening, Michaelis, looking weary, his cropped hair prematurely gray, kept her and Harold Martin of the *Saturday Evening Post* scribbling steadily as he regaled them with the story of the tenacious attack mounted by one of his tank battalions that very day.

Early the next morning, while she was feasting on a comparatively deluxe meal of powdered eggs with Michaelis and a half dozen of his officers, communist infiltrators ambushed the command post. "A coffee pot knocked off the breakfast table by machine gunfire was the first warning this correspondent and most of the regimental officers had of the attack," Maggie reported in the *Herald Tribune*.

A fusillade of small-arms fire hit the building, crackling through the broken windows and splintering the paper-thin walls. Then came the deep clatter of a machine gun. A grenade sent fragments flying off the roof. Another pulverized the wooden grill where she had been sleeping an hour earlier. The vicious cross fire made it demonstrably clear that they were surrounded. During the night, the enemy had sneaked past the defense lines in camouflaged uniforms and crept onto the hillside behind the schoolhouse, while others set up machine guns in the rice paddy on the far side of the yard. The surprise attack against the dozing American soldiers wounded many before they could reach for their weapons.

Maggie and Harold Martin hugged the floor. They lay flat, noses in the dust, for fifteen minutes as bullets ripped past, tearing up the walls and floorboards. In the far corner of the room, three enemy prisoners were moving aimlessly about on their hands and knees, moaning. The next time she looked in their direction, they were lying dead in a pool of blood. Then one of the officers yelled, "I'm getting out of here!" He dove through one of the open windows. In what Maggie described as "the swiftest series of leaps ever seen outside the Olympics," six officers and two correspondents followed him.

They found shelter from the rain of fire behind a low stone wall. The courtyard was in chaos. Some of the terrified soldiers were shooting without aiming. An officer shot and wounded a GI machine gunner who had gone berserk and was firing at his own vehicles and troops. Maggie tried to say something to Martin, who had pulled out his notebook and was recording the progress of the battle, but she discovered to her shame that her teeth were chattering so uncontrollably she could not form the words. She broke off "after the first disgraceful squeak."

She later recalled her reaction to her first close brush with death: "Then suddenly, for the first time in the war, I experienced the cold, awful certainty that there would be no escape. My reactions were trite. As with most people who suddenly accept death as inevitable and imminent, I was simply filled with surprise that this was finally going to happen to me. Then, as the conviction grew, I grew hard inside and comparatively calm. I ceased worrying."

A few minutes later, when Michaelis came around and called out, "How you doin', kid?" Maggie was relieved to find that she had stopped shaking. She was able to say, "Just fine, Sir."

By 7:45 a.m., the battle was in full fury. At a time when many American units seemed to crumble and retreat under assault, Maggie wrote, the Twenty-Seventh held fast: "Colonel Michaelis suddenly emerged from the schoolhouse, and his appearance rallied the men." He steeled his troops and launched a counterattack. Machine-gun squads crept up the hill under the cover of rifle fire and mowed down the communist soldiers as they tried to swarm the schoolhouse. Huge artillery guns were lowered into place and fired at the enemy within point-blank range. By noon, the Americans had repulsed the last onslaught. More than six hundred dead North Koreans littered the hills.

At the end of her riveting account of the schoolhouse siege, Maggie described the sudden onrush of casualties as the Americans began advancing, and of the unparalleled skill and dedication of the doctors who tended to them even as bullets provided a nerve-racking accompaniment: "Medical corps men began to bring in the wounded, who were numerous. One correspondent learned how to administer blood plasma." When the battle was over, five Americans were dead and forty wounded.

In her August 4 dispatch, she did not name the journalist who helped to care for the influx of bodies. But after her story appeared, Colonel Michaelis took exception to her omission and wrote a letter to her editors at the *Tribune* praising her performance under duress:

[It] struck me as being the height of understatement insofar as the personal activities of Miss Higgins were concerned. During the attack, which lasted over four hours, and which reached within 75 yards of the Command Post, Miss Higgins, completely disregarding her own safety, voluntarily assisted by administering blood plasma to the many wounded as they were carried into the Temporary Aid Station. This Aid Station was subject to small arms fire throughout the attack. The Regimental Combat Team considers Miss Higgins' actions on that day as heroic, but even more important is the gratitude felt by members of this command towards the selfless devotion of Miss Higgins in saving the lives of many grievously wounded men.

The *Herald Tribune* published the letter in full, in a special squared-off section on page four, under the heading "Tribute to Marguerite Higgins." Michaelis, who courted publicity, might have guessed that in calling attention to her courage he would also be highlighting his regiment's extraordinary valor. But Maggie was touched that he had gone to the trouble of writing the letter, and it became one of her most treasured possessions.

Time, which had been giving Michaelis and his redoubtable Twenty-Seventh lavish coverage, reprinted the letter and called Maggie the "Pride of the Regiment." The article was accompanied by another striking Carl Mydans photo of her at the front. The magazine noted that "slender, durable Newshen Higgins who covers Korea in tennis shoes, baggy pants and shirt and a fatigue cap that usually conceals her bobbed blonde hair, has done more than win the admiration of soldiers in her front-line reporting. She has also forced her male competitors to admit grudgingly that she was their match when it came to bravery and beats." As one colleague told the magazine, "She's either brave as hell or stupid."

Wittingly or unwittingly, in according her the highest accolades, Michaelis turned Maggie into a latter-day GI heroine. "Woman Writer Helps Medics," applauded *Stars and Stripes.* "No one could be more surprised here on the Korean front than the dirty dust-covered GIs when they spot a blond-headed slip of a girl roaming the battlefield in quest of news. Especially when this same girl pitches in at a forward aid station."

Thereafter, Maggie was always linked to the Twenty-Seventh Regiment. By continuing to send home sizzling stories about the outfit's engagements, she was instrumental in establishing a battlefield personality for the Wolfhounds in the press, which benefited both the unit and its commander and helped keep morale high in the bloody confusion of the first months of war. "My Wolfhound Regiment became the darling of the public because Marguerite Higgins stayed with us for months," recalled David Hackworth, who was awarded three Silver Stars and three Purple Hearts during his time in Korea, and went on to become a respected military journalist. "She made us famous and we loved her for doing it."

Later, there were those who would snidely suggest that Maggie's flattering dispatches about Michaelis helped him earn two battlefield promotions in six months, to full colonel and then brigadier general. Those same people would also hint there was more to their relationship than soldier and scribe. Michaelis vigorously rebutted the accusation that he had been involved with Higgins. The idea of anything sexual going on at the front was absurd, he explained, referring graphically to the toll the filthy conditions took on their bodies, along with the lice, fleas, bad food, and constant diarrhea. "People charged her with sleeping around to get stories but it sure as hell didn't happen in Korea," he said. "In my own case, I didn't have my clothes off in a hundred days. It was hardly a time for romance."

The speculation about Maggie and MacArthur was "equally silly." He dismissed the gossip as malicious, putting it down to jealousy. "Her driving ambition forced competitors into positions they didn't particularly enjoy," he said. "She became successful; she stood out. Some people never forgave her for that."

As Maggie's fame spread, so did her popularity with the troops. Like Beech and Mydans, she adopted the perspective of the foot soldiers as the best way of showing what the war was like, a bias that got her compared to the grunts' favorite World War II correspondent, Ernie Pyle. Anecdotes about her support and sympathy for the fighting boys abounded. According to one tale, just after a group of GIs under enemy attack complained to Higgins that the U.S. army tanks were failing to provide backup, a retreating tank passed and the commander yelled down at her, "Hey Lady, you're in the wrong place."

Maggie shouted back, "So are you!" and the beleaguered infantrymen got up out of their foxholes and cheered.

Her insistence on sharing the hardships of the front on equal terms with the men also won her kudos. She covered the war in her cut-down khakis for weeks on end, lived off canned rations, and choked on the same brown dust without complaint. Because she was a woman, she was often offered special accommodations. She invariably turned them down, asking no special favors.

A rugged Australian reporter named Jack Percival told of bedding down one night on the floor of a house in Taejon filled with correspondents, only to discover that the fellow who kept rolling over in his sleep "wasn't a he, but a she." Higgins had arrived late, doused herself with flea powder, and wedged herself in a gap between the prone bodies. Percival woke up to find himself lying between the only two women reporters at the front, Higgins and Charlotte Knight of *Collier's*. "One can brag about having slept with Maggie without becoming an indiscreet villain," quipped a colleague.

Not everyone appreciated her reportorial zeal. Eyeing her with distaste as she hopped out of a jeep after a particularly dusty drive, one colonel commented to the *Denver Post's* Bill Hosokawa, "No American woman should let herself get so dirty." Hosokawa disagreed. He thought Higgins had guts. "She displayed remarkable physical courage and stamina," he said, "and went out of her way to live down the handicap of her sex."

On August 21, *Time* reported that "honors for outstanding coverage by a single newspaper" went to the *Herald Tribune*, whose two war correspondents were soundly beating the *Times's* four-man team. Commenting editorially on their feat, the magazine called attention to their remarkable coverage of one of the saddest, most dangerous wars in American military history: "Pulitzer Prizewinning Homer Bigart and hard-driving

Marguerite Higgins spurred each other on in a perpetual competition for top billing on the *Tribune*'s front page. To get it, both were taking chances that many other reporters shied away from." The magazine then ran snippets of their dueling dispatches:

> Bigart reported: "This correspondent was one of three reporters who saw the action and . . . the only newsman to get out alive."
>
> Wrote Miss Higgins last week: "A reinforced American patrol, accompanied by this correspondent, this afternoon barreled eight miles deep through enemy territory . . . Snipers picked at the road, but the jeep flew faster than the bullets which nicked just in back of our right rear tire."

Hanson Baldwin of the *Times* contingent asked Beech how it was that Homer and Maggie were beating a virtual armada of reporters. "That's easy—they hate each other," Beech told him. "The competition is a lot fiercer between them than between you and them."

Junior wire-service men somberly predicted that the reckless Higgins would be the death of Bigart before she was done. "As soon as Homer kills off Maggie or Maggie kills off Homer," said Lambert, "the competition will wane and so will the coverage of the Korean War." It was a conviction Bigart privately shared. He told a *Trib* colleague that she took chances no sensible correspondent would dare take except when forced to by her stubbornly foolhardy example. Beech thought Homer was just crying in his beer. He was old and tired and ready to go home but for Higgins. In Beech's opinion, Higgins took no more risks than himself, and perhaps a dozen other consummately courageous reporters, and not nearly as many as the photographers, who by virtue of their profession needed to be even closer to the action.

DURING THE WEEKS THAT followed, Maggie usually went out to the front with Beech. In the beginning, this was for the simple reason that it was his jeep. As he noted sardonically, "Miss Higgins valued her transportation." This did not mean that they got along. By this time, Higgins was covering the war for both the *Tribune* and the *London News Chronicle*, and Beech for the *Chicago Daily News* and *London Evening Standard*. While they pooled all their information, they did not necessarily agree about when, where, or how to report their stories. They fought, often, and about everything.

Scorn, he recalled, was her chief weapon when angry or frustrated: "Her pale blue eyes went a shade paler, her jaw muscles bunched, and her voice took on a flat, metallic quality that made each word sound like a hammer driving nails into a two-by-four." On one occasion, their bickering back and forth grew so loud and expletive-laced that Beech found himself apologizing to Tom Shaw, a very gentlemanly British correspondent, who was in the back seat.

Early in their working relationship, Maggie, in a fit of temper, called the crusty ex-marine the most disagreeable son of a bitch she had ever known. Beech's reply was that he could think of no one who could bring out the SOB in him quite the way she did. But misery makes for strange bedfellows, and he was soon sharing her sleeping bag. If they had not been thrown together by circumstance—and he was a man of many ifs, buts, and onlys—Beech conceded his life would have been "more serene but less interesting."

Neither of them was under any illusion that their relationship was about anything more than sex. They may have shared the same foxhole but they were both in love with someone else: Maggie with Bill Hall, and Beech, despite being married, with another blue-eyed blonde named Linda Mangelsdorf, a secretary who worked in MacArthur's headquarters. Once Beech, well into a bottle of scotch, asked Maggie if she was sure the air force general was the man for her, or if it was a kind of perverse challenge, and he was all the more desirable because he was unobtainable. Utterly frank as always, she admitted she had her heart set on the married general. Her main concern was that Hall, who was known as a great swordsman in Berlin, was not the faithful type. He was willing to leave his wife of twenty years for her, but Maggie worried about his philandering. Beech, who found this pretty rich given her own proclivities, scolded her for wanting a "double standard in reverse."

While never so smitten that he was blind to her faults, he forged a close bond with his frisky, fearless jeep mate. He could not help but like her. She had a bawdy sense of humor that made him laugh. He remembered once asking which half of her was French. She replied without missing a beat, "The lower half."

There was nothing prudish or puritanical about Higgins. She never played hard to get. When in a carnal mood, she would "practically knock on the windshield" to get him to pull over someplace private, which in Korea was not always easy to find. "She had a male attitude toward sex," he recalled. While she took many lovers, mostly fellow reporters, he did not consider her undiscriminating or dissolute. In the war zone, where life was grim and death a constant companion, you sought comfort where you could. "[But] she didn't deliberately sleep with men to get stories," he said. "That's a lot of crap."

More importantly to Beech, Maggie never violated his journalistic code of honor. She never gave her editors what they both suspected they really wanted from her—which was the "woman's angle" on the war. "Higgins never stooped to that," he said.

She earned her keep by purloining gasoline for his beloved jeep. After a while, they worked out a pretty good routine, which Gibney observed with jaded amusement: Maggie would drive up to the motor pool on her own, smile sweetly, and in her little-girl voice ask if she could just top up the tank. The enthralled sergeant would let her cut the line and even offer to handle the pump. While he chatted her up, hoping to get lucky, Beech would hop in and they would drive off into the sunset, calling a cheerful thank-you behind them.

Most of the time, Beech monopolized the driver's seat, so Maggie, by default, rode shotgun. They had learned by then that this was a very different kind of conflict, and this enemy had no qualms about shooting unarmed civilians. By August, eleven war correspondents had been killed in Korea, more than in the entire first year of World War II. Many reporters took to carrying a weapon. Beech instructed Maggie in the proper use of a carbine, and the volley of bullets distracted the enemy long enough for him to floor the accelerator. She never panicked, even when passing through sniper territory going to and from the front. "She was the best combat buddy I ever had," he said.

On the few occasions her gender became an issue, however, he was predictably impatient. Though his whole body ached as a result of tearing over the rough roads, Beech rolled his eyes when he saw Maggie wrap her arms around her chest to restrain her painfully bouncing breasts, groaning aloud that she had lost her "goddamn bra." He was even more long-suffering when she unexpectedly got her period on the eve of a planned invasion, and he had to race back twenty miles through a whole army of trigger-happy marines to a nurse's station in Pusan for a supply of Kotex. "I was particularly ungracious that night," he admitted.

But Higgins single-handedly disproved the axiom that the female is the weaker of the sexes—"she could take more physical punishment than most men." There was an evening in late August, on their way back from a dinner at the residence of Ambassador John Muccio, high above the hills of Pusan, when the brakes on their jeep suddenly gave out. To avoid going over the embankment, he steered the car straight into a concrete gatepost. He yelled a warning to Maggie, but not before her head collided with the windshield. When Beech looked over, she was bleeding from the nose and mouth.

The crash was loud enough to bring Muccio and his aides running. By the time they helped Higgins into the house, there was a bump on her head the size of a doorknob. While they waited for the army doctor, she demanded to know how she looked. Told she looked like hell, she got up to check in the mirror and fainted. When the ambulance arrived, she refused to lie down on the stretcher. Instead, she sat up front with the driver while the indignant doctor rode in the back. At the hospital, she insisted on walking in on her own steam, only to collapse after a few steps. The doctor just managed to catch her, though as Beech recalled, by then he was so furious she could have dropped dead for all he cared.

The next morning, when Beech called to check on her, Maggie was in a state. The nurses had ordered her to remain in bed, and they had taken her things and would not give them back. When he suggested that she needed the rest, and he needed to return to the front, her anger grew to open fury. She insisted he bring her a bag of clothes so she could go with him. He finally agreed, with some misgivings, muttering that it was "her funeral."

The mishap made all the papers. "Marguerite Higgins Hurt," reported both the *Tribune* and the *Times*. Despite a slight concussion, two black eyes, and a swollen nose, Maggie said she would "stay on the job." Mydans snapped a photo of her bruised mug for posterity. The accident only added to her reputation for regularly cheating death and then shrugging off her narrow escapes in a cavalier fashion.

Back in Tokyo, she and Beech maintained a polite distance. He was trying to patch things up with Linda. And by late August, Maggie was pining for Bill Hall. She had been over the moon when he called to tell her of his upcoming jaunt to the Far East as an official observer for the air force. They would have time for a brief reunion in Tokyo before he left on a ten-day tour. Knowing he liked her to look like a lady, Maggie got a much-needed makeover. She had her hair done, sat for a manicure, and dug out a little black dress and heels.

In the months since she had last seen him, she and Bill had fallen madly in love over their passionate letters and phone calls. The long-distance courtship had only increased their ardor. They had discussed marriage and the many difficulties it would entail—not the least of which was that he would have to sign over the bulk of his savings to support his ex-wife and children—but they were willing to do whatever it took to be united. He was making an enormous sacrifice to be with her, and Maggie, who was as determined to win Hall as she was to succeed at her work, knew she would need to draw on all her resources to secure the future she desired.

At the end of August, a scribbled entry in her notebook in anticipation of his visit reveals the tension she felt between the demands of her career and dreams of domesticity:

> *Thrilled and so excited about Bill's arrival that I can't settle down to work. Feel enveloped with longing and desire for the affection and passion I've sometimes found with him. The pull between wanting to live with Bill and wanting to finish*

*out this war is terrible. But it won't be acute until he finally
gets his divorce. The prospect of a 3rd world war makes me feel
that all this worry about houses and finances is ridiculous. I
wonder how much longer any of us have. Disgusted with my
lack of concentration. I've had a day of happy daydreaming
and that's about that.*

She practically fell through the revolving doors of the Imperial
Hotel and into his arms. On September 3, Hall took her out to celebrate her thirtieth birthday. He told her again that he was leaving his
wife. Over champagne, he proposed a spring wedding. All the time he
was making plans for their life together, her mind was on another, more
urgent plan, too secret to share even with him. An important military
mission loomed, and she, along with the rest of her colleagues, had been
told to stay in Tokyo and hold themselves in readiness for the big show.
Every fifteen minutes, she excused herself from the table to make a call to
headquarters. Nervous, she was up and down six times before the meal
was over.

By the time Hall returned from his swing through the East, Maggie
had departed for the front. With characteristic optimism and fortitude,
she left behind a note expressing her own hopes for a happy outcome:
"I am going on a great adventure which, if successful, should bring this
situation to a conclusion." Jotted notes in her diary indicate that as she
was preparing to leave on her most dangerous assignment yet, she drew
strength from the knowledge that he was "so near," and from the constant
of "Bill loving me."

IN SEPTEMBER, GENERAL MacARTHUR had decided to gamble that he
could stop the relentless North Korean offensive, and gain back all the
ground he had lost, with an amphibious landing 110 miles behind enemy
lines, along the beaches of Inchon. It was a hazardous undertaking, rife
with risks. His advisers said it was impossible—the geography was all
wrong, the beaches too exposed, the tides too unpredictable. But Mac-
Arthur was convinced the sheer difficulty of the scheme recommended

it. They would take the enemy by surprise, and use American air and sea power to strike at the invaders' rear and cut off their supply lines.

Maggie learned of the landing plans, a huge invasion fleet of more than 260 ships, the largest since Normandy, weeks in advance. The secret was so well known at the press club that the correspondents dubbed it "Operation Common Knowledge." After so many close calls in recent months, she had debated whether to accompany the assault troops or seek out the comparative safety of a destroyer. On September 7, another three correspondents had died when their C-54 plunged into a fog-shrouded mountain. It was the latest in a series of press-corps tragedies and plunged her into an "I'm-going-to-get-killed-today" funk, the opposite of the "nothing-can-touch-me" mood that usually propelled her forward.

She was still undecided when a naval public relations officer informed her of the regulations barring women from combat ships. Once again, the facilities were the problem. Maggie reflexively balked at this latest prohibition. Her request to go to Inchon on one of the assault crafts had apparently been greeted by the brass with "the same degree of horror as might have met a leper's request to sleep with the admiral." Told she had been relegated to a hospital ship, the *Consolation*, and might not even be allowed to disembark, she boiled with resentment at the "anti-female navy." Her earlier hesitation forgotten, she immediately petitioned the top brass to be afforded the same opportunity as the other eighty reporters, from six countries, going to cover MacArthur's offensive.

Maggie cabled Whitie Reid that the navy was "hampering *Herald Tribune* coverage and competitive position." Reid wired Francis P. Mathews, secretary of the navy, and Admiral Forrest P. Sherman, chief of naval operations, requesting their assistance. He argued that the army generals had accepted Higgins for battlefront assignments, and hoped the navy would send a similar message to its admirals in Korea. No such announcement was forthcoming.

But by some strange twist of fate, when she went to pick up her travel orders, the busy captain in charge of logistics made a mistake—the four mimeographed sheets he handed her stated that Miss Higgins could board "any Navy ship" in pursuit of press duties. As soon as she grasped the wonderful implications of this snafu, she raced to catch a flight for Korea, and then hitched to Pusan Harbor, where the assault force was set to depart the next day. The only problem with her reprieve was that she was still on the passenger list for the *Consolation*. She would need to talk her way onto another transport.

Her first request for a place on a ship was refused, ostensibly on the grounds that it was already overcrowded. She offered to sleep on the deck, but it was no use. Tense and dispirited, she decided to try the USS *Henrico*, a command ship ferrying a unit of the Fifth Marines. The captain studied her orders, then nodded his approval. As she stood there trembling in elation, he mentioned that there was even a spare room, a sort of emergency cabin. A typhoon threatened, so he would be moving up their departure time to get out of the congested harbor. Thanking her Irish luck, she went straight to her cabin and locked herself in. She lay on the bunk with her heart racing, afraid every approaching sound meant someone was coming to throw her off.

On the morning of September 15, after a massive bombardment, she approached Red Beach with the fifth wave of marines, the first to face serious opposition from the surprised enemy. By the time she dropped into one of the small assault boats, the last of thirty-eight to clamber down the swaying rope ladder, they could hear the sound of enemy machine-gun fire coming from shore. There were two other correspondents and a photographer in their group. According to Private First Class Thomas Shay, "No one knew there was a woman on board until we reached the harbor." With her helmet and heavy overcoat, Higgins looked just like another GI. "When the Gooks opened up with small arms fire, it didn't seem to bother her," he added, "though she didn't say much."

After circling for almost an hour, the channel reverberating with the earsplitting sound of warship guns and rockets, they went in. As they neared the seawall, an amber star shell burst over the beach. It was a good sign—the initial objective of the Fifth Marines, Cemetery Hill, had been taken. Before she could let out a sigh of relief, brightly colored tracer bullets ripped across the bow of their landing craft. Everyone hunched down low in the open boat. Maggie peered up at the men to try to gauge how things were going and saw that their faces were contorted with fear. Then their boat smashed into the seawall.

"Come on, you big, brave marines!" yelled Lieutenant R. J. Schening. "Let's get the hell out of here." He gave the man in front a shove. Another burst of fire and she got out fast, landing in three feet of water.

Red Beach was not a beach at all, but a rough seawall composed of giant boulders. They were immediately trapped against a portion of the crumbled canyon, down which the North Koreans were rolling grenades. Their group crawled on their stomachs to a gouged-out spot in the wall that provided some cover and remained pinned there for hours. She watched wave after wave of marines hit the beach. Another assault boat swept up, disgorging more men into their crevice, until marines were stretched out all along the top of the seawall.

It was nearing twilight when the strong tidal currents shifted and a sudden swell of water came rushing into the dip in the wall. They saw a huge landing ship tank (LST) bearing down on them, its platform doors open and ramp half lowered. All at once, their whole group rose up and vaulted the trenches on the inland side of the seawall. The marines fanned out across the open area. Maggie and the other correspondents raced to a raised mound for protection from the gunfire. Two men in the back got caught by the churning tide, their legs crushed by the steel ramp before they could be pulled clear.

In the half dark, marines were zigzagging toward the cliffs. Maggie had an anguished view of a half dozen as they were hurled to the ground by a hail of bullets. Crouching down, she took what would become an iconic photograph of the battle, showing Marine 1st Lt. Baldomero Lopez leading his men over the seawall under fire. Minutes later, Lopez was shot in the act of throwing a grenade. He crawled onto the explosive to save his men. (He was posthumously awarded the Medal of Honor.)

By about 7 p.m., Red Beach was secure and there was only intermittent small-arms fire. As night fell, the marines advanced inland without too much difficulty. Lt. John Counselman had just taken a ricochet and was lying on the ground injured when he saw her on shore. "A round skipped off the side of a tank and hit my leg," he recalled. "It hardly drew blood, but my leg immediately turned blue black. A corpsman had my pants around my ankles. I looked around and, Oh, God!, there was Maggie Higgins. Every time you looked around, there she was!"

Maggie emerged unscathed. She and two other correspondents threaded their way across the beach through the heavy traffic of tanks, artillery guns, and trucks until they were back at the seawall. The tide had turned, and they were stunned to see the boats were now twenty-five feet below where they stood. After a shaky climb down the rope ladder, their small boat had to fight the rip current to reach the flagship, the *Mount McKinley*. It had started to rain, and it was all Maggie could do to balance precariously on the gunwale, grab one of the slippery steps of the ship, and haul herself aboard.

When she stumbled into the *McKinley*'s wardroom, which seemed to her the last word in luxury and warmth, she immediately ran afoul of the navy brass. After angrily demanding to know what the hell she was doing there, the captain treated her like a criminal on the lam. He refused to allow her to remain on the flagship, citing the lack of suitable facilities. After a prolonged debate, Maggie insisted on seeing the senior ranking officer, Rear Adm. James H. Doyle, the commander of the amphibious phase of the Inchon operation.

"Naturally I agreed to see her and she was brought to my cabin," Doyle later recalled. He could still picture her, tall and slender, her damp hair in ringlets, a smudge of dirt on one cheek. "She was beautiful."

Higgins pleaded to be allowed to stay at least the one night to file her story. Doyle, an officer and gentleman of the old school, had a problem. Vice Adm. C. Turner Joy, commander of naval forces, Far East, had decreed that women correspondents had to be billeted in a hospital ship. Not only was Doyle bound by this order, but there was no cabin on the *McKinley*, as MacArthur and his staff were taking up every spare room. If she stayed, he explained, it would deprive four officers of a room and tie up a head for her personal use. Higgins dismissed his objections, and continued to argue her case, concluding vehemently, "Furthermore, you'd be surprised how long I can go without using the head."

Doyle, momentarily flustered by her retort, responded he had no choice. But before he could off-load her, the weather intervened. When he realized he could not get rid of her, a cot was made available in the sick bay, and she was put ashore at first light. "I was grateful that it made my inevitable defeat acceptable," noted Doyle, adding that he had never come up against a woman of such indomitable will.

Admiral Joy's decree remained in effect. Women were banned from any navy vessel between 9 p.m. and 9 a.m.—the only time the correspondents actually wanted to be aboard in order to file and get some rest. For the remainder of her time in Inchon, as the marines fought their way to Seoul, Maggie handed her copy to Keyes Beech each evening. But she cursed the navy for leaving her to sleep on the docks, while he and the other reporters enjoyed dry bunks, hot showers, and a hearty breakfast.

Maggie's account of the invasion made page one of the *Herald Tribune*:

WITH THE UNITED STATES MARINES AT INCHON, KOREA—Sept. 15. Heavily laden United States marines, in one of the most technically difficult amphibious landings in history, stormed at sunset today over a ten-foot sea wall in the heart of the port of Inchon and within an hour had taken three commanding hills in the city.

I was in the fifth wave that hit "Red Beach," which in reality was a rough vertical pile of stones over which the first assault troops had to scramble with the aid of improvised landing ladders topped with steel hooks.

Despite a deadly and steady pounding from naval guns and air planes, enough North Koreans remained alive close to the beach to harass us with small-arms and mortar fire.

The invasion was a rousing success. Only 20 marines were killed, and 174 wounded, along with one cameraman. MacArthur's great gamble at Inchon had paid off, and the marines blazed a bloody path to Seoul. She and Beech were with a battalion of marines when they advanced on Kimpo Airport. It was tough going, and they were stalled for thirty minutes at a time by enemy fire. Just ahead of them, the lead tank was blown up. They dove for the ditches, and Maggie filed another first-person eyepopper for the *Tribune*.

The Americans recaptured the old walled capital on September 25, though it would take three more days to subdue the North Korean resistance. She and Beech were among the first correspondents there. They were trailing Charlie (C) Company, which was spearheading the First Marine Battalion's drive through the city, when they realized they were within a block of the old, red-brick Chosun Hotel, a familiar landmark. They helped to liberate the hotel staff, who broke into cheers when the two correspondents burst through the gate flanked by twenty South Korean soldiers.

Maggie was there when MacArthur triumphantly handed the keys to the city to the tearful, white-haired Syngman Rhee, restoring the South Korean president to the capital seat he had been forced to abandon three months earlier. The pursuit and destruction of the retreating North Korean army was underway. The war seemed all but over. She had never seen quite so much bright, shiny army brass collected in one place. She and Beech, along with most officers from the First Marine Division, kept to the rear. They had no time to make themselves presentable after the battle for the city, which had ended only the night before.

Catching sight of her in the crowd after the ceremony, MacArthur feigned surprise at her disheveled appearance and called out, "Hello, there, tall, blond, and ugly. Come up and see me sometime." Judging by the astonished faces of the officers, dignitaries, and reporters around him, she knew the general had succeeded in launching a fleet of rumors.

The marines' victory allowed her to make good on the promise she had made to herself—she had walked back into Seoul. She celebrated another personal victory of sorts. Her Inchon dispatch had been the news lead in the *Tribune*. In the early edition, the copydesk had accorded her an unusual compliment, simply headlining the piece: "Miss Higgins' Story of the Landing." Meanwhile Bigart, who somehow wound up on an official transport, was not allowed to go ashore and had to file an overview of the historic operation.

The relationship between Bigart and Higgins was so strained by then that when she encountered him in a village outside Seoul a few days later, Beech found himself having to play "peacemaker." Maggie glowered at Homer, who was watching the progress of the marine battle from across the road. When a *Times* reporter hurried by, presumably on his way to the rear to dictate his story over a field line, she said, "One of us ought to go back and file." By "us" she meant either herself or Bigart. Beech suggested she go ask Homer what he was going to do. She shook her head. "If I speak to him, he'll just ignore me or bawl me out," she said.

It was apparent that after not having spoken to each other for two and a half months, this breach of mutual silence would have to be negotiated with the formality of armistice talks. Beech walked across the road and told Homer that Maggie wanted to talk to him. Homer considered the matter for a few minutes and gave a curt nod of assent. The two met in the middle of the road and conversed. Afterward, Beech was tempted to erect a commemorative plaque on the spot: "Homer and Maggie spoke here."

A month after the Inchon invasion, the navy amended its rules and made the necessary provisions for female correspondents. This concession, Maggie was amused to learn, meant she could board any ship as long as she was "chaperoned at all times by a navy nurse." She later exacted a measure of revenge by including a detailed account of the navy's discriminatory policy in her book about the war in Korea. Doyle, who had bought her a conciliatory drink in the Imperial Hotel in Tokyo, had no hard feelings about her "giving me my comeuppance but good." He thought she was a woman of remarkable courage, so he sent her a note: "Dear Maggie. Have read your book. Love anyway."

Maggie had not set out to be a reformer—merely an exception to the rules—but along the way she revolutionized the status of her female colleagues in both the army and the navy. Her ambivalent attitude toward this achievement, and the recognition she received as a barrier breaker, was best expressed by an editorial that ran in the *Louisville Courier-Journal*, which said in part: "Miss Higgins shows no desire to win fame simply as a woman who dares to write at the spot where men are fighting. Her ambition is to be recognized as a very good reporter, sex undesignated."

Inchon was the critical moment in Maggie's career. It sealed her reputation for derring-do and made her immortal in journalistic circles. From the press-club bar in Tokyo to the press billet in Taegu, she threatened to replace the war as the main topic of conversation. A week after the invasion, *Stars and Stripes* published a long piece about the more than three hundred correspondents from nineteen countries accredited to Mac-Arthur's Far East Command, and it identified Maggie as a new star in the reporting galaxy, who was outshining the competition.

"Of the special papers which have sent top-notch correspondents to Korea, the New York *Herald Tribune* has attracted the largest amount of publicity, through its 29-year-old reporter Marguerite Higgins," wrote Esther Crane, the Tokyo-based wife of *Times* correspondent Burton Crane. "Scarcely a week passes without Maggie's picture in either *Time* or *Newsweek.*" The *Tribune*'s prize-winning Homer Bigart, she noted mischievously, "is rumored to be having a difficult time of it, keeping up with Maggie's frontline energy in Korea. Her ceaseless activity keeps both her and Homer on the go, but from all reports they go in opposite directions."

Bigart had taken a terrible drubbing at the hands of his plucky colleague. *Stars and Stripes* rubbed his nose in it, reporting that his friend, the *Times*'s William Lawrence, had provided much comic relief on a slow Sunday by coaxing a chorus of Korean children to stand outside the press barracks during happy hour and chant the refrain, "Homer loves Maggie—Homer loves Maggie!"

Other correspondents composed an ode to Maggie and Homer with taunting lyrics, set to the tune of "Lili Marlene":

Marguerite Higgins
Telephones the news
She gets exclusives
Front line interviews
While Homer crawls
Through rice fields wet
To scrounge some stuff
That she can't get

Before the conflict was four months old, the epic feud between Maggie and Homer was part of the lore of the Korean War. Despite all the songs, limericks, and wisecracks, it was not in any sense a friendly feud, according to Mydans, even though Maggie tried to think of it that way. "It was bitter, and everyone knew it was bitter," he said. "Homer was a giant among correspondents. He felt sincerely that he was being taken advantage of by the *Herald Tribune*, which encouraged coverage of the feud." The Reids, he added, "played it for all it was worth because, of course, it was interesting to the reading public, had great appeal, and sold newspapers."

Years later, Whitie Reid commented on the intense rivalry that developed between Higgins and Bigart:

> In the case of the Far East, she became increasingly aggressive, and the kind of competition she gave her contemporaries was exceedingly tough. Homer Bigart, who had been our star correspondent on almost every front, was placed in a cruel dilemma. He had been sticking his neck out . . . for several years. All of a sudden a woman appears on the scene ready to finagle and maneuver and stick her neck out a little further. I am afraid he was driven up the wall by her. Her willingness to sleep on the docks with the troops and seek no privileges as a woman was impressive. She had grit and courage and an ability to get her way.

Beech, who was her staunchest defender and harshest critic in Korea, summed her up best. "In her quest for fame Higgins was appallingly, almost frighteningly, single-minded in her determination to overcome obstacles," he wrote. "But she had more guts, more staying power, and more resourcefulness than 90 percent of her detractors. She was a good newspaperman."

12

✳ ✳ ✳ ✳ ✳ ✳ ✳ ✳

Perils of Fame

From somewhere deep inside her was a desire "to
show those male chauvinist sons-a-bitches" who
thought wars were theirs alone, and she surely did.
Army nurses in the forward areas used to speak of
her with the awe which they saved for celebrities.
Once in Taegu, one told me, "Marguerite Higgins
came by our field hospital last night for a shower,"
said with the same sense of admiration up-market
real estate agents speak of George Washington.

—Pat Conger, UP

IN THE MIDST OF SOME OF THE WORST FIGHTING IN KOREA, MAG-
gie received a telegram from Emmet Hughes, the articles editor at *Life*
magazine, inquiring: "What does it feel like to be a lone woman correspondent among all those men?"

The answer came in the form of a feature-length article in the October 2, 1950, issue of *Life*, entitled "Girl War Correspondent," by Carl
Mydans. The spread ran six pages, included ten photographs, and was
penned in the breathless style usually reserved for actresses on goodwill tours. The magazine gave her the full star treatment: There is Maggie, front and center, looking fabulous in army fatigues and flashing her
thousand-watt smile; there is a montage of Maggie, boyishly insouciant,
attempting to trim her blond locks in a roadside barbershop at Pusan Air

Base; and there is Maggie in action—conferring with MacArthur on his first visit to Korea, crouching in an infantry battalion observation post, and punching out a story in a primitive press shack. The final shot is of Maggie in glamour mode, back in the Tokyo bureau, her short bob tamed and sporting pearls and a frilly dress.

At the front, Mydans reported, the slight, blonde *Herald Tribune* correspondent had proved extraordinarily brave, durable, and pretty even in her fighting clothes. A thick coating of dust and dirt failed to disguise her attractiveness, though she did little to emphasize it. Her standard battle attire consisted of GI pants and shirt, cap, and a pair of muddy tennis shoes. She wore no socks and carried with her only a toothbrush, a towel, and a lipstick. Observed an admiring soldier, "Maggie wears mud like other women wear make-up."

In a more serious vein, Mydans asserted that Maggie, despite the controversies that swirled around her, had done some excellent reporting—her dispatches were exciting if not always brilliant—and her achievements in some fourteen weeks of war had been substantial. "The question of what makes Maggie run so hard and so fast fascinates her nearly 300 male competitors in Korea almost as much as the war itself," he wrote in a remarkable piece for the time, arguing that in her daily battle for the front page she was winning the war of the sexes.

Mydans went on to explain that since the beginning of the Korean War Maggie had been engaged in three separate campaigns: one, to be allowed to cover the actual fighting, and she had convinced both her colleagues and the troops of her courage and professional capability; two, a fierce, intensely personal competition with her *Herald Tribune* rival Homer Bigart; and three, a concerted effort "to deny that sex has anything to do with war corresponding."

The unprecedented exposure turned her into an overnight celebrity. She was the most famous war correspondent in the world. "Maggie already has become a legend," *Life* told its readers, "both in Korea and the U.S." The weekly magazine, which boasted that it was America's most potent editorial force, had tremendous reach, with a total circulation of some 62.5 million, representing roughly 40 percent of the population.

Henry Luce's formidable publication made Maggie a household name, far beyond her wildest dreams. From that moment on, the way opened out to far wider acclaim than any female journalist had ever enjoyed. Her star power was not lost on Hollywood. Here was a young, eye-catching beauty who had burst onto the scene like a comet. Her daring "I was there" war reports had made her the darling of the press, defying conventional ideas about what women could and should do at the front while outdoing all the men. She had created a stir in Korea and was now an international sensation. Not since Rosalind Russell's fast-talking Hildy Johnson in Howard Hawks's *His Girl Friday* had a female reporter so completely captivated the public's imagination. Magazines, radio, and the early days of television were transforming American popular culture, and members of the media were just beginning to emerge as public figures and promotable personalities. When it came to Maggie, the marketing possibilities were endless. The offers poured in. Everyone wanted a piece of her.

"LIFE DISPLAY BEWITCHING HAVE YOU PICTURE RIGHTS?" cabled George T. Bye, a New York literary agent known for representing newsmakers, with a specialty in stunt books. A film star wanted to make a movie about her and "WANTS TO BE YOU IN PICTURE. METRO AND WARNER WARMLY INTERESTED," he added, using the showbiz shorthand for the motion-picture studios Metro-Goldwyn-Mayer (MGM) and Warner Bros.

"INTERESTED IN SECURING RIGHTS TO YOUR LIFE STORY FOR FILMS," cabled Douglas Whitney of the Music Corporation of America (MCA). Under the direction of the studio executive Lew Wasserman, MCA had become a major player in the entertainment business. Wasserman, who handled such stars as Bette Davis and Jimmy Stewart, contacted her personally and proposed that MCA represent. Two days later, Wasserman cabled her again, stating that Paramount, MGM, and Warner Bros. "insisted" on bidding on the rights to her story.

Several more cables arrived in rapid succession from a producer at Paramount, William Perlberg, who a few years earlier had scored a huge hit with *Miracle on 34th Street*. Maggie had met Perlberg in 1949 when he was in Berlin filming *The Big Lift*, the story of the airlift told through two air force pilots, and starring Montgomery Clift and Paul Douglas. Perlberg urged her to go with Wasserman and invited her to visit him at the Paramount studio.

At the same time, she received word from Whitie Reid that Spyros Skouras, president of Twentieth Century-Fox, was inquiring about "having a full-length motion picture made on your activities as a foreign correspondent. If you give the green-light he will start preliminary planning and want to discuss the matter in detail on your return."

Whitie added that they wanted her to come back to New York as soon as possible, by October 22 at the very latest, for myriad publicity events. Helen Reid cabled her separately asking if she would speak at an important forum she was convening at the end of the month. It was not a question, of course. She was being summoned home by the newspaper's proprietors.

Sounding slightly overwhelmed, Maggie cabled the Reids her agreement:

> PLEASE TELL SKOURAS FILM IDEA SOUNDS MOST
> INTERESTING AND EXCITING TO ME AND EYE AM
> ALL IN FAVOR OF IT STOP HOWEVER SINCE IN
> PAST TWO WEEKS A NUMBER OF STUDIOS HAVE
> SENT ME QUERIES AND I AM IN THE DEPARTMENT
> OF UTTER CONFUSION ON ANYTHING HAVING
> TO DO WITH HOLLYWOOD I HAVE ASKED LEW
> WASSERMAN OF MUSIC CORPORATION OF
> AMERICA TO ACT AS MY AGENT STOP IF SKOURAS
> COULD TALK WITH WASSERMAN WHOLL BE IN NEW
> YORK MONDAY EYE WOULD MUCH APPRECIATE IT
> AND EYE WOULD OF COURSE MUCH LIKE TALK TO
> SKOURAS MYSELF WHEN EYE GET TO NEW YORK
> STOP SEE ON TWENTY SECOND

Her publisher at Doubleday, Ken McCormick, joined the cable traffic with a brief message saying he was looking forward to meeting her, and to please bring the manuscript of her Korea book with her. Magazine-serial and movie interest was keen. He suggested "Woman Correspondent" as a title, or "War Is My Affair." He concluded: "URGE TALK TO NO ONE."

Maggie dealt with the dizzying spate of offers by going straight back to the front, where she covered the Fifth Cavalry Regiment's advance into North Korea. Determined to show she had not let her sudden fame go to her head, she kept working as if nothing had happened. But her life had changed forever. She was recognized everywhere she went. She was no longer an obscure young reporter, but a VIP in her own right. "She was the queen of the ball, she enjoyed the admiration, and had a very nice way of handling it," said Bob Miller. "The word would get out, 'Maggie Higgins is here!' You must remember, you had several thousand virile young males and the sight of a sexy blond female was a very exciting thing in their lives, and of course, they all had wonderful stories—and hallucinations and what not—about her."

Not all of her colleagues were as kind. The men who had envied her early success, and cordially disliked her, now loathed her on sight. The *Life* story confirmed their suspicion that she courted publicity as avidly as she did danger. She unfailingly made matters worse, appearing even more arrogant and aloof to those who already thought of her as bigheaded. Higgins had a "genius for bad public relations," confirmed Beech, whose own popularity suffered as a consequence of his choice of jeep mate. As far as he could tell, Maggie could have cared less. She was an implacable creature, bent on gaining her ends. She rarely remembered what she put herself or others through in her pursuit of glory.

When she arrived in Honolulu on October 19, after a two-day plane trip from Seoul via Tokyo, Maggie was besieged by the local press. She was stopped on the tarmac, garlanded with leis, and snapped by a photographer in the act of applying a fresh coat of lipstick. On first inspection, the reporter for the *Honolulu Advertiser* found the "GI's Maggie"—as she was known to all the boys at the front—was "still photogenic in spite of the rigors of war." The Korea correspondent, who had forsaken her combat trousseau, appeared "slim and trim in a maroon wool skirt and white silk shirt, topped by a perky little pancake of a hat."

Maggie, carried by her Chinese nurse, was born in Hong Kong and spent the first three years of her life in the Far East.

Lawrence Higgins, a World War I flying ace, taught his daughter to "never fear anything."

A tomboy at heart, Maggie excelled at sports and led her classmates in daring exploits.

Maggie, age sixteen, graduated at the top of her high school class and won the athletics prize.

Maggie, at a sorority
party at Berkeley,
was very pretty but
it was her brash
self-confidence that
made her stand out.

Maggie talked her way
into the Columbia
University Graduate
School of Journalism just
ahead of the deadline.

Maggie married Berkeley philosophy professor Stanley Moore, but the war soon separated them.

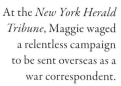

At the *New York Herald Tribune*, Maggie waged a relentless campaign to be sent overseas as a war correspondent.

Helen Rogers Reid, the tiny but regal publisher of the *New York Herald Tribune*, flanked by her sons, Whitelaw (left) and Ogden Reid, recognized Maggie's raw ambition.

Maggie (far left), unrecognizable in a fur hat with earflaps, was with a reconnaissance party of the Forty-Second Infantry "Rainbow" Division when they liberated Dachau on April 29, 1945. She is standing next to the acting commandant of the camp, 2nd Lt. Heinrich Wicker, who is talking to *Stars and Stripes* reporter Peter Furst (center), who acted as interpreter for Brig. Gen. Henning Linden (right), assistant division commander of the Forty-Second Infantry. Victor Maurer of the International Red Cross is holding the white flag.

While General Linden (front center) was negotiating the official terms of surrender, Maggie and Peter Furst heard the sound of shooting and took cover behind a jeep.

American soldiers guarding the surrendered Waffen-SS troops at Dachau as Maggie (far right), her blond hair hidden by a bandanna, confers with Lt. Col. Walter Fellenz of the 222nd Infantry Regiment, Rainbow Division.

At the war's end, Maggie fell madly in love with the dashing British reporter turned spy George Millar.

Maggie covering the Nuremberg trials of Nazi war crimes, where she earned a reputation as an indefatigable reporter and shameless operator.

As bureau chief, Maggie led the *Herald Tribune*'s reporting of the Berlin airlift. She is shown here with a group of correspondents being briefed on "Exercise Harvest."

Maggie Higgins, sporting her usual fatigues and sneakers, arriving in South Korea carrying just the essentials—a portable typewriter and trench coat.

The veteran *Chicago Daily News* correspondent Keyes Beech shared his jeep, and sleeping bag, with Maggie.

The *Herald Tribune*'s star military correspondent Homer Bigart began an epic feud with Maggie.

Maggie interviewing Gen. Douglas A. MacArthur, Supreme Commander for the Allied Powers, at the start of the Korean War. When another officer ordered her out of the country, MacArthur lifted the ban and allowed her to return to the battle lines.

Korea correspondents: Keyes Beech, Tom Lambert, Carl Mydans, and Maggie Higgins, with an unidentified soldier, after the fall of Seoul in June 1950.

Despite her time in the trenches, Maggie— grabbing a nap at Oryong, Korea— continued to face charges that she "slept her way to the top."

Maggie and Gen. William E. Hall, all smiles on their honeymoon in Novato, California, became part of the Georgetown set in Washington, DC.

The Rover Boys: Vietnam correspondents David Halberstam (left), Neil Sheehan (center), and Malcolm Browne (right) regarded Maggie as a superpatriot and Kennedy shill.

Maggie was thrilled by the arrival of a son, Lawrence, and insisted he be christened Catholic.

Maggie, about to embark on a book tour, was fueled by a sense of mission.

She was required to give more interviews when she landed in San Francisco, where she made a brief stopover to see her parents, and then continued on to Los Angeles to meet with Hollywood executives. Bill Perlberg threw her a dinner and took her around the Paramount lot. Gossip columnists from Hy Gardner to Louella Parsons reported that studios were vying for the rights to her life story, and that Twentieth Century-Fox head Darryl F. Zanuck, a colonel in the army during World War II, was rumored to have the inside track. More than one commentator observed that the battlefield bombshell had sufficient beauty to play herself on the screen.

Before leaving LA, Maggie made her first radio broadcast on Mutual Network's *Newsreel* program. "I feel slightly like a deserter, leaving the front now," she said in her whispery voice. "It is only natural when you are with soldiers under fire that you wish to stay with them until the end of the war."

She returned to New York in time to appear at the *Herald Tribune* Forum, a prestigious three-day, celebrity-packed conference hosted annually by Helen Reid at the Waldorf Astoria Hotel. Owing to her sudden notoriety, Maggie was easily the most important attraction of the glittering media summit. Her appearance, the highlight of the final evening, was advertised in advance by the paper, which had flown her home especially for the occasion. She was introduced by the forum's grande dame herself, the diminutive, gray-haired Helen Reid, who could scarcely be seen over the lectern.

Small but imperious, she began by lamenting the "stupidity of nations" in allowing war to be invoked by men: "A number of years ago Amelia Earhart made the statement that war would never end until women went to the front as well as men. Perhaps if the aggressor Reds had seen Marguerite Higgins they would have withdrawn more rapidly. In any event she showed that professional responsibility and human courage have no sex."

The *Tribune's* proprietress went on to cite Higgins's brilliant European war dispatches and coverage of Korea, and her valiant fight against discriminatory work practices, a cause near and dear to Helen Reid's own heart. "Perhaps the greatest tribute paid to Maggie Higgins, a newspaper-woman, came from another correspondent at the time of her ouster from Korea," she continued. He said he "felt sorry for the Eighth Army because Higgins, who was often described as 'winsome' by the press, was about as winsome as a maddened adder."

Maggie made her way to the rostrum, which was bristling with two dozen microphones. Just below stood a battery of photographers, snapping away. Her blond hair curled to gleaming perfection, she had donned an off-the-shoulder black taffeta dress and long sparkling earrings to talk of the uphill fight in Korea. She spoke not of her own feats that night but of the soldiers in the field, delivering a rousing call to arms on behalf of their boys in Korea:

"Unpreparedness," she explained, her voice tired but her smile bright, "is hearing a battalion commander like Colonel Jensen bitterly predicting on a hilltop observation post: 'This position will be untenable in 24 hours,' and hearing his operations officer interrupt with, 'No Sir, about 24 minutes. Enemy tanks are breaking through.' Nor do I ever want to talk again to a young American like Lt. Edward James of Columbus, Ga., who, after seeing his outfit decimated by the communists, asked us, 'How can the United States throw us into such a useless, hopeless battle with so little to back us.'"

Praising the marines' performance in a savage war, she blamed the missteps on policy blunders. Korea had taught them some hard lessons, among them the danger of overconfidence and half-hearted measures. If Truman's "police action" in Korea did not live up to the public's expectations and the still-remembered victories of 1945, it was because they did not have enough trained troops in the field. Korea meant more to Maggie than just another war to cover, and her ideological fervor came to the fore. Peering out over the packed ballroom, her voice soft but impassioned, she said that the U.S.'s intervention in Korea had been necessary because unless they made a stand there, they risked seeing all of Asia taken over by the communists. The Soviet-supplied Asian soldier was a formidable adversary, who could fight with one-fifth the food, clothes, and transportation considered essential by one of their own. And, she added, speaking from personal experience, "he is a very good shot."

A legion of invitations showered down on her in the days that followed. People loved her bravery, her gumption, her gameness, and the hint of playfulness. The *Tribune* arranged a busy schedule of personal appearances during her six-week stay in the States, including advertising-sales luncheons, executive dinners, and charity functions. Her every move in New York was chronicled in the daily papers, most dotingly in her own, accompanied by photographs of a svelte Higgins stylishly attired. Helen Reid was always by her side, eager to introduce her protégé, though after a seemingly endless series of banquets, she joked wearily, "Everywhere Marguerite went, her Reid was sure to go."

Increasingly newsworthy for her bold foreign policy pronouncements, Maggie told the 1,200 guests gathered at the Roosevelt Hotel that unless China capitulated to U.S. demands to leave Korea there would be a "third world war." At the National Women's Press Club in Washington, she argued that America must mobilize to stop the spread of communism and, echoing MacArthur, urged that "every weapon, including the atomic bomb" should be used. Her "alarmist" message earned frequent mentions on editorial pages, and played well in the context of the Cold War, and the anticommunist political atmosphere that had taken hold in the U.S.

She was so outspoken that when her remarks were repeated before a UN session, John Foster Dulles, a special adviser to the administration, was forced to remonstrate with Russia's foreign minister, Andrei Vishinsky, "President Truman makes American foreign policy and not the *New York Daily Compass* or Miss Marguerite Higgins of the *New York Herald Tribune.*" Though Dulles hastened to add that he found the war correspondent "charming."

On November 18, she was honored by her peers at the New York Newspaperwomen's annual "Front Page" dinner. Maggie was named the outstanding woman reporter of the year. She received a special citation commending her for her "courage under fire" and bravery in helping administer blood plasma to the wounded. When she accepted the scroll, the four hundred reporters, editors, and publishers in attendance rose to their feet in a standing ovation. Maggie later confided that the honor from her peers meant more to her than any other tribute.

She thrived on all the attention. From the very beginning, she consciously strove to burnish her image as a heroic war correspondent, not just as the lone woman in the field but as one of the best of the big-league reporters. With an eye to capitalizing on her newfound fame, and solidifying her reputation as a serious journalist, she retained the W. Colston Leigh Bureau, a preeminent speakers' agency, to handle all the invitations she was receiving to lecture and appear on topical radio and television programs. But she could not resist the high-paid commercial offers and impulsively agreed to pose in an absurdly large hat for an ad for Blue Bonnet margarine, which did not exactly enhance her reputation as a gritty reporter.

A few weeks later, *Mademoiselle* magazine selected her as one of the ten "Young Women of the Year" who had distinguished themselves in their field. She made *The Book of Knowledge*'s annual list of the "12 Smartest Women in America," along with Eleanor Roosevelt, the anthropologist Margaret Mead, the author and activist Helen Keller, the *New York Times* columnist Anne O'Hare McCormick, and her longtime idol, Dorothy Thompson, among others.

As the prizes piled up, Maggie found herself becoming fodder for the gossip columns. She discovered the perils of being a public figure. Her romantic interludes with Bill Hall in New York and Washington had not gone unnoticed. Inevitably, the pair were photographed together at intimate dinners, sitting side by side in banquettes, holding hands and gazing into each other's eyes. In his syndicated column, Walter Winchell predicted that Higgins and a certain "major general" would soon wed.

Winchell's column, which at its height was read by fifty million people a day, caused them both problems. The main problem was that their romance was supposed to be a secret, as Bill was still married. There was talk that by detaching him from his family, Maggie had denied Hall the chief of staff's position that had been earmarked for him. At the same time, some of the tabloids were speculating that she was fielding proposals from her jeep mate, Keyes Beech. This was awkward for everybody concerned, as Beech was also married, and in the midst of divorcing his wife so he could marry someone other than Higgins.

Three days later, Maggie was in Winchell's column again. This time the muckraker, making nice, lauded her as a "daredevil angel of the press," who was deservedly the toast of the town for her reporting in Korea. "She is back there now," he disclosed, "recording the agony of her countrymen."

MAGGIE ARRIVED BACK AT the front on December 5 as the First Marine Division, the core of X Corps, was preparing to fight its way out of an icy trap at the frozen Changjin Reservoir in North Korea. Although the U.S. had been warned that the Chinese communists would enter the war if the UN forces crossed the 38th parallel, no one in high command believed Mao would intervene. MacArthur was sufficiently unconcerned that on Thanksgiving Day, November 23, he promised the troops that they would spend Christmas at home if they reached the Yalu River at the North Korean–Chinese border. The next morning, the Eighth Army and X Corps resumed their advance. Two marine divisions pushed north with orders to cut off and destroy the retreating enemy, and what was supposed to be only a few token units of the Chinese People's Volunteer Army (CPV).

On the night of November 27, 250,000 bugle-blowing, cymbal-clashing Chinese troops struck, surprising and encircling the American divisions that were strung out along seventy-eight miles of slender road between Hungnam and the Changjin Reservoir. By the time the marines recognized they were fighting a vastly superior force, it was too late— they were trapped. When the order to advance was changed to a withdrawal, they realized the desperate nature of their predicament. A brutal fourteen-day siege in freezing weather followed. MacArthur had gambled again, but this time he lost. The Yalu offensive was a military debacle.

Day after day, night after night, the marines battled their way through the snow and ice, and masses of Chinese troops, to break a bloody trail across more than one hundred miles of hostile terrain. The mercury was fifteen below zero as they embarked on their terrible trek back through snowy mountain passes and over frigid gray ice fields the leathernecks dubbed "Nightmare Alley," carrying with them nearly five thousand dead, wounded, and frostbitten men. Maggie described the disaster as a "Korean Valley Forge, worse than anything in the Marine Corps' history." Her gut-wrenching reports, like those of Beech and Bigart, were colored with bitterness at the poor logistics and "faulty generalship" that had allowed the X Corps to be so precariously exposed and was responsible, at least in part, for their entrapment. The marines had to endure colossal difficulties and sickening losses before they could extricate themselves from their plight. She caught up with the last beleaguered stragglers of the Fifth and Seventh Marine Regiments at Hagaru-ri, on the tip of the reservoir, where a C-47 had deposited her after a shuddering landing on the pitted, snow-covered plateau. On seeing the exhausted, disoriented X Corps survivors, she wired back an unsparing account of the horrific cost of their reverse journey.

"The men were ragged," she wrote, "their faces swollen from the cold and bleeding from the raw bite of the icy wind, their lips blue. Their mittens were torn and raveled. Some were without their fur hats. A few walked barefoot. They had to—they could not get their frostbitten feet into their frozen shoe-pacs."

From Hagaru, she cadged a lift on a bomber to the bleak city of Kot'o-ri, only ten miles farther south as the crow flies, but another torturous two-day ordeal for the troops, who had to fight all the way, buffeted by winds so strong it was hard to stand or walk on the ice-glazed reservoir. Guns and vehicles froze. They had to chip ice off the mortars to fire them. The wounded could not be treated because the plasma turned rock hard and the bottles shattered. The marines told her their boots had not been adequate for the arctic temperatures and the deficient gear decimated up to half the troops in some companies.

By the time they reached Kot'o, there were so many casualties that three mass graves had to be dynamited out of the frozen earth. "The chaplain spoke the psalm, 'The Lord is my Shepherd,' but the tobogganing wind swept away his words," wrote Maggie, who was part of the tiny group of mourners who huddled together for warmth.

A portable bridge, dropped by the air force in a last-ditch effort to save the badly mauled marines, enabled thousands to cross a river under heavy fire and finally complete their escape. Maggie was asked by a company of the Fifth Marines, with whom she had made the landing at Inchon, to "walk out with them" to the secure beachhead of Hungnam for evacuation. But Maj. Gen. Oliver P. Smith, gripped by a "seizure of chivalry," intervened and ordered her out of there. Lt. Gen. Lemuel Shepherd, commander of all marines in the Pacific, who had flown in to inspect the situation, found himself unexpectedly saddled with Higgins. "Just as I was about to board the plane, my old friend Lewie Puller [Col. Lewis "Chesty" Puller] showed up with a very irate Marguerite Higgins in tow," he recalled. "It was clear that he was interested in getting rid of her. 'General,' he said, 'would you take this woman with you?'

"Poor Maggie," recounted Shepherd. "She wanted me to intercede and ask O.P. [Smith] to let her stay. 'This is the biggest story of the war,' she pleaded. 'I don't want to miss it, General.'" Smith brooked no argument. Maggie flew out with Shepherd.

On December 7, she filed a dispatch on the hellish retreat under the headline "How Marines Cut Way out of Red Trap." The subhead read: "Miss Higgins Describes Bloody Battle." In a follow-up story on the epic withdrawal, Maggie observed that courage was perhaps the greatest virtue on display in Korea, where the ninth anniversary of Pearl Harbor tragically found American soldiers once again fighting against a relentless enemy. "The marines came out of their ordeal in the freezing wasteland of the Changjin Reservoir plateau as well-organized units," she wrote admiringly of the orderly retreat, "even though some units were only remnants of what they had been. The spirits of the men were high, and their assault backward to the sea had the precision which characterized their offensives."

While her support for the troops was unwavering, it did not lessen her anger at the military's deceptive and self-serving propaganda and its eagerness to downplay the crushing defeat she had just witnessed. She was affronted by any attempt to put a rosier slant on the ill-fated "home by Christmas" offensive, and her growing cynicism was evident in the tone of her stories. As the haggard marines staggered into Hungnam, hardly able to take in the fact that they were safe at last, Maggie turned a jaundiced eye on the newsreel cameramen, who shouted at them, "Wave and look happy." The marines, she wrote, "merely waved." Every officer and enlisted man she spoke to told her plaintively, "If only we had more troops, we could have licked them." Even more telling was the view expressed by a marine colonel who, after surveying the losses, said: "I'm afraid we are all part of a sad piece of history."

The problem was not with the troops in Korea, Maggie's reporting suggested, but with their leaders in Washington. While she focused on the human angle in an implicit challenge to the official line, Bigart, who was responsible for the broader strategic perspective, went even further. He explicitly criticized MacArthur's insistence on pushing for Yalu, revealing that "already some of the thoughtful officers are beginning to question the sanity of recent military decisions."

The *Herald Tribune* reveled in the controversial reports of its two high-profile correspondents, confident the caliber of their reporting and solid sourcing could stand up to the angry blasts from the Pentagon. While papers like the *New York Times* and *Christian Science Monitor* usually opted for a detached, factual approach to the war, relying on army press releases and wire-service accounts, and making little attempt to analyze the cause or consequences, the *Herald Tribune* tended to be less timid, allowing for more powerful, penetrating reports. In an editorial on December 7, the paper cited the grim side-by-side dispatches of Higgins and Bigart—"both told better than a hundred communiqués"— and argued that they demanded an official accounting, and raised the question that was being asked on the battlefield, and at home: "How did this happen?"

The recriminations had only just begun. The intervention of the Chinese had come as a shock. Korea was now a very different war, and MacArthur's command was held responsible for the growing sense of disaster. The press had lost faith in the military's assessment of the war, and their reports took a negative turn. On January 3, in a gloomy dispatch about the third fall of Seoul in seven months, Maggie wrote that the shattered city had a "calm air of approaching doom, while along the

Han River, the refugees crowd southward." Once again, the roads were clogged with civilians fleeing communist rule and the inevitable blood-letting. This was where she "came in," she noted, and it was depressing to see history repeat itself. "Never have I seen so many tears."

At the end of the month, Maggie left Korea. A telegram was wait-ing for her in the Tokyo bureau from Whitie Reid: "CONGRATU-LATIONS YOUR EXPLOIT ON REACHING MARINES AND CRACKING GOOD STORIES."

Like many of the Korea correspondents, she was headed home for a rest. She had seen fourteen weeks of action and it had used up all her strength and endurance. The cold of the Korean winter had seeped into her bones and she could not shake off a bad chill. She was hoping two weeks of R & R at Chabot Court would restore her to fighting fit before she had to embark on another round of publicity for the paper and a lec-ture tour. Even the indestructible Bigart had left the front. He was back in New York, taking a bow, while the paper was preparing to submit his work to the Pulitzer Prize committee. She had read that his next job would be in Europe, and he had let it be known that he would "refuse to work" in any area being covered by her.

Before returning to the States, Maggie took the bold step of broach-ing the topic of the Pulitzer nominations with Whitie Reid. She knew such decisions were made entirely at the discretion of the editors, and any lobbying by a staff reporter was seen as bad form. But she had lit-tle faith in the masculine hierarchy. The Pulitzers, which had been given out annually since 1917, had only twice recognized the contribution of women.* Moreover, the *Trib* was certain to back Bigart. She fretted that his memorable, history-in-the-making articles would overshadow her straight-up action pieces. If she did not toot her own horn, she felt certain her work would be overlooked. "Members of the Tokyo press corps have been flattering enough to suggest that some of my stories—fall of Seoul,

---

* The first time was in 1918, when Minna Lewinson was a joint winner of the prize for news-paper history with her Columbia Graduate School of Journalism classmate, Henry Beetle Hough; and the second was when Anne O'Hare McCormick won in 1937 in the category of correspondence.

the Inchon landing and the marine escape—might at least be a candidate," she wrote. "Even though my chances might be slim indeed, I have the normal human desire to be in on the competition."

Whitie cabled back that she was on the list of nominees and the paper was doing all it could on her behalf. "Trust you'll be feeling better soon," he wrote. "Your stories are tops."

On January 27, 1951, the *Saturday Evening Post* published her harrowing account of the Christmas retreat from Changjin Reservoir, entitled "The Bloody Trail Back." Higgins had become one of the biggest names reporting from Korea, and the magazine's editors, who only months earlier had consigned her to second fiddle to Bigart, now gave her top billing. In a box next to her byline, they noted, "Marguerite Higgins, famous and pretty war correspondent of the *New York Herald Tribune* has won herself an unexcelled reputation for courage and skill in covering the frontline fighting in Korea."

The article was an excerpt from her upcoming book, *War in Korea: The Report of a Woman War Correspondent*, which Doubleday was rushing into print that April. The book, which was heavily promoted and widely excerpted, was a bestseller long before it arrived in stores. *Woman's Home Companion* serialized highlights of her war adventures as the "Front Line Diary of Marguerite Higgins," advertising it as "a woman's magnificent story of our fight as she saw it, felt it and reported it." The *Tribune* also ran dramatic snippets in its Sunday magazine, boosting Higgins as "one of the few American women ever to share the grim realities of the front lines and to report the day-to-day struggles of our fighting men during a desperate campaign."

War in Korea was published to rave reviews and was a Book of the Month Club selection. In the *New York Times Book Review*, Quentin Reynolds hailed his courageous fellow correspondent in a glowing write-up capped by the memorable headline "In Korea, It Was Blood, Thunder, and Maggie Higgins."

After acknowledging that it was not the done thing to admire a colleague's tome without qualification, he justified his position by declaring, "No matter how you consider it, this is one hell of a book." Higgins was a force of nature. How she ever found time to write the book was one of the many miracles of her crowded career. In the daily *Times* review, Charles Poore commended the "beautiful, able, and exultantly competitive Marguerite Higgins," noting that her experience of facing enemy fire, obstructive army officials, and displeasure of a *Trib* colleague in the field "made for remarkably interesting reading."

In the *Herald Tribune Book Review,* the UP columnist and author Marquis Childs perceptively observed that Higgins, who described MacArthur as a "prisoner of his own legend," was in a sense herself also the victim of a legend: "It is the legend of a woman war correspondent, beautiful yet relentless, trading on her charm in an effort to compete successfully in a sphere in which men have traditionally and jealously dominated." Her appealing femininity did not win her the scoops and stories, but her persistence, plain endurance, and extraordinary determination. Throughout the book, "La Higgins," as he called her, was continually at war with this legend, which had wide currency in the newspaper world, but she was "a sufficient realist to understand that it was in no small part responsible for catapulting her to fame."

The most comprehensive review was by S. L. A. Marshall, an eminent military historian and World War II colonel, who was only recently returned from Korea. He thought her informal account of the Korea campaign lacked a proper sense of proportion when it came to war, and was inaccurate in minor details, but he praised her for refusing to dissemble about American reverses. He found much to admire in its pages, and about the author herself: "This Maggie's eye view of the Korean police action is downright irresistible in its candor, in its simple expression of things which many of us feel strongly but can't say very well, in its change of pace between the tragedy of the battlefield and the high comedy of much human behavior in close relationship to it." Marshall concluded, "I have never met Marguerite Higgins, but I would be standing in line; she takes a nice picture and she writes a whale of a war story."

Winchell gave her the ultimate seal of approval, plugging Higgins as the "female Ernie Pyle." Doubleday saw dollar signs and used the line in all the print ads for the book.

Awards continued to pour in. Over the next weeks and months, she received every laurel imaginable, a haul of more than fifty prizes, plaques, medals, and certificates. In April, as expected, she collected the Overseas Press Club's George Polk Memorial Award as best foreign correspondent for having demonstrated "courage, integrity and enterprise above and beyond the call of duty." The award, named for a CBS newsman murdered in 1948 while covering the Greek civil war, was one of the most prestigious in their industry, and carried with it a hefty $500 check.

In May, she grabbed journalism's brass ring—the Pulitzer. A record six correspondents were awarded prizes in the international affairs category for their Korean War coverage. It was the first time in the organization's thirty-four-year history that more than one prize had ever been given for foreign reporting. It was also the first time a female correspondent had ever won for frontline reporting, with the jury noting that Higgins was "entitled to special consideration by reason of being a woman, since she had to work under unusual dangers."

Casting her eyes down the list of recipients, Maggie read the names in alphabetical order: At the top was Keyes Beech, followed by Homer Bigart. The other three recipients were the AP correspondents Relman Morin and Don Whitehead, and Fred Sparks of the *Chicago Daily News*.

The *Herald Tribune* patted its own back in an editorial, telling its readers that the paper was pleased and proud that two of its correspondents should number among the six to get the nod, and noted that Higgins had "demonstrated that to be a woman is no bar to being a first-rate combat correspondent." It also ran a huge ad, featuring side-by-side photographs of Bigart and Higgins, bragging that the duo's copious Korea coverage was the reason the *Trib* was "the only morning newspaper in New York to show a daily circulation gain over the past 12 months."

The June issue of *Vogue* featured the strikingly feminine combat correspondent in their "People Are Talking About" section, observing that Higgins "was now a celebrity, a role she accepts with matter-of-fact simplicity." The piece was accompanied by a stunning full-page portrait of her in a black bouclé jacket and pearl choker, taken by the renowned fashion photographer Erwin Blumenfeld. Magazines from *Elle* and

Harper's Bazaar to the French newsweekly *Paris Match* followed up with profiles.

She was a hit on the lecture circuit. A crowd pleaser, she was in constant demand, receiving more than two thousand requests for personal appearances in her first month back. Her voice gave out after the first week. With practice she learned how to speak in a lower register and to project loudly enough to be heard in the back of the room. She discovered that lecturing was a lucrative business. Her agent was demanding fees of $500 to $1,000 a pop, plus expenses. The entire time she had been in Berlin and Korea, she had been making $135 a week as a foreign correspondent. Suddenly, she was raking in what seemed like stupendous sums.

She celebrated with friends and colleagues at the Stork Club, at El Morocco, and at 21. She went to the ballet and opera and saw all the best Broadway plays. Winchell observed that the new musical *Messer Marco Polo* featured a feisty gal reporter "not unlike Maggie" and that the war correspondent was "getting famous." In his Newsreel column, Hy Gardner suggested the rivalry between Higgins and Bigart was destined for movie theaters and that the last scene would end with a fade-out of the two "walking arm-in-arm down the beach."

Conscious of always being on display, Maggie shopped compulsively, better able to meet the world with composure in smart clothes. Although she was making more money than she had ever had in her life, it burned a hole in her pocket. She went through her unaccustomed riches with the same reckless abandon with which she pursued her stories. As soon as the checks arrived, she cashed them. She was so busy juggling her various commitments, and accommodating the Reids' myriad requests, that she hardly had a minute to think about what it all meant, or how long she would be the flavor of the moment.

When the *Tribune* suggested it was time to do some honest work, Maggie pitched her dream assignment of being a globe-trotting foreign correspondent. The Reids were not blind to the value of her services. They offered her the most important slot in the paper—the opportunity to temporarily fill in for their liberal columnist Walter Lippmann, who was going on a six-month sabbatical. Lippmann was rumored to be in hot water over his repeated attacks on the administration and State Department, at a time when the *Tribune* was being accused of being soft on communism. Senator Joseph McCarthy of Wisconsin had launched a hunt for communist sympathizers in the government, and his "Red Scare" crusade was creating a climate of fear and suspicion across the country. The Reids were afraid the paper was in danger of losing major segments of its conservative readership, which would further undermine its already wobbly financial stability. Maggie's staunch anticommunism was more in tune with the times and just what they needed to disarm the charges of leftism.

The foreign editor, Joe Barnes, dreamed up the idea of having Higgins do a ten-week, around-the-world tour to report on key persons and places in the cold and hot wars on communism. The series would give her a much wider canvas, a place where her ideas could have real impact. It was an offer she could not resist. In addition to being paid for the "Around Russia's Curtain" column, she would get 50 percent of the gross revenue from the syndicated rights. Her dispatches from Europe, as well as the Near and Far East, would appear three times weekly in the paper beginning on August 1, in the form of news stories, think pieces, and editorials, and her byline would appear in syndication in newspapers all over the country.

She sailed for Europe on the *Île de France* on June 28. Word of her selection as the 1951 Headliner of Theta Sigma Phi, the national fraternity for women in journalism, reached her just as she was packing to go. Maggie sent her regrets.

In Paris, she was feted by old friends and colleagues. She had a warm reunion with Mike Michaelis, now a brigadier general, who was working with Eisenhower to create an overall military-defense plan for Western Europe. Maggie and her old lover, Ed Morrow, now a member of the *Times* Paris bureau, took Michaelis and his wife, Mary, out for a "gastronomic splurge" at Tour d'Argent, a restaurant known for its superb food and views of the city. The next day, she met with Eisenhower, who was still supreme allied commander in Europe, at his austere new headquarters at Marly-le-Roi. He stressed that rearmament was an urgent necessity. "If we let this drag on and on," he told her, "we will not be ready at a time when there could conceivably be extreme danger."

She spent the summer hopping from one trouble spot to another, interviewing foreign heads of state: she met with the Spanish dictator General Francisco Franco, at the royal palace in Madrid, who promised "to fight with fervor" against the communist thrust on the continent; the tough-looking Yugoslavian dictator Marshal Tito, who pledged to "do battle" on the side of the West in the event of a Soviet attack; the handsome, progressive shah of Iran, Mohammad Reza Pahlavi, and his beautiful queen, in Marmar Palace on the Caspian Sea; King Paul and Queen Frederica of Greece, who stood ready to fight Soviet imperialism; the shy, young twenty-two-year-old King of Siam, whose country was "very much part of the oriental cold war"; India's Prime Minister Nehru, with his "aura of selflessness and sincerity," in his high-ceilinged office in the parliament building in New Delhi; and Liaquat Ali Khan, the first prime minister of newly independent Pakistan, who was assassinated shortly thereafter.

The *Tribune*, eager to display its attentiveness to the communist threat, gave her series major play and encouraged her to report on the "Red infiltration of Asia." Maggie pushed on to Hanoi, toured the Indo-Chinese front and the forts being hastily built by the French and loyal Vietnamese in anticipation of a communist attack. She chatted with the "playboy emperor" Bao Dai, the chief of the state of Vietnam, on his yacht in the resort town of Nha Trang, and noted that she was pleasantly surprised to find him urging land reform and vehemently opposed to communism. In Taipei, she dined with the slight, dignified Generalissimo Chiang Kai-Shek and Madam Chiang in their modest brick house, where they had lived in exile since 1949, when his Nationalist government took refuge on the island of Taiwan. "Events have since proved that whatever the faults of Chiang's regime," she wrote, "he was right in estimating that compromise with the communists was impossible."

On her return to Korea in mid-October, she reported on the tense peace talks between the communists and the UN forces, which had only recently resumed after being suspended for two months. The impasse had finally been settled earlier that month when the Chinese agreed to move the venue to the village of P'anmunjom, in a no-man's-land between the two sides. She was amazed to find her old friend Peter Burchett, now in the employ of France's communist paper *Ce Soir*, filling the role of spokesman for the enemy camp. The photographers wanted to get a picture of the famous Higgins being briefed by Burchett. As they faced the cameras, he jokingly warned her that she "better look stern or you will be purged." Maggie retorted that she thought he had "more to worry about" in that regard.

She compiled a glamorous travelogue of her globe-circling jaunt for *Woman's Home Companion*, which ran three long installments of "Marguerite Higgins' Round the World Diary." The magazine ran photographs of an elegantly clad Maggie, pictured in a Christian Dior travel ensemble and silk shantung evening dresses, hobnobbing with world leaders in exotic locales, and reporting from Indochina, looking impossibly cool in summer khakis and aviator sunglasses alongside French air force officers.

In the autumn, she was asked to write an essay for *Collier's*, as part of a special issue entitled "Preview of the War We Do Not Want," a reference to the growing national hysteria about the impending atomic war with the Soviets. As part of their Cold War compendium, they consulted the era's "great men of letters," including the playwright Robert E. Sherwood and novelist Arthur Koestler, as well as some of the country's foremost journalists, including Edward R. Murrow and the Pulitzer Prize winners Hanson Baldwin and Hal Boyle. Maggie, amazed to find herself in such exalted company, ransacked her old reporters notebooks for inspiration. Her contribution, "Women of Russia," based on her experience in postwar Berlin, was a nightmarish, postapocalyptic imagining of Moscow in the year 1960, a decimated city where millions of women find themselves alone "in a country shorn of men."

She returned to New York in October, in time to pick up her second award from the New York Newspaper Women's Club. In her absence, she had been presented with the Veterans of Foreign Wars Gold Medal, which Whitie Reid had accepted on her behalf. Her "Around the Curtain" series had been a huge hit, and the syndicate sales had been strong. Her book, a bestseller, was going into its fourth printing.

Seventeen magazine asked about her unparalleled success in the traditionally antifemale profession—"Is It a Man's Game?"—and reported that Higgins "doesn't think so." But the writer observed that Maggie looked "nearly as thin and fragile as a Dresden china figurine," and her advice to any young woman interested in being a newspaper correspondent was to "prepare to be better than all the men in your field, and to suffer because you are better."

Her fame was at its peak. Her speaking agent was preparing another busy lecture tour for November and December, with a second leg planned for the West Coast in the New Year. Life should have been wonderful, only it was not. Far from it. The demanding journey had left her exhausted. A persistent cold had developed into acute bronchitis and sinusitis. She was also suffering from a recurrence of malaria and jaundice, as well as dysentery. Her ailments, together with a case of nervous tension, made her feel like a "social menace." In addition to feeling sorry for herself, she was nursing an aching heart. She had returned to rumors that Bill Hall had been seeing someone while she was away.

When an old pal took her to lunch at the Stork Club on her release from the hospital, she burst into tears over the first martini. "He had made the mistake of saying something kind," she recalled. "It was even worse than the unintentional emotional torture provided by well-meaning clubwomen, who would exclaim, 'Ah, what a wonderful life you must lead.'"

The pressure of her stratospheric rise took its toll in all sorts of unforeseen ways. Crisscrossing the globe, she had little time to sort out her problems with Hall, whose petition to dissolve his marriage had been denied. His wife filed a counterpetition, charging extreme cruelty and gross neglect, which was eventually granted. But by then, Maggie and Bill had quarreled and were barely speaking. She had solved the problem by going abroad, hoping that some time apart would allow them both to see things more clearly. What she had thought of as just another temporary separation nearly finished them.

It hit her unexpectedly hard when she learned Beech had cashed his Pulitzer check and flown to Mexico for a quickie divorce. Then he and the lovely Linda had gotten hitched in Fairfield, Connecticut. Frank

Gibney was best man. Maggie was left with a strange hangover from their battlefront days, a profound sense of loss and dismay, as if a trusted friend had suddenly gone in a time of great need.

On Sunday, December 15, the day she was named "Woman of the Year" by a poll of female newspaper editors, Maggie learned that the man she loved was leaving her. She had pinned her hopes on Hall and he had let her down. All the time she had been chasing headlines, she still secretly believed she could "have everything"—a big job, fame, and a fairy-tale ending. "In my conceit," she wrote, "I had thought I would top it all off with something far rarer: a love both true and deep; a man to whom I could be both friend and lover; a man who would need no other love than mine."

Her profession had come first for eleven years. She had finally felt ready to pause her career and rearrange her priorities in order to make time for a personal life. She cherished a naive fantasy of a traditional marriage—of a family, a house with a white picket fence, and a dog in the yard. She longed for a sense of balance, inner serenity, and security. As always, she had dashed ahead, not bothering to look where she was going. Just when everything was going her way, she had been tripped up by her own hubris and sent sprawling. Blindsided by Hall's rejection, she felt more alone and miserable than she had ever been.

Her sense of irony was too well developed for her to ignore the timing. It was a spectacular and permanent reminder that life was a great leveler. "Whatever it was—fate, destiny, Kismet—I had perhaps more than my share in Korea," she ruminated in her memoir. "And perhaps this is why, in the period directly after I went home from the wars, fortune was so often absent."

13

* * * * * * * * *

Winging It

Ride a fast plane, from Moscow to Maine,
To watch a bright lady wing upward again.
Rings on her fingers (but none on her nose)
She shall make headlines wherever she goes.

—Harry Evans, editor, *Family Circle*

AT THE START OF 1952, MAGGIE WAS SICK AND TIRED. SHE WAS
also broke. Despite all the easy money from prizes, magazine pieces,
serial rights, and syndication deals, she had little to show for it. She had
requested six months' leave from the *Tribune* to extend her speaking tour
to the West Coast, with the idea that it would give her time to bank some
savings, relax, and enjoy the fruits of all her labor, but things had not gone
according to plan.

She spent Christmas holed up at Chabot Court, recuperating from
her assorted ailments and being fussed over by her parents. Pale and
depressed, she was reluctant to show her face in public. But her publi-
cists had taken out ads promoting her speaking tour, and hundreds of her
young admirers in the local YWCA had spent the holiday selling tick-
ets to her upcoming charity lecture. According to the local papers, the
teens would be "turning out en masse to hear from the local girl made
good." There was no way she could disappoint them. When January 3
rolled around, she had to drag herself from bed to speak at the Oakland
Auditorium Theater, where she was given a huge hometown reception.

Afterward, there was a party in her honor hosted by her former Gamma Phi Beta sorority sisters. Apparently, all was forgiven.

Maggie had always shown herself to be astoundingly resilient, but between her poor health and private despair, she could not seem to regain her stamina. When she showed up at a San Francisco women's civic club in mid-January, she was still so out of sorts that she was unable to make it through her prepared speech. It was such an embarrassing, rambling performance that the club president wrote her speaker's agency, W. Colston Leigh, demanding the group's money back.

Days later, she was chided in an editorial in the *Santa Fe New Mexican* for rudely skipping out on an engagement and leaving her fans in the lurch. It turned out she had checked into the Alta Bates Hospital in Berkeley, still battling a stubborn bacterial infection. She later admitted in a telephone interview with the *New Mexican* that she had suffered a "semi-nervous breakdown." On doctor's orders, she was forced to curtail her future bookings.

All her lecture dates for January and February had to be canceled. Maggie was inundated with angry letters. The Duluth Women's Institute sent a bill for damages for her failure to appear in December. Several other women's clubs followed suit. In the end, the Leigh agency filed a claim against her for $1,300 for nonfulfillment of her contract, which it noted was nothing compared to the hundreds of hours it had spent on telephone calls, telegrams, and letters trying to undo the problems created by her disappearing act.

Miss Higgins has been "ill from overwork," wrote Harry Evans in a snarky piece for *Family Circle*. "Living these war experiences has brought her a lot of satisfaction. Cashing in on them is bringing her a raft of headaches. She is more at home with a gang of soldiers than at a literary tea, and she finds it more difficult to keep up the commitments of her New York lecture bureau than she did with her Japanese news bureau."

During her first few months back home, Maggie was so besieged by editors, agents, and producers that she had just wanted to be left alone. The searing glare of fame had been confusing and more than a little destabilizing. At the height of the publicity frenzy, she had felt harassed by the invasive scrutiny. "It seemed to me that just about everybody in America wanted me to do something, most of them were willing to pay me, and all of them acted as if it were a mortal insult if I didn't comply at once," she recalled. "I was able to respond to only a small fraction of these offers, partly because such high-pressure offers came all at once. Partly because I was in bad health, and partly because I had an extraordinarily cavalier attitude toward money."

She turned down a television program based on her life—a deal that would have netted her thousands of dollars—because she considered the character of the heroine "to be inane as well as an insult to journalism." Then, just as fast as they appeared, all the movie offers that had been dangled before her vanished. At the time, she had not realized how quickly the tidal wave of publicity that had buoyed her up would recede. Her sudden fame had seen her income jump from $7,020 to over $26,000, almost half of which was from her book advance and royalties. Given her new celebrity status—and earning potential—she found herself questioning whether she should return to the comparatively low-paid profession of newspaper correspondent.

While she appreciated the validation the Pulitzer had conferred, the prize did not provide her with the same sense that she had "made the grade" that it had for some of her peers. Dan De Luce said that after he won his Pulitzer in 1944, he felt like he had arrived and no longer had to work as hard to prove himself. But Maggie, who was conscious of having been such a "unique phenomenon" in Korea, believed she had received more acclaim than she deserved. As a consequence, the prize weighed more heavily on her. She felt more was expected of her, forever demanding that she demonstrate her worthiness.

She also observed that many of her fellow prizewinners were moving on to greener pastures. "It is in the very nature of the genus Foreign Correspondent to transfer to more lucrative fields when he becomes famous," observed Russell F. Anderson, who in his glory days covered everything from the Spanish Civil War to the Battle of Dunkirk. For the most part, it was a transitory profession. The average foreign correspondent returned after three to five years abroad, "with his toothbrush and his duodenal ulcers," and sought better-paid work at home. But the weary adventurers always hung on to the label—and its romantic association with strange and distant places—no matter how faded.

In the beginning of 1952, she began exploring the possibility of breaking into broadcast television, which producers promised would bring her national exposure and allow her to reach an even larger audience for her written work. It was also a ticket to the top income brackets. Toward that end, she wrote a friend, she had purchased a pricey console in its custom mahogany cabinet "to familiarize myself with the medium." Edward R. Murrow had recently debuted a new documentary series, *See It Now*, on the CBS network, and the possibilities were tantalizing.

Her first foray into television was an hour-long program for *Pulitzer Prize Playhouse*, "Marguerite Higgins' Hill 346: A Report on Korea," based on her *Herald Tribune* dispatches and personal recollections. The show consisted of newsreel footage of the Korean front, interspersed with narration by Higgins, as well as dramatic reenactments staged in the studio. Unfortunately, the story was told in flat, static terms, with an uneven script and Hollywood actors playing a succession of wooden stereotypes. Maggie was not surprised by the poor reviews.

When KPIX, the local CBS affiliate in San Francisco, approached her about doing a weekly interview program on Sunday evenings at eight o'clock, she agreed, although she did not relish the prospect. She viewed the nickel-and-dime operation, with its tiny studio, and even tinier budget, as beneath her. It was just an experiment, she told a friend, so she could continue "practicing the art of tv." The twelve-part series, *Marguerite Higgins News Close-Ups*, would cover national and international issues, using newsreel clips to illustrate the relevant scenes, interspersed with her commentary. Each program would feature one of her much-vaunted "exclusives" in the form of an interview with a high-profile political figure or personality.

It was not a happy experience. Local television, still in the tender stages of development, was not ready for Maggie's sharp, confrontational style. In a vexed letter to her new manager, Joseph Bailey of the John E. Gibbs Agency in Manhattan, she complained that people on the West

Coast "gasp at the questions I ask, but they wouldn't startle anyone regularly acquainted with Washington or New York reporting." KPIX offered to extend her deal indefinitely, but Maggie had other ideas. "It's very small time and I think I wouldn't have gotten involved if all those doctors bills hadn't frightened me into thinking that I better have some income, even if picayune, or have my financial morale undermined completely," she griped. "I only wish I was doing it from the East, cuz as you know I loathe it out here."

She expected all the recognition she had received to make the next steps in her career come more easily, but instead she was finding it harder. Television was unrewarding, and too much effort for too little return. For the first time in many years, her work was going unnoticed—and it was unnerving. Stuck out in the boondocks, her star power had dimmed. She needed to get back to the East Coast, where her name meant something. "To me the devilish part of experiencing fame to any degree," she observed ruefully, "is the human reluctance to let go of it."

So far as the public at large was concerned, however, Maggie was still the glamorous ace correspondent. On April 8, on a cloudless Oakland morning, she collected the Marine Corps Reserve Officers Association's "Non Sibi Sed Patriae" ("Not for Self, but for Country") Award. Maggie was deeply moved by the citation, which not only credited her splendid reporting but stated that her presence at the front had lifted the troops' morale. "She looks more like a movie actress, blond and beautiful, describing the difficulties of filming a war," raved the *Oakland Tribune*. "It's almost incredible that she's been an eyewitness to the carnage of a real war."

Standing unobtrusively in the back was Bill Hall, who had proudly accompanied her to the event. In January 1951, Hall had been made commanding general of the Fourth Air Force at Hamilton Air Force Base in nearby Marin County. He had spent the last few months trying to mend his relationship with Maggie. The fun-loving, hard-drinking officer had admitted to keeping company with a bevy of Bay Area ladies while she was away, but there was never any question that she was the one he loved.

Maggie forgave him. She had never been one of those women who was attracted to the straight arrows. "You get a cockeyed notion of masculine charm when you've knocked around as I have," she once confided to a fellow reporter. "For months you associate with men who spend most of their time dodging bullets in mudholes. Then you come home and hear men talking about the problem of dodging traffic on 5th Avenue."

While they were working through their differences, Hall offered to take her out target shooting one February afternoon for fun. Choosing not to remind him that she had acquired ample firearms experience in Korea, she allowed him to show her the finer points of handling a rifle. Then, when it was her turn, she proceeded to outshoot him. After inspecting the damage, Hall labeled the holes—all bull's-eyes—inflicted by the object of his affection. He added a signed testimonial: "I certify that this target is mute but irrefutable evidence of the results of Marguerite Higgins' first lesson in rifle marksmanship, which I witnessed personally with mixed emotions of admiration and horror." Maggie kept the perforated paper as a valentine.

Herb Caen, whose daily column in the *San Francisco Examiner* was a local institution, dropped hints about a spring reconciliation. Maggie was "hiding out" in a Telegraph Hill apartment, and she was secretly seeing the general "whose name has been linked with hers so long and so hush-hushily." Jean Craig remembered visiting the Lombard Street apartment and finding her old school friend restored to good health, blooming, and bright-eyed again. Maggie was in a happy-go-lucky mood. She kept chirping snatches of the popular tune from *Oklahoma*, "I'm Just a Girl Who Cain't Say No." She said it was her theme song.

Underneath the carefree facade, however, she was still brittle. "After many, many months, the rift was healed," Maggie wrote in her memoir. "Despite the scars, and the risks, we were married." She did not kid herself that a partnership with the forty-five-year-old Hall would amount to wedded bliss, but she had been humbled by illness, and sorrow, and the pain and loneliness of their separation. "I was thirty-one years old," she added. "It seemed too late in my life to start turning back. Also, I was in love."

On Thursday, April 24, the couple flew to Reno. After picking up rings, flowers, and two strangers as witnesses, they were married in the briefest of civil services. Then they polished off a bottle of champagne, and took the train back to Oakland. The ink was barely dry on Hall's divorce decree, the marriage license revealing that it became final earlier that same day. Maggie did not invite her parents, who had been less than enthusiastic about the nuptials. She did not get on with her disapproving mother. And her father, who took a dim view of the age gap between his daughter and the general, had been rather too vehement in letting Hall know that his intentions had better be good.

News of their elopement, along with a smiling portrait of the newlyweds, made the front page of papers around the world. The *Tribune* announced, "Marguerite Higgins Becomes a Bride." *Time* reported that the dauntless correspondent had once vowed: "I will marry only when I find a man as exciting as war."

They spent their honeymoon in Novato, California, in the small, ivy-covered cottage Hall had rented by the base. They were both too over-scheduled and underfunded to go anywhere. After much debate and discussion, Hall had decided to retire from the air force and look for a new line of work, possibly in the private sector. As soon as the powers-that-be made it official, they planned to head back east. Maggie was anxious to return to the *Trib*—and she needed the paycheck. The divorce had cleaned Hall out. Under the alimony agreement 80 percent of his income would go to his ex-wife and children. "This was not begrudged," Maggie wrote, "but it meant that I had no choice but to make a very substantial contribution to our mutual finances."

The day before she left for Reno, Maggie wrote a typically candid letter to Helen Reid about her situation:

> Since I consider the *Herald Tribune* to be a kind of family,
> I wanted to be sure to inform you, before the columnists
> did, that I am marrying General Hall.
>
> I also wanted to tell you that the marriage will not, so

far as we are concerned, affect my plans for resuming my work with the *Herald Tribune* very shortly. I see no point in being coy about our problems. Briefly they stem from the fact that Bill's alimony leaves him less per month than I used to earn per week. So even if I wanted to stop being a reporter—which I don't—I couldn't.

Despite all the manifold difficulties, we decided to go ahead with our marriage on the theory that it was better to face the difficulties as a team than apart. . . .

I'm looking forward to being back in New York. I detest California, but I'll have to admit the weather has been wonderful and at last I appear to be completely cured of all my ills including the sinus. This bout with the bugs has been quite an exhausting one and I'm glad that particular battle is over.

Maggie's tone was one of muted defiance and weary realism. Her personal woes and professional struggles had worn her down. She had learned that money and fame could not shield her from unhappiness. At the start of her career, she had been so set on achieving her goals that she had unhesitatingly accepted the demands of the job. She did not care that being a peripatetic foreign correspondent was inimical to long relationships, or that "aloneness was the price." Now she felt differently. Women did not age well in the profession, and she was haunted by the spectacle of some of the older female correspondents she knew who were divorced, beginning to show the miles, and becoming messy drunks. She could see herself in them ten years hence, and it scared her. She would not, if she could help it, end up that way. She did not want to "live so narrowly, having to do without the bonds of love."

When she was younger, she had been filled with such a great sense of injustice that she had raged against anyone or anything that got in her way. She was older now, and knew life was not fair, especially if you were a woman. She was fully prepared to compromise, to cut back, and stay closer to home, in order to have the family she desperately wanted.

It was with a half-amused self-awareness that she observed her altered approach to life: "I used to feel aggrieved when things went very wrong," she reflected wryly. "Now I feel astonished (and sometimes suspicious) when things go very right. The practical and rather steadying result is that when the kicks, inevitably, are delivered, I am better braced."

14

✳✳✳✳✳✳✳✳✳

Between the Lines

Time to play—After 12 years of following war,
revolution and peace conferences all over the
world, reporter Marguerite Higgins is finding
time for quieter pursuits these days. Her favorite
form of relaxation is tending her garden.

—*Washington Post*, March 11, 1956

IN FEBRUARY OF 1953, MAGGIE WROTE TO CARL MYDANS OF SET-
tling into a surprisingly contented life as a general's wife: "Here I am living, believe it or not, on an Air Force post!" Hall had been appointed
vice commander of the Continental Air Command at Mitchel Air Force
Base, responsible for overseeing both the Air Force Reserve and National
Guard programs nationwide. After all that time roughing it on army
bases in Korea, she had come home to one on Long Island, of all places,
albeit one with the cushy atmosphere of a military country club.

Sounding determinedly upbeat, she told him that the *Trib* had given
her "a very easy assignment," so she could enjoy the leisurely routine of
a roving correspondent and pundit. She would do one major interview
a week, with a national or international figure of her own choosing. In
addition, she would write two columns, with some topics expanded for
the editorial page. Her exclusives could "range from Taft to Tito," so she
expected to begin traveling again soon. She was planning a trip to the Far
East, and another to Europe. What she did not say was that in exchange

for her flexible schedule she had been forced to take a pay cut, but Mydans would have guessed as much. The *Trib*'s bottom line was in bad shape. The ranks of foreign correspondents were being trimmed. Old-timers complained that the inexperienced Reid sons, Whitie and Brownie, were running the business into the ground. Every week there was a new rumor—the paper was up for sale, a merger was in the works, investors were being sought.

Between the lines, Maggie sounded restless, and a bit bored. "Bill and I are getting along pretty much as one would expect," she added dryly at the end of the letter, "and I'm going to let you figure that one out for yourself."

She and Hall were polar opposites, and living together necessitated some adjustments on both their parts. While he was an early riser, neat and punctilious, a creature of barracks life, she lived in a state of sustained chaos. Her office was filled with cascading stacks of books, newspapers, and magazines. "I'm so organized I never get anything done," he observed. "She was so totally disorganized everything would fall right into place. I never knew what time of day she was going to get up, or *if*, because every-thing was dictated by what she had in mind, what she was working on." Maggie stayed up late. She slept in. "No schedule. Liable to work *all night. Anytime*," he said, drawing out the words for emphasis.

At the start of their relationship, they were not quite as in sync politically as she led people to believe. They were both big personalities, with strong views. Their arguments could get loud. "We had our politi-cal quarrels," said Hall, a died-in-the-wool Oklahoma conservative and 32nd Degree Freemason and proud of it. "She told me I was so far to the right she couldn't even see me at times," he said with a laugh. Maggie had been a "screaming liberal" in her college days, but Hall believed that as she saw more of the world and matured, she had come round to his way of thinking. Their views had become closer. She still had her "causes," and wrote checks for the needy—she could be breathtakingly gener-ous to the war widows and orphans she encountered—but they were "in total agreement" about what should be done to counter the Soviet threat. In the months after their marriage, her increasing identification with his hawkish nationalism and hard-line foreign policy was evident in her lectures and magazine articles, which were devoted to the communist menace.

Maggie stayed in Long Island most of that winter, playing house with Hall and phoning in her assignments. She did a timely interview with Chiang Kai-Shek, who called on the free world to give "moral and material support" to an all-out war with communist-held mainland China, which he argued was "a fundamental step toward ending the Korean war." This "exclusive statement" was obtained from Taiwan via New York, with Maggie cabling her questions, printing his cabled responses, and fleshing out the story with insights gleaned from their previous meetings. For several months, she managed to get away with this sleight of hand, conducting long-distance interviews with heads of state and foreign ambassadors without ever getting on a plane. But it made her feel like a sedentary hack. She worried her reputation was not what it was when she was filing dramatic dispatches from the front.

She was buoyed by a droll note from Mydans congratulating her on getting the Chiang scoop without leaving home, joking about what all those "high-priced" foreign correspondents in Taiwan were telling their editors when she pulled off the exclusive from an Air Force base in New York. "I've been reading you My Dear, all that the Paris Tribune will carry of yours," he wrote, "and I am not surprised to say you're a Hell of a reporter. I'll even confess I miss you."

She was frustrated by what she perceived as the *Tribune's* reluctance to allow her to transition from foreign correspondent to foreign affairs columnist. The paper had "more or less condescended" to let her start with the interview series, she complained to Lucius Clay, her husband's former boss and now a close friend. She was trying to persuade her editors that all her years of experience overseas, most of which had been spent documenting communist aggression in Europe and Asia, "could be put to some use in this country." In April, the *Trib* announced a new Cold War series by Higgins, but these were short contracts and did not pay well.

Maggie felt like she was in a career slump and her self-esteem sank. She was laboring over another book for Ken McCormick, who was now married to her old friend Mackie. It was taking longer than anticipated, and seemed to be turning into a midlife autobiography. The audit of her early achievements was making her feel like a has-been. Raised in the city room, and almost neurotically obsessed with status and byline success, Maggie was depressed by how much her stock had fallen.

Her father, aware she was floundering, tried to cheer her on. "I don't agree with you as to your status in the journalistic world," he wrote. "I think everybody here thinks that considering the fact that you have been back barely 4 months that you have done a fine job under very *difficult circumstances*," and he heavily underlined his penciled scrawl for emphasis. "This is a *flat period professionally*, but time and patience will take care of the situation."

He told her not to worry about money. Now a prosperous securities broker, Larry had taken on the role of financial adviser to his spendthrift daughter. He had persuaded her to put some of her book earnings into property to take advantage of the postwar real estate boom, including the purchase of a small townhouse in Washington, DC. While her portfolio was steadily accruing in value, the mortgage payments still had to be met, and he offered a small loan to tide her over. The letter was signed, "Loads of love, Daddy."

That spring brought a new crop of journalism prizes, which gave her ego a badly needed boost, and galvanized her to get back in the saddle. She was particularly pleased to win a second Polk Award for foreign coverage, which commended her as a "daring, restless reporter ... [who] made bold and unprecedented expeditions behind enemy lines and returned with some of the outstanding stories to come of the bloody war in Asia." Homer Bigart had also been designated twice in the past, which made it that much sweeter.

By June, she was back in Korea, her fifth trip to the embattled country, to report on the peace talks. After two years of protracted and complex negotiations, Eisenhower and his team had finally managed to reach a settlement. But there was little to celebrate: the fighting in Korea would end, after more than three years and 140,000 American casualties, but the wider struggle against communism in the region was far from over.

Eisenhower, in a somber speech, told Americans this was merely "an armistice on a single battleground—not peace in the world."

Outside the new straw-thatched pagoda at P'anmunjom, which had been built specially for the occasion, Maggie gathered with several of the old gang of correspondents to watch the UN delegates sign the historic document. She had managed to immediately antagonize the Eighth Army censors by refusing to submit her interview with the president of South Korea, a story that one press officer characterized as "a typical piece of inflammatory Rhee propaganda." In the article, the stubborn seventy-eight-year-old patriot threatened to oppose any truce that would divide his country, and said South Korea was prepared to "proceed on its own." His threat to continue fighting caught the administration off guard and caused a measure of anguish until he could be placated. Ultimately, Rhee's objections were overcome, and in deference to Maggie's stature, her indiscretion was diplomatically ignored.

For the next two and a half months, she reported from Japan, Taiwan, Hong Kong, and China—with Nationalist guerillas on the Shang Ta Chen islands near Shanghai. Then on to cover France's long, losing effort to maintain its colonial empire in Indochina, which it had occupied since the late nineteenth century. She returned in late August, weary, and visibly pregnant. The baby was due in December.

On October 9, Maggie went into labor two months early. She gave birth to a daughter, Sharon Lee Hall, at Harkness Pavilion at New York–Presbyterian Hospital. Although premature, Sharon weighed almost four pounds, and the doctors gave her a fighting chance. When Maggie and Bill went to admire her through the glass partition that separated them from the small preemie incubators, they were overwhelmed—she was an adorable baby, with black hair, long lashes, and smooth pink skin.

Five days later, Maggie was awakened by a nurse and a white-coated doctor at 4:30 in the morning and told that her baby was in distress. They were administering oxygen. Maggie watched as Sharon struggled to breathe, gasping hard, every breath emptying her tiny diaphragm, and then on the intake expanding and pulling her skin taut against her bird-like ribs. She fought a gallant battle, but it was over in two hours. After

Sharon died, all Maggie could think was that she never even held her baby daughter in her arms.

She spent the weeks that followed, she told a friend, in a "haze of hurt, self-accusation and bewilderment." She wrote in her memoir of wallowing in self-pity. Nothing was of any comfort:

> At the time, my body was still torn and bruised from the birth of the child. But it was nothing to the wounds of the heart. There was nothing new, and certainly nothing brave, in my reactions. Over and over I put the question that has been asked through the ages and will be asked through other ages because it is not answerable by humankind: "what sense is there in a universe that took the life of a beautiful, perfectly formed little child who was deeply loved and deeply wanted?"

"It was an awful blow to Marguerite," recalled her husband. "It was her first child and she wasn't any youngster. And the baby was beautiful." After Sharon died, Maggie went back to church. All her adult life, she had rebelled against her mother's Catholicism and rejected the dogmatic tenets. But now she needed faith, if only to find a way to cope. She may have been in need of absolution, to rid herself of the burden of guilt and pain that accompanies such a loss. "It was the first time I saw that [spiritual side of her]," said Bill Hall. "After that, whenever she got in trouble, she would turn back to religion."

The birth notices had been published in all the papers. In the days and weeks that followed, Winchell and other columnists printed the sad tidings of the baby's passing. Whitie Reid and his wife, Joan, sent their condolences. The pile of notes and letters from friends and admirers grew. Like many public figures, who do not have the luxury of mourning in private, Maggie worked through her shock and grief by writing about the experience. "As Sharon died, I made the discovery that I had seen death, yet I had not known it," she wrote in a raw, emotional essay for *Good Housekeeping.* She had been sorry for the thousands she had seen die in Korea, "but sorry in a detached way." Castigating herself for her faults as a mother, she thrashed herself in print for not comprehending the tears of the bereaved as a reporter, "for I had not known the meaning of compassion."

Anyone in the public eye can confirm the pain of glib pronouncements on personal tragedies. Many of her newspaper colleagues were critical of her work habits. Some even suggested that she had somehow brought this on herself by bouncing all over the globe while expecting. The newsroom jokes that made Bigart a favorite with his colleagues still hung in the air. On first being told Maggie was pregnant, he had joked, "Oh, g-good. And wh-wh who is the mother?" When the baby was born, he cheerily inquired if the mother had "devoured her young." A witty man, warm and generous to friends, Bigart could also be cruel, one coworker recalling that he knew how to perfectly time his stammer to yield the most laughs.

Bigart's remarks, which he later surely would have liked to retract, revealed the extent to which he did not like being shown up by a woman correspondent. Thirty years later he conceded, "No way I can make my behavior toward her appear in a favorable light." But in the fifties, women who operated so far outside the norms of society were easy objects of ridicule. Maggie had bumped up against the limits of what was considered appropriate for a woman, and her choices were harshly judged.

Throughout it all, Maggie was stoical. A week after losing the baby, she traveled to Richmond, Virginia, where she spoke to a women's club audience. She looked thin and drawn, but put on a brave smile for the photographer. Four days later, her poise still shaky, she was in Pennsylvania, to collect an honorary degree from Lafayette College. Sharing the stage with her were Gen. Matthew Ridgway, U.S. Army chief of staff, and Admiral William F. Halsey, a hero of the Pacific war. At her side was Hall, who had been named assistant chief of staff for reserve forces and assigned to U.S. Air Force headquarters in Washington, DC.

WITH BILL TRANSFERRED TO the capital, they had to move again that fall. It would be a fresh start for them both. Fortunately, Maggie had the little one-story white brick row house at 1693 Thirty-Fourth Street in Georgetown that she had bought as an investment with her book advance. As soon as the tenants vacated the premises, she set about turning it into a beautiful, welcoming home, and someplace Hall's children would enjoy visiting on weekends.

The house was formerly the guest wing of "Friendship," the old Evalyn Walsh McLean mansion, and guests used to promenade through the wide hall and massive oaken doors to the ballroom. It had since been remodeled, and now the heavy doors opened onto a disproportionately small dining room. But there was a book-lined den, where Maggie kept her awards, a top-of-the-line record player, and shelves and shelves filled with her huge record collection. The furniture was white and starkly modern, serving as a backdrop for the souvenirs of her travels—inlaid Japanese cabinets, three-hundred-year-old Chinese wall tapestries, and richly colored silk rugs. She also designed the small back garden in an Oriental style, planting bamboo, Chinese fringe trees, and dozens of Japanese azaleas.

Maggie was a passionate woman, and it was with the same fervor and glorious zeal Hall had seen on display in Berlin that she now devoted herself to making a home for them in Washington. "Everything she did, she did with the same enthusiasm," he said, recalling the novelty of her domestic impulses. Improbably, she enjoyed gardening. "She was very good at it. We had a whole roomful of books on gardening. Every damn one of which she read and remembered what was in them." She quickly accumulated a menagerie of pets. Reno the dog, adopted after their impromptu nuptials, was joined by the first of four cats, a big buck rabbit, and an antisocial parakeet named Fred Unfriendly (after Murrow's CBS producer, Fred W. Friendly). She clucked over them like a mother hen. "She loved animals," said Hall. "We had them all over the place."

Maggie had a traditional feminine side, a desire to nurture and nest that belied her driven war-correspondent image, and she happily played hostess, pondered menus, and tried out new recipes. She was a proficient cook, though she was too busy to bother most of the time, but she always maintained a good staff to clean, make the beds, and cater her popular buffet suppers. "She loved having a well-run house," said Hall. "And it was never empty. We must have entertained or been entertained damned near every night. It was a pretty hectic circuit at times."

Their cobblestoned Georgetown neighborhood was a haven for journalists. Ruth Montgomery and her husband, Robert, deputy chief of the Small Business Administration, lived next door and shared an adjoining garden, and the two couples became inseparable. Her debonair *Tribune* colleague Joe Alsop had a lavish home on Dumbarton Avenue, which was the scene of convivial dinner parties with politicians, foreign dignitaries, intelligence officers, intellectuals, and society figures. Together with his brother Stewart, he wrote the much-quoted column "Matter of Fact," which appeared in more than two hundred newspapers. Hall once observed that Joe's parties were like transactional summits with cocktails and canapés.

Maggie thrived in Washington's social milieu. Since everyone in town was more or less in the same business—politics—national and international policy issues dominated every conversation, so that work enveloped their lives. An early guide to this vortex of power and privilege was the tall, sophisticated Letitia "Tish" Baldrige, who had worked as secretary to Clare Boothe Luce. Baldridge was also friends with Ruth Montgomery, and they helped Maggie to make important political and social connections, to develop sources, and to become something of a local personage in her own right. It was the first time in her life that she cultivated close friendships with women whom she genuinely liked and admired. She was older now, wiser, and consciously trying to be nicer.

Maggie wowed the stuffy Georgetown set with her wit and verve and lack of pretension. In a roomful of mascaraed ladies, only she was without the heavy eye makeup and elaborate teased and combed updo that were then in vogue. Her forte was her naturalness, from her scrubbed complexion to her complete lack of artifice. She was gorgeous, casual, and self-possessed. "I recall being very impressed with Marguerite when I first met her at a cocktail party at the Montgomerys," recalled Hope Ridings Miller, the genteel former society editor of the *Washington Post* and newly appointed editor of *The Diplomat* magazine, where Maggie soon became a contributing author.

Effortlessly chic in a narrow Chinese silk shift, Maggie had held forth on a variety of subjects from world affairs to foreign travel and fashion. She spoke animatedly about Hong Kong and how she tried to get back there as often as possible to shop, purchasing all her shoes there—handmade—which made her the envy of all the ladies present. She insisted her favorite city was Paris, and one of her ambitions in life was to own a Latin Quarter bistro patronized by writers and artists. "Everyone in the circle of journalists in which I moved respected her ability," said Miller, "and was impressed with her forceful personality."

Washington was the nation's nerve center, and Maggie, who was looking for new worlds to conquer, was delighted to be there. At the same time, she was dismayed by the antediluvian attitude toward women in the corridors of power, where even distinguished female columnists were treated as second-class citizens. In some ways it was worse than dealing with the army. Women were barred from membership in the National Press Club and the Gridiron Club, and even from attending the White House Correspondents Dinner. Ruth Montgomery, who came to the city in 1943 as the first woman member of the Washington bureau of the *New York Daily News*, shared Maggie's disgust with the pervasive chauvinism of the capital press corps. But neither of them allowed the discrimination to hold them back. "Both of us seemed to do better in our profession and received higher salaries than most of the men reporters," she noted in the decided tone of a woman with a healthy view of her own worth.

In the fall, Maggie was invited to appear on the prestigious news program *Meet the Press*. She relished the chance to join the elite circle of on-air interrogators. The program was created by her friend Martha Rountree, a pioneering journalist and broadcaster, whose previous hit, *Leave It to the Girls*, was a panel show where Maggie had been a frequent guest. The December 13 installment of *Meet the Press* featured Senator Joseph McCarthy, billed as "America's most controversial figure." Maggie, wearing a fixed smile, and speaking in her breathy little-girl voice, asked the rabble-rousing demagogue whether American policy toward the Soviet Union, which had achieved nuclear parity, was too soft. Her query drew a scowling response: "The answer, Miss Higgins, is no." Two quick follow-up questions drew the same monosyllabic reply.

Maggie was not a natural on TV. She sat there stiff as a Saks Fifth Avenue mannequin in her pearls, her dulcet voice and sweet demeanor strangely at odds with her persistent interrogation. She presented quite a contrast to May Craig, the stern silver-haired Gannett reporter, known for her "Inside Washington" column, whose bristling manner signaled her indignation at every word McCarthy uttered. Maggie was not a firebrand of the same order, but she was articulate, nimble, and managed to pose some nettlesome questions. She made enough of an impression to be asked back many times.

Five days later, she was the featured guest on Murrow's new television show, *Person to Person*. Smiling demurely like a fifties housewife who has just been complimented on her casserole, Maggie fielded questions about her life and career, and the war in Korea. She would become a familiar face on television in the fifties, even making an appearance on the popular celebrity guessing game, *What's My Line?*, where the actress Arlene Francis made quick work of identifying her as the star *New York Herald Tribune* correspondent.

Where Maggie had once wanted fame, she now craved influence. It was a Washington disease. What she needed was not to be better known but to be more highly regarded as an expert in her field. She decided to shore up her Cold War credentials, and applied for a Guggenheim Fellowship to underwrite a journalistic mission to the Soviet Union. Part of her rationale for going to Russia was that by establishing herself as an authority on the communist threat, she would be better placed to negotiate a lucrative contract as a syndicated columnist. Word had it that the sixty-year-old Dorothy Thompson, whose column alternated with Lippmann's at the *Trib*, was in decline—and that she had become too much of a crabby propagandist for her leftist point of view. Some papers had begun dropping her "On the Record" column. Maggie was busy fashioning herself as a younger, more conservative alternative for the Eisenhower era.

She needed the syndication money to underwrite her increasingly expensive lifestyle. On a whim, she had bought a $21,000 share in a new

Jamaican resort called Round Hill, complete with a villa overlooking Montego Bay. It was a somewhat risky endeavor—a "pleasant insanity," as she put it. A socially connected hotelier named John Pringle carved the hundred-acre development, on a private peninsula, out of a former coconut plantation. Round Hill was the first luxury retreat of its kind in the Caribbean, but she had been assured that it would quickly turn a profit. Maggie and Bill had fallen in love with the place on their first visit, and were persuaded to invest another $9,000 in one of the whitewashed "cottages" that dotted the hillside.

In 1953, Round Hill opened with Noel Coward as its first customer. That fall, John F. Kennedy, the boyishly handsome freshman senator from Massachusetts, honeymooned at Round Hill with his beautiful bride, Jacqueline. The Halls flew down for the holiday season, returning for several visits over the winter. But before the finishing touches were put on their cottage, Maggie wrote to Pringle that she was forced to "retreat from the Round Hill project." The long illness following the loss of her baby meant that their finances had suffered a setback. "Not being one of your tycoons but a mere working gal," she noted frankly, "I don't have the margin of safety and flexibility I'd like."

To help supplement her income, Maggie began endorsing products for advertisers, lending her name to commercials for a slew of products, everything from Packard cars and Rolex watches to Camel cigarettes. At the time, many well-known journalists, from Edward R. Murrow to Dorothy Kilgallen, pitched products for the companies that sponsored their radio and television shows. The *Trib*'s syndicate manager, Bill Weeks, even sent Maggie a note saying he thought her Camel ad was "mighty pretty." The camera loved her, but he advised her to think twice about doing a TV spot until she had improved her acting skills.

By the year's end, even her movie prospects were looking up. Mrs. Lela Rogers, mother and manager of the Hollywood star Ginger Rogers, was interested in making a film based on Maggie's book about her adventures as a war correspondent in Korea. A successful screenwriter and producer, Lela Rogers was also negotiating for Ginger to star in a European television series—in color—about the reporter's life. "Contracts are now being drawn up," a Hollywood columnist reported in his weekly run-down of industry gossip.

The Maggie Higgins Story never materialized, on either the large or small screen. Why the project fell through is unclear, though Maggie had quibbled with the terms of the deal. She was also worried about the script, especially the suggestion that parts of her personal history might be fictionalized to make it more dramatic. In one letter during the negotiations, she wrote Lela Rogers that she had been thinking about the proposed narrative arc showing "the tough woman correspondent who softens in the end," which was actually the reverse of what happened.

To Maggie, it was no trifling matter. She wanted the story told as she saw it: "Why not have everybody more as they were—men hostile to the idea of a woman war correspondent, and then have the love interest melt when the woman went out on patrol and behaved courageously."

15

✳ ✳ ✳ ✳ ✳ ✳ ✳ ✳

The Fine Print

> So well-known had she become that her articles
> generally bore her name not merely as a byline
> but in the headline. A typical dispatch of hers
> out of Hong Kong carried a "kicker" or smaller,
> underscored italic line reading "Marguerite Higgins
> Reports" followed by the main, larger head,
> "Russia Sending Peking Long-Range Bombers."
>
> —Richard Kluger, *The Paper*

IN THE SPRING OF 1954, MAGGIE WAS BACK IN VIETNAM COVER-
ing the last agonies of the Indochina War for the *Tribune*. She reunited
with her old jeep jockey, Keyes Beech, and together they drove out to
inspect a quiet village near Hanoi that was controlled by the straw-hatted
Franco-Vietnamese militia. The governor of North Vietnam, Nguyen
Huu Tri, was pleading for more military assistance to repulse the communist rebels, and he wanted to show the American reporters that the
civilian population was predominantly on his side. "As if to underline
the absurdity of our mission," Beech recalled, "we rode in a red Chevrolet
convertible driven by the governor's secretary. The top was down."

   To the two correspondents, there was something dreadfully familiar
about it all. During the war in Korea, they had commuted frequently to
the war in Vietnam, which seemed like another front in the same struggle. "Here we go again," said Beech, heading once more into the fray.

The French were struggling to retain their old colonial interests in Vietnam. The U.S. was supporting them in what the Eisenhower administration viewed as an anti-colonial war to prevent a new aggressive imperial power, the Chinese communists, from taking over. Meanwhile, Ho Chi Minh, a wily, dedicated nationalist leader who had declared Vietnam's independence at the end of World War II, was fighting to free his country from foreign control. The problem was that Ho Chi Minh was also a communist—trained by the Soviets, and aided by the Chinese. The U.S. regarded him, and his communist forces, the Viet Minh, as a threat.

Vietnam was a muddle. America was once again trying to draw a line in the sand. But trying to make sense of the complex political and military issues in the region, and figure out whom to trust, was an almost impossible task. To Maggie, it looked as if the enchanting tropical land where she had been taken as an ailing baby, and where her grandfather had died fighting with the French colonial forces, was being torn apart by another pointless civil war. "It seemed to me that the villagers of Vietnam have about the same attitude that the villagers of Korea used to have," she wrote. "They would like to be left alone to cultivate their rice."

On May 7, Dien Bien Phu, a heavily fortified French village in northern Vietnam near the Laos border, finally surrendered after an eight-week siege with the communist insurgents. A red flag was hoisted over the French command post. The battle ended eight years of struggle between the French and the Vietnamese nationalist forces, and it marked the end of seventy-five years of French colonial rule in Indochina. It was a decisive military and propaganda victory by the communists—a small feudal country had beaten a great European nation.

Maggie was in Hanoi when news came that at the international conference underway in Geneva to resolve the problems in Asia, the French had agreed to withdraw their troops from northern Vietnam. Vietnam would be temporarily divided along the 17th parallel, between the Communist North and the South, pending elections in two years to choose a president and unite the country. Ho Chi Minh reluctantly signed the Geneva Agreements, even though he felt he was denied the spoils of victory. The noncommunist puppet government in South Vietnam, set up under the new premier Ngo Dinh Diem, a fanatical nationalist and devout Catholic, refused to sign, but without the French military its opposition meant little.

The U.S. also refused to sign, privately viewing the outcome a disaster, but it agreed to abide by the accords. Diem was hardly an ideal choice to lead the new South Vietnam—a French-educated Catholic was never going to win much popular support in a predominantly Buddhist country—but the U.S., with no clear alternative, was committed to bolstering his fledgling government, and sent in the first of two hundred military advisers.

At the time, few Americans could identify French Indochina. Weary of years of war, they had little interest in carrying on the fight. But the fear that this defeat might signal to the world that communism was the wave of the future, and would send hordes of Chinese communists sweeping over Vietnam and the rest of Southeast Asia, suddenly rendered the situation in Indochina of critical importance. President Eisenhower described this ominous possibility as the "domino" effect, and it would become the prevailing theory that guided U.S. policy in Vietnam for the next decade. He believed America needed to act boldly to stop the Chinese and to preserve these vital areas from communist domination.

In the aftermath of the French capitulation, Maggie toured the strategic Red River delta, where she reported that "village after village is being lost by default to the communist enemy." She described the plight of nearly a million North Vietnamese refugees making an attempt to reach the sanctuary of the South. It was a dreary repeat of what she had seen in Korea.

On Tuesday, May 25, she went out with a French military convoy, along with a group of reporters, including the famed *Life* photographer Robert Capa, a friend through many conflicts. At Doai Than, the French flags had already been lowered at the old, crenellated Beau Geste–style fort, which was about to be demolished ahead of the advancing Viet Minh. They could hear heavy small-arms fire from a nearby village. Maggie was three jeeps away when Capa, who had wandered into a rice paddy for a better shot, stepped on a land mine and was killed.

Her editors at the *Tribune* asked her to stay in Indochina and continue following the developments there. But Maggie had just received
word that she had been awarded a Guggenheim Fellowship for $5,000.
Her travel papers for the Soviet Union had been approved. As the first
American journalist to be issued a visa to visit Russia in the post-Stalin
era, the trip represented a unique opportunity—and one of the biggest
exclusives of her career. She wired Whitie Reid that she was sticking to
her original plan:

THINK INDOCHINA WILL BE STORY LONG TIME
WHEREAS OPPORTUNITY TO GO RUSSIA UNLIKELY
COME AGAIN STOP HIGGINS.

She returned to Washington in early July for a month's respite with
Bill. In mid-August, she would be taking off again for a ten-week tour of
Russia. She had just been away for ten weeks. It was a long time to be an
absent wife. She knew that if she stayed away long enough, there was a danger her husband would not be home when she got there. They were both
drinking too much and it led to terrible fights. Her nights were fueled by
martinis often chased with a morning bout of self-loathing. But Hall was
no paragon. There were the chronic infidelities—some woman or other was
always hovering on the periphery. His Pentagon duties also kept him on the
move, and their schedules were rarely in accord, so it often seemed that they
inhabited separate worlds. It was a worry, but it would ever be thus.

They had gone into the marriage with their eyes open and had vowed
to find a way to make it work and maintain their mutual regard. "If I
wasn't overseas, she was," said Hall. "Somebody was always gone. But we
were a little older than most in getting married, and we had a good deal of
respect for each other's privacy. I did a lot of things that she didn't know
about, she did a lot of things I didn't know about."

Like every woman correspondent of her generation, Maggie was forever being asked how she intended to keep a husband when she was continually running to catch a plane. Once, after watching her dancing at El
Morocco with a group of journalist friends, Harry Evans, the small, spry,

Georgia-born founder of *Family Circle*, had teased her about the "demon ambition" that possessed her very attractive form. She was a "paradoxical person," he mused, intrigued by the degree to which her femininity disguised a ferocious drive to succeed.

In his subsequent magazine profile of her, Evans observed that Maggie was "a social freak, a complete contradiction of every rule in the book governing the social reflexes and behavior pattern of the successful female." Despite her brutal endeavors, she showed no outward signs of wear and tear, nothing of the "hard, masculine edge." He went on to predict that she was in for an ordeal, because it was going to be difficult to continue being so agreeable in her private life and ruthless at work. He framed her predicament for his magazine's readers: "What does a career woman sacrifice for what she wins?"

Maggie had been annoyed at the time, but he had gotten to the heart of the matter. "But was it really worth it?" the clubwomen would always ask after one of her lectures. "Such a question, it seems to me, presupposes some ready alternative," she wrote in exasperation. "As if one could approach life like a Horn and Hardart cafeteria, and after depositing the right coin emerge with a pleasantly laden tray consisting of 'nice husband, nice home, happy marriage.'" At this point, she was resigned to the idea that her life, personally and professionally, would continue to be a bumpy ride—"rough, but interesting." Her response to problems at home was to burrow into work. She and Bill usually solved their problems with distance, so it seemed to her that this was probably the best frame of mind in which to depart for an extended tour of Russia.

She also wanted to get out of Dodge. Another scandalous roman à clef had just been published featuring a "five-star bitch"—said to be some ungodly combination of Higgins and Clare Boothe Luce—who roiled the newsroom of a fictional New York newspaper. The book, *The Iron Maiden*, written by a *Trib* copyeditor turned novelist named Edwin Lanham, was the talk of the Washington bureau and the delight of Georgetown dinner parties. A review in the *Times* that August noted, "In the course of the story some brilliant little facets of newspapers and newspaper folk are polished off."

Lanham had known Maggie back in the early days. Many people thought they recognized her in the description of the main protagonist of his novel, a cunning girl reporter named Carolyn Brown: "She was as lustrous as storm-kissed kelp, with eyes a clear and exciting blue, a smile that was gentle and shy and intimate, with a way of walking and moving that reminded every muscle in her body that it had a function." The editors liked to use her as "a catalyst," he wrote. "Where Carolyn went, something usually happened." There was lots of sex, and lots of spurned lovers—Lanham was rumored to be one—whom she dropped after they outlived their usefulness and then "drove the spikes in."

Maggie had had enough of being cast as the alluring and destructive newsroom siren. The idea that the old rumor mill was starting up again drove her to despair. After the permissiveness of the war years, the country had become more prudish, and she fretted that the gossip about her florid love life would undermine her reputation. Publicly, she held her head high, but privately she admitted it made her miserable. She seemed to attract the kind of enemies who liked to settle old scores. "She shrank from controversies," said her old friend Peter Lisagor, who had joined the Washington bureau of the *Chicago Daily News* and occupied a neighboring office in the National Press Building. "She just did not want to go through the [whole] business again."

She needed to get away. As she prepared to go on the road, her spirits lifted. There was the familiar thrum in her veins, the rising of the blood, which she recognized as "the exhilaration and excitement that accompany the prospect of a big journalistic opportunity." She always felt most herself in pursuit of an important story.

There was also an element of uncertainty. Reporting from Korea was not without risk, but she knew where the battle lines were; in Russia, there would be no lines, no safe haven. As a Western journalist, she could expect her every move to be closely monitored by the secret police. TASS, Russia's state-owned news agency, had once labeled her a "hyena of the press" for her rabid anticommunist views, which would make Maggie even more suspect than most reporters.

On her last night in her Helsinki hotel on August 24, she took the precaution of notifying the American minister in Moscow of her itinerary, so that if he received no word of her safe arrival he could begin checking with Russian officials on her whereabouts. Having lost none of her flair for drama, she then sat down and wrote out a prepared statement, signed it, and mailed it to a contact in the State Department. It would later serve as the opening paragraph of her book about her adventure in the hostile East.

To Whom It May Concern:

> This is being written to counteract any statements made by me in the event that I should be arrested in the Soviet Union. This letter constitutes advance denial of any injurious utterances whatsoever against the United States that might be attributed to or actually delivered by me as a result of duress or torture.

> Sincerely,
> Marguerite Higgins

Maggie's trip lasted two and a half months and took her 13,500 miles around the Soviet Union, including Siberia, Soviet Central Asia, the Caucasus, White Russia, and Ukraine. Many of the places she visited, such as Samarkand, Yalta, and Simferopol, had been forbidden areas until very recently. She had taken a crash course in Russian, knowing she would need to rely on her language skills if she had any hope of drawing back the curtain on everyday life under the new Soviet premier, Nikita Khrushchev. Before she was done, she filled fifteen notebooks with her observations of the long-suffering Russian people, who had to endure the mass regimentation and restrictions of an all-pervasive police state. She was arrested sixteen times—usually for taking pictures with the little Lubitel camera she bought in Tashkent—something that got huge play back home.

Maggie's trip behind the Iron Curtain was another journalistic coup.

Just as she had hoped, her solo journey greatly added to her fame and stature as a Cold War correspondent. In one of several promotional editorials, the *Trib* applauded her success in piercing the veil of the mysterious East: "Miss Higgins herself represents a new aspect of Russian policy—an American, without obvious surveillance, photographing her way through the secret heart of the U.S.S.R."

The *Washington Post, Times Herald*, and hundreds of other newspapers across the country ran her series of fourteen articles, illustrated with her own photos. *Reader's Digest* ran excerpts, and *Woman's Home Companion* printed another travelogue that appeared as Higgins's "Russian Diary." She spun off still other parts of her reporting for *U.S. News & World Report*, which she was assiduously courting if and when she had to leave the *Tribune*. Maggie hastily converted her articles and diaries into a book, *Red Plush and Black Bread*, which was published a year later, setting another speed record in publishing history.

By the time Maggie returned to work in the spring of 1955, she found the *Trib* in turmoil, and in the midst of generational change. Helen Reid, age seventy-two, had announced she was retiring to give her sons a chance at running the paper. However, because of his dubious handling of the paper's financial problems, Whitie was getting the boot. He would be yielding his position as president and publisher to his much younger brother, twenty-nine-year-old Brownie.

Many reporters resisted the change, even though there was no doubt that if the business did not improve the old *Trib* was done for. Brownie had already begun making changes in an attempt to reinvigorate the paper and attract more advertising, but not everyone liked the zippy new tabloid, with its mint-green sports section, and focus on crime stories, contests, and quizzes. There was unrest among the rank and file as the paper eased up on solid reporting and writing in favor of frothy features. Close to twenty reporters had left the city room alone, as well as some illustrious correspondents. Bigart, appalled at the changes, defected to the *Times*.

So it was with the dark-haired, fast-talking Brownie, an ex-paratrooper who was in every way the opposite of his quiet, thoughtful ex-Navy aviator brother, that Maggie had to negotiate her future at the paper. After much back-and-forth, she agreed to produce a column focusing on the Cold War that would appear every Monday on the editorial page, and to be available—anytime, anywhere—for "special spot assignments." Brownie had wanted her to do another stint abroad, but Maggie was determined to spend more time at home with her husband. There had been too many rows and the cracks were beginning to show in their relationship. She got her way. The *Trib*'s longtime editors watched with dismay as she rolled over their boy publisher like a tank crushing new growth in its path.

On May 16, Maggie took her place in the Washington bureau as a somewhat glorified diplomatic correspondent. She was greeted warily by the new bureau chief, Walter Kerr, the bright, tightly wound former foreign editor with whom she had sparred on more than one occasion. Aware of her reputation as an inveterate poacher, Kerr reminded Maggie of the complications that could arise when working alongside reporters in close quarters. That said, "I let her cover any story she wanted, because she had contacts in the State Department and at the Pentagon, provided there was no encroachment on another member of staff," he recalled. "I asked only that she clear her intention. So far as I remember, she always did."

The timing of her arrival was not ideal. Her autobiography, *News Is a Singular Thing*, was published that month to enthusiastic reviews and another avalanche of publicity. But even the write-up in her own paper credited her success primarily to her "competitive instinct," and described her, next to MacArthur, as "the most contentious personality to come out of the Korean war." Ditto the snippy *Times* review by Tania Long, who praised the book as a good primer for would-be reporters but noted that she had worked in competition with Higgins and emphasized her "burning ambition."

When Maggie strode into the *Trib*'s cramped offices in the National Press Building that spring, the air turned electric. Heads turned, knowing looks were exchanged. "Higgins was not admired by her colleagues, to put it mildly, especially her male colleagues," recalled Ben Bradlee, then a reporter in *Newsweek*'s Washington bureau. Everyone had heard the tales about her in Berlin, and then Korea, and the feud with the great Homer

Bigart. "The men charged that she got more than her share of exclusive stories in ways not available to them," he added, repeating what had become a tired cliché. Another colleague put it this way: "People either liked Marguerite or thoroughly detested her. There was no middle ground."

After spending the summer cranking out editorials praising German chancellor Konrad Adenauer's attempts to unify his country, and warning of the dangers of an illusory détente with Russia, she accompanied him to Moscow that autumn. While she was there, Maggie, as always, managed to make herself the center of the story by announcing that she had been granted a permanent visa to reestablish the *Tribune's* Moscow bureau. It was a major accomplishment: the paper had been without a bureau there since 1949, when its chief correspondent, Joseph Newman, left on a brief visit to Paris and was denied a reentry visa by the Soviet government. The *Trib* ran the news flash of Maggie's latest feat, accompanied by her picture.

On December 11, the *Tribune* debuted a new series of articles on the Soviet Union by Higgins, who had just returned from another three-month trip there. The first story, "Terror Still the Public Boss," describing her impressions of Khrushchev's velvet glove policy, ran on page one, next to a large photo of Maggie eating an ice-cream cone in Moscow. No other *Trib* reporter was allowed to make such frequent use of the perpendicular pronoun or was so frequently pictured in the paper.

U.S. News & World Report dedicated the better part of an entire issue to her insights on the new ruler in the Kremlin, with the magazine's board of editors putting questions to "one of the world's best-known reporters of international affairs." In the ten-page Q&A on "What the Top Russians Are Like," Maggie spoke of "having a nodding acquaintance with every member of the Politburo." She described Khrushchev as shrewd and engaging, but she saw that beneath the polished performance was a tough-minded, unmovable character. When asked to predict whether he would become an all-out dictator after the Party Congress in February, she quoted a Moscow diplomat who said, "Watching the top-level politics in Russia is like watching a dog fight under a blanket—you know something is going on, but you don't know just what."

Once again at the top of her game, Maggie moved to solidify her position at the *Trib*, which had been frustratingly uncertain for years. She informed her editors that the International News Service was wooing her with a better salary. They would have to top it if they wanted her to stay. Afraid to call her bluff, Brownie took the unusual step of giving her a special employment contract. Only hugely successful and influential syndicated columnists like Lippmann and Roscoe Drummond were rewarded with employment contracts. No staff reporter had ever enjoyed such a privileged position, except Maggie.

On January 19, 1956, she signed a two-year contract, with a two-year renewal clause, that would keep her at the *Tribune* for the foreseeable future. The key clause in the agreement defined her duties as "a Correspondent attached to the Washington Bureau...on White House assignments, or on top-flight assignments as mutually determined from time to time by the Editor of the *Herald Tribune* and the Author."

As bureau chief, Kerr was unaware Maggie had cut a special deal for herself. When Robert J. Donovan, the longtime White House correspondent, asked for a leave of absence to write a book about Eisenhower, Kerr offered the job to the *Trib*'s New York political reporter, Robert Mazo. The decision was approved by all the top editors. But when Maggie heard about it, she decided she wanted the White House beat for herself, and asked Kerr if she could discuss it with Brownie. Without explanation, Brownie reversed his decision and gave the job to Higgins. Kerr, who was never told of the language in her contract giving her first call on any assignment—he did not learn of it until decades later—felt betrayed and quit. "The circumstances were somewhat humiliating to me, because Mazo had sold his house and moved to Washington at my urging," recalled Kerr, who left to run the international edition.

Kerr's departure made Maggie even more of a divisive presence at the bureau. Various versions of his falling on his sword made the rounds, but always with her as the villain of the piece. When Bob Donovan returned, and later became head of the Washington operation, he took steps to curb the headstrong Higgins, who in his view "could not go on freewheeling the way she did with blow-ups all over the place."

Donovan would soon be called on to adjudicate another brouhaha involving Higgins, when the Standing Committee of the Congressional Press Gallery Correspondents revoked her membership on the grounds that her commercial endorsements violated their rules against "paid publicity or promotion work." Maggie had been caught plugging Crest toothpaste. She had pocketed the $500 fee and thought nothing of it until someone riffling through *Reader's Digest* saw the advertorial—"One Billion Unfilled Cavities Must Be Wrong"—and sent it to the committee.

Maggie apologized and huffily relinquished her press-gallery credentials, stating that she was unaware of the rules: "Shows you should always read the fine print, doesn't it." But she remained defiant, refusing to give up her advertising gig and insisting her outside jobs did not interfere with her newspaper work. She also took a jab at her colleagues who regularly appeared on "sponsored television panel shows," pointing out the obvious conflict of interest.

In his "Capitol Stuff" column, John O'Donnell, the older brother of her friend Jim, wondered why they were picking on the *Trib*'s golden-haired correspondent: "If the standing committee wants to kick out such a swell reporter as Maggie Higgins, we can suggest that they kick out about 50 or 75 other Washington reporters—including this one—who over the years have been picking up checks for $125 or $150 a show for appearing on sponsored tv and radio panels." This was not an issue her male colleagues wanted to raise because programs like *Meet the Press*, *Face the Nation*, and *Reporters Round-Up* were all welcome additions to their domestic budget. Now, because of Maggie, the whole issue would have to be probed. "Well, the boys asked for it," he concluded, "and we have a hunch she planned it that way."

A "Tempest in Toothpaste," decreed *Newsweek*, noting that Higgins "seems to make almost as much news as she reports." When reached for comment, she groaned, "Oh God! Not another controversy," apparently a reference to her recent dustup with Kerr.

Maggie did not let the contretemps cramp her style. As the *Tribune*'s undisputed star correspondent, she was used to generating good copy. Living in the Washington fishbowl meant the gossip columnists commented on everything she did, from her fashion choices, bountiful tulips at the annual Georgetown Garden Tour, and growing friendship with the Kennedys. Jack and Jackie were frequent guests at her popular dinner parties, and the younger Kennedys Robert ("Bobby") and Ethel were part of her Georgetown crowd and regular dog-walking companions.

Maggie continued her old practice of salon diplomacy, hosting intimate brunches and buffet suppers that brought people together, fostered alliances, and furthered her own interests. "She ran a helluva good Sunday salon," recalled Walter Cronkite, describing relaxed gatherings peppered with a mix of politicians and military types, and leading journalists like Bourke-White. Ruth Montgomery recalled a memorable night when Maggie's carefully laid plans to entertain JFK went awry: "Jacqueline arrived on time, as did an assortment of senators, but dinner cooled on the back burners while we waited for Jack to appear. Jackie became increasingly agitated, as she tried vainly to telephone him at his office, but he finally arrived with the casual explanation that he had been detained." Maggie was less understanding the next time, though this time it was Cronkite who was so late that he missed not only dinner but his meeting with Kennedy. Maggie was so angry that when she saw the tardy newsman standing in the doorway, she hurled a vase of flowers at his feet.

It was testament to her clout that only ten days after being reelected to office, President Eisenhower took the time to send his "personal commendation" to Maggie when she was feted by the American Woman's Association tribute to women in the press and presented with the Award for Eminent Achievement for foreign reporting. His message, which was read aloud to the gathering at the Waldorf Astoria, said in part: "There is no reporter more deserving of praise than Miss Marguerite Higgins. She gets the facts with courage, thoroughness and insight. Her service in Korea was in the highest tradition of American journalism, and by keeping the home front informed she added strength to the nation's will."

BY THE SPRING OF 1958, Maggie was expecting again. There was much rejoicing all around. Winchell noted in his column that Washington was buzzing about the anticipated "Blessed Event." On June 19, the

Halls welcomed the arrival of a healthy baby boy, Lawrence O'Higgins Hall, named for her father and using the original Irish spelling of the family name.

Maggie was determined the child would be christened and raised a good Catholic. "If you don't think we had some trouble," Hall said, noting that they were both divorced, and that he was no saint in anyone's book. "We finally went to Cardinal Spellman and he said, 'If those jerks in Washington won't do it, I'll send somebody down who will.'" The difficulties did not end there. Maggie had asked Ruth Montgomery to be the baby's godmother, but she had to obtain special dispensation because her friend was a Protestant. There were no objections to Ambassador Robert Murphy, a friend from their Berlin days, serving as godfather.

After the arrival of their son, the Halls found their Georgetown home was too small for a growing ménage that included a housekeeper and nanny, so they moved to an elegant four-story townhouse at 1832 Twenty-Fourth Street, just off Massachusetts Avenue. Maggie told everyone it was her dream house because it had once belonged to the bandmaster John Philip Sousa, famous for his military marches, but in reality it was in such poor repair they were able to pick it up for under $20,000. It had seemed like a good deal at the time, but Maggie proceeded to spend another $180,000 renovating it from top to bottom, and turning it into a stunning showplace.

During the same period, Maggie and Bill bought a lovely old farmhouse in The Plains, Virginia. The Fauquier County spread sat on eighteen acres of land sandwiched between two sprawling cattle ranches. "It was a little enclave," said Hall, with room for a large garden and pool for Maggie, who had rediscovered her girlhood passion for swimming and liked to do twenty laps each morning. She had negotiated with the owners and gotten the place for a steal. "That was the French peasant coming out," said Hall of his wife's ability to drive a hard bargain.

They began to spend a lot of time at the nearby McLean estate of Bobby and Ethel Kennedy, who entertained an endless stream of guests at their big, white antebellum house known as Hickory Hill. There were backyard barbecues for fifty, boisterous pool parties, and a lot of the youngest brother, Teddy, shoving fully dressed guests into the water. Maggie was most impressed with the aplomb of Pierre Salinger, the senator's press secretary, who once emerged from the pool with black tie in place and cigar still firmly clenched between his teeth. Bobby and Ethel's four offspring romped around, trailed by the children of friends, and a troupe of animals.

Feisty and flirtatious, Maggie, with her Irish wit, fit in easily with the Kennedys. She was learning to enjoy the family sport of politics and was eager to become a team player. Soon she was on a first-name basis with the parents, Rose and Joseph P. Kennedy, and quickly became a particular favorite of the old man's. It was a close-knit clan, and all of them, one way or another, were already working for Jack's 1960 presidential campaign. Nixon was by far the front-runner, and Kennedy, while insisting he was not a candidate, endured a backbreaking schedule of speeches across the country. In the months to come, Bobby would resign his job as chief counsel for the Senate Labor Racketeering Committee to direct the campaign.

Maggie got on the bandwagon early. She did what she could to help behind the scenes, writing articles, providing informal media advice, and introducing Jack to key military and diplomatic figures who could suggest important areas of legislation and help prepare foreign policy position papers. It was a time when much of the Washington press corps was openly skeptical of JFK, who was seen as too young, too Catholic, too East Coast. Maggie busied herself writing articles that would help convince the critics that he was not "just another pretty boy from Harvard."

In February, she held a luncheon for him at her home that was designed to be an informal get-together for members of the press to meet the senator and size him up. "He [JFK] gave the shortcomings of all of them [the other possible Democratic presidential candidates] ... and himself, giving what he thought were his own assets and liabilities, his shortcomings," recalled Peter Lisagor, noting that it was the first time many of the reporters realized that Kennedy was seriously considering throwing his hat in the ring.

Her bureau colleagues, noticing her fondness for long lunches and frequent absences from the office, made the mistake of thinking perhaps the thirty-eight-year-old peripatetic correspondent was morphing into a Georgetown doyenne. With her busy social schedule, the obligations of being a general's wife, and the responsibilities of motherhood, it would be understandable if she was tired of the harness and wanted to slow down. They could not have been more wrong. When she heard that Eisenhower was sending Vice President Nixon to Russia on an official visit, she went to Donovan and demanded the assignment for herself. No one in the bureau was better qualified or had more Kremlin contacts. But Donovan had already decided to send Mazo, who had been covering Nixon. The two locked horns over the issue. Donovan would not be dictated to by Higgins and told her he was sending Mazo alone. She went anyway.

Maggie was six months pregnant when Nixon and his entourage took off from Idlewild Airport on July 22, 1959. The vice president's hectic tour of the Soviet hinterland was grueling for most of the press contingent, forced to cover long distances, endure uncomfortable lodging, and get by with little sleep. For Maggie, it felt like a marathon. They tramped through kindergartens, youth camps, steel mills, and vast copper mines. Khrushchev and his wife, Nina, worried she was overdoing it. They urged her to go home and put her feet up.

She managed to keep her expanding belly discreetly hidden under the loose-fitting tent dresses that were then in style, but she found it more difficult to outsprint the phalanx of *Times* reporters to call in her stories. The final indignity came in Sverdlovsk, the Pittsburgh of Siberia, when she had a scoop and made a dash for the nearest telephone. Miraculously, she made a quick connection to the *Tribune* office in Paris. "She pantingly told the editor that she had an important story to dictate," recalled Ruth Montgomery, a member of the press party. "But he replied, 'Sorry. Everyone's out to lunch now. Call back in an hour.'"

On November 20, Linda Marguerite Hall was born. Months later, when Maggie was attending a reception for Khrushchev at the Soviet mission in New York, he recognized her as the reporter he had admired for pushing her way through the crowds when heavily pregnant. Speaking through an interpreter, Khrushchev asked: "What was it? A boy or girl?" *Newsweek*, impressed by his familiarity with the American correspondent, picked up the story, and noted that upon hearing that it was a girl, the alternately jovial and testy Soviet leader remarked, "Then you'll be forgiven in heaven for all the tripe you've written."

"But Mr. Chairman," Maggie shot back, "I thought you didn't believe in heaven."

Just in case her editors were inclined to write her off now that she was a mother of two, Maggie sent a pointed reply to Robert White, the new president of the *Tribune*, who had sent a note of congratulations on Linda's birth in which he wondered whether the baby would be following in her famous mother's footsteps. After thanking him, Maggie, writing with vinegar, expressed the hope that her arrangement with the paper would continue. Her new contract, increasing her salary and range of her correspondent duties, included covering international conferences. She was glad to hear, therefore, that it was "merely uncertainty over Linda's arrival" that kept them from sending her to the recent Paris-Western summit meeting. She would be going to the "April in Paris" summit as well as the Ike-Khrushchev summit.

"I hadn't intended, really, to inject a professional note," she added, "but it just goes to show that the old habit of putting the newspaper business first is still with me":

> As to Linda, my bet is on a newspaper career. After all, not many babies have had such a newspapery pre-natal conditioning as Linda gained in all the time she passed in July and August following Mr. Nixon through Russia and Siberia, and last autumn in whistle-stopping across the United States in the company of Mr. K.
>
> Do you suppose her first word will be "Nyet?"

16

✳✳✳✳✳✳✳✳✳

The Maggie Higgins Hour

In the early sixties in the Washington bureau of
the *Times*, the period around 9:00 pm used to
be known as the Maggie Higgins Hour.... Her
frequently exclusive stories obviously had
to be checked out, and the Maggie Higgins
Hour arrived when the bureau phone would
start ringing with calls from New York on
the latest Higgins headlines, just out in the
Herald Trib. Could the bureau match?

—Tom Wicker, *On Press*

ON DECEMBER 12, 1960, A BANNER HEADLINE ON THE FRONT PAGE
of the *Herald Tribune* announced Maggie's latest exclusive: "Kennedy
Sr. Tells of His Family." Much to the consternation of her competitors,
the ubiquitous Higgins had somehow managed to establish herself as an
insider in the new Kennedy administration, and she had been rewarded
with a long, intimate interview with the controversial patriarch of the
president-elect's sprawling Irish Catholic family. The subhead of her story
read, "He Urged His Son to Run for President? Nonsense."

Her exclusive was picked up by the *Washington Star*, and the AP, and
was quoted in the daily papers and the nightly news broadcasts. When
calls poured in from reporters at other publications wanting to know
how Higgins scored her sit-down with Joe Kennedy just one month after

his son's election, she sounded smug, explaining that she had pitched the story while at the family's Hyannis Port compound along with a handful of other correspondents "personally known to the president." Tidbits from the interview continued to circulate for days afterward, including the tycoon's insistence that there was "absolutely no truth" to rumors that he planned to be the power behind the throne, and was hunting for a house in Washington and would soon be taking up residence near 1600 Pennsylvania Avenue.

A week earlier, when Jack Kennedy ignited a firestorm by nominating his brother for attorney general, Maggie devoted an entire column to pushing Bobby for the post. In "His Brother's Keeper," she reported that the thirty-five-year-old Democratic campaign manager, who had contributed greatly to JFK's victory, was sensitive to the charges of nepotism, but the president-elect would not be deterred from giving him the job, and they hoped the public would come to see it as a well-deserved reward. Before the column came out, she sent Bobby a draft, along with a note that conveys how involved she had become in helping to advance his political fortunes:

Bobby:

I left many details about you out because your situation is so uncertain even though the observations your father made about you are my sentiments exactly. But just wait. One day I'm going to blow the myth about the "ruthless" Bobby Kennedy so high it will never be put back together again. I hope this article is satisfactory. I tried to lay to rest the old bogey about your father manipulating the white house and it was easy to do because any first-hand observer can see this is utterly contrary to the truth.

I'll call or perhaps you could call me at North 7 7070.

All the best,
Maggie

BOBBY SENT A HANDWRITTEN reply: "Your article was certainly most kind—and most appreciated." He added that he and Ethel were "looking forward to seeing you next Saturday," a reference to baby Linda Hall's christening day. At the church, the new priest who had taken over the parish declined to let Ruth Montgomery serve as godmother. Bobby and Ethel Kennedy offered to stand in, and they became Linda's official godparents.

By the time the new administration was being sworn in, Maggie was at the forefront of Washington social life. When the Women's National Press Club gave a reception for the new members of the president's cabinet on January 21, 1961, she introduced the new attorney general, who, in typical Kennedy fashion, was half an hour late for the party in his honor. Waving away his apologies, Maggie took the breathless Ethel by the arm and steered the couple into the ballroom, presiding over a private party for all the guests who stayed.

Maggie continued to help burnish the Kennedy image. She penned a glowing profile of the family matriarch, Rose Kennedy, for *McCall's*. The magazine was so pleased it put Maggie on a $1,000 monthly retainer. She followed up with another puff piece. Packed with admiring quotes from Kennedy cronies, "The Private World of Robert and Ethel Kennedy" underscored her own position as a trusted friend and member of the clan.

She and Peter Lisagor teamed up to write a flattering profile of Tish Baldrige, who had been appointed Jackie Kennedy's social secretary, and another gauzy feature about the Kennedys' new style of entertaining, "RSVP—The White House," detailing the scandalous changes the young, modern president and his wife were introducing to the "forbidding, museum-like atmosphere of the White House," including a switch from the torturous white tie and tails to black tie at formal affairs, and abandoning the traditional receiving line.

Maggie's enviable access was observed up close by Jim O'Donnell, who left journalism to join the Kennedy administration in 1960. "Jack always cultivated newspapermen, he brain-picked, which I think a good politician should do," he said, noting that Kennedy had a dozen or so favorites among the press corps, including Higgins, Lisagor, Lippmann, Cronkite, and Elie Abel of the *Times*. The president valued Maggie for her candor—she could be counted on to tell it like it was, with no sugar-coating. "Kennedy would call her, much more often than he called me. He was much closer to her. She was a power in the press those days."

Once, after she had written a piece that angered Kennedy, he expressed his disappointment in her. As she related the conversation to O'Donnell later in the day, the president had complained, "Marguerite, I thought you were a friend of mine. You could at least have called me up. You're going with this thing. It's critical. You could have called me up."

"But Jack, it was eleven in the evening," she had protested, trying to explain that she was on deadline and unable to put in a call to his secretary, Evelyn Lincoln, at such a late hour.

"Look, I don't care what time of day or night," Kennedy had said. "If you're going to be on the front page of the *Herald Tribune* with something that concerns my government, you can roll me out at three in the morning. I'll only be angry if you didn't check it. Because (a) you got it wrong, and (b) I could have given you some added information."

O'Donnell marveled at Maggie's relationship with the president, whom she called "Jack," something he could never bring himself to do. "She had a really fine relationship with President Kennedy," he said, adding unprompted that their after-hours contact was strictly "platonic." For a reporter to be given the president's private number was incredible, he added; "she could literally call him at midnight and get through."

The lure of the Kennedys was irresistible, and not just for Maggie. Many journalists shared her exhilaration at the arrival of the New Frontiersmen, who seemed so bright, energetic, and full of ideas. "Few presidents ever had a more adoring press corps," observed Lippmann biographer Ronald Steel, who detailed the conversion of the *Trib*'s influential political columnist into "one of the shining ornaments of the Kennedy administration."

Even in this period of adulation, friendly columnists and correspondents did not suspend all critical judgment. Ben Bradlee, who went on to become a legendary editor of the *Washington Post*, wrote about the excitement and fascination of unexpectedly having a friend elected president, but he noted, "For a newspaperman it is all that, plus confusing: are you a friend, or are you a reporter? You have to redefine 'friend' and redefine 'reporter' over and over again, before reaching any kind of comfort level." There is a line reporters know they should not cross. It is a boundary that denotes separate and distinct professional agendas, distance, and if not impartiality then at least some semblance of neutrality. During the first weeks after Kennedy was elected, Bradlee admitted that he often found it difficult to toe that line, and it took time before he "got it right."

Maggie waltzed across the line without missing a beat. There is no sign she experienced so much as a twinge of ethical queasiness about her overfamiliarity with the first family. The more time she spent as a special columnist, the less attention she paid to the ordinary rules of journalism. Confident she could negotiate what Bradlee called the "complicated perimeters of friendship," and the conflict between the private and public spheres, she ignored all the textbook warnings about compromising relationships.

As she morphed from foreign correspondent to Cold War pundit and anticommunist crusader, she became increasingly partisan. She saw herself as an advocate, identifying areas of instability, advancing her interpretation of events, and recommending courses of action. Promoting the Kennedys—their policies, their appointees, their cult of personality—was all of a piece with her worldview; she was their emissary, and they were part of her larger cause. The martial sentiment of the president's inaugural address was music to her ears, and she liked his public pronouncements on combating communism. Even though they sometimes differed on issues, there was a shared sense that this was their generation's turn to lead, and the beginning of a new period of global commitment.

Maggie and the Kennedys were made for each other. The brothers shared her insatiable appetite for news and political gossip, and they enjoyed the lively give-and-take of journalistic shoptalk, the no-holds-barred, who's-in-who's-out roundup of state officials, politicians, reporters, friends, enemies, and acquaintances. For her, the Kennedys were the holy grail of sources—the highest of high-placed authorities—providing unparalleled access, allowing her to be first with the news and the most complete with the background and context of events. Her files during this period are crammed full of correspondence with Bobby, including notes, telegrams, call slips, meeting dates, and dinner plans. She was a regular recipient of RFK's leaks, and reciprocated with stories he found useful.

She also wrote regularly to Jack, her easy rapport with him evident in the telegram she sent after he clinched the nomination at the Los Angeles convention on July 15, 1960:

> CONGRATULATIONS ON NOMINATION, LAST
> NIGHT'S SPEECH, AND, IN FACT, ON PRACTICALLY
> EVERYTHING STOP HOPE YOU WILL TIDY UP SUCH
> MATTERS AS THE CONGO, CUBA, ETC, SO I CAN
> ATTEND NEXT CONVENTION STOP WISH I'D BEEN
> THERE.

Kennedy wrote back a week later, noting that the "chaotic last hours" at the Biltmore had prevented him from responding that night. "I, of course, regret that you were left behind on the war fronts of the Congo and Cuba," he added. "I shall, however, do my best to provide a breathing spell in the summer of 1964."

Maggie had missed the convention because she was stuck in Washington writing a series of articles about the Congo, and the future of the new African states, sixteen independent nations that had just been admitted to the United Nations. In one of her better recent scoops, "Summer Scandal," she reported that the NATO base in Greece was being used as a stopover for Russia's Ilyushin planes, which were being sent "to win friends and influence the Congolese on communism's behalf."

In March of 1961, when trouble erupted in the Belgian Congo Republic, Maggie jumped on a plane to cover the hostilities. The page-one headline was classic Higgins: "Congolese Hostile to U.N., but Welcome an American." The American was Maggie, of course. Her story opened in familiar dramatic style with her arrival in Leopoldville:

> As we stepped out of the tiny blue and white Cub plane that had flown us across the river at Brazzaville, a helmeted Congolese

soldier, complete with paratroop boots and grenades on his belt, waved a burp gun somewhat indecisively in our direction.

"Go back," he said. "We don't want any more United Nations people here."

"Pay no attention," said an Air France hostess, who was armed with only a pert blue uniform and an air of supreme confidence.

Readers who plowed on would learn that Congolese president Joseph Kasavubu's government had tried to topple the communist-backed rebel leader Antoine Gizenga by cutting off supplies to his regime in Stanleyville. European civilians were fleeing across the border and the province was beset by violence. Maggie scored a world beat by being the first reporter to send word from Leopoldville of the arrival of Indian combat troops. She did it by locating the only open wireless circuit in the republic, and punching out her own story on the teletype machine in the communications center. A week later, she pinned down Gizenga for an hour-long talk in his house in Stanleyville. The interview made even bigger news: he told her that unless the Western powers officially recognized him by April 15, he would expel British, French, and U.S. consuls from his city. More headlines followed, and more Higgins fanfare.

Newsweek reported that in the space of two weeks, Maggie, showing a touch of her old "fire-horse flamboyance," had filed two world exclusives to the *Herald Tribune*. Making her entrance in a posy-printed dress in place of her usual fatigues, and gobbling anti-dysentery pills, Higgins had apparently refused to take no for an answer when the media-shy Gizenga turned down her interview request. The fact that no *Trib* correspondent had been in Stanleyville since 1877, when the famed reporter and explorer Henry Morton Stanley visited the spot after tracking down the long-lost Dr. David Livingstone, made her scoop all the more newsworthy.

"Is it courage, initiative, or sheer blind luck that gives Marguerite Higgins her exclusive stories from the Congo?" *Newsweek* asked rhetorically. "Her envious male colleagues, who have been there for months, have good reason to debate this stickler."

Not wanting to lose her momentum, Maggie planned to fly to Vienna to cover Kennedy's first meeting with Khrushchev, a superpower conference to be held in June. When Donovan told her he was sending their White House correspondent, David Wise, Maggie was livid. Ignoring his objections, she took leave and paid her own way, later claiming it was for a freelance piece.

Donovan's patience had been tried past endurance. He told the higher-ups he was tired of being saddled with the "care and feeding" of Higgins. She answered to no one. Every assignment became a test of wills. She was obstinate, obsessive, and impossible to control. Maggie, in turn, complained of being "frozen out" and threatened to resign. Tittle-tattle about the bureau squabbling made the columns and added to her growing reputation as a diva. But the bottom line was that her name was an asset to the paper. Donovan had little choice but to put up with her.

On the second day of the Vienna summit, Kennedy and Khrushchev got around to the subject of Berlin and the ongoing debate over reunification. Khrushchev, who had little respect for the inexperienced young president, demanded a peace treaty and recognition for East Germany. Berlin needed to become a strictly neutral city, and the Western powers would have access to the city only with East German permission. Kennedy was amazed. He maintained the Western powers had every right to be in Berlin, having defeated Germany in the Second World War. He declared that the national security of the U.S. was directly linked to that of Berlin. Khrushchev exploded, banging his fist on the table, and said, "I want peace, but if you want war that is your problem." The meeting ended ominously, with the Soviet leader insisting his decision to sign a peace treaty with East Germany in six months was irrevocable. The president responded, "If that's true, it's going to be a cold winter."

Kennedy was badly shaken by the encounter. He had been in office only four months, but the Soviets had handed him one bruising setback after another. The glorious New Frontier he had outlined in his inaugural address was not rolling out as expected. A few weeks before the meeting, the Russians announced they had won the race to put the first man in space—cosmonaut Yuri Gagarin aboard the *Vostok*. Just days after that, the CIA-backed invasion of Cuba, a secret plan to have a group of Cuban exiles overthrow the communist leader Fidel Castro, proved a fiasco, and was crushed after a landing at the Bay of Pigs. On his way home, a gloomy Kennedy admitted to reporters that it had been "a very sober two days," but that "our most somber talks had been on Berlin."

Kennedy was incensed by Maggie's column wondering whether their young president, who was still not sure of himself, was going to screw up his courage and stick by his obligations to their allies and the people of West Berlin. Under the headline "The Next to the Last Straw," she quoted high German officials saying they had their doubts about Kennedy; "in Laos for instance, the president has said something was the last straw, then retreated."

Over the summer, the situation in Berlin steadily deteriorated. Maggie wrote several columns warning that rumors were spreading that a wall would be erected to surround West Berlin. A flood of five thousand East Germans a week were crossing the border. People were in a panic to get out while they could. Before leaving for her August vacation, she wrote about the huge numbers of refugees overwhelming West Berlin, and the fear it could become a mass uprising.

Then, in the early hours of Sunday, August 13, the Soviets moved to close the borders and stop the exodus. Maggie, who had been monitoring the situation, learned of the sudden appearance of a barbed-wire fence that zigzagged its way through the center of the city. By two-thirty that afternoon, the entire twenty-eight miles separating the Soviet sector from the three Western sectors had been sealed. Interrupting her holiday with her family on Cape Cod, she immediately tried to reach the president. But Kennedy had retired to Hyannis Port for the weekend, and she was told he had planned a day of sailing.

After a morning phone call from Secretary of State Dean Rusk informing him that the Russians were closing the border—a move that the Allies had come to view as inevitable—Kennedy had breathed a sigh of relief. Khrushchev had found a solution to the East German refugee crisis short of war. There was no need for the West to mount a military response. Kennedy told Rusk to go ahead to his ball game, as he was taking his father's sloop, the *Marlin*, out for a relaxing cruise on Nantucket Sound.

By the time the *Marlin* put in at Hyannis Port, Maggie was waiting impatiently for him on the dock. Planted between two Secret Service men, she looked and sounded extremely agitated. "Take it easy, Maggie," a tanned and relaxed Kennedy said as he disembarked.

She launched right into her argument: "If you do not grasp the reins firmly in your hands," she said, "Berlin will slip through your fingers."

"Why are you excited, Maggie?" the president asked, still puzzled.

"The situation in Berlin is becoming acute," she explained. "There are many heavily armed communist troops on the borders of Berlin, and not one American soldier has been seen. Has no one given you the picture? You can call it hysteria if you wish, but the Berliners have suffered a fearful shock."

"What do you propose?" Kennedy asked.

"Permit me to speak to General Clay," she said. The president's reply was guarded. He was not yet convinced he should take any action.

Later that same evening, Maggie and Bill Hall went to see General Clay, whose cottage, in Chatham, was nearby. Clay felt exactly as she did. But he was a prominent Republican and had actively supported Nixon in the election. He did not feel it was his place to offer unsolicited advice to the new president. He agreed, however, that someone needed to go to Berlin immediately to try to salvage the situation, and he might be willing to volunteer. Clay advised Maggie to call Bobby Kennedy.

When she got the attorney general on the telephone, he did not seem to think the crisis was serious. Only the East was affected. "No American has had a hair on his head disturbed," Bobby told her. "It was," he suggested, "a question of nerves. The West must hold back. If, however, the Berliners wanted General Clay, they could have him, not as a commandant in the city, but as a morale booster."

No sooner had she put down the phone than it started to ring. Jim O'Donnell was calling from his office in the State Department to confer. Like Higgins, he had been hearing from his contacts in Berlin, who had reported that "all hell had broken loose." Among them were Peter

Boenisch, the editor of *Bild*; and the newspaper's influential publisher, Axel Springer. "Wake them up in Washington," Boenisch had warned, "or they'll have lost Berlin by morning."

"Call them back," Maggie told O'Donnell in her self-appointed role as German policy adviser to the administration. "Tell them we are going to send General Clay."

By Thursday, August 17, it was all arranged. Kennedy had returned to Washington and summoned his brother, Dean Rusk, National Security Adviser McGeorge Bundy, and Intelligence Director Allen Dulles. After weighing the pros and cons, they agreed they needed to send a Democrat along with the high-profile Republican Clay. They decided to send Vice President Lyndon B. Johnson to Berlin as a special envoy, and Clay, the bullish commander of the airlift and symbol of American strength, would accompany him. The president also agreed to send military reinforcements—a show of force to help quell the panic.

At 9:15 p.m. on Friday, August 18, Maggie flew out of Andrews Air Force Base for Berlin as a member of the vice president's small party. When Johnson and Clay spoke at Berlin City Hall the next day, and pledged "our lives, our fortunes, and our sacred honor" to protect the surrounded city, they received a tumultuous ovation from the crowd of more than a quarter million. Maggie described Johnson's triumphant motorcade, the royal welcome he received, and the resounding firmness of his words—"Tyranny's days are numbered."

Her appraisal of the disastrous consequences of doing nothing in Berlin had been correct, and the tremendous response of the citizens was indicative of their gratitude to the American government for standing with them. Finally, in divided Berlin, they had shown the flag. West Berliners were reassured they would not be abandoned. "The Clay mission was by no means a complete success, but it was a partial success," said O'Donnell. More importantly, it was Kennedy's first foreign policy success.

All that fall, Maggie continued to write about Berlin. Her columns were filled with warnings that the crisis was not over. The city remained in turmoil. The Soviets were clamping down even further, reducing the number of border crossings. She returned to West Berlin in September in time to see the arrival of additional American reinforcements, for an army of just over fifty thousand. It was still only a token force to keep the enemy at bay. She lambasted a State Department official for declaring that the wall—now a permanent concrete barrier—was visible proof of communism's unpopularity, and therefore a symbol of America's victory and the Soviets' failure. In a stinging column, she quoted one European official's reaction: "Five more 'victories' like the last one in Berlin and you Americans will be fighting on Cape Cod."

Annoyed by her endlessly alarmist reports, McGeorge Bundy, in a memorandum to the president, called Higgins "the firebug"—she was a kind of catalytic force, always excitedly rushing to the scene of the next disaster, and the next headline. The woman was maddening.

AFTER THE BERLIN CRISIS, Maggie's relationship with the Kennedys grew even closer. By the end of 1961, she was negotiating with Harper & Brothers to do an extravagant art book on the refurbished White House with her friend David Douglas Duncan, a famous combat photojournalist, who was also known for his stunning book on Pablo Picasso. "I am most anxious to see the Red Room and all the exciting changes that have been made since Pam [Turnure] gave Dave and I our tour," Maggie enthused in a letter to Jackie about their joint project.

She was also working on a book about the president's boyhood, *Young John Kennedy*, based on forty-odd letters he wrote as a youth. She had pitched the idea to Sterling North at Houghton Mifflin, who had earlier asked her to write a short biography of the pioneering American writer and political activist Jessie Benton Fremont as part of its North Star series for young adults. It was a sign of just how fast Maggie was moving that when she inked the deal on February 14, 1962, the president felt like he was the last to know. The project was promptly flagged by Pierre Salinger, his press secretary, who viewed the publication of the letters as an invasion of JFK's privacy.

On March 8, Maggie sent the president an apologetic note, saying that she was "surprised to hear from Pierre that you did not know of the project." She hastened to fill him in, explaining that he had no doubt forgotten—"having a few other things to think about"—that she had cleared the project with both him and Bobby, who had made the letters available. To stave off any more interference from the pesky Salinger, she added that she would prefer to deal directly with the president and his brother: "Bob and I understand each other. Besides, it is more rewarding to cooperate with someone who has a measure of confidence in my judgment and integrity which I believe Bob has and which Pierre obviously does not."

She wrote an even blunter letter to Bobby, informing him of the unpleasant call she had received earlier that day from Salinger demanding the immediate return of JFK's letters, and reminding him that he had consented to the project. She concluded hotly, "I resent being put in the category of an untrustworthy type even when it's done by a press secretary." In a postscript, she added, "Pierre has at least proved to me that age has not dimmed my Irish temper."

Bobby took full responsibility for the mix-up, confessing it had completely slipped his mind. His high regard for her was evidenced by the effort he put into stroking her reporter's ego, thanking her profusely for "a number of articles on the family," and noting that "the article on my mother, in my judgment, was the finest of any that has been written." He added, "You have always been most understanding and I never ever had the slightest qualm or hesitation in telling you anything personally or in the line of business because of any fear it might be published or handled in bad taste." As to JFK's letters, however, he recommended they be returned forthwith.

In the end, Maggie persuaded the president to allow her to proceed with the *Young John Kennedy* story. Had he known just how many books she had on the back burner, he might have thought twice about it. Before the year was out, Maggie had accepted a commission to write a biography of his mother for Harper & Row. She would soon begin yet another book, in conjunction with Peter Lisagor, about the foreign service, inspired in part by an off-the-record speech the president gave to a group of young diplomats about how the highly charged present moment was "the Golden Age of the State Department."

Maggie even had the cheek to write to him and suggest, "We thought that in light of your interest in the morale of the foreign service, you might like to write the forward [*sic*]." The president agreed to provide the duo with the text of his extemporaneous remarks—albeit a sanitized version—to include in the book.

By now, Maggie and Pete were a recognized, highly visible team in Washington. They were the closest of colleagues. They were always together. They went to West Wing meetings together. They traveled around the country and overseas together. They coauthored articles and collaborated on a book. All these things are possible without sleeping together, but the grapevine always knows better. Bill Hall, who retired from the air force that fall, had taken a job as director of the Madigan Electronic Corporation in New York and commuted back and forth to Washington on weekends. In his absence, it was Lisagor who squired Maggie to White House receptions and Georgetown dinner parties.

"They were having a not-very-secret affair," according to Carl T. Rowan, a prominent Black journalist who had been made deputy assistant secretary of state under Kennedy. Rowan recalled a number of press luncheons cohosted by Higgins and Lisagor at her Twenty-Fourth Street home, where he enjoyed her French cooking and did "a little choice leaking on instructions from officials as high as the president."

Serious, married, far from being a ladies' man in character and bearing, Lisagor was one of the most respected correspondents in Washington. He was known as "a reporter's reporter," the highest praise, and he had a breezy, irreverent, down-to-earth approach to his job. Maggie's free-wheeling, slam-bang style of journalism differed markedly from Lisagor's finely measured reporting, but he had a lot of time for her. Maggie could be "very intense," he conceded. "She had the quality of draining you, if you had something she wanted." For the most part, they worked well together. "We had a fairly amiable relationship. She had a great sympatico with a lot of people, and was getting a lot more reflective as time went on."

Lisagor indulged her excesses with tolerant affection. She was a complicated combination of tough-mindedness, sexy irreverence, and subtle frailties. "She was one of the rare feminine people in our business," he mused. "Marguerite, for all her deep competitive instincts remained an extremely feminine woman to an extensive degree. Womanly in almost every way. You couldn't look at it in terms of weakness. . . . Somewhere was the hell-cat behind the baby-blue eyes and girlish manner."

That fierceness earned her the enmity of nearly every reporter she went up against, and every official she held accountable. For all the official favors she did, Maggie did not forfeit her watchdog role. She was not afraid to address policy lapses or publish a leak from a concerned source. On March 14, she found herself in hot water with the administration over her exclusive story of a behind-closed-doors conversation between Secretary of State Dean Rusk and Soviet Foreign Minister Andrei Gromyko in Geneva. The discussion centered on Soviet harassment of Allied planes in the Berlin air corridors, and her story reported word for word Rusk's remarks and Gromyko's icy replies.

Since their communication was highly restricted—provided only to select members of the National Security Council (NSC), White House, and General Maxwell Taylor's staffs—it was apparent that someone had given a transcript of the conversation to Higgins. Her article represented the "unauthorized disclosure" of classified material, and it immediately triggered an investigation by the executive office of the NSC. As a consequence, a half dozen of the president's top advisers were forced to fill out security questionnaires forswearing any knowledge of how Higgins came by her scoop.

Never were her formidable skills more fully on display than in the walk up to the Cuban missile crisis in October 1962. Months earlier, long before most of her colleagues, Maggie had warned about the ominous buildup of military matériel in Cuba, and that Russians were entering the country in large numbers. Back in February, she had reported, "It is understood that communist-bloc deliveries of tanks, machine guns, and jets to Cuba have been increasing steadily beyond anything the Castro regime itself could absorb."

The weekend before the missile crisis, Maggie received a tip that the reason the U.S. military was activating its units was because of the presence of Soviet missile sites in Cuba. On Sunday, she phoned the intelligence into the Washington bureau, offering to do more legwork on the story. But when the desk reporter Warren Rogers checked with his Pentagon and State Department sources, they told him it had to do with the situation in Berlin. Rogers could not confirm her tip, and he could not risk running a faulty story on something so sensitive that might result in an embarrassing retraction. Higgins tended to go off on tangents and that could lead to trouble. She had such a powerful urge to compete, her editors sometimes worried it could cause her to make rash judgments or breach editorial standards in the heat of the chase.

Not all of Maggie's exclusives panned out. But when her Cuba tip turned out to be on the money, and the dreaded nuclear showdown with the Soviet Union suddenly loomed into view, she gave Rogers an earful. On Monday, October 22, the president ordered a naval blockade of Cuba. In the days that followed, tensions mounted, and the world teetered on the edge of nuclear war. Khrushchev responded that the blockade was an "act of aggression," and the Soviet ships bound for Cuba would proceed. In the end, it was Bobby, engaged in back-channel negotiations, who broke the stalemate and proposed a peaceful solution: if the Soviets dismantled their missile sites, the U.S. would withdraw the blockade and guarantee there would be no invasion. In a separate, secret deal, the U.S missiles in Turkey, which were sighted at the Soviet Union, would be quietly removed. On the morning of Sunday, October 28, Kennedy made a brief national broadcast accepting a statement from Moscow that the Soviets would dismantle the arms.

Maggie treated Kennedy's successful Cuban brinkmanship as a major Soviet defeat. She extolled the president and his policy advisers for standing firm in the missile crisis. Kennedy had kept his cool and called the Soviets' bluff. He had gone head-to-head with Khrushchev and won. A true knight of the Cold War, he had picked up the torch and was ready to advance the "cause of freedom" all over the world. On December 31, in a year-end review, she wrote, "The New Frontier is approaching 1963 with an unprecedented sense of expectation arising out of its victorious confrontation with the Soviet Union."

Maggie remained a vigilant crusader against communism everywhere.

Her Cold War ideology framed every new crisis along the same familiar axis of conflict, a bipolar struggle between democracy and totalitarianism. As she saw it, the Cuban confrontation demonstrated that Soviet aggression could be checked. But incalculable dangers remained: American planes were still flying daily reconnaissance missions over Cuba; there had been a string of antidemocratic eruptions in Latin America; the Congo was heating up again; and the communist aggression in Laos and Vietnam was growing steadily worse. In the euphoria of the moment, she thought it prudent to remind the administration, and the American people, that "one battle does not win a war—especially a global cold war."

17

✳ ✳ ✳ ✳ ✳ ✳ ✳ ✳

War of Words

A few weeks ago, a correspondent flew
out of the U.S. to Saigon for a firsthand
look and, ignoring the assessments of the
resident newsmen, reached independent
conclusions. Club members were furious.

—*Time*, September 20, 1963

IT WAS LATE ON A STEAMY JULY NIGHT IN WASHINGTON WHEN
Maggie was awakened by a telephone call. Just back from covering Kennedy's state visit to West Germany, she groped for the phone through a
fog of sleep and fever. The voice on the other end of the line was that of
Vic Wilson, the night desk manager in the Washington bureau. After
apologizing for the midnight call, he said he had an urgent message
from the New York office: "Could she go to Vietnam at the earliest possible moment?"

The assignment came from the *Tribune*'s top brass. Too tired to care,
Maggie mumbled something unprintable about their request and asked
Wilson to relay the message. Wilson, accustomed to all manner of profane outbursts, suggested she might want to reconsider. Why not wait
and see how she felt in the morning?

Three days later Maggie was on a plane bound for Saigon.

On June 11, 1963, Americans had been shocked by the images on television and in their morning papers of a saffron-robed Buddhist monk ablaze. He had sat in a lotus position in the middle of a Saigon square and been doused with gasoline by two young monks. Then he lit a match and dropped it in his lap. Thich Quang Duc never uttered a sound while the more than three hundred monks and nuns who had been marching in protest with him wailed and cried as his body was engulfed in flames. Malcolm Browne, the AP bureau chief in Saigon, had caught the grisly scene on film and it was front-paged around the world.

Her editors wanted to know what the hell was happening in Vietnam. Maggie was to fly to Saigon for six weeks and get to the bottom of this headline-making crisis. Instead of filing day-to-day reports, they wanted her to dig deep and find out how the war was really going, and explain how the U.S. embassy and military officials there had allowed the South Vietnamese leader Eisenhower once lauded as the "miracle of Asia" to turn into such a monster.

The predeparture briefings provided by the State Department did not help clarify the confused reports from Saigon. The U.S. had spent over $2 billion trying to prevent a communist takeover in South Vietnam. President Kennedy had pledged that the U.S. would stay "until we win." His administration had signed an aid treaty with Diem's beleaguered government, and approved a new counterinsurgency plan for South Vietnam, steadily increasing the number of military advisers and soldiers to fourteen thousand. The military buildup had begun in earnest in February 1962, when U.S. Special Forces began training the South Vietnamese soldiers to fight the new onslaught of guerrilla attacks by the National Liberation Front, or Viet Cong, directed by Ho Chi Minh, the communist chieftain in the North.

The State Department officials Maggie spoke to were clearly angry and exasperated with Diem. He had failed to institute the recommended reforms to restore confidence in his government and seemed incapable of winning the loyalty of his own people. The current religious crisis was a case in point: on May 8, residents of Hué, the imperial capital of old Vietnam, protested Diem's ban on flying religious flags on Buddha's birthday, and government troops had fired on the crowd, killing nine and wounding fourteen. The Buddhist demonstrations followed. The U.S. was getting "a black eye" in the world media because of Diem's repressive regime, a State Department spokesman told her.

Before Maggie left, Bobby Kennedy gave her a high-level backgrounder on the administration view of the limited war in Vietnam, which was as much a public relations war as a military one. The bad press was alarming. What disturbed him the most was that the conflict between Diem and the Buddhists might jeopardize the U.S. mission in South Vietnam, as well as their efforts to keep the clandestine military intervention out of the papers. Bobby closed out their conversation with the injunction: "Don't leave the country without talking to General Krulak. He's just back from Vietnam and has the best perspective of the situation there of anyone I've heard."

Maggie headed straight for his office at the Pentagon. Marine Maj. Gen. Victor "Brute" Krulak was an imposing figure despite being only five feet, four inches tall. A much-decorated World War II hero, he enjoyed a special relationship with the president dating back to the Pacific war, when as a young navy lieutenant Jack Kennedy captained a PT boat that rescued a group of Krulak's marines. Fresh from a recent tour of Vietnam, Krulak, a counterinsurgency adviser to the Joint Chiefs of Staff, had an entirely different take on the situation. He told her the Buddhist upheaval was political, not religious, and was irrelevant to the war being fought in the countryside, which he maintained was improving. The problem was that the true story of the war was not being told by the Saigon press corps.

"What is needed," he advised in a July memorandum to the Joint Chiefs, "is a few venturesome newsmen who are willing to forgo the comforts of the city and endure a little mud and discomfort. Those so inclined would be rewarded with a picture of resolution and progress which they would not quickly forget."

Krulak as good as gave Maggie her marching orders. A soldier's daughter, and a soldier's wife, she was always inclined to side with the troops in the way of the bullets while discounting the cheap shots from newsmen anchored to their desks. Until now, the events in Vietnam had received only modest attention in America. It was easy to attribute the misleading, spotty coverage to the handful of obscure news-agency reporters who were based in Saigon, a picture she would soon put right with her trademark frontline reporting.

Maggie, like Kennedy, viewed Vietnam as a crucial Cold War battle-field, one that could not be abandoned without grave consequences. In column after column that spring, she had underscored the importance of the administration's ongoing commitment to defeating communist aggression in South Vietnam. She was so personally committed to the success of their mission that she charged off to Vietnam, armed with White House credentials, determined to show that the U.S. was justified in pursuing its policy of containment.

As soon as she landed, Maggie headed for Xa Loi Pagoda, the largest temple in Saigon. Far from being the familiar shrine to meditation and mysticism, she found it had become the command post for the Buddhist propaganda campaign against the Diem regime. By using their grievances to whip up a larger movement—organizing demonstrations, printing posters, cranking out press releases, and tipping off the media in advance of the fiery death spectacles—the Buddhists were shrewdly exploiting the tensions with the primary goal of insurrection, without caring if "they were softening up the country for a takeover by the Communist Viet Cong." Maggie concluded that Krulak was right—the American report-ers had been taken in.

As proof, she related how the Buddhist leader, Thich Tri Quang, had summoned her to Xa Loi with the express purpose of laying out their political aims. Taking the White House credentials hanging from her neck to mean that she reported directly to the president, Tri Quang then gave her a message for Kennedy to the effect that "it would be hard to get rid of the Diem regime without explicit American support."

Not certain that he understood that she did not work for the admin-istration, Maggie told him: "I don't *represent* the White House, I am *accredited* to the White House."

Tri Quang nodded sagely, certain he knew better. He warned her that the American president should not be too closely associated with the Diem regime. There would be more self-immolations—"10, 15, maybe even 50"—and the images of burning monks would destroy both Kennedy's and Diem's reputations. Maggie took his comments as a threat. On her return to Washington, she passed on Tri Quang's message to Kennedy as requested. Only she added that in her opinion the blackmailing Buddhists were political opportunists and planned to keep up the horrifying headlines until Washington agreed it was time for Diem to go.

"What did the Buddhists want?" she asked in an article. "Diem's head, and not on a silver platter but wrapped in an American flag."

Her analysis of the Buddhist crisis immediately put her at odds with the Saigon-based press corps, the small band of young, male, rambunctious resident correspondents she disparagingly called the "Rover Boys." The head boy was a tall, black-haired, square-jawed twenty-nine-year-old general-assignment reporter for the *New York Times* named David Halberstam. In September 1962, he had replaced a burned-out Homer Bigart, who left in disgust, tired of watching the U.S. back one tin-pot dictator after another in the vain hope they would be better than the communists. The grizzled war correspondent was an unqualified hero to Halberstam, who had come to Vietnam after fifteen months of covering the UN peacekeeping operation in the Congo, and whose total acquaintance with frontline reporting, by his own admission, consisted of "one session with live machine guns and one visit to a field hospital."

Picking up where Bigart left off, the Rover Boys—chiefly Halberstam, Malcolm Browne, Neil Sheehan and Ray Herndon of UPI, Peter Arnett of AP, and Mert Perry and Charles Mohr of *Time*—had spent months bashing the Diem regime for being Roman Catholic in a predominantly Buddhist country, authoritarian, and, as Halberstam would later sum it up, "an incompetent and hostile instrument of American policy." They believed victory was remote, and that the U.S. would soon have to remove Diem in a military coup.

When the Rover Boys read Maggie's first dashed-off piece on the Buddhist crisis in the *Tribune*, taking the Diem line that the protests were entirely political and a made-to-order sideshow for a Western audience, they took it as the ultimate affront. Twenty-six-year-old Neil Sheehan was indignant: she was kissing off the crisis as "the invention of the Machiavellian monks and the gullible reporters," he fumed. Halberstam, who had not yet interviewed Tri Quang, was seething: "Four days on the ground and she's feeding people the whole line of crap."

Halberstam was even more outraged when the palace doors, firmly shut against the skeptical young men who were resident correspondents, magically opened for Maggie, a sympathetic outsider. She was granted an audience with Tran Le Xuan, known as Madame Nhu, the tiny, diabolically beautiful wife of Diem's brother and chief adviser, Ngo Dinh Nhu, who was head of the secret police. Dubbed the "Dragon Lady" by the American press for her dramatic lacquered hairdos and savage comments about the Buddhist "barbecues," she proudly boasted to Maggie that she would clap and say the same thing again if it helped put the monks' fraudulent acts in "their true grotesque perspective." Maggie, who just let her talk and talk about the scheming Buddhists, was then rewarded with interviews with Diem and Nhu.

When Halberstam and the gang gathered at the Caravelle Hotel's rooftop restaurant, a nightly ritual, they downed martinis and compared notes on the big-byline Washington columnist who had flown in for a look-see. As they saw it, war reporting was a young man's game, and Maggie, at forty-two, a general's wife and a mother, was past her prime. She was no longer the dimpled girl wonder of the *Life* magazine spread, and her super-patriot diatribes made her seem like a relic of the glory days of World War II.

Halberstam thought she came with way too much baggage. "Marguerite Higgins was very much a Pentagon spokesman," he recalled. "She was also, I think, a very dedicated conservative and quite a serious Catholic. So she hated the idea of what we were reporting. Those were her identifiable credentials. Almost everyone knew that. She was not just a straight reporter, but she was a real voice of a certain segment."

In addition to getting Bigart's job, Halberstam inherited his feud with Higgins, the pesky *Tribune* thorn in the *Times*'s side. He had heard all about the infamous, much-photographed Maggie of the trenches, high priestess of her profession, come to uncover the true story of what was happening in Vietnam. She was a shrill, ill-informed Cold War idealogue dispatched by the president to discredit his reports on how badly the war was going. Already at odds with Gen. Paul Harkins, Kennedy's can-do commander of the U.S. mission in Vietnam, and sparring with the military censors, Halberstam viewed her as little more than an administration lackey.

The dislike was mutual. Maggie bristled at the very mention of Bigart and his smart-alecky disciples. "Those arrogant upstarts" was how she described the two Harvard grads, Halberstam and Sheehan, to Malcolm Browne, implying that their loyalty to their country was questionable at best. Browne, a maverick correspondent who at thirty-two was the oldest of the group, did not like feuds. He took Higgins out to dinner in hopes of persuading her to bury the hatchet, but she spent the whole evening railing against Halberstam.

Maggie was tired of strutting young male reporters, especially ones with Halberstam's towering ego and ambition. He was new to Asia, had never seen any real action, and she regarded his thin résumé with utter disdain. He was a rookie, as earnest as he was irresponsible. He was trying to make his reputation in Vietnam, but his stories were creating a false impression of the situation and turning public opinion against Diem without a clue of the dangerous consequences. He did not grasp the impact on the Vietnamese people—and on American credibility, principles, and prestige—that might result from encouraging the overthrow of a democratically elected government of their foremost ally in the region.

At the end of a contentious embassy briefing, Peter Arnett remembered Higgins pulling him aside and telling him, "You know, you shouldn't blindly follow Halberstam's direction on this story." Arnett responded, "No, we are reporting what we are seeing. It's what I'm paid for." Maggie just wanted them to stop criticizing Diem's inept leadership and let the U.S. and South Vietnamese army get on with the important objective of trying to contain the Viet Cong.

She was encouraged in her views by the U.S. officials in Vietnam, who regarded the Rover Boys as unruly children and attempted to conceal from them the extent of the covert American military campaign against the Viet Cong. The newsmen responded by treating all official communiqués with the contempt they deserved. They made no secret of the fact that they considered Kennedy's handpicked ambassadors, advisers, and generals to be a bunch of liars. They were so skeptical of officialdom that they dubbed the daily press briefings the "Five O'Clock Follies" for the ubiquity of overly optimistic, vague, and inaccurate information. On one occasion, when Admiral Harry Felt, commander of all U.S. forces in the Pacific, was giving the briefing, Malcolm Browne queried the casualty figures. "Why can't you get on the team?" Felt snapped.

Maggie took a couple of public swipes at the Rover Boys, who she thought were unnecessarily antagonistic and were not providing a fair and balanced picture of the war. While she may have led the initial attack on their slanted stories, there were other members of the press who shared her concerns that the junior Saigon correspondents were too emotionally involved in the story, and too naively moralistic. Her Korea partner, Keyes Beech, now based in Saigon, admired their dedication and drive, but he also rapped their knuckles for being "young and inexperienced." Beech felt some of the same anger Higgins did over their "boorish behavior," "Diem must go" consensus, and unrelievedly gloomy view of the conflict.

The split was due in large measure to the "generation gap," Beech observed later, saying he felt caught in the middle. "Men of my generation already knew war was hell and reacted stoically to the horror of it. The younger men were learning about death for the first time and often reacted emotionally. As the bitterness grew, the press corps divided into two camps—those who wanted to win the war and those who wanted to lose it."

THE JOURNALISTIC DISPUTE WAS still simmering when Maggie left Saigon, just as the Buddhist demonstrations that had been gathering force all summer exploded into a violent uprising. On August 21, the secret police raided the pagodas in Saigon and arrested hundreds of monks, hauling them away in trucks. Martial law was imposed. The Kennedy administration issued a statement deploring the brutal raids, but behind the scenes a debate ensued about where to place the blame, and whether or not it was time to ditch Diem and the vengeful Nhus. Maggie, en route to Washington, was not heard from as the story broke wide open. By the time she got back to Washington, she had to scramble to report the burgeoning crisis, which the *Tribune* was covering with wire-service copy, and which she would try to refute with her stories.

By Aug. 24, the fast-moving events in Saigon had overtaken her reporting. The State Department suddenly did an about-face, reversing their earlier position, and now placing the blame for the religious strife, and brutal pagoda raids, squarely on Diem, implying he had abdicated too much power to Nhu. American dailies were blanketed in anti-Nhu, anti-Diem articles, editorials, and cartoons. Suddenly, the view from Saigon was that Halberstam and the Rover Boys had been right all along.

Maggie had been routed. She had been misled by Pentagon officials and the duplicitous Roger Hilsman, assistant secretary of state for Far Eastern affairs. A recent Voice of America (VOA) broadcast made it clear that the administration was holding Diem responsible for the unrest and believed the crisis was beginning to disrupt the war effort. Furious, she called Hilsman at his office and demanded to know what was going on. "The embassy says the Buddhist crisis is having no effect on the war, but your VOA broadcast said there is. What did you base it on," she asked sarcastically, "the *New York Times?*"

"Partly that," Hilsman said. "The *Times* and other dispatches out of Saigon."

There had been a sudden switch in policy and the State Department was now signaling Saigon that Washington condoned a coup. They were throwing Diem and the Nhus to the dogs. A source, an old friend at the State Department, informed her that weekend that the regime would be overthrown "in a matter of days." The pagoda raids were the turning point. The U.S. had long been dissatisfied with the weak Diem regime. Now the Kennedy administration had run out of patience. Rumors of a palace coup—with the blessings of the U.S.—were swirling around Saigon and Washington.

Refusing to be beaten by the competition, Maggie managed to insert herself into the headlines out of Saigon. She let Diem use her as his conduit to the White House: instead of cabling President Kennedy his assurances that Nhu had not taken over, Diem gave Higgins an exclusive statement that he was still in charge of the army, declaring, "I maintain control over the situation." But his claim—and her story—did not reflect reality, and many of Higgins's colleagues wondered why she was willing to act as a mouthpiece for the embattled regime.

Maggie was at her wit's end. She felt her reputation was at stake. Her dispatches from Saigon had consistently argued the opposite line, and now it looked like she had been duped by dissembling State Department officials. She did what she could to salvage her material, quickly cranking out a six-part series of articles the *Tribune* provocatively packaged as "VIETNAM—FACT AND FICTION." The first installment appeared on the front page on August 26, accompanied by an editorial promise that Marguerite Higgins would "cut through rumor and contradictions in a search for the facts of the Buddhist-government dispute."

To present the "seldom told other side of the story," Maggie wrote, she headed into the Vietnamese countryside, "deep into the dull, flat muddy delta" where the war was really being fought and few reporters bothered to go. She went on to provide a completely different assessment of the situation, arguing the suicides by fire were a distraction—staged "media events" by a few dissident monks and their followers— and should not be confused with the real progress of the U.S. military mission: "After 18 months of buildup, setbacks, and false starts the war in Vietnam is beginning to be won."

She continued to challenge the Rover Boys' reporting, from their sloppy, incorrect assertion that Buddhists represented a "majority" in South Vietnam—they were actually a minority of "perhaps fifteen percent" in a region that included Confucianists, Taoists, Moslems, and Montagnards—to more serious misrepresentations, such as consistently identifying Diem as "Catholic," harping on his religion and colonial roots, while obscuring his anti-French, Vietnamese nationalist background. "Why do American correspondents insist on calling my government 'Diem's Catholic regime'?" the country's president once asked her. "I notice they never say 'Kennedy's Catholic regime.'"

Maggie traveled the length of South Vietnam, from Hué to Da Nang in the north to Can Tho and Bac Lieu in the south, with stopovers in dozens of hamlets and combat areas, including those near Cambodia and at the bottom of Laos. She found U.S. military officials who were frustrated that the Saigon press corps exaggerated their defeats, like the one at Ap Bac, but were reluctant to give splash coverage to successful operations. In a clear dig at Halberstam and his long series of articles documenting how the military situation in the Mekong Delta had "deteriorated," she quoted General Harkins insisting that the "opposite is true."

She concluded: "The tragic irony of South Vietnam today is that its worldwide image is being tarnished at a period when the war is going better than ever. Is the United States going to jeopardize these real accomplishments in exchange for a coup d'etat and military dictatorship that may or may not supply the image that Washington desires?"

MUCH OF MAGGIE'S REPORTING was valid, though the best that could be said at that moment about the war was that U.S. forces were beginning to hold their own. Progress was marginal. But her public condemnation of the Saigon press corps for going out of their way to print negative stories about the war, and "anything scurrilous" about Diem, was wrong, and a mistake in more ways than one.

Maggie was so blinkered by her Cold War outlook, and fervent belief that the U.S. had to stop the march of communism, that she went too far. She simply could not accept the wholesale military and diplomatic failure the young correspondents were foretelling. Her attempts to counter Halberstam's carefully reported account of the collapse of the South Vietnamese army in the field—and the fruitless "strategic hamlet" program, which was doing nothing to discourage the communist guerillas roaming the countryside—with the canned optimism of the very same generals responsible for the policy, sounded hollow, and only confirmed to many that she was a Kennedy shill.

The Rover Boys may have seemed green compared to her class of war correspondents, but in terms of raw talent they exceeded all expectations. With every week that passed, Halberstam, Sheehan, and company were proving themselves to be serious, hardworking reporters, determined to try to evaluate the convoluted advisory policy being followed by the

U.S. military and what appeared to be the increasing unlikelihood that it would succeed in defeating the Viet Cong.

The young Saigon newsmen were certainly not faultless, but calling them out—though not by name—for bias and careless errors in their dispatches was an extraordinary slap in the face that was guaranteed to cause a ruckus. Maggie was an old Asia hand, and her opinion packed a punch. On September 20, *Time* magazine wrote about the press dispute in Saigon, taking her side and scolding the regular reporters on the scene for "helping to compound the very confusion that it should be untangling for its readers at home," and leaving people so thoroughly perplexed they would have been justified in thinking their newspapers were "printed in Vietnamese."

The magazine traced the problem to the unusual solidarity among the tight-knit group of young Saigon correspondents, who had formed an unofficial club *Time* dubbed "Caravelle camaraderie." The worry was that this small, incestuous clique of bar regulars pooled not only their information but also their misinformation, prejudices, and grievances. "But the balm of such companionship has not been conducive to independent thought," the magazine opined. "The reporters have tended to reach unanimous agreement on almost everything they have seen." The Caravelle gang was so confident of its own convictions that any other version of the story was "quickly dismissed."

This was strong stuff. The editors of *Time* were blatantly impeaching the young Saigon correspondents for distorting the news. Days later, another heavyweight Washington columnist, Joe Alsop, who visited Vietnam briefly, joined the chorus of critics. He supported Maggie's claims and accused the Saigon press corps of carrying on an "egregious crusade" to oust Diem. The conservative Hearst columnist Frank Conniff chimed in, opining that the *New York Times*'s reporting in Vietnam had misled President Kennedy and was "a political time bomb." The local boys were clearly too young and too tendentious, and they lacked the abilities of "a Marguerite Higgins, whose byline carries authority."

Worried by the young Saigon crew's insistent anti-Diem, pro-Buddhist, we're-losing-the-war attitude, editors in New York began sending senior correspondents to Saigon for a fresh look. Mohr and Perry were so upset at being pilloried in their own magazine that they resigned. *Time* did a follow-up piece that was somewhat more moderate, but by then the press mess had become a story in itself, with Higgins and Halberstam as the main protagonists. Malcom Browne and Neil Sheehan both got into heated arguments with their home offices over their coverage, and AP told Browne to take a month's leave to cool off.

When the *Times* began nervously querying their man in Saigon about Higgins's contrary claims in the *Tribune*, Halberstam went ballistic. Exhausted and under enormous pressure, he found the daily barrage of nagging cables from New York intolerable.

First came:

> INFORMATIVELY HIGGINS YESTERDAY REPORTED
> SITUATION IN HINTERLANDS RE BUDDHISTS QUITE
> DIFFERENT . . .

Followed by:

> WHAT IS THERE TO MAGGIE HIGGINS STATEMENTS
> THAT IN COUNTRYSIDE WAR ACTUALLY BEING
> FOUGHT . . .

Halberstam was having none of it and doubled down on his censure of Higgins. Her main source, General Harkins, was a fool and wholly unreliable. He and Sheehan placed their faith instead in the popular Lt. Col. John Paul Vann, a guerilla-warfare expert, whom they regarded as the rare military leader of great integrity and adopted as a kind of mentor, sharing his pessimistic view of the war. Annoyed that his editors in New York were giving any credence to Higgins's reports, Halberstam fired off a series of angry rebuttals:

> ON THAT LITTLE GIRL I THINK IT SHOULD BE CLEAR
> WHICH SIDE IS SLANTING STOP . . .

And then more heatedly:

> MAGGIE COPY NOT TAKEN SERIOUSLY HERE AND
> PLEASE UNWORRY SINCE ENTIRE BUSINESS IS
> DELIBERATE PHONY STOP LONGER MEMO ON THAT
> FOLLOWS . . .

On and on it went, with missives flying back and forth between New York and Saigon. When the badgering cables about Higgins's reporting kept on coming, Halberstam pounded out his final, furious reply:

> IF YOU SEND ME ONE MORE CABLE REFERRING
> TO THAT WOMANS COPY YOU WILL HAVE MY
> RESIGNATION FORTHWITH BY RETURN CABLE AND I
> MEAN IT REPEAT MEAN IT

Halberstam would not, could not, calm down. His emotions were so inflamed he was beyond reasonableness. "I'm combative not just with ambassadors and generals, but I'm combative with my own editors," he later admitted, adding, "I was very full of myself." The *Times* sent their Hong Kong bureau chief to Saigon to try to soothe their overwrought correspondent and reassure him that they still had faith in him.

But Halberstam and the Rover Boys were in a fighting mood, and they were quick to defend every dispatch. One night that August, over dinner at l'Amiral, a French bistro in Saigon, an exasperated Charley Mohr told Higgins exactly what he thought: "Anything—even a military junta—would be better than Diem," he declared. Provoked, she retorted, according to Mohr: "Reporters here would like to see us lose the war to prove they're right." He passed on her comment to *Time*, which printed it. She denied ever making the remark, but it was widely circulated and she would never live it down.

Maggie retaliated. She began needling the young Saigon reporters with the Krulak barb that they were "typewriter strategists" who rarely ventured to the front, and preferred to cover the shooting war from the air-conditioned comfort of the Caravelle. When it got back to Halberstam, he had a fit. He had spent months slogging through the mud of the Mekong Delta, and here was Higgins, after only three weeks in the boonies with the Green Berets, calling him a coward. She was driving him crazy, playing on his insecurities and planting stories out of spite. "People in the Pentagon were leaking," he recalled. "Generals would leak stories: 'Marguerite Higgins says that young boy Halberstam was shown a photograph of Viet Cong bodies and he burst into tears.'"

The tale knifed into his psyche no less dramatically than had she stabbed him in the back. Higgins had gone around telling people that when she returned from the field one day with photos of butchered Viet Cong, she showed some of the pictures to Halberstam, who cried at the sight of so much butchery.

The anecdote quickly made the rounds at the Caravelle, and eventually reached the ears of Brute Krulak. The marine general took it as confirmation that the belligerent *Times* reporter, the scourge of the military brass, was actually a sissy. When Krulak repeated it to the editors of *Time*, they checked it with their Saigon correspondent. Mohr told his pal, who promptly erupted. For Halberstam, who was notoriously thin-skinned, it was not merely a slight, it was an unforgivable slur—"the penultimate assault on my manhood." He never knew whether the story was Krulak's or Higgins's invention, but the damage was done.

"Tears were for women, of course, and not only had I wept, but I had wept for the wrong side," he later wrote, explaining that the insult went against his ideal of the virile war correspondent. "Hemingway heroes did not cry."

A few weeks later, Halberstam, still nursing his wounded vanity, confronted Krulak at the military airfield near Saigon. His six-foot, two-inch frame looming over the squat general, the *Times* reporter thundered: "My name is David Halberstam and I hear you've been telling people I was crying on the roof of the Caravelle Hotel."

"Yes," Krulak replied. "I was quoting Maggie Higgins, as you probably know."

Halberstam proceeded to have a complete meltdown. "I want to tell you that story is a bunch of shit!!!" he shouted, his voice easily carrying over the full-throttle engines. He went on shouting—it was not true, he had never been shown any photos, and he had certainly never broken into tears. "And I just want you to fucking know it," he added, "and don't *ever* put out shit like that again!"

"Well, it's not a GI Joe war, is it?" said Krulak, unintimidated by the reporter's tirade. "It is not a war with an Ernie Pyle, is it?"

The reference to the revered World War II correspondent was too much for Halberstam. He started shouting again and carried on shouting another five minutes. His tarmac tantrum, which by all accounts was unforgettable, upset his editors and earned him a reprimand.

"It was a cat-and-dog fight between two great journalists," recalled Beverly Deepe, then a twenty-eight-year-old stringer for *Newsweek* and the only resident female correspondent in Saigon. She was not part of the Caravelle fraternity. "I never got in on those bar room conversations about Maggie," she said, "but I knew of the feud."

Deepe had no interest in ganging up on Higgins. The claim that she once spotted the famous correspondent in Saigon and purposefully avoided her, convinced her girlhood idol had "sold out" and become a cheerleader for the military, was not true. Deepe had never dreamed of being a war correspondent and did not learn about the *Herald Tribune* phenom until later, when she was hired as a freelancer by the paper. "She covered a lot of ground in a big way," said Deepe of her predecessor, adding that she took her hat off to her. She seconded the opinion of another female member of the press corps: "Being the Maggie Higgins of the Vietnam war was what women journalists talked about."

Maggie's Vietnam series proved to be highly controversial, but not for the reasons she hoped. All that autumn, the *Times*, the wire services, and newsmagazines ran stories contradicting the central points she had made. On September 20, she sent Bobby Kennedy a strongly worded letter summarizing her impressions of the sorry situation in Vietnam. After thanking him for putting her in touch with Krulak, she laid into the "allegedly informed" officials in the State Department, whose misguided view of

Diem and the war was "based on the distorted U.S. press dispatches from Saigon." She added, "See last week's press section of *Time*."

Referring to Walter Cronkite's September 2 television interview with the president, she thought she detected Hilsman's handiwork in Kennedy's statement that the war could be won only if there were "changes in policy and perhaps with personnel," which was widely interpreted as a green light for a military coup. "It seems to me that whoever briefed the President before the Cronkite show did the President and the country a disservice," she concluded sourly. "Our Vietnamese client has a bad enough image without making it worse than it is."

She sent a copy of her letter to the president, hoping to register her ideas where they would count. In a separate note, she insisted Diem still had a lot of support and it would be unwise to depose him. "Unless the Viet Minh yield to the temptation to escalate, I believe those Americans in Saigon who say the war is on the way to being won." She had a lot more to tell him about the Americans and Saigon: "Could I come see you here or in Hyannis Port at your earliest convenience? Could Mrs. Lincoln call me?"

Then Maggie went on the offensive. By September 23, she had tracked down the source of a secret August 24th cable sent to the new ambassador in Vietnam, Henry Cabot Lodge, from the State Department, instructing him to advise the South Vietnamese generals that the U.S. would not oppose a military coup. She did not spare her friends in the White House, although she did not realize then that the president was implicated. She reported: "A diplomatic cable that back-fired in South Vietnam is the fuel stoking a white-hot Pentagon-State Department feud involving high Kennedy administration officials." Hilsman had sent the cables as "a kind of invitation to the Vietnamese Army to get rid of President Diem and his brother and sister-in-law, the highly publicized Ngo Dinh Nhus."

By October 2, she had more details of the skullduggery. Her damning revelations about the secret cable authorizing the coup, and resulting tensions between the players—the "get-Diem" team led by Lodge and

Harkins versus the outmaneuvered CIA chief John Richardson—created such an uproar that Kennedy had to address it in a press conference.

"Higgins's reports were cannonballs," wrote the press critic Russ Braley. "But they were propelled by a half charge." Her report on the fatal cable was her last scoop for the *Trib*, which was drowning in debt and on the verge of going under. On October 12, just as she had the State Department on the defensive, came the ill-timed denouement: Maggie announced she was leaving the paper that had been her home for twenty-one years.

The old *Trib* was dying, mortally wounded by a 114-day newspaper strike from which it could not recover. The Reids had been forced to sell to Jock Whitney, a Wall Street investor and family friend, who was using his many millions to try to keep it afloat. The new editor, James Bellows, desperate to breathe life into the paper, decided to shake up the aging all-star roster on the editorial page and dropped Higgins's column. For Maggie, that was the "last straw" and she headed for the door. Despite her profound devotion to the *Trib*—she called it her "Holy Mother Church"—the paper's future looked grim.

She had known this day was coming for a long time and had another suitor waiting in the wings. Harry Guggenheim, the president and publisher of *Newsday*, a thriving Long Island paper with a circulation of four hundred thousand, offered her a lucrative deal to write three columns a week on foreign and domestic affairs, which would be syndicated to sixty newspapers. Eager to entice her away from the *Tribune*, he was prepared to pay her a generous starting salary of $20,000 a year—subject to upward revisions—as well as her usual 50 percent of the syndication gross, plus a $5,000-a-year travel allowance. It was too good a deal to turn down. "Leaving the *Trib* was a terrible wrench," she told colleagues mournfully. "I have such affection for it." But she did not know how much longer the paper would last—it lingered on another three years—and she did not want to go down with it.

On November 1, Diem and Nhu were killed, murdered in an armored car after surrendering. Maggie had just returned from Germany and was delivering an exclusive to *Newsday*—the first interview with Konrad

Adenauer, the former chancellor of West Germany, since his retirement. It was late on Saturday night, November 2, when, returning home from a party, she heard the news on the radio. There was an urgent message from Madame Nhu, who had been on a public relations tour of the U.S., only to find herself a widow, and without allies. Stranded in Los Angeles, she reached out to Higgins for help. Sobbing into the phone, Madame Nhu asked her plaintively, "Are they going to kill my children too?"

It was 2 a.m. when Maggie, her Irish temper roused, woke Hilsman out of a sound sleep at home in Washington. "Congratulations, Roger," she said. "How does it feel to have blood on your hands?"

"Oh, come on now, Maggie," he replied. "Revolutions are rough. People get hurt."

She demanded the State Department do something about getting Nhu's four-year-old daughter, and two sons, aged eleven and fifteen, safely out of Vietnam. Hilsman said he would have General Harkins send his personal plane to fetch them.

Three weeks later Jack Kennedy was dead, assassinated while riding in a motorcade in Dallas, Texas, on November 22. Maggie was in Hong Kong when she learned the president had been shot, and she cabled a reaction story expressing her grief to *Newsday*. She was just back from My Tho in the Mekong Delta, reporting on the "new mess" in Vietnam in the aftermath of the military coup, and the accompanying riots and police terror that she had predicted.

Her reporting linking the assassinations in Saigon and Dallas resonated with Kennedy's successor, Lyndon Johnson. The day after Kennedy's funeral, and before moving into the White House, Johnson walked down the hallway of his home and, pointing to a portrait of Diem on the wall, told a visitor, "We've had a hand in killing him. Now it's happening here." He feared the assassination of JFK was payback. He would later call the coup "the worst mistake we ever made."

Maggie would continue to try to prove that U.S. officials decided to "play God" by ordering the overthrow of the government, and that they were accountable for Diem's death and the debacle in Vietnam that followed. "It was a valiant effort that would cost her life," wrote Russ

Braley, "but now the effort was doomed. It could not be done without blackening the name of the martyred president, too much for the nation to take."

There was little support for her views in the media. Halberstam's five-thousand-word anatomy of the coup had appeared on the front page of the *Times*, detailing the many intrigues by the Vietnamese generals and including only one paragraph on the role of the Americans. The administration was hiding behind plausible deniability, and rationalizing that what had happened was an entirely Vietnamese affair.

Determined to vindicate her reporting, Maggie began work on a book, *Our Vietnam Nightmare*, building a case that the constant criticism by Halberstam and the Saigon press corps aided the anti-Diem forces, and weakened U.S. support for the regime to the point where the Kennedy administration eventually acquiesced to a military coup. In the tumultuous period that followed, Hanoi quickly moved in to capitalize on the confusion. As Maggie had predicted, the fall of Diem opened a Pandora's box of local conflicts. South Vietnam went through five governments in fourteen months, and she showed how the Buddhist leader Tri Quang engineered the end of each one. "By becoming a party to the coup," she contended, "the Saigon press corps and the U.S. government turned what had been a Vietnamese war into an American war, making large-scale American intervention and casualties inevitable."

Halberstam left Saigon not long after the coup, telling colleagues that it had become too dangerous. His hasty retreat did not impress Beverly Deepe. "Who was he to criticize Higgins for all her exploits?" she asked. Deepe stayed and covered the war in Vietnam for seven continuous years, giving her a long "institutional memory" and a unique perspective. As for the self-aggrandizing *Times* reporter, who was so convinced he had the corner on truth, all Halberstam did, she said, "was parrot John Paul Vann, who, as it turned out, was a big liar, and womanizer, and rapist, and helped to deceive the American public."

Maggie would make three more extended trips to Vietnam between 1963 and 1965 to try to uncover the story of the Diem plot, painstakingly gathering evidence of how the decision was reached. She wrote a full indictment of the administration's role in the shameful episode, "Saigon Summary," which appeared in *America* magazine in January 1964.

It was Halberstam who had the last word. In the spring, in a nod to the changing of the reportorial guard, he and Malcolm Browne were awarded the Pulitzer Prize for their courageous Vietnam reporting. Halberstam's byline was the best known of the Saigon press corps, and he would go on to become one of the most celebrated reporters and nonfiction writers of his time, sealing his reputation with his best-selling 1965 book about Vietnam, *The Making of a Quagmire.*

Despite all the accolades that came his way over the years, he never got over Maggie's attack on his patriotism, masculinity, and accuracy. He bore a grudge against her for the rest of his life. Over the next four decades, in interview after interview, he seldom missed an opportunity to vilify her work and character. "Her name was never mentioned without his uttering the most awful epithets," said Peter Arnett. "He hated her viscerally."

Then again, Halberstam was known for his grudges. He famously carried on a thirteen-year feud with the writer Gay Talese, his best friend and a fellow *Times* alumnus, over a disagreement about a book idea about the auto industry that Halberstam pigheadedly claimed as his own. "He cared about a story more than he cared about anything," recalled Talese. "He had an ego like nobody else's." (The two finally made up in 1990.) Shaking his head, Talese added, "He was the most arrogant, self-centered, determined, loving, beautiful guy."

But he more than met his match in Maggie Higgins. Interviewed for an adulatory 1964 *Esquire* cover story on Halberstam, certifying him as a new pop-culture figure and antiestablishment hero, she stubbornly refused to let him and his cohorts off the hook. "I think the boys are entitled to their viewpoint," she said. "Some of us don't happen to agree—and we've been to a few more wars."

The bitter press dispute that developed between the Saigon reporters, the U.S. government, and the World War II generation of correspondents was much more complex and far-reaching than the petty spat between Halberstam and Higgins. The White House, Pentagon, and embassy officials all piled on. "It was a great storm," Halberstam said of the intensifying, orchestrated attacks on his critical reporting that culminated with President Kennedy asking the editor of the *Times* to have him reassigned. Decades later, the 1963 "war of words" would be the subject of dozens of books and doctoral theses, and government and military think tanks would still be doing studies analyzing the tactics, and anti-Diem advocacy, of the crusading young correspondents, and the contrary view voiced by veterans like Higgins and Beech.

In 1971, when transcripts of the *Pentagon Papers*—the government's classified history of the war—became public, the secret cables confirmed Maggie's account of American complicity in toppling the regime: "For the military coup d'etat against Ngo Dinh Diem, the U.S. must accept its full share of responsibility. Beginning in August 1963 we variously authorized, sanctioned and encouraged the coup efforts of the Vietnamese generals and offered full support for a successor government." The transcripts were courtesy of Neil Sheehan, then the Pentagon reporter for the *New York Times*, who obtained the seven thousand pages of classified government documents about the Vietnam War.

In the end, the transcripts proved that the Vietnam reporters got some things right and some things wrong. Maggie, who had no problem with the larger administration lie—that in fighting a limited war, the American military commitment was actually unlimited—could not countenance the State Department's unscrupulous behavior in overthrowing the regime. Halberstam, who fought so passionately to expose the government's covert military campaign, did not particularly mind minimizing the truth about the coup, considering Diem to be hopeless and the dark motives behind the secret Lodge cable to be not worth probing too deeply.

By the time the first of the many Vietnam memoirs by the Saigon press corps and Kennedy advisers began to reach bookstores in 1965, "they were all the same side," observed Russ Braley of the "alibi books" absolving the authors of any part in the coup. "Hilsman, [Averell] Harriman, [George] Ball, Halberstam, Sheehan and the *Times*," he ticked off the names, "their wagons were drawn in a circle" to defend against attack.

They reinforced one another's accounts, provided complimentary blurbs for each other's book jackets, and the *Times* book review praised them all, "closing the circle of mutual admiration and mortaring in the building blocks of history reposing in the nation's libraries."

The most dangerous outlier, the fiercely independent Maggie Higgins, was not among them.

18

✳ ✳ ✳ ✳ ✳ ✳ ✳ ✳

A Legend

To underestimate Maggie Higgins could be
disastrous. If, like an aging ballplayer, she had
lost her reporter's legs, she had also found a
new playing field. Her home turf was now
Washington, that strange city where, knowing
the right people and making the right changes
in your game, a reporter can play on bad pins
forever. In the nation's capital she remained
what she had always been—a holy terror with
the most outrageous tactics in the business.

—William Prochnau, *Once upon a Distant War*

BY THE TIME MAGGIE HAD RECOVERED FROM THE SHOCK OF KEN-
nedy's assassination, some of the sheen had worn off his administration.
She did not write any paeans to the fallen leader who had signed Diem's
death warrant. She was too heartbroken, and at the same time conferring
accolades at that moment did not feel appropriate. In the sad, unsettled
weeks that followed, she moved quickly to shore up her relationship with
the new president, writing columns praising Johnson's grace under pressure and remarkably smooth transition to the White House.

On December 28, a month after Kennedy was buried, Maggie was
rewarded with an invitation to the LBJ Ranch in Texas and an exclusive
interview with Lady Bird Johnson. Speaking at length for the first time

about the tragedy, the new first lady confided the "torrent of emotions" that assailed her after she heard the shots ring out over Dealey Plaza in downtown Dallas. Later, at the hospital, when an aide approached them in the waiting room and addressed LBJ as "Mr. President," she remembered feeling "infinite compassion for my husband."

Lyndon Johnson liked Maggie—he always sought her out for a dance at White House functions—and he was grateful for her support. He had gotten to know her on the trip to Berlin during the wall crisis of 1961, the occasion of his first diplomatic triumph. The new West German chancellor Ludwig Erhard was visiting the ranch the same weekend as Maggie's Lady Bird interview, and the president asked her to stay and give him a few pointers. Johnson was hosting a big barbecue in the chancellor's honor, attended by a gathering of foreign press, in an effort to improve East-West relations. Maggie was happy to oblige. She was delighted to find she still had a friend in the Oval Office, one who was even more eager to flatter and woo the press.

From the very beginning, the gregarious Johnson made it clear he was not going to be fenced in by White House security and protocol. He continued his practice, developed as Senate majority leader, of solicitously phoning newspaper pals for their opinion, and dropping in unannounced for a chat. On January 27, 1964, he took Maggie by surprise.

She and Pete Lisagor were cohosting a luncheon at her Georgetown home to talk politics and policy with Bill Moyers, the precocious, bespectacled thirty-year-old assistant to the president, and Carl Rowan, who that very morning had been named head of the U.S. Information Agency, which would make him the highest-ranking Black official in the government. Moyers had rung to say he was running late, and to ask if he could bring Jack Valenti, another top White House aide. Maggie told him there was a pot of French ragout on the stove and more than enough for everyone. Half an hour later, a cortege of limousines rolled into Twenty-Fourth Street. Coming up the walk were Moyers, Valenti, and a smiling President Johnson, who kissed Higgins on both cheeks for all the neighbors to see.

When Bill Hall arrived at one-thirty, he amused Johnson by describing how he had to run a gauntlet of Secret Service to get to his own home.

"Who are you?" four large men carrying walkie-talkies demanded, barring the door. "I could ask the same of you," Hall replied.

After laughing, the president turned serious, as he always did after a few drinks. "I got a lot of problems," he said. "I've got a brazen communist attempt to conquer Asia on my hands. I've got Negroes revolting in America—and I know Mr. Roe-*ann* sides with the revolution. I got troubles in Central America that the people don't even know about. I gotta figure out how to pay for these fucking wars and keep my commitment to feed, educate, and care for the people of this country. Now, I can't do it if Maggie and Pete Lisagor abandon me and echo the know-nothings on social policy and the goddamn liberals like Mary McGrory [a *Washington Star* columnist] on foreign policy."

Changing the subject, Maggie told Johnson that Henry Cabot Lodge ought to be recalled from Vietnam and he should appoint a new ambassador. She had already made the same suggestion in a recent column. Lodge had made the removal of Diem and the Nhus his primary objective, and she would not rest until he was held accountable. Johnson let the remark slide, unwilling to address it. When Maggie next brought up General Clay, LBJ said, "Bill, let's get General Clay down here next week, he's a great American." She noted with satisfaction that Moyers whipped out his little white notebook and jotted down a reminder.

Naturally, she wrote about the president's impromptu visit, leaving out his off-the-record remarks. "He was a zestful, engaging and responsive guest, full of stories and anecdotes, some serious, some funny," she gushed over the flamboyant Texan, whose manners were often criticized as crude or corny but which on that occasion charmed everyone present. "Johnson is a person whose awesome energies and determination to do a good job keep him working all the time. At lunch, over coffee, on the way to the front door, he is probing, thinking out loud, exchanging ideas, occasionally giving orders." The new president seemed genuinely fond of the press, she observed, and was gracious enough to tell his hostess that he "enjoyed the ragout."

She also wrote a column praising Johnson for appointing Rowan to the powerful post of director of the USIA, where he would be responsible for beaming America's story to the Soviet Union, China, Poland, Hungary, Cuba, Vietnam, and scores of other countries where there was no free press. Rowan, who was up for a tough fight for Senate confirmation, was not only an admirable choice to replace Edward R. Murrow, she asserted, but his appointment would underline the fact that the president's ideas on racial equality were not just words but policy: "Johnson has now surely given the final blow to the stubbornly prevailing myth that in racial matters he 'talks liberal but really doesn't mean it.'"

Maggie, who disliked prejudice based on race, color, creed, or sex, noted that the president also said that another of his priorities would be "more top jobs for women," as part of his commitment to recruit more talented female professionals into high-level civil service positions. He had already offered the post of ambassador to Finland, made available by Rowan's move to Washington, to the philanthropist Mary Lasker.

Johnson's secretary later told Rowan that the president said, "I could almost cry," after he read the Higgins column. Rowan also appreciated the vote of confidence. It was "nice, temporarily consoling stuff," he recalled of her kind words, especially for a "black person who was under attack in powerful parts of the media."

Maggie was off and running, helping to build support for Johnson in the upcoming 1964 election and, along with the rest of the "Irish mafia," pushing Bobby Kennedy as a vice-presidential prospect. Since it was an open secret that LBJ loathed the Kennedys, she had her work cut out for her. A week after the official mourning period was over, and the black crepe that had draped the White House was being replaced with Christmas decorations, Bobby gave her a disarmingly candid interview. Maggie had recently sent Ethel flowers on the christening of their eighth child, the latest addition to their brood. Bobby spoke thoughtfully of his decision to stay on as attorney general, telling her, "If I had walked out on Johnson, it would have made it seem as if Kennedys were only willing to serve other Kennedys."

But there was no denying his dynastic ambitions, and it was obvious that Bobby was already eyeing the role of vice president—and president— for himself. As if in answer to her unspoken question, he predicted

Johnson would be elected in '64 and would most likely run again in '68. With Teddy now occupying Jack's former Senate seat, that was also not an option, but Maggie speculated the attorney general would soon find another influential role for himself in Washington. The surviving head of the Kennedy clan, Bobby, new lines etched in his chiseled face, had emerged from the grief of his brother's death with a raw determination to follow in his footsteps. "He is back at his enormous work pace," she wrote, "his wit at the ready and composure such that he can even talk of the past with outward calm."

To Maggie, nothing was off-limits in an interview. She invaded his privacy remorselessly, posing a question few reporters would have dared ask so soon: Did Jack ever have a premonition of his fate?

"President Kennedy and I often talked about how easy it would be to kill an American president," Bobby replied. "We would speculate, in a specific situation, how the gunman could most easily go about it." But Jack never took the possibility seriously. In the aftermath of his assassination, Bobby admitted, everything about his life had changed forever. "I am no longer the president's brother," he said. "With my brother there were so many conversations—not just about official duties—but about many things . . ." His voice trailed off, his expression bleak.

Her Kennedy projects—the book on Jack's boyhood, and another on Jackie's redecorated White House—had to be scrapped. For a while, she and Pete Lisagor even thought their tome about the Foreign Service, with JFK's off-the-record speech as the epilogue, would end up in the dustbin. They had not managed to clear the speech, which had been carefully censored by Bundy, but the final version had been in Pierre Salinger's dispatch case on November 22 awaiting the president's approval. At Maggie's request, Bobby expedited the matter, and *Overtime in Heaven* was published in June.

Her book about Rose Kennedy was still "up in the air," Maggie informed Bobby in August after returning from a summer holiday on the Cape. She had seen Ethel and the children, "but I wish you had been there." After LBJ lowered the vice-presidential boom, Bobby had decided to switch states and declare for senator from New York. With the nominations becoming official on September 1, he was already on the campaign trail, trying to persuade New Yorkers that he was not just another carpetbagger. Maggie tried to help him combat some of the adverse press, and oft-repeated criticism that RFK was too cold to win over voters, insisting that he displayed the "Kennedy magic"—at times heart-wrenchingly like that of his brother—and the same "instinctive rapport with the crowds."

While busily turning out columns, Maggie had spent her first six months at *Newsday* battling with the paper's editorial director, William Woestendiek. She kept the adrenaline flowing by banging out long, belli-cose letters listing all the reasons she was dissatisfied with her new terms of employment, from the strict noon deadlines that made it all but impos-sible to write "close to the news," to Guggenheim's assurances that her column would run regularly in the *Washington Star*, giving her a voice in the capital, but it had appeared only erratically. "Those 'assurances,'" she wrote in one scorching missive, had "proved empty."

On her return from a trip to Los Angeles, she received Woestendiek's response—filled with the usual complaints about her trips abroad dupli-cating the efforts of other correspondents and racking up exorbitant travel expenses—which had Maggie threatening to quit in another scathing let-ter if they could not "negotiate their differences." She had plans to go to Panama, and then on to Zanzibar and Greece to cover the political unrest. Noting acidly that her column was called "On the Spot" for a reason, she added, "My specialty has been, and for some time must continue to be, to go to places that other columnists are either too lazy or too fearful to go to."

A measure of her unhappiness with *Newsday* was reflected in an uncharacteristically deferential note she sent Jock Whitney on the flimsy pretext of having never paid him a "formal farewell call." She admitted that she missed the *Herald Tribune* and "hoped that the *Herald Tribune* misses me." She wanted to correct the impression that she had quit over money—she had turned down jobs that offered twice as much on more than one occasion—and maintained she left solely because Bellows dropped her column. "If Jim should ever find that circumstances have changed," she hinted broadly, "I should be interested in hearing from him."

About this time *Newsday* hired Thomas Dorsey to grow their syndication business, and he offered Guggenheim and his editors some tips on handling their obstreperous, budget-busting columnist. A charismatic salesman given to grand gestures and bold assertions, Dorsey understood the marquee value of a name like Higgins and exactly what it would take to make her column work. "I had known Maggie and fought with her at the *Herald Tribune* and I said to them: 'You know, she's terrific, but you'll never make any money on her because she'll spend it all up. You'd better put a tight rein on expenses.'"

He knew all about her formidable Irish temper. And her fondness for ultimatums. After taking some careful soundings in the industry, he was also convinced it was mostly bluster. Maggie was nothing if not predictable. As soon as he curtailed her expenses, she did what she had always done at the *Trib* and went straight over his head to the boss to complain. "Whatever Maggie wanted, she got," said Dorsey. "She was a good reporter, and she was also a dish. I mean, she could look like the wrath of God, or she could look like a model for *Glamour* magazine, whichever suited her."

Dorsey told Guggenheim he did not know what was going to happen, but either he won this battle with Higgins or he was gone. When the three met to try to resolve their differences, Dorsey stood his ground. Maggie, as expected, began listing the other papers interested in her services. "Well, I tell you what," Dorsey said, cutting her off mid-rant. "I think if that's what Maggie wants to do, we ought to tear up the contract." From that day on, he had no problems with Higgins. "Maggie and I got along great," he said, adding that she developed some discipline with the noon deadlines, in part thanks to a very good assistant who brought order to the mayhem of her Washington office. Her column was going well, and was soon expanded to four times a week, in addition to her "On the Spot" dispatches.

On August 4, Maggie broke a big story that landed her on page one of newspapers across the country. The lead was a humdinger: "The best kept secret of the Cuban crisis is now coming to light." Maggie poured out the story of how John Scali, an ABC news correspondent, became a go-between for the State Department in secret meetings with a Soviet intelligence officer and was entrusted with "delivering a Soviet outline of a Caribbean compromise that in all probability meant the difference between peace and war in the Cuban missile crisis of October 1962." She had learned of Scali's "historic mission" two years earlier, and had discussed it with then-president Kennedy, who had declined to release it for publication at the time. When Maggie was tipped that Roger Hilsman, who had been cast out of the State Department had written an article about the negotiations for *Look* magazine, she decided to steal a beat on her old foe.

Editor & Publisher highlighted her Cuba scoop, calling it "an exclusive of world-wide significance," and used it as an excuse to do an updated profile of the star correspondent. "This national recognition of the importance of her work is nothing new in the experience of Marguerite Higgins," the editors noted, adding that the reporter, known for the hard-to-get interview, was a "living legend."

Dorsey launched a promotion campaign quoting the *Editor & Publisher* piece in an effort to hook more subscribing newspapers for her column. The tagline read: "Lady on the Spot . . . Fusing the tough realism of a combat reporter with the human insights of an informed and perceptive woman."

While never a standard-bearer for feminism, Maggie's celebrated journalistic barnstorming made her stand out as an example to young women entering the profession. "Small wonder my generation of cub reporters saw Higgins not as a role model (an anemic phrase) but as an idol," recalled Bernice Buresh, who became a correspondent and bureau chief for *Newsweek*. She remembered that one of her colleagues, the writer Caryl Rivers, as a seventeen-year-old copy girl, used to stake out places around the capital that might give her a glimpse of the fabulous Higgins at work, saying, "I gladly would have kissed her feet."

1964 WAS A TURBULENT YEAR, and there were so many important issues to cover—the shifting domestic political currents after JFK's assassination, the civil rights marches, the anti-war movement, and the ongoing debate over the nuclear nonproliferation treaty—but America's moral failure in Vietnam nagged at Maggie. She could not let it go.

She wrote another lengthy condemnation of Kennedy's misguided war policy for *America* magazine, entitled "Ugly Americans of Vietnam." The title was a nod to the Graham Greene novel *The Quiet American*, a literary interpretation of U.S. arrogance narrated by a British journalist in Vietnam. She considered Greene's text required reading and advised the *Evening Star* editor Newby Noyes to "dip into it" before his upcoming trip, adding, "When you get there, it will give you the creeps to see all those 'quiet Americans' of today."

In her opinion the folly dated back to Washington's decision to meddle in Vietnamese affairs, and to impose Western concepts of "reform" on a country with profoundly different traditions:

> The good Americans had acted on the very false assumption that somehow an Oriental country that had never experienced nationhood or known peace could none the less develop "instant democracy" and operate responsibly in the middle of a war. . . . Such a false assumption is a bungle that history does not lightly forgive. And today Vietnam's survival is in doubt. The impossible, if well-meaning, American demands for the trappings of democracy brought near chaos instead.

She sent a copy of her article to David Halbertsam in New York, but his editor informed her that the reporter, whose blood pressure surely would have gone up after reading her piece, had already left for his new assignment in Eastern Europe. She adapted the main ideas in her "Ugly Americans" piece for a television documentary about the war in Vietnam, writing the commentary for an hour-long program for National Educational Television (WNET). Her view of the conflict had crystallized into one of cynical disillusionment, reflected in the program's opening lines, in which she quoted an allied diplomat describing American policy in Vietnam as "friendly to the neutrals, neutral to the enemy, and hostile to its friends."

She returned again and again to this theme of a tragedy of errors, preoccupied with the idea that her reputation might have suffered as a result of being on the wrong side of history, and that she needed to get her views on the record. It was as if she hoped that, by endless repetition, she could prove that she had been just as correct in her journalistic judgments about the war as Halberstam had been in his. At one point, she even considered taking out a full-page ad in one of the trade publications citing all the predictions she had made in her column that were being borne out by the disastrous turn of events over the past year. In the end, Dorsey talked her out of it. He argued that no one really knew or cared who was right and who was wrong about Vietnam, and the "I told you so" technique would work against her, not for her.

In August, after an allegedly unprovoked attack by North Vietnamese gunboats on the U.S. destroyers *Maddox* and *Turner Joy* in the Gulf of Tonkin, American war planes bombed North Vietnamese naval bases. Congress, in the form of the Gulf of Tonkin Resolution, authorized the president "to take all necessary measures" to protect American forces. "The torpedo boats in the Tonkin Gulf were testing the 'paper tiger' image," she wrote, referring to Mao's description of America as threatening in appearance but actually unable to stomach a fight. "No doubt they were hoping to cause the Yankees to go home." Maggie, along with other hard-liners, was demanding more vigorous action. Within weeks, she got her wish, and the administration embarked on a sustained bombing program against the North.

That fall, she heard from her longtime editor, Ken McCormick, that Doubleday was already committed to publishing John Mecklin's Vietnam chronicle, *Mission in Torment*, so Maggie offered her book to Harper & Row, the publisher of her much-delayed Rose Kennedy memoir. She wrote her new editor, Evan Thomas, that what she had in mind was a short exposé that would illuminate "the great American bungle in Vietnam."

A spate of books by the Saigon correspondents—first and foremost Halberstam's *The Making of a Quagmire*—and Kennedy advisers were being published, and she wanted to get her points across before she was drowned out by the coup apologists. "The thesis of the book—the Ugly Americans in Vietnam—stands irrespective of Vietnam's fate," she wrote. "If Vietnam falls, the book would explain why. If Vietnam somehow miraculously pulls itself together with American help, this outcome would merely confirm that Bismarck was right when he said: 'God is on the side of dogs, drunkards and the United States of America.'"

On November 14, Maggie left on a State Department junket to Vietnam. After a year's absence, she found Saigon—referred to as the "twilight zone" by the GIs—still in the grip of political plots, Buddhist riots, and an atmosphere "heavy with unreality." Thich Tri Quang was still stage-managing protests. Maggie recognized some of the "professional agitators" and waved at them. One waved back.

Her *Newsday* series, "What's Happening in Vietnam," reiterated the well-intentioned but costly errors that had been made by Americans and documented the intensifying war against the South after Diem's death, evidenced by the mounting infiltration of men and equipment from the North, down the supply chain known as the Ho Chi Minh Trail, in support of the Viet Cong. The enemy was growing stronger by the day.

Vietnam was turning into a major war, and she summed up the magnitude of the opposition in an unadorned, fact-based dispatch that was her strong suit. Her source, Capt. Tram Quoc Ba, who had defected to the South after sixteen years of service with the Communist Viet Minh, told her that in his province alone, more than one thousand regular Viet Minh troops had passed through in the past eight months: "The weapons they brought were far better and heavier than before. Every unit had mortars. Many units came south in company strength ready to fight without further reorganization. And for the first time, thirty-man antiaircraft units came south to fight with each battalion."

For someone just back from the front, she wrote, "it is strange to listen to talk here at home of 'escalating the war' in Vietnam sometime in the future. For the war in Vietnam has already been escalated, and very dangerously." The widening scope of the operation meant that it was going to require a lot more troops, and a lot more years of fighting. President Johnson and his new commanding general, William Westmoreland, now had to decide what to do about the communist buildup, and whether Vietnam was "to be fought as a real war, not a toy one."

She was still in Saigon when she received a cable from Hall that her father, who had long been ill with multiple sclerosis, had suffered a heart attack. Maggie was distraught. She had secured an exclusive interview with Prince Norodom Sihanouk of Cambodia on the ramifications of the U.S. involvement in the overthrow of Diem. If she went on to Phnom Penh and did the interview, her father might die before she could get home. She was torn between her devotion to her father and her dedication to the job. "She was in terrible conflict over her feelings about her father and asked for my advice," recalled Lisagor, who was also on the junket. "I finally said, 'Go do the interview. He won't live long.'" Maggie did the interview, but it was a hard decision and nearly broke her heart.

Larry Higgins died two days later, on November 26. The *San Francisco Chronicle* reported that her mother had to delay the funeral so their daughter—"the internationally-known news correspondent, who was still en route"—could attend.

Dorsey sent a brief condolence note, saying he had heard that she had remained in Southeast Asia to get the Sihanouk interview and that her service to the paper was beyond the call of duty. It was a great scoop. Her front-page story about the Cambodia–Viet Cong pact revealed that South Vietnam's neighbor had lost faith in America and was now negotiating with the communists to ensure his country's survival.

Maggie made it to Oakland just in time to see her father buried. Losing him meant she had lost the one person she had always wanted most to impress, and it left her feeling bereft and strangely unmoored. She called the New York office and numbly dictated a message for Dorsey thanking him for his kind words, then added, "But I would be less than candid if I claimed to stay out there that extra day in Cambodia for *Newsday*:

> I did it for Dad. You see, he had been unconscious by the time I heard of his illness. And then when he died, I had to think—sentimentally perhaps, superstitiously even—what he would want. He was a true man of adventure from his

early volunteer days in the French air force to the moment in middle age when he parachuted into Formosa. And in his declining years, his great joys were the journalistic adventures and achievements, such as they were, that I once had.

I have returned depressed by many things, including me. I am really beginning to doubt I have a place anymore in the newspaper business.

I want to make it clear that I blame no one but myself. . . . In Washington a columnist is nothing unless they appear regularly on the editorial page. I feel that I have failed and while I blame myself completely, I would appreciate knowing what Newby Noyes [foreign editor of the *Washington Evening Star*] has against my product.

On December 10, Dorsey sent a brief note complimenting her on her most recent column. He added that she was quite mistaken about Noyes being prejudiced against her. The *Evening Star* editor liked her work very much, and he had made ample use of her reporting from Vietnam. But it was the last line that lifted her spirits. Noyes was going to make a concerted effort to find a place for her column on the editorial page of the *Star* once a week after the first of the year. "Give me just one day—any one day—on the editorial page," she implored, "then the needles, messages, points that I want to get across most to Mr. Johnson, Rusk, French embassy, etc. can be written that day."

Guggenheim also sent her an encouraging letter, telling her he was going to ignore her comment about feeling like failure, most likely written in a low moment, and advised her to buck up. Her column was a magnificent success, as evidenced by its now being carried by ninety-two papers and counting. He knew how much she yearned to be on the editorial page of the *Star*, but her reporting kept landing her on page one instead, which in his opinion was not a bad place to be and was perhaps where she belonged.

A few weeks later, Guggenheim wrote again to confirm a happy rumor. *Newsday* was nominating her for another Pulitzer Prize, once again in the category of Distinguished International Reporting, based on her continuing coverage of the war in Vietnam and her analysis of the tragedy of errors perpetrated by the Americans since the murder of Diem. She was also being nominated for the Sigma Delta Chi Award. They had put together a package of articles they felt reflected her prescience, plus a very handsome picture of her. There was little chance that she would win, given the *Times*'s powerful lobby and the growing public sentiment against the war. Still, to Maggie, who had come to *Newsday* with such high expectations, it was a sign her column was at last gaining some traction.

Maggie had her dream job, but the truth was that she was finding the relentless grind draining. She had insisted on a clause in her *Newsday* contract guaranteeing her four weeks a year of vacation, "but the joke," she wrote Dorsey in January 1965, "is on me." The constant pressure to drum up sales for her column was such that "I wouldn't dare stop for even a week, and I have a feeling that you would agree." Bemoaning her "untakeable vacations," she wrote that she would have to get by with "work-and-play" trips such as the one she was planning in Antigua in February, before flying to Puerto Rico and then on to the Dominican Republic, where a communist takeover threatened.

Apart from all the travel, the reason she was so tired was that she had, as usual, taken on too much freelance work. There was the new "Letter from America" column for the *Welt am Sonntag*, a German weekly magazine. The lengthy features for the *Saturday Evening Post*, *Cosmopolitan*, and *Mademoiselle*, among others. A damning profile of Henry Cabot Lodge for *The Diplomat*, in which she included the newsworthy nugget that President Johnson had lobbied against the coup the ambassador endorsed. And then there were the many television appearances on *Meet the Press* and other news-panel programs.

She delivered commencement addresses and received honorary degrees, and seemed destined to turn her string of "firsts" for women into an esteemed sinecure, but observed her own progress dourly. She often expressed regret at not being able to spend more time at home with her family, but it was a luxury she could not afford. Journalism "hardly pays anymore," she griped to a female colleague, explaining that her salary only just covered the cost of the housekeeper and nanny she needed to keep things running smoothly while she was gone. But it was her compulsion to do it all, as much as the need for the extra cash, that led her to overextend herself time and again.

A recurrent note of weariness crept into her public utterances. The image she had created of the intrepid, globe-trotting dynamo required all her energy and willpower, and it was proving harder to maintain with every passing year. She confessed in an interview that she no longer enjoyed going off to war zones; the thrill was gone. "But I do like having been there," she explained. "There's a difference you know. It always frightens me, but it is absolutely necessary."

After a lecture in Los Angeles that winter, she responded to yet another query about why she still rushed off to cover revolutions now that she had achieved so much and was married and the mother of two. "I was typecast as a war correspondent, and I seem to have been covering them ever since," she replied reflexively, implying she had no choice but to carry on. It was a revealing comment, and a sad one. Beneath the career glitter, she felt trapped by the swashbuckling persona she had fashioned for herself two decades earlier.

In her early days at the *Trib*, she used to go down to the composing room and watch them print the paper. She would stand in the back and listen to the presses roll, the rumble infusing her with the same awe and reverence others feel at the sound of the pounding surf. She had loved everything about the newspaper business. Not anymore. Her malaise ran deeper, recalling the brooding hopelessness about finding happiness and fathoming the true meaning of life that filled the last pages of her memoir. But she had little patience for introspection. The deadline hour was approaching. There was always a last fact to chase. And the urge to register her opinion on matters of global importance. She did not know the answer to the frequently asked question, "What makes Maggie run?" She was a mystery to herself, and concluded that for her, life "would always be a riddle."

She worked like a fiend on her book. By spring, she was submitting the chapters as soon as she finished them. The tone of the book was angry and deeply personal, that of an embittered observer who felt betrayed by the "furiously conflicting judgments and furiously conflicting advice that was to unfold under both President Kennedy and President Johnson." She fought her corner just as fiercely, and when she stopped to catch her breath between broadsides, she worried about how it would be received. Thanking Evan Thomas for his encouraging note saying he found the first installment fascinating, she confessed that, like most writers, she was plagued by doubts—"nervous and prone to melancholy."

By July, the book was in galleys. *Our Vietnam Nightmare* was a detailed, step-by-step analysis of how the Kennedy administration's self-deluded hubris led to the downfall of Diem, the continuing deterioration of the country, and "a sadly unnecessary tragedy." She relitigated the Buddhist crisis, hammered away at Hilsman and Lodge for their role in the coup, and described President Kennedy as conflicted and indecisive and ultimately misled by his advisers, who ignored embassy dispatches in favor of erroneous news reports. Bobby Kennedy, who cautioned the president against removing Diem, told her that his brother had "second thoughts" about the cable green-lighting the coup, and had hoped to the last that Lodge might reach an agreement with Diem. But it was too late for regrets. "Our Vietnamese nightmare was in great part one of our own making," she wrote. "And our responsibility for creating the nightmare that followed the anti-Diem coup d'etat only heightens our obligation to bring it to an end."

As always, for Maggie, communism was the enemy, freedom the issue worth fighting for. Delivering what she called her "minority report" on Vietnam, she concluded that although Johnson had inherited a terrible mess, there was still time for him to turn it around. She was guardedly optimistic that America could prevail, though it would take patience and as long as ten years. "Dangerous as such prophecies are," she wrote in the book's last lines, "I believe America will in Vietnam somehow muddle through—with the accent on muddle."

There was no question the book was going to be controversial. After all the publicity about her dissenting views on Vietnam, she should have been prepared for some editorial jitters on the part of Harper & Row. Arthur Schlesinger and Theodore Sorensen had just published histories of the Kennedy administration, and each had wrestled with her version of the secret cables ordering the coup. But as Evan Thomas's occasional nit-picking comments gave way to larger queries about her reporting, Maggie's anxiety quickly changed to anger. On July 1, she sent a testy letter saying that she "sensed a feeling of uneasiness."

When she discovered that Thomas not only had serious questions about the narrative as presented in the book but had felt the need to fact-check her reporting, Maggie was incandescent. In a heated three-page letter that was by turns emotional and acrimonious, she responded to his suggestion that she should hedge her account in places. "It seems to me that one fundamental problem is that you have difficulty in accepting my version of events," she wrote on learning that he had spoken to a few of her sources. "May I point out that you have talked, however, only to three or four of the principal characters in the Saigon drama. I have talked to virtually all of them. . . . Hopefully, this gives me a basis of judgment that is perhaps broader than yours, if you will pardon the presumption."

When Evan Thomas persisted in asking her to "blur" the charge that Lodge gave the order to unleash the generals on Diem and knowingly sealed his fate, Maggie was intractable. She was righteous in her rejection of his suggestion that it might be in the "national interest" to minimize the involvement of the infinitely civilized ambassador in the murder of the chief of state of an allied nation. "I don't know how to say this without sounding stuffy," she wrote, "but in twenty-seven years of covering hot wars and cold wars, I have found that a suppression of truth rarely serves the national interest except in such cases as movement of troops, revelation of weapons and secrets." Before the book went to the printers, she agreed to soften a few phrases about the coup to make it "more palatable," as she put it.

On August 10, she left for Europe, a bundle of galleys tucked under one arm. She and Bill were taking seven-year-old Larry and five-year-old Linda on a much-anticipated holiday to France to meet their cousins.

Maggie planned to spend a few days in Paris at the Hôtel Athénée, where she would file a few quick stories on de Gaulle's recent anti-U.S. pronouncements; he was telling allies that America could not be counted on and sympathizing with the plight of Vietnam. She and her family would then decamp to the palatial le Provençal, a shabby but chic art deco hotel in the Riviera resort of Juan-les-Pins in Antibes.

"I'm utterly exhausted and need some time in the sun," she wrote Dorsey. At the end of the two-week holiday, Bill and the children would fly home and Maggie would travel on to Rome to interview Madame Nhu, who had chosen Italy as her country of exile. But "hassle over the book" forced her to cut her trip short and fly back to Washington for a last round of wrangling with her publisher and the lawyers. "The censors took out a dismaying amount," she lamented in a follow-up note, "but think the basic picture has been salvaged."

In the autumn of 1965, she made her tenth trip to Vietnam to report on the fighting. In Bac Lieu, deep in the lush Mekong Delta, Maggie flew over the recently bombarded areas where the Johnson-approved air strikes—known as Operation Rolling Thunder—had decimated the countryside in an attempt to stop the enemy aggression and drive the Viet Cong from their tunnels. Maggie defended the use of aerial warfare against its increasingly vocal critics, even to the point of reciting the official line that the bombing campaigns were being conducted as humanely as possible. "Beginning with WWII and including both Korea and the first Indochina war," she asserted, "this correspondent has never seen so many military minds so devoted to the effort to accomplish maximum military impact on the enemy with minimum damage to innocent civilians."

She was making her way back via India in early October when Tom Dorsey received a call from a mutual friend, who told him he had just seen Higgins and was concerned about the reporter's health. She had come down with a bad case of dengue fever, a mosquito-borne illness that caused vomiting, high fever, and severe flu-like symptoms, but was trying to push through it despite the fact that she was on her last legs. He warned that Maggie was sicker—much sicker—than she would admit.

"You should order her home," he urged. It took Dorsey almost a full day of ringing round the various bureaus to track her down in Indonesia. When he finally found her and made her come to the phone, he said, "Maggie, I want you to come home right now."

"Oh, I can't, I'm seeing Sukarno," she said, referring to the Indonesian leader, who was clinging to power after an abortive coup, while the army purged the country of the purported communist insurgents.

Dorsey insisted. "Look, you're not feeling well. Come home. If we have to pay for another trip back to go see Sukarno, we'll pay for the trip, but come home." Reluctantly she agreed.

By the time Maggie landed in Washington, she was desperately ill. All through the long plane flight home her body ached and shuddered. Her fever spiked to 105 degrees. For the first few weeks, she resisted going into the hospital, determined to finish the series of articles about her trip. She struggled valiantly to keep up her three-times-a-week column. Despite raging fevers and a debilitating blood ailment, she worked from bed, typing her column on the same battered portable machine she had dragged through Germany and Korea.

She sent Dorsey an apologetic note declining an invitation to attend an *Oakland Tribune* event honoring the top columnists in California, saying that she was "not unwilling," just unable. On October 25, she sent another brief line that she was still unwell: "I'm afraid the effects of this Dengue fever I picked up in Delhi are still with me." She apologized for the overdue expenses from her trip and promised to sort out the bills as soon as she could. "If you will just bear with me," she added, "it's all I can do to gather the strength to clean out my notebook and get all the Vietnam material down on paper while it is still fresh in my mind."

On November 3, she was admitted to Walter Reed Army Medical Center after her white-blood-cell count dropped alarmingly. The doctors were baffled by her symptoms. At first, they thought she had contracted the drug-resistant malaria that had reached almost epic proportions in South Vietnam. Then they suspected she might have cancer. She underwent surgery to remove abdominal tissue for laboratory examination, but the tests revealed nothing. No parasite could be identified. Then she developed uremic poisoning and began to hemorrhage internally. For several days it was touch and go before her condition stabilized.

After running a battery of tests, the doctors finally surmised that she had contracted a rare tropical parasite called leishmaniasis, in which protozoa from the bite of a sand fly enter the bloodstream and attack the liver and spleen. As a rule, patients who receive the proper drug regimen rarely die of the infection, but in Maggie's case, the doctors were unable to arrest its progress.

A week later, when *Our Vietnam Nightmare* was published on November 10, Maggie was frustrated that she was unable to participate in the book launch. If she was not out there flogging her book, it would never make the bestseller lists. Too weak to stand, she could not stay away from her cherished limelight. Invited to appear on NBC's *Today Show*, Maggie secretly conspired with the children's nanny to take her by taxi to the airport, and then on to the broadcast network's Manhattan studio and back. Fueled by a sense of mission, she was determined to go, even though her husband and doctors advised against it. "I wasn't going to stop her," said Hall. "Well, I couldn't have. The doctor told her she was endangering her life. But she was just back from Vietnam and she felt like she had a message that she had an opportunity to deliver on TV and she was going to do it if it killed her."

Lisagor also thought she was too frail to appear on the TV program, but Maggie would not listen. "She could be resolute," he said. "One of the syndicated columnists said she looked like she was dying. In fact, she was dying. But she went to New York to promote the book, complete with wheel chairs at both ends."

The book received the mixed reviews one might expect for a fiery polemic, which her publishing company marketed as "certain to stir up a storm." The *New York Times* snubbed it, while the right-wing papers gave it raves. It was a selection of the Conservative Book Club. The majority of critics gave Higgins her due, stressing her hard-hitting report, unsparing in its criticism of the State Department, and calling *Our Vietnam Nightmare* a valuable contribution, even if not everyone would agree with her conclusions.

By mid-December, Maggie's once-boundless reserves of energy depleted, she agreed to cut her workload to one column a week. Any suggestion that she take a break, or temporarily hand over the column to someone else, was met by hysterical protests. Not wanting to cause her any unnecessary distress, Dorsey consulted her doctor, who was of the opinion that it was important for her state of mind that the column continue.

Faced with a difficult dilemma, Dorsey, together with Maggie's close friends Peter Lisagor and Michael O'Neill, the State Department correspondent for the *Daily News*, entered into a conspiracy to create the illusion that they were "helping her" to write the columns, though it went way beyond that. Lisagor had suggested it as a temporary arrangement. Maggie was only forty-five; she would soon rally. "She's going to be fine," he kept saying, "she's going to be fine." Dorsey did not have the heart to argue. From then on, Lisagor and O'Neill took turns visiting Maggie in the hospital, where they would sit and talk over the latest news, get the thrust of what she wanted to say, and then one or the other of them would go back to the office and type it up. The two prominent Washington reporters told no one about the ghostwritten columns.

While she was in the hospital, the war was accelerating. After the devastating siege at Plei Me in the Central Highlands, when the Viet Cong attacked an American Special Forces camp, Maggie advocated the use of defoliants to strip the dense jungle to prevent enemy infiltration from the North. "The bravery is history at Plei Me," she declared. "The scandal is the hypocrisy about the use of crucial but nonlethal chemicals that could have saved thousands of American lives. . . . This war won't even start coming to an end until those border points used by Ho Chi Minh's troops are finally cleared and, at the very least, open to surveillance."

In what would be her final column, she criticized Johnson's timid Vietnam War policy, and his tendency to "treat the problem as a pesky but peripheral one in an atmosphere of business-as-usual." Hawkish and uncompromising to the end, Maggie believed only a massive show of force would demonstrate American resolve and persuade the North Vietnamese to sue for peace.

But Johnson did not need to be goaded into expanding the war. The devastating mid-November battle in the Ia Drang Valley, and the high body count—an estimated 3,561 North Vietnamese killed versus 305 American dead—convinced the president and his military leaders that the enemy could never sustain such losses. Despite the carnage, the "kill ratio" was twelve to one. Westmoreland claimed the bloody encounter an "unprecedented victory" and would use it to justify a war of attrition against a guerrilla force. The U.S. was about to vastly increase the number of troops in Vietnam, but Maggie would not live to see it.

She went downhill quickly in December. Her kidneys began to fail; she was in a great deal of pain and on a dialysis machine almost constantly. "She suffered a lot, and it aged her terribly," Dorsey recalled. "There were days when I'd go down to see her and she would not be coherent at all, and then there would be times when she would be as coherent as could be." Once, as he approached her hospital room, he heard someone shouting profanities. When he entered the room, Maggie was screaming into the phone. Dorsey had no idea who was at the other end of the line, so he gently took the handset from her and inquired who was there. A man's voice said urgently, "Yes, this is Dean Rusk. Will you tell me how she is?"

Ruth Montgomery was the first to report that Higgins had been hospitalized with a virulent infection, including the news in a favorable review of her book for the *New York Journal-American*. She had covered so many wars with hardly a scratch, but Maggie's luck had finally run out. But then Vietnam was unlike any other conflict. Only weeks earlier, it had claimed the life of Dickey Chapelle, one of the bravest female photojournalists of her time, who was killed while on patrol with the marines. It felt like a bad omen.

Shortly before Christmas, Montgomery stopped in to see Maggie, who seemed to be doing a bit better. The antimonial drugs were finally beginning to have an effect. The pain had subsided and her kidney function improved. She was feeling well enough that morning to fret about how she could get home for a few hours on Christmas to see the children. Montgomery, who had almost not come that day because she had a column due, tried to distract her. She had brought a bright red bed jacket as a gift, and a festively bedecked tree for her hospital room.

"Did you think I was going to die?" Maggie asked with the poignant candor of one who already knew the answer. Montgomery could see that her friend, never one to kid herself, sensed the end was near. Maggie never veered into the maudlin, but she spoke a trifle wistfully of things she would have liked to have done differently—would do differently, given the chance. She swore she would curtail her travel. She would spend more time with Bill and the children.

Suddenly, unaccountably, she took a turn for the worse. On Christmas Day, President Johnson and Lady Bird called from Texas to wish her well. They talked for a few minutes, but Maggie's voice soon grew so faint it was barely more than a whisper. "Thank you so much for calling," she said before ringing off, "but I'm awfully tired, Bird."

She was stoic right to the end. Used to running the show, she spent her last days issuing instructions about the family finances and the children's future. She wanted Larry and Linda to attend parochial school and made her husband promise that he would see to it. "She was an absolutely devoted mother," said Hall. "She wanted absolutely everything in the world for her children and she was pushing them every inch of the way. It didn't matter what they were involved in, she wanted them to be the best." When Hall brought Larry and Linda to the hospital to see her, Maggie kept up a warm, bantering front, talking cheerfully about school and their plans, never letting on that it might be the last time. "She was sick but she was able to speak to us," recalled Larry, who was too young to remember any parting words.

Maggie died on Monday, January 3, 1966, after slipping into a coma. Before Hall could bring himself to tell the children that their mother had passed away, Larry saw a photograph of her on the front page of the *Washington Post*. The headline read: "Marguerite Higgins, Newswoman, Is Dead."

The *Post* gave her a large, three-column obituary, describing her reporting in World War II and in Korea, and stating that her last trip to Vietnam was made to gather material for her column and a book. No mention was made of her feuds and knack for controversy. It was an unmistakably sedate eulogy for the enfant terrible of the journalism world, who had charmed and cajoled soldiers and officers in the wars she so ardently covered, chastised and provoked foreign heads of state and presidents from de Gaulle and Khrushchev to Kennedy and Johnson, and vexed two generations of foreign correspondents.

Ironically, it was the *New York Times* that gave the famed war correspondent and syndicated columnist the kind of lavish write-up editors reserve for legends in their field. "There was steel in Marguerite Higgins's character," the paper observed of the indelible archetype created by her dispatches and magazine features, "but it was concealed in a feminine figure, and the femininity always showed, even when she was slogging along the muddy roads of Korea in baggy pants and a man's shirt with her blond curls tucked into an Army fatigue hat."

The *Times* went on to laud her as one of the most accomplished women reporters in history:

> Marguerite Higgins got stories other reporters didn't get.
>
> She did it with a combination of masculine drive, feminine wiles and professional pride. She had brass and she had charm, and she used them to rise to the top of a profession that usually relegates women to the softie beats of cooking, clothes and society.
>
> Miss Higgins made it big in a way any man would have been proud of. She won a Pulitzer Prize for her reports from the Korean warfronts for the New York Herald Tribune, after she fought her way into that war over the objections of an American general.

She was buried at Arlington National Cemetery, a rare honor for a civilian. Half of Washington turned out for the funeral. There were so many congressmen, beribboned generals, and Defense Department officials at Fort Myer Chapel it looked like she was being given a military send-off. Although it was a debilitating parasitic disease that ultimately vanquished her, most of those present regarded her as a "combat casualty," one writer observed, "just as certainly as if she had been felled by a bullet."

Political leaders sent messages of praise and sympathy, including Bobby Kennedy, Hubert Humphrey, and Dean Rusk, among others.

Elizabeth Carpenter, press secretary to Lady Bird Johnson, who had known Higgins for fifteen years, said, "She had soldier-like qualifications, determination and no fear of covering the front lines. Reporters the world over, particularly women, have been professionally enhanced by the high quality of her performance."

Friends and colleagues who had worked with her, and competed against her, sent telegrams expressing shock and sadness at her untimely demise. Margaret Parton, who had toiled alongside her on the *Trib*'s city desk, felt strangely shaken. "For twenty years—in the same profession but more famous than I had ever been—she had been the shadow-dancer on the other side of the screen, the glimpsed figure beyond the looking glass," she recalled after the memorial service, surprised to find her eyes full of tears.

Wes Gallagher, AP general manager, who had first encountered Higgins in Germany when she was still a young cub, called her death a loss to journalism as a whole. Longtime admirers from Ralph McGill and John Chamberlain to Clare Boothe Luce penned testimonials to her heroic career. "Maggie was a cross between Alice in Wonderland and Eleanor Roosevelt," one competitor told *Newsweek*. "She regarded the world with wide-eyed excitement. Then rolled up her sleeves determined to do something about it."

Perhaps the best tribute came from her old rival, Homer Bigart. Eschewing sentimental epitaphs, he said, "She made me work like hell."

ACKNOWLEDGMENTS

THIS BIOGRAPHY WOULD HAVE BEEN VERY DIFFERENT HAD IT NOT been for my fortuitous discovery, in the depths of that first shuttered Covid winter, of the collection of Marguerite Higgins's papers assembled by Kathleen Kearney Keeshen. Kay, a single mother who worked her way up the ladder in the personnel department of IBM for three decades until her retirement in 1992, became impatient with the slow rate of promotion for women and so pursued—at the company's expense—a master's degree in 1973, and then a PhD in 1983, from the University of Maryland, focusing both times on the trailblazing career of Marguerite Higgins. Over a period of twelve years, Kay corresponded with and interviewed dozens of Maggie's journalistic contemporaries, several generals, various lovers, and two husbands. She generously shared with me her cache of unpublished interviews with these key figures, all long deceased, as well as bursting folders of yellowed clippings, magazine articles, and related material. In the process, we developed a lively telephone and email friendship and spent many hours dissecting and analyzing our mutual obsession—Maggie. It is impossible to adequately acknowledge her help.

I am also grateful to her son, John Day, for packing up and shipping this treasure trove to me from a storage facility on the West Coast to my home on the East Coast. It is our hope that the Kathleen Kearney Keeshen Papers will eventually become part of the Marguerite Higgins archive at the Special Collections Research Center at Syracuse University, where they will be made available to future generations of journalists and scholars.

I am indebted to the Pulitzer Prize–winning historian Richard Kluger for giving me access to his collection of interviews conducted for his definitive book, *The Paper: The Life and Death of the New York Herald Tribune.*

His invaluable archive is deposited at the Sterling Memorial Library of Yale University. I must also acknowledge the librarians there for doing a splendid job despite the onerous Covid restrictions. For permission to use portions of his unpublished interview with Thomas Dorsey, I would like to thank Robert Keeler, the author of another mammoth history of a New York paper, *Newsday: A Candid History of the Respectable Tabloid.* Also, a thank-you to Shelley and Seth Mydans for permission to quote from one of Carl Mydans's letters.

I benefited greatly from the wisdom of John McManus, who helped me to make sense of the many competing Dachau liberation stories. His superb analysis of the ensuing controversy sheds light on a still-murky chapter of World War II history and restores some semblance of truth among all the grandiose claims to glory.

Heartfelt thanks to the many people who shared their recollections, chief among them Gay Talese, Beverly Deepe, Peter Arnett, Jurate Kazickas, and Janine di Giovanni. For their help and advice, I must also thank Richard Cohen, Howard Rosenberg, and David Sacks, chief of the Intracellular Parasite Biology Section of the NIH, and an expert on leishmanial infections.

I am especially grateful to those who took the time to listen to, read, and comment on the work in progress: Tav Holmes, James Jacoby, and Amandine Isnard, who also acted as my French translator. I am lucky to have Perri Peltz and Victoria Gordon in my corner, and am grateful for their friendship and generous support.

As always, I owe an enormous debt of gratitude to my longtime research assistant, Ruth Tenenbaum, who helped me track down Maggie's dispatches through three wars and found valuable documents that might otherwise have been lost to the ash heap of history. Also, Carin Wolfe, who helped me to plunder the Higgins archive in Syracuse when Covid made travel difficult.

Above all, I would like to express my immense gratitude to Lawrence Hall for permission to quote from Marguerite Higgins's private letters, diaries, and books, as well as for permission to publish photographs from her archive. I was deeply touched by his willingness to share memories of the mother he lost at the age of seven, and I cannot thank him enough for his faith in this project.

My deepest thanks to my agent Kris Dahl, and to my editor, John Glusman, and to Helen Thomaides, for their care and attention.

Finally, I wish to thank my husband, Steve Kroft, a former *Stars and Stripes* correspondent in Vietnam, and the most rigorous journalist I know, for being my best source, sounding board, and sharpest critic. He and my son, John, were my champions, and their love and encouragement got me through the long, bleak days of Covid. They both showed great patience while I talked endlessly about Maggie, morning, noon, and night, and I am more grateful than they will ever know.

Jennet Conant
Sag Harbor, September 2022

NOTES

PROLOGUE

1   "We did all kinds": Peter Furst, Oral History Interview by Nancy Dahl, Dec. 30, 2009, Veterans History Project, Library of Congress, Washington, DC.

2   "taking cities": Marguerite Higgins, *News Is a Singular Thing* (Garden City, NY: Doubleday, 1955), p. 86.

2   "Let's drive": Furst, Oral History Interview, Dec. 30, 2009.

4   "frozen in place": John H. Linden, *Surrender of the Dachau Concentration Camp 29 April 45: The True Account* (Elm Grove, WI: Sycamore Press, 1997), p. 11.

6   "Heil Hitler": Furst, Oral History Interview, Dec. 30, 2009.

6   varyingly self-serving accounts: The only fact about the liberation of Dachau that is agreed upon is that the concentration camp was overrun by American forces on April 29, 1945. For the record, the U.S. Army Center of Military History in Washington, DC, recognizes both the Forty-Second and the Forty-Fifth Infantry Divisions, along with the Twentieth Armored Division, as liberators. But over the decades, the debate over who was first to arrive at the camp has degenerated into a "blood feud," in the words of Ron Jensen, who wrote about the controversy in the April 23, 1995, *Stars and Stripes* magazine cover story on the fiftieth anniversary of Dachau's deliverance.

The exact details concerning when the camp was liberated, which American units arrived first, what they did at the camp, who was first to reach the enclosure area where the prisoners were kept, and what transpired there continue to be matters of dispute. Everyone's recall is slightly different. The story is plagued by all the usual problems of frontline reporting, only greatly magnified by the importance of the event, with many factors contributing to the confusion. There is the inevitable glory seeking on the part of the Forty-Second and Forty-Fifth Infantry Divisions and their commanding officers; the official lies meant to conceal the errors and excesses committed by the liberating troops; inaccurate and sensational news accounts; and faulty and/or embellished individual accounts. Importantly, there was also considerable confusion about the geographical layout of the vast Dachau complex that has led to various U.S. military divisions claiming they were first to reach Dachau when they had probably stumbled upon one of the many smaller, satellite camps.

Central to the Dachau liberation controversy is the angry confrontation that took place at the *jourhaus* gate between the leaders of the two competing divisions—General Linden of the Forty-Second Division and Lt. Col. Felix Sparks of the Forty-Fifth—a confrontation in which Maggie Higgins plays a key role. In an account written four decades after the fact, and no doubt colored by the bitter rivalry between their two divisions, Sparks presented a very different version of the standoff at the prison enclosure. He has clung to his story over the years, and it has influenced Hollywood, as well as many popular accounts of this chapter of history. I will not rehash his conflicting account here, except to say that the bulk of the documentary evidence does not corroborate Sparks's self-aggrandizing account, and there are so many inaccuracies that his whole narrative strains credulity.

For anyone in search of scholarly clarity on the liberation of Dachau and ensuing controversy, I recommend the excellent, even-handed examination of this episode of the Holocaust presented by John C. McManus in his book *Hell before Their Very Eyes: American Soldiers Liberate Concentration Camps in Germany, April 1945*.

There are multiple witnesses—military officers, journalists, and prisoners— whose description of the events at Dachau roughly parallels Linden's account of their arrival at the camp, being fired upon, the enthusiastic reception of Higgins and Furst by the inmates, and the fact that they remained at the camp with the general until that evening. *Time* correspondent Sidney Olson was also present, and in a cable to his editors wrote that he had heard that "a German tried to surrender to *NYHT* correspondent Marguerite Higgins, and that the Nazis raised a white flag when she arrived." The Belgian journalists wrote their own accounts of accompanying Linden and Higgins, and took a series of photographs of the surrender scene and prison enclosure, several of which are included in this book.

There are a few notable discrepancies between Linden's version and that of Higgins and Furst: Lt. Col. William J. Cowling III, who was Linden's aide-de-camp, states that he was the one who hollered up at the SS guards in the tower to descend; and that twelve guards surrendered, not twenty, as Higgins claimed in her July 1945 *Mademoiselle* article and later memoir. Furst's *Stars and Stripes* story of May 2, 1945, states that he saw Higgins call out to the guards, and that a group then surrendered with their hands in the air, and that another eight followed. (The two accounts are not mutually exclusive, and it is possible that different groups of SS guards surrendered to the two parties at different times.) Furst repeats the same story in his 2009 Oral History Interview, where he also states that he was present when Higgins "slapped" Wicker. It should also be noted that the other reporters at Dachau that day also wrote detailed personal accounts of what they had witnessed, believing them to be more powerful. Either way, Maggie's wartime memoir must be seen as a highly selective version of events, with her at its center. She is not the first—and will not be the last—journalist (or military leader) to exaggerate their own heroics.

For my rendering of the Dachau liberation, I relied on the contemporaneous accounts of Marguerite Higgins and Peter Furst, published in their respective newspapers, *NYHT* April 29, 1945, and *Stars and Stripes* May 2, 1945. Higgins later amplified and embellished her story in an article, "Finale in the West," which appeared in the July 1945 issue of *Mademoiselle*, and again, in an even more heroic version, in her 1954 memoir, *News Is a Singular Thing*. Peter Furst recounted his version of events in his December 30, 2009, Oral History Interview, which is included in the Veterans History Project in the Library of Congress. Another corroborating account can be found in the Father Francis Cegielka's Oral History Interview, October 2, 1990, in the Jeff and Toby Herr Oral History Archive in the United States Holocaust Memorial Museum Collection.

The following books offer similar accounts, though some details differ: *The Day of the Americans* by Nerin E. Gun; *Dachau 29 April 1945: The Rainbow Liberation Memoirs*, edited by Sam Dann; *Surrender of the Dachau Concentration Camp 29 April 45: The True Account* (self-published monograph) by John H. Linden; *Dachau Liberated: The Official Report*, by the U.S. Seventh Army; and "Long-Forgotten Cables Reveal What Time's Correspondent Saw at the Liberation of Dachau" by Olivia B. Waxman, *Time*, April 21, 2020. Several in-depth accounts of the so-called Dachau Liberation Controversy are available at the USC Shoah Foundation, https://remember.org/witness/sparks2. An alternative version of events can be found in the oral history account of Brig. Gen. Felix L. Sparks, as well as a monograph on Dachau written by him, and an accompanying historical overview of the controversy by his friend, Lt. Col. Hugh F. Foster III, https://www.45thinfantrydivision.com/index14.htm; *Inside the Vicious Heart: Americans and the Liberation of Nazi Concentration Camps* by Robert H. Abzug; and finally, a full-length biography of Sparks, *The Liberator: One World War II Soldier's 500-Day Odyssey* by Alex Kershaw.

7 **"Kommen Sie hier"**: Marguerite Higgins, "Finale in the West," *Mademoiselle*, July 1945; Higgins, *News Is a Singular Thing*, p. 91; *New York Herald Tribune*, April 29, 1945; Furst, Oral History Interview, Dec. 30, 2009; *Stars and Stripes*, May 2, 1945.

7 **"Arbeit Macht Frei"**: Linden, *Surrender of the Dachau Concentration Camp*, p. 28.

7 **"There was not"**: *New York Herald Tribune*, April 29, 1945; Higgins, "Finale in the West"; Higgins, *News Is a Singular Thing*, pp. 91–93; *Stars and Stripes*, May 2, 1945.

7 **"Mon Dieu"**: Higgins, *News Is a Singular Thing*, p. 92; Nerin E. Gun, *The Day of the Americans* (New York: Fleet, 1966), p. 22.

8 **"Golden locks"**: Gun, *Day of the Americans*, p. 22.

8 **"What the hell," "God dammit"**: Higgins, *News Is a Singular Thing*, p. 94.

10 **"She shouted"**: *Stars and Stripes*, May 2, 1945; Furst, Oral History Interview, Dec. 30, 2009.

11 **"covered the news"**: Marion Marzolf, "Marguerite Higgins," in *Notable American Women: The Modern Period*, ed. Barbara Sicherman and Carol Hurd Green (Cambridge, MA: Belknap Press of Harvard University Press, 1980), p. 340.

11 **"girl correspondent"**: Carl Mydans, "Girl War Correspondent," *Life*, Oct. 2, 1950.

11 **O'Daniel's victory party**: Higgins, "Finale in the West."

12 **"gaunt blazing ruin"**: *New York Herald Tribune*, May 7, 1945.

12 **"no place for a woman"**: Higgins, *News Is a Singular Thing*, p. 40.

CHAPTER 1: FREAK

14 **"Good candidates"**: Ishbel Ross, *Ladies of the Press* (New York: Harper & Brothers, 1936), p. 5.

14 **"noted for"**: Higgins, *News Is a Singular Thing*, p. 26.

14 **"to darken"**: Herbert Molloy Mason Jr., *The Lafayette Escadrille* (New York: Random House, 1964), p. 231.

15 "the human," "flabby routine," "neat little": Higgins, *News Is a Singular Thing*, p. 27.

16 "Lucky Lindy": Tony Long, "Lucky Lindy Flies His Way into the Celebrity Ranks," *Wired*, May 21, 2007.

16 "And so": Higgins, *News Is a Singular Thing*, p. 26.

16 "Gri": Eileen Summers, "2,000 Bulbs Are Keeping Marguerite Higgins Here," *Washington Post*, March 11, 1956.

16 Dalat: Marguerite Higgins, *Our Vietnam Nightmare: The Story of U.S. Involvement in the Vietnamese Tragedy, with Thoughts on a Future Policy* (New York: Harper & Row, 1965), pp. 2–3.

18 "She was possessed," "feeling superior": Higgins, *News Is a Singular Thing*, pp. 30–31.

19 "I'd never": Antoinette May, *Witness to War: A Biography of Marguerite Higgins* (New York: Beaufort Books, 1983), p. 23.

19 "Irish-French": Higgins, *News Is a Singular Thing*, p. 36.

19 "start her": Estes Kefauver, "Memo to Tom Colman."

19 "Dirty Chinamen!": Higgins, *News Is a Singular Thing*, p. 38.

20 "From the time": Kefauver, "Memo to Tom Colman."

20 "She led," "There was only": Ibid. Additional background information from Jean Craig Clack, interview by Kathleen Kearney Keeshen, Dec. 5, 1975, Kathleen Kearney Keeshen Papers (KKKP); Kathleen Kearney Keeshen, "Marguerite Higgins: Journalist, 1920–1966" (PhD diss., University of Maryland, 1983).

20 "She preferred": Marguerite Higgins, *Jesse Benton Fremont: California Pioneer* (Boston: Houghton Mifflin, 1962), p. 13.

21 "what force": Higgins, *News Is a Singular Thing*, p. 30.

21 "They used to fight": Lt. Gen. William E. Hall, USAF, recorded interview by Kathleen Kearney Keeshen, Feb. 26, 1973, KKKP.

22 "worst moment": Higgins, *News Is a Singular Thing*, p. 17.

22 "justify her free": Ibid., p. 39.

22 "Every time," "a stable personality": Ibid.

23 "which would become," "numbness": Ibid., p. 32.

23 "financial misfit": Ibid., p. 38.

24 school records: Anna Head School for Girls, *Nods and Becks* (Oakland, CA: Anna Head School, 1937), p. 13.

24 "Horoscope," "Probable End": Higgins, *News Is a Singular Thing*, p. 16; Marguerite Higgins Scrapbooks, Marguerite Higgins Papers, SCRC.

24 "bookworm": Higgins, *News Is a Singular Thing*, p. 39.

25 "It was pretty rough": Kefauver, "Memo to Tom Colman."

25 "gone the limit," "though she": Letter, Anne Duhring Cooper to Kathleen Kearney Keeshen, November 28, 1979, KKKP.

26 "desperately wanted": May, *Witness to War*, p. 34.

26 "party girl," "She tended": Katrina J. Lee, '94, "She Wrote the War," *Daily Californian Alumni Association Newsletter*, Winter 1999.

26 "without fail": Marguerite Higgins, "Autobiographical Essay," Application to Columbia University Graduate School of Journalism, September 1941.

26 **"wearing one blue"**: Jean Craig Clack, "Marguerite Higgins '41," *California Monthly*, Oct. 1950.

27 **"You wouldn't," "a very equestrian"**: Letter, Jean Kelly Stock to Kathleen Kearney Keeshen, May 20, 1975, KKKP.

28 **"Household Science," "looking for," "poor little"**: *Daily Californian*, Nov. 7, 1938.

28 **"We were a very"**: Letter, Marjorie Barker Malmquist to Kathleen Kearney Keeshen, Oct. 28, 1979, KKKP.

29 **"do away with"**: Higgins, *News Is a Singular Thing*, p. 128.

30 **"Fascism and"**: "Lessons Learned," *Reed Magazine*, Aug. 1997.

30 **"pretty far out"**: Letter, Malmquist to Keeshen, Oct. 28, 1979.

30 **"only to those"**: *Daily Californian*, Nov. 10, 1938.

30 **"It was very"**: Lee, "She Wrote the War."

30 **"Mexico," "There are no"**: *Daily Californian*, Feb. 2, 1940.

31 **"What's done"**: Hall, interview by Keeshen, Feb. 26, 1973.

31 **"petit bourgeois"**: Higgins, *News Is a Singular Thing*, p. 26.

32 **"practically on a"**: Letter, Malmquist to Keeshen.

32 **"There is much talk"**: *Oakland Tribune*, Sept. 3, 1940; *Berkeley Daily Gazette*, Dec. 3, 1940.

32 **"pink communist"**: Letter, Malmquist to Keeshen.

32 **"tomato-throwing"**: *Daily Californian*, Dec. 7, 1940.

33 **"What about the Women?"**: Ibid., Feb. 23, 1940.

33 **"blonde," "the war"**: Ibid., March 1, 1940.

33 **"Time and again," "She was seen"**: Letter, Cooper to Keeshen, Nov. 28, 1979.

33 **"The Ins and Outs"**: *Daily Californian*, Oct. 18, 1940; Letter, Michael Emery to Kathleen Kearney Keeshen, July 8, 1975, KKKP.

34 **"the practical proof"**: Higgins, "Autobiographical Essay."

34 **"symbolized the epitome"**: Higgins, *News Is a Singular Thing*, p. 16.

35 **"She was eager"**: Barbara Belford, *Brilliant Bylines: A Biographical Anthology of Notable Newspaperwomen in America* (New York: Columbia University Press, 1986), p. 287.

35 **"last-chance job"**: Higgins, *News Is a Singular Thing*, p. 16.

35 **"dubious merit," "That is the penalty"**: Ibid., pp. 15, 36.

CHAPTER 2: HUSTLING

36 **"She was not the best"**: John Chamberlain, *A Life with the Printed Word* (Chicago: Regnery Gateway, 1982), p. 94; John Chamberlain, "Marguerite Higgins, RIP," *National Review*, Jan. 25, 1966.

36 **"It was just," "Where is"**: Higgins, *News Is a Singular Thing*, pp. 16, 19.

37 **"Engel"**: Richard Kluger, *The Paper: The Life and Death of the New York Herald Tribune* (New York: Alfred A. Knopf, 1986), pp. 309–11; Margaret Parton, *Journey through a Lighted Room* (New York: Viking Press, 1973), pp. 73–74.

37 **"misleading air," "You know, kid"**: Higgins, *News Is a Singular Thing*, pp. 20–21.

38 **"a tremendous"**: Higgins, "Autobiographical Essay."

39 **"Sorry if you," "The professors"**: Letter, Higgins to her parents, undated 1942, Box 1, Family Correspondence, Marguerite Higgins Papers, SCRC.

39   **"The odds," "dirty tricks":** May, *Witness to War*, p. 51.

40   **"paper dolls":** Stanley Frank and Paul Sann, "Paper Dolls," in *More Post Biographies: Articles of Enduring Interest about Famous Journalists and Journals and Other Subjects Journalistic*, ed. John E. Drewry (Athens: University of Georgia Press, 1947), p. 206.

40   **"Even women," "Maggie":** May, *Witness to War*, p. 51.

40   **"This young," "She knew," "not mere":** Chamberlain, "Marguerite Higgins, RIP"; Chamberlain, *Life with the Printed Word*, pp. 93–94.

41   **"get down," "a great driving force":** Higgins, *News Is a Singular Thing*, p. 22.

41   **"didn't want to hire," "But I had to try":** Ibid., p. 25.

41   **"intensely competitive":** Marzolf, "Marguerite Higgins," p. 340.

41   **"She made the first":** John Chamberlain, "The Making of a Female War Correspondent," *Wall Street Journal*, Dec. 22, 1983.

42   **"cold to women," "face of":** Julia Edwards, *Women of the World: The Great Foreign Correspondents* (Boston: Houghton Mifflin, 1988), pp. 189–91.

42   **"What's an hour's":** May, *Witness to War*, p. 51.

43   **"An air of dignity," "Stanley gave":** Letter, Higgins to her parents, undated 1942.

43   **"Now, about Stanley," "He is radical," "Though he":** Ibid.

44   **"advanced notions," "quite a sentimentalist," "The point is":** Ibid.

45   **"I am only":** Letter, Higgins to her mother, May 29, 1942.

45   **"excellent shape," "I am still determined":** Letter, Higgins to her parents, Thursday, undated 1942.

46   **"It is a splendid":** Letter, Higgins to her parents, undated 1942.

46   **"Meanest cat":** Higgins, *News Is a Singular Thing*, p. 48.

46   **"What high school," "an agony":** Higgins, *News Is a Singular Thing*, p. 20.

47   **"looked like":** Ibid., p. 50; *New York Herald Tribune*, July 18, 1942.

47   **"Smoothing her stories":** M. C. Blackman, "Rewrite Man," Interview by Richard Kluger, undated, Richard Kluger Papers, Manuscripts and Archives, Yale University Library, New Haven, CT.

48   **"a newspaperman's," "a literate Tammany":** Fred C. Shapiro, "The Life and Death of a Great Newspaper," *American Heritage* 18, no. 6 (Oct. 1967).

48   **"The city editor":** Edwin Lanham, *The Iron Maiden* (New York: Popular Library Edition, 1954), p. 54.

48   **"district work":** Joseph F. Barnes, "Reminiscences of Joseph F. Barnes," 1954, Oral History Project, Columbia University, New York; Darnton, "Writing News and Telling Stories."

49   **"the greatest school":** *New York Herald Tribune*, Oct. 20, 1980.

49   **"Miss Higgins," "complete non sequitur":** Higgins, *News Is a Singular Thing*, p. 54.

50   **"He was not":** Ibid. p. 60.

50   **"cyclonic energy":** Kluger, *The Paper*, p. 440.

50   **"The Berkshire":** *New York Herald Tribune*, Aug. 29, 1942.

51   **"So right now," "his farewell," "And I don't":** Letter, Higgins to her parents, undated 1942.

CHAPTER 3: TRICKS OF THE TRADE

53   **"Was it feminism"**: Kluger, *The Paper*, p. 441.

53   **"My life"**: Letter, Higgins to her parents, undated 1942.

53   **"cocktails-for-freedom"**: Viola Ilma, *The Political Virgin* (New York: Duell, Sloan and Pearce, 1958), p. 103.

53   **"the wrong place"**: Sam Roberts, "The Clubs That Broke Barriers," *New York Times*, Aug. 14, 2009.

53   **"the whole evening"**: Letter, Higgins to her parents, undated 1943.

54   **"This was the beginning," "We were sloppy"**: Ilma, *Political Virgin*, pp. 132–134.

55   **"incredibly girlish," "Higgie looked"**: Ibid.

55   **"Drink is the curse"**: Shapiro, "The Life and Death of a Great Newspaper," *American Heritage*, Oct. 1967.

55   **"a lot of rah-rah boys"**: Earl Ubell, interview by Richard Kluger, 1981, Box 14, Richard Kluger Papers, Manuscripts and Archives, Yale University Library, New Haven, CT.

56   **"You are both"**: Ilma, *Political Virgin*, p. 133.

56   **"snake pit"**: Robert Darnton, "Writing News and Telling Stories," *Daedalus* 104, no. 2 (1975): pp. 175–94.

57   **"derided her babyish," "whether she was"**: Kluger, *The Paper*, pp. 440–41.

57   **"Few men could wield"**: Ibid., p. 441.

57   **"preying on"**: Janet Malcolm, *The Journalist and the Murderer* (New York: Vintage, 1990), p. 3.

57   **"manipulativeness," "Men didn't do that"**: Kluger, *The Paper*, p. 441.

58   **"She had to"**: Ibid., p. 440.

58   **"Hell, she just liked"**: Robert Shaplen, interview by Richard Kluger, Aug. 18, 1982, Box 12, Richard Kluger Papers, Manuscripts and Archives, Yale University Library, New Haven, CT.

58   **"[She] blew through," "In what was"**: *Philadelphia Inquirer*, Jan. 30, 1984.

58   **"thorough," "On these occasions"**: Parton, *Journey through a Lighted Room*, pp. 75–76.

59   **"professional"**: Stanley Walker, *City Editor* (New York: Frederick A. Stokes, 1934), pp. 248–64.

59   **"For newspaper men"**: Parton, *Journey through a Lighted Room*, p. 75.

59   **"The anti-Higgins group"**: Ilma, *Political Virgin*, p. 134.

60   **"chips on male"**: Higgins, *News Is a Singular Thing*, p. 204.

60   **"In the New York newspaper"**: Ibid.

61   **"She had a"**: Kluger, *The Paper*, p. 440; Judith Crist, interview by Richard Kluger, 1981, Box 4, Richard Kluger Papers, Manuscripts and Archives, Yale University Library, New Haven, CT; Letter, Judith Crist to Kathleen Kearney Keeshen, Nov. 8, 1981, KKKP.

61   **"all drive," "warm," "the rampant"**: Judith Crist, interview by Richard Kluger, 1981.

61   **"hogging," "She was a *very good*"**: Ibid.

62   **"a saga in itself"**: Higgins, *News Is a Singular Thing*, p. 46.

62   **"Queen Helen," "hostess to the famous"**: Mona Gardner, "Queen Helen," *Saturday Evening Post*, May 6, 1944, p. 9.

63   **"I was so violently"**: Higgins, *News Is a Singular Thing*, p. 40.

64   **"She put in hours"**: Ilma, *Political Virgin*, p. 135.

65   **"But all the other"**: "What Makes Maggie Run?," *Newsweek*, May 23, 1955.

65   **"Into the very masculine"**: Ibid.

66   **"running down"**: Ted Laymon, interview by Richard Kluger, 1981, Richard Kluger Papers, Manuscripts and Archives, Yale University Library, New Haven, CT.

66   **"less than ten minutes"**: *New York Herald Tribune*, July 7–9, 1944.

66   **"If she hasn't talked"**: Laymon, interview by Kluger, 1981.

67   **"Where did you get," "That was Maggie"**: Ibid.

67   **"The *Herald Tribune*"**: Letter, Tania Long Daniell to Kathleen Kearney Keeshen, July 2, 1982, KKKP.

67   **"projected"**: Ross, *Ladies of the Press*, p. 137.

67   **"drive and ingenuity"**: Helen Rogers Reid, "Remarks Introducing Marguerite Higgins at West Side Association Dinner," Nov. 10, 1950, Reid Family Papers, Manuscript/Mixed Material, Library of Congress, retrieved from https://lccn.loc.gov/mm82065491.

67   **"You are all set"**: Higgins, *News Is a Singular Thing*, p. 55.

CHAPTER 4: LATECOMER

68   **"I cannot tell you"**: Letter, Walter Kerr to Kathleen Kearney Keeshen, Nov. 30, 1982, KKKP.

68   **"G.I. Shuttle"**: Eric Niderost, 2018, "RMS Queen Mary's War Service: Voyages to Victory," Warfare History Network, retrieved from https://warfarehistorynetwork.com/rms-queen-marys-war-service-voyages-to-victory/.

69   **"She looked so"**: May, *Witness to War*, p. 66.

69   **"people often"**: Marion Marzolf, *Up from the Footnote: A History of Women Journalists* (New York: Hastings House, 1977), p. 78.

69   **"whispered certainty"**: Eric Hawkins, *Hawkins of the Paris Herald* (New York: Simon & Schuster, 1963), p. 234.

70   **"The lavish appointments"**: Ibid.

70   **"The Berlin Radio"**: *International Herald Tribune*, Feb. 12, 1945.

71   **"keep quiet," "The English reporters"**: Ibid., Nov. 27, 1944.

71   **"As a foreign," "run-along," "[They] seemed"**: Higgins, *News Is a Singular Thing*, p. 56.

71   **"She was beautiful," "There were"**: Letter, Charles Bernard to Kathleen Kearney Keeshen, Feb. 9, 1982, KKKP.

72   **"Male reporters"**: Letter, John MacVane to Kathleen Kearney Keeshen, Jan. 25, 1982, KKKP.

73   **"admiration and affection"**: Higgins, *News Is a Singular Thing*, p. 107; Letter, Clack to Keeshen, Dec. 5, 1975.

73   **"My ideas"**: Higgins, *News Is a Singular Thing*, p. 12.

74   **"just turned"**: Editor's note, *Mademoiselle*, February 1945.

75   **"more than just"**: Marguerite Higgins, "The Press: Foreign Correspondent," *Mademoiselle*, February 1945.

75   **"It was my first," "No one"**: Ralph McGill, "Salute to Maggie," *Daily Reporter*, Jan. 11, 1968.

CHAPTER 5: EARLY MANEUVERS

76   **"She didn't need"**: Letter, Russell Hill to Kathleen Kearney Keeshen, Feb. 17, 1982, KKP.

76   **"as clamorous"**: Higgins, *News Is a Singular Thing*, p. 41.

76   **"War Correspondent," "status as a novice"**: Ibid., pp. 41–42.

77   **"Young, blonde"**: Letter, Daniel De Luce to Kathleen Kearney Keeshen, Jan. 11, 1980, KKKP.

77   **"1 Rue Scribe"**: Higgins, Diary, March 1945, Box 41, Notebooks, Marguerite Higgins Papers, SCRC.

78   **"Hill introduced me"**: Higgins, *News Is a Singular Thing*, p. 43.

78   **"well, almost," "I'm on a no-drinking," "Well, you won't"**: Ibid., p. 44.

78   **"I, war correspondent"**: Higgins, Diary, March 1945, SCRC.

79   **"You do speak"**: Higgins, *News Is a Singular Thing*, p. 45.

79   **"Don't you think," "terribly, terribly"**: Ibid., p. 55.

80   **"still on a semi-starvation"**: *New York Herald Tribune*, March 7, 1945.

80   **"This attracted attention"**: Higgins, *News Is a Singular Thing*, p. 61.

81   **"When the three"**: Kerr to Keeshen, Nov. 30, 1982.

81   **"Those wartime," "I'm sorry"**: Hill to Keeshen, Feb. 17, 1982.

81   **"Marguerite liked," "I shared"**: Ibid.

82   **"When the war," "plucking"**: Phillip Knightley, *The First Casualty: From the Crimea to Vietnam; The War Correspondent as Hero, Propagandist, and Myth Maker* (New York: Harcourt Brace Jovanovich, 1975), p. 325.

82   **"The war"**: Higgins, *News Is a Singular Thing*, p. 68.

82   **"go no further"**: Barney Oldfield, *Never a Shot in Anger* (New York: Duell, Sloan and Pierce, 1956), p. 189.

83   **"It was the lure"**: Ibid., p. 191.

83   **"excellent ammunition"**: Higgins, *News Is a Singular Thing*, p. 72.

84   **"made ready"**: *New York Herald Tribune*, March 17, 1945.

84   **"in the heaviest"**: Ibid., March 25, 1945.

84   **"Here roofs"**: Ibid., April 1, 1945.

85   **"How is it"**: Antony Penrose, *The Lives of Lee Miller* (New York: Holt, Rhinehart & Winston, 1985), p. 138.

85   **"requisition"**: Higgins, *News Is a Singular Thing*, pp. 68–69.

85   **"A good part," "minx"**: Helen Kirkpatrick Milbank, interview #2 by Anne S. Kasper, Washington Press Club Foundation, April 4, 1990, Williamsburg, VA.

87   **"Get 'em the hell"**: Oldfield, *Never a Shot in Anger*, p. 156.

87   **"Rhine Maidens"**: Letter, Wes Gallagher to Kathleen Kearney Keeshen, Jan. 7, 1982, KKKP.

87 **"She was very"**: Gallagher to Keeshen, Jan. 7, 1982; "The Rhine Maidens," *Newsweek*, March 19, 1945.

88 **"The reason"**: Letter, Russell Hill to Kathleen Kearney Keeshen, Nov. 10, 1981, KKKP.

88 **"She was smart," "None except"**: Letter, Andrew A. Rooney to Peter Noel Murray, Aug. 6, 2003, KKKP; Peter Noel Murray, "Marguerite Higgins: An Examination of Legacy and Gender Bias" (PhD diss., University of Maryland, 2003).

88 **"The double standard"**: Edwards, *Women of the World*, p. 196.

89 **"the general's mattress," "the news"**: Vicki Goldberg, *Margaret Bourke-White: A Biography* (Reading, MA: Addison-Wesley, 1987), p. 263.

89 **"[They] faced," "slept their way," "Indeed"**: Letter, Carl Mydans to Kathleen Kearney Keeshen, July 9, 1980, KKKP.

90 **"Don't be deceived"**: Martha Gellhorn and Virginia Cowles, *Love Goes to Press: A Comedy in Three Acts* (Lincoln: University of Nebraska Press, 2009), p. 12.

91 **"wasn't going to fall," "a mood"**: Higgins, *News Is a Singular Thing*, p. 74.

91 **"The most awful," "As if to emphasize," "At Buchenwald"**: Ibid., p. 76.

92 **"relentless persistence"**: Ibid., p. 75.

93 **"The stench"**: Gordon Fisher, Oral History Interview, 1945, Louise Gignoux Papers, United States Holocaust Memorial Museum Collection, retrieved from https://collections.ushmm.org/search/catalog/irn523424.

93 **"The reaction"**: Higgins, "Finale in the West."

93 **"Horror Comes Home," "the vast"**: *New York Herald Tribune*, April 16 (delayed) and 18, 1945.

93 **"One thousand"**: Ibid., April 18, 1945.

94 **"really wanted"**: Higgins, *News Is a Singular Thing*, p. 77.

95 **"some very," "constant vigilance"**: Ibid., pp. 73, 81.

95 **"blithe disregard," "Many," "As far as"**: *New York Herald Tribune*, April 26, 1945.

96 **"stony-faced and grave"**: *New York Herald Tribune*, May 5, 1945.

96 **"rumpled white pajamas"**: Ibid., May 18, 1945.

96 **"manacled and silent"**: Ibid., May 25, 1945.

97 **"We lived it up"**: Furst, Oral History Interview, Dec. 30, 2009.

97 **"What are you," "Hold on," "General"**: Ibid.

CHAPTER 6: UNCHARTED TERRAIN

99 **"When I first met"**: Letter, George Reid Millar to Kathleen Kearney Keeshen, Nov. 3, 1981.

99 **"Four months"**: Marguerite Higgins, "Paris—Heartbreak and Hope," *Mademoiselle*, Sept. 1945.

99 **"liberated," "I might have"**: Higgins, *News Is a Singular Thing*, pp. 103, 98.

100 **"Golden Millar"**: Ben Lowings, *The Chancellor: George Millar, a Life* (Cowes, Isle of Wight, UK: Taniwha Press, 2021), e-book; *London Times*, Jan. 20, 2005.

100 **"Here, suddenly"**: Eric Sevareid, *Not So Wild a Dream* (New York: Alfred A. Knopf, 1947), p. 468.

101 **"This annoyed him," "girlish softness"**: Higgins, *News Is a Singular Thing*, p. 100.

102 **"unaccepting of"**: Ibid., p. 104.

102 **"international set":** Lowings, *The Chancellor.*

102 **"We would sail":** Higgins, *News Is a Singular Thing*, p. 98.

103 **"an idyllic two days":** Marguerite Higgins, "Voices of the Defeated," *Mademoiselle*, Aug. 1945.

103 **"knew too much," "Who's Afraid":** *New York Herald Tribune*, May 23, 1945.

103 **"What Long Teeth":** "What Long Teeth, Adolf," *Newsweek*, June 4, 1945.

103 **"Gay Paris":** Higgins, "Paris in the Spring," *Mademoiselle*, May 1945.

104 **"The only notification," "risk of":** Higgins, "Paris—Heartbreak and Hope."

104 **"He was certainly":** Hill to Keeshen, Feb. 17, 1982.

104 **"My marriage":** Higgins, *News Is a Singular Thing*, p 107; Divorce complaint, Stanley W. Moore vs. Marguerite H. Moore, Oct. 30, 1946; Stanley M. Moore vs. Marguerite H. Moore, Authorization for Counsel to Appear on Behalf of the State of California, Nov. 25, 1946; Letter, Stanley Moore to Kathleen Kearney Keeshen, April 19, 1982, KKKP.

104 **"I don't think," "I discovered":** Higgins, *News Is a Singular Thing*, pp. 107–8.

105 **"You can't be":** Sonia Tomara, interview by Kathleen Kearney Keeshen, Oct. 13, 1979.

105 **"For a while":** Higgins, *News Is a Singular Thing*, p. 98.

105 **"selling out":** *New York Herald Tribune*, July 28, 1945.

105 **"The solution":** Ibid., Aug. 12, 1945.

106 **"inconsequential and tawdry":** Higgins, *News Is a Singular Thing*, p. 111.

106 **"How I would," "You Americans," "In our":** Ibid., pp. 109–11, 108.

106 **"If it had," "As everyone learns":** Ibid., pp. 111–12.

107 **"The truth is":** Millar to Keeshen, Nov. 3, 1981.

107 **"I deeply," "I have read," "She has":** Ibid.

107 **"love-struck":** Higgins, *News Is a Singular Thing*, p. 105.

108 **"Voyage of the *Truant*":** Lowings, *The Chancellor.*

108 **"I hoped," "After George":** Higgins, *News Is a Singular Thing*, pp. 105, 113.

110 **"As a correspondent":** De Luce to Keeshen, Jan. 11, 1980.

110 **"living in," "a look," "writes," "like Keitel":** *New York Herald Tribune*, Sept. 8, 1945.

110 **"human animals," "They had been," "slave labor":** Ibid., Dec. 12, 1945.

111 **"was always among":** De Luce to Keeshen, Jan. 11, 1980.

111 **"She dug," "Maggie," "sort of":** Walter Cronkite, interview by Richard Kluger, 1982, Box 4, Richard Kluger Papers, Manuscripts and Archives, Yale University Library, New Haven, CT.

112 **"as competent":** Letter, Clinton "Pat" Conger to Kathleen Kearney Keeshen, March 4, 1982, KKKP.

112 **"It developed," "I finally," "Maggie":** Ibid.

113 **"I am honored":** *New York Times*, Feb. 16, 1946.

133 **"It has only," "super newsgathering":** Hal Johnson, "So We're Told," *Berkeley Daily Gazette*, May 22, 1946.

CHAPTER 7: ROVING CORRESPONDENT

114 **"Whenever she showed":** Bernard to Keeshen, Feb. 2, 1982.

114 **"better than average":** Conger to Keeshen, March 4, 1982.

115 **"It has an atmosphere"**: Marguerite Higgins, "Berlin: City of Women," *Mademoiselle*, Dec. 1945.

115 **"did not bode"**: *New York Herald Tribune*, Sept. 8, 1945.

116 **"a hero's death," "Fascist trick"**: Ibid., May 3, 1945 and May 2, 1945.

116 **July 1945 Allied headquarters' press release on Hitler's death**: "Hitler: The Cremation," *Newsweek*, July 2, 1945.

117 **"When competing," "with a drawn pistol"**: James P. O'Donnell, *The Bunker* (New York: Houghton Mifflin, 1978), pp. 373–74.

118 **"Marguerite and I"**: Ibid., p. 374.

119 **"zest of danger," "It left no"**: Higgins, *News Is a Singular Thing*, p. 181.

119 **"Her success," "She was"**: Hill to Keeshen, Nov. 10, 1981.

120 **"She drove"**: Gallagher to Keeshen, Jan. 7, 1982.

120 **"Marguerite evidently," "I ordered"**: Kerr to Keeshen, Nov. 30, 1982.

121 **"iron curtain," "sphere of influence"**: Ronald Steel, *Walter Lippmann and the American Century* (Boston: Atlantic Monthly Press, 1980) pp. 426–27.

121 **"kind of man," "to serve," "isolated"**: Higgins, *News Is a Singular Thing*, pp. 118–119.

122 **"kidnapped, robbed"**: Ibid., p. 132.

122 **"free and unfettered"**: *New York Herald Tribune*, April 25, 1946.

122 **"I was still"**: Higgins, *News Is a Singular Thing*, p. 138.

123 **"dirty capitalist"**: *New York Herald Tribune*, Feb. 12, 1947.

123 **"Poland's Police Ape"**: Ibid., Dec. 25, 1946.

123 **"a mere formality"**: Ibid., Jan. 1, 1947.

123 **"It was a terrible"**: Higgins, *News Is a Singular Thing*, p. 139.

123 **"nothing to complain," "The picture"**: *Daily Worker*, Jan. 23, 1947; "Clear Picture," *Time*, Feb. 3, 1947.

124 **"The *Herald Tribune*'s"**: Clack, "Marguerite Higgins '41."

124 **"The volatile"**: Higgins, *News Is a Singular Thing*, p. 142.

124 **"bright hope," "His tragic"**: Ibid., pp. 139, 117.

125 **"She became"**: Peter I. Lisagor, interview by Kathleen Kearney Keeshen, Dec. 12, 1972, KKKP.

CHAPTER 8: DATELINE—BERLIN

126 **"A careless, unauthenticated"**: Quentin Reynolds, *Leave It to the People* (New York: Random House, 1948), p. 305.

126 **"I was wearing"**: Higgins, *News Is a Singular Thing*, pp. 157–58.

127 **"coming of age," "a little slip"**: Ibid., pp. 156, 159.

127 **"I'd never trust"**: Ibid., pp. 57–58.

128 **"She was sitting"**: Letter, Barney Oldfield to Kathleen Kearney Keeshen, Jan. 4, 1982, KKKP.

128 **"solemnly assured," "moments," "I felt"**: Higgins, *News Is a Singular Thing*, p. 161.

129 **"Professor"**: Ibid., p. 162.

130 **"Only the sleekest," "Life in"**: Marguerite Higgins, "At Home in the Ruins," *Mademoiselle*, Aug. 1946.

130 **"purpose parties"**: Higgins, *News Is a Singular Thing*, p. 160.

131 **"That's ridiculous," "I was proving," "In order"**: Ibid., pp. 170–71, 164.

133 **"What are you," "No, nothing," "WHAT'S GOING ON"**: May, *Witness to War*, p. 119; *New York Herald Tribune*, Feb. 14, 1947; "Cardinal of Berlin," *Newsweek*, Feb. 24, 1947.

134 **"Can you imagine"**: May, *Witness to War*, p. 121.

135 **"She was ruthless," "rather nice," "After all"**: Sonia Tomara Clark, interview by Kathleen Kearney Keeshen, Oct. 13, 1979, KKKP.

135 **"American forces"**: *New York Herald Tribune*, March 25, 1948.

135 **"he rather liked"**: Jean Edward Smith, *Lucius D. Clay: An American Life* (New York: Henry Holt, 1990), p. 440.

136 **"The United States"**: *New York Herald Tribune*, April 2, 1948.

136 **"baby blockade"**: Smith, *Lucius D. Clay: An American Life*, p. 473; Daniel F. Harrington, *"The Air Force Can Deliver Anything!": A History of the Berlin Air Lift* (Washington, DC: USAFE Office of History, Jan. 1998), p. 9.

136 **"completing the split"**: *New York Herald Tribune*, June 19, 1948.

137 **"As far as we"**: Ibid., June 25, 1948.

137 **Operation Vittles, Operation Plainfare**: Harrington, *"Air Force Can Deliver Anything,"* p. 31.

138 **"absolutely impossible," "I may be"**: Marguerite Higgins, "Obituary of a Government," in *This Is Germany*, ed. Arthur Settel (New York: Houghton Mifflin, 1950), p. 322.

140 **"tensest city"**: Marguerite Higgins, "The Night Raiders of Berlin," *Saturday Evening Post*, June 17, 1950.

140 **"Clay felt that"**: Marguerite Higgins, "What I Learned from the Russians," *Saturday Evening Post*, Dec. 27, 1952.

140 **"coiled snake," "first team"**: Quentin Reynolds, "In Korea, It Was Blood, Thunder and Maggie Higgins," *New York Times*, April 15, 1951; "Scream with Delight," *Der Spiegel*, July 10, 1951.

140 **"It might not be," "That gal"**: Reynolds, "In Korea, It Was Blood"; "Scream with Delight."

141 **"great personal courage"**: Ibid., p. 164; Higgins, "What I Learned from the Russians."

141 **"The pistol"**: "Maggie," *Newsweek*, January 17, 1966.

142 **"If you mention," "whose was"**: May, *Witness to War*, p. 118.

142 **"personal disaster"**: Higgins, *News Is a Singular Thing*, p. 161.

142 **"The Soviet soldiers"**: *New York Herald Tribune*, Sept. 7, 1948; *New York Times*, Sept. 10, 1948.

143 **"Are you planning," "Of course," "Because"**: Higgins, *News Is a Singular Thing*, pp. 185–86.

144 **"something adolescent," "very aggressive," "Maggie treated"**: Letter, Stephen White to Richard Kluger, Oct. 15, 1981, Box 16, Richard Kluger Papers, Manuscripts and Archives, Yale University Library, New Haven, CT; Stephen White, interview by Richard Kluger, Richard Kluger Papers, Manuscripts and Archives, Yale University Library, New Haven, CT; Kluger, *The Paper*, p. 442.

144 **"Marguerite did"**: Michael Emery, *On the Front Lines: Following America's Foreign Correspondents across the Twentieth Century* (Washington, DC: American University Press, 1995), p. 102.

144 **"Yes indeed," "Noncommital"**: Higgins, *News Is a Singular Thing*, p. 187.

CHAPTER 9: POISON PENS

146 **"In the bars"**: Toni Howard, *Shriek with Pleasure* (New York: Pyramid Books, 1950), dustjacket.

147 **"I steered shy"**: Hall, interview by Keeshen, Feb. 26, 1973.

147 **"Heads turn"**: *Washington Post*, April 10, 1947.

148 **"Nothing for now"**: Georges Pernoud, "Le marriage de Marguerite Higgins," *Paris Match*, May 24, 1952.

148 **"She was," "a lot of fun," "She and I"**: Hall, interview by Keeshen, Feb. 26, 1973.

149 **"mil-gov requisitioned," "I don't think"**: De Luce to Keeshen, Jan. 11, 1980.

149 **"That was"**: Hall, interview by Keeshen, Feb. 26, 1973.

149 **"the only luggage"**: Pernoud, "Le marriage de Marguerite Higgins."

150 **"I tried to"**: Higgins, *News Is a Singular Thing*, p. 205.

151 **"offered more"**: May, *Witness to War*, p. 52.

151 **"I always thought"**: Carl Levin, interview by Richard Kluger, 1982, Box 7, Richard Kluger Papers, Manuscripts and Archives, Yale University Library, New Haven, CT.

151 **"do anything," "This is, frankly"**: Howard, *Shriek with Pleasure*, dustjacket.

152 **"She seems to do"**: Ibid., pp. 80–81.

152 **"Carla has learned"**: Richard McLaughlin, "Boudoir Blitzkrieg: Shriek with Pleasure," *New York Times Book Review*, June 4, 1950.

152 **"Indeed, her hoppings"**: Patricia Highsmith, "Amber Correspondent & Beaux: Shriek with Pleasure," *Saturday Review of Literature*, June 3, 1950.

153 **"a biased fictionalized"**: Hill to Keeshen, Nov. 10, 1987.

153 **"Correspondents," "Since the locale"**: Keyes Beech, *Tokyo and Points East* (Tokyo: Charles E. Tuttle, 1955), pp. 168–69.

154 **"According to," "such a," "consciously"**: Higgins, *News Is a Singular Thing*, p. 206.

155 **"Despite the grim"**: Ibid., p. 180.

CHAPTER 10: SCOOP TROUBLE

156 **"A fatherly general"**: Beech, *Tokyo and Points East*, p. 168.

156 **"Western style"**: Parton, *Journey through a Lighted Room*, p. 93.

157 **"Higgins found"**: Higgins, *News Is a Singular Thing*, p. 205.

158 **"This unpublicized"**: *New York Herald Tribune*, May 29, 1950.

158 **"for at least ten"**: Ibid., June 21, 1950.

158 **"Very, very," "press hostility," "good start"**: Higgins, *News Is a Singular Thing*, pp. 194–95.

159 **"The Red invasion"**: Marguerite Higgins, *War in Korea: The Report of a Woman Combat Correspondent* (Garden City, NY: Doubleday, 1951), p. 15.

159 **"Like Dalmations"**: Frank Gibney, introduction to *Foreign Correspondents in*

Japan: Reporting a Half Century of Upheavals; From 1945 to the Present, ed. Charles Pomeroy (Rutland, VT: Charles E. Tuttle, 1998), p. xiii.

159 **"land running"**: Keyes Beech, interview by Richard Kluger, 1982, Box 2, Richard Kluger Papers, Manuscripts and Archives, Yale University Library, New Haven, CT.

160 **"no place," "For me"**: Higgins, *War in Korea*, pp. 17–19.

161 **"Be of good," "momentous," "world scoop"**: Ibid., pp. 20, 19.

161 **"Get up!," "My God"**: Marguerite Higgins, "The Terrible Days in Korea," *Saturday Evening Post*, Aug. 19, 1950.

162 **"safe and smug," "What's the matter"**: Higgins, *War in Korea*, pp. 27–30.

163 **"Any story-making"**: Beech, *Tokyo and Points East*, p. 167.

163 **"Korean Reds," "Seoul's Fall"**: *New York Herald Tribune*, June 25 and 29, 1950.

164 **"its" war correspondent**: "This Time, Korea," *Newsweek*, July 10, 1950.

164 **"few who got," "winsome blonde"**: "The Press: Drawing the Line," *Time*, July 10, 1950.

165 **"the palace guard"**: Emery, *On the Front Lines*, p. 95.

165 **"News of MacArthur's"**: *New York Herald Tribune*, June 29, 1950.

165 **"talked her way," "first-class scoop," "Scoop Trouble"**: "This Time, Korea."

165 **"Miss Higgins," "untrue statements," "I wish"**: "Letters: Miss Higgins Speaks," *Newsweek*, August 7, 1950.

166 **"Pay no attention"**: Higgins, *News Is a Singular Thing*, p 195.

166 **"A Corporal," "Point No. 4"**: "Letters: A Corporal Speaks," *Newsweek*, Sept. 11, 1950.

167 **"strenuous objections"**: "The Press," cartoon caption, *Newsweek*, Sept. 11, 1950.

167 **"about as popular"**: Higgins, *War in Korea*, pp. 108–9.

167 **"On the Line," "Their bravery"**: Bob Considine, "Inside INSIDE," *Esquire*, June 1951, collected in *Off the Record: The Best Stories of Foreign Correspondents*, ed. Dickson Hartwell and Andy A. Rooney (New York: Doubleday, 1953), p. xxiv.

167 **"in a fine," "a rush of fear," "He was," "I wouldn't," "Hey, lieutenant"**: Higgins, *War in Korea*, pp. 38–39.

168 **"Get to," "Those sons," "From then on," "The Reds"**: Ibid., pp. 41–42.

169 **"It is most"**: *Chicago Daily News*, June 30, 1950.

169 **"You may be"**: Higgins, *War in Korea*, p. 47.

170 **"Certainly not," "We will hurl," "We'll hurl"**: *New York Herald Tribune*, July 1, 1950.

170 **"Never once"**: Higgins, *War in Korea*, pp. 50–51.

171 **"Death of the First," "My God"**: *New York Herald Tribune*, July 6, 1950; Higgins, "Terrible Days in Korea"; Emery, *On the Front Lines*, pp. 99–100.

172 **"The youngsters," "strategic withdrawal," "the long retreat," "Within minutes"**: Higgins, "Terrible Days in Korea."

173 **"a blow," "giving aid," "bruising truth"**: Higgins, *War in Korea*, pp. 95–96.

173 **"for ladies," "In Korea," agreed to depart**: Higgins, "Terrible Days in Korea."

174 **"bum's rush"**: Higgins, *War in Korea*, p. 101.

174 **"This is just not"**: *New York Herald Tribune*, July 18, 1950; *New York Times*, July 18, 1950; UP, July 18, 1950.

174   **"Army orders," "I am going"**: *New York Herald Tribune*, July 18, 1950.

174   **"personal strength," "[Walker's ban]"**: Kluger, *The Paper*, p. 446.

175   **"The *Herald Tribune***": *New York Herald Tribune*, July 18, 1950.

175   **"And you can," "Am I," "Don't pull"**: Higgins, *War in Korea*, pp. 106–7.

175   **"Maggie was," "I don't think"**: Audiotape letter (cassette), Robert "Bob" Miller to Kathleen Kearney Keeshen, Feb. 23, 1982; UP, July 18, 1950, KKKP.

176   **"I have been with"**: *New York Herald Tribune*, July 18, 1950.

176   **"ZEBRA ONE"**: Helen Rogers Reid, Reid Family Papers, Manuscript/Mixed Material, Library of Congress, retrieved from https://lccn.loc.gov/mm82065491; *New York Herald Tribune*, July 19, 1950.

176   **"it was not the type"**: *New York Herald Tribune*, July 19, 1950.

177   **"Miss Higgins"**: *New York Times*, July 19, 1950.

177   **"You have"**: Letter, Mary Hornaday to Whitelaw Reid, Aug. 8, 1950, Reid Family Papers, Manuscript/Mixed Material, Library of Congress, retrieved from https://lccn.loc.gov/mm82065491.

177   **"The First Victory"**: *New York Herald Tribune*, July 28, 1950.

177   **"indispensable"**: Letter, Marguerite Higgins to Thomas E. Elwell of Paillard, Aug. 16, 1950, Marguerite Higgins Papers, Correspondence, SCRC.

177   **"The *Herald Tribune*'s"**: *New York Herald Tribune*, Aug. 23, 1950.

CHAPTER 11: THE FEUD

179   **"The competition"**: Miller to Keeshen, Feb. 23, 1982.

180   **"bring the house"**: Beech, *Tokyo and Points East*, p. 170.

180   **"Help Homer"**: Beech, interview by Kluger, 1982.

180   **"What is more"**: Higgins, *War in Korea*, p. 58.

180   **"It's all very"**: Letter, Marguerite Higgins to her managing editor, Bill Robinson, undated, Marguerite Higgins Papers, SCRC.

181   **"the paper's senior"**: Higgins, Diary, July 1950, Box 41, Notebooks, Marguerite Higgins Papers, SCRC.

181   **"If the Racing Form"**: "The Press: Homer's Odyssey," *Newsweek*, Jan. 22, 1951.

181   **"Going forward"**: Higgins, Diary, July 1, 1950, SCRC.

181   **"There was"**: Beech, *Tokyo and Points East*, p. 171.

182   **"SHE'S AS INNOCENT"**: William Prochnau, *Once upon a Distant War: David Halberstam, Neil Sheehan, Peter Arnett—Young War Correspondents and Their Early Vietnam Battles* (New York: Vintage, 1995), p. 342.

182   **"straight reporting"**: Steven Casey, *Selling the Korean War: Propaganda, Politics, and Public Opinion 1950–1953* (Oxford: Oxford University Press, 2008), p. 58.

182   **"YOU HAVE SENT"**: Cable, Whitelaw Reid to Marguerite Higgins, July 13, 1950, Reid Family Papers, Manuscript/Mixed Material, Library of Congress, retrieved from https://lccn.loc.gov/mm82065491.

183   **"Maggie intently"**: Letter, Max Desfor to Kathleen Kearney Keeshen, Feb. 19, 1982, KKKP.

183   **"It was less"**: Homer Bigart, interview by Richard Kluger.

183   **"The Higgins competitive"**: Beech, *Tokyo and Points East*, p. 171.

183 **"Orders were orders," "absolutely," "The American":** Higgins, *War in Korea*, p. 114.

184 **"missing in action":** Sheila Miyoshi Jager, *Brothers at War: The Unending Conflict in Korea* (New York: W. W. Norton, 2013), p. 77.

184 **"We were sent," "Well, the story's," "I thought":** *Stars and Stripes Korea* 8, no. 5 (July 11–24, 2019).

185 **"Battle," "Remember":** "Battle of Bowling Alley," *Time*, Sept. 4, 1950.

186 **"A coffee pot," "I'm getting," "the swiftest":** *New York Herald Tribune*, Aug. 4, 1950.

187 **"after the first," "Then suddenly," "How you doin'":** Higgins, *War in Korea*, p. 127.

187 **"Colonel Michaelis," "Medical corps":** *New York Herald Tribune*, Aug. 4, 1950.

188 **"[It] struck me":** Letter, Colonel J. H. Michaelis to the Editors of the *NYHT*, Aug. 29, 1950, published as "Tribute to Marguerite Higgins," *New York Herald Tribune*, Sept. 14, 1950.

188 **"slender, durable Newshen," "She's either":** "Pride of the Regiment," *Time*, Sept. 25, 1950.

188 **"Woman Writer," "No one":** *Stars and Stripes*, Aug. 22, 1950; Harold H. Martin, "The Colonel Saved the Day," *Saturday Evening Post*, Sept. 9, 1950.

189 **"My Wolfhound":** David Hackworth, "Learning How to Cover a War," *Newsweek*, Dec. 12, 1992.

189 **"People charged," "equally silly," "Her driving":** May, *Witness to War*, p. 166.

190 **"Hey Lady," "So are you!":** Mydans, "Girl War Correspondent."

190 **"wasn't a he," "One can brag":** "The Press: Covering Korea," *Time*, Aug. 21, 1950.

190 **"No American," "She displayed":** Bill Hosokawa, "Maggie and the War in Korea," *Denver Post*, April 12, 1951.

190 **"honors for," "Pulitzer Prizewinning":** "The Press: Covering Korea," *Time*, Aug. 21, 1950.

191 **"That's easy," "the competition":** Beech, interview by Kluger, 1982.

191 **"As soon as":** Mydans, "Girl War Correspondent."

191 **"Miss Higgins valued," "Her pale blue":** Beech, *Tokyo and Points East*, pp. 168, 173.

192 **"double standard":** Beech, interview by Kluger, 1982.

193 **"The lower half," "practically knock," "She had a male":** Ibid.

193 **"[But] she didn't":** Emery, *On the Front Lines*, p. 118.

193 **"woman's angle," "Higgins never":** Beech, interview by Kluger, 1982; Kluger, *The Paper*, p. 447.

194 **"She was the best":** Beech, interview by Kluger, 1982.

194 **"goddamn bra":** "Scream with Delight," *Der Spiegel*, July 10, 1951; Beech, Letter to Kathleen Kearney Keeshen, Nov. 28, 1979, KKKP.

194 **"I was particularly":** Beech, interview by Kluger, 1982; Kluger, *The Paper*, p. 447.

194 **"she could take," "her funeral":** Beech, interview by Kluger, 1982; Beech, *Tokyo and Points East*, p. 180.

195 **"Marguerite Higgins Hurt," "stay on":** *New York Herald Tribune*, Aug. 27, 1950.

195 **"Thrilled and":** Higgins, Diary, Aug. 30, 1950, Box 41, Notebooks, Marguerite Higgins Papers, SCRC.

196 **"I am going":** May, *Witness to War*, p. 167.

196 **"so near," "Bill loving":** Higgins, Diary, undated 1950, Box 41, Notebooks, Marguerite Higgins Papers, SCRC.

197 **"Operation Common":** Higgins, *War in Korea*, p. 136.

197 **"I'm-going-to-get," "nothing-can":** Higgins, *News Is a Singular Thing*, p. 211.

197 **"the same degree":** Higgins, *War in Korea*, pp. 136–37.

197 **"hampering *Herald Tribune*":** Cable, Marguerite Higgins to Whitelaw Reid, Sept. 9, 1950, Reid Family Papers, Manuscript/Mixed Material, Library of Congress, retrieved from https://lccn.loc.gov/mm82065491.

197 **"any Navy ship":** Higgins, *War in Korea*, p. 149.

198 **"No one knew," "When the Gooks":** *Daily Boston Globe*, March 13, 1951.

199 **"Come on":** Higgins, *War in Korea*, p. 144.

199 **photograph of Marine 1st Lt. Baldomero Lopez:** Samuel J. Cox, Director, *NHHC*, "H-054–1: Inchon Landing and Naval Action in the Korean War, September–October 1950," Sept. 2020, Naval History and Heritage Command, retrieved from https://www.history.navy.mil/about-us/leadership/director/directors-corner/h -grams/h-gram-054/h-054-1.html.

199 **"A round skipped":** Donald Knox, *The Korean War: Pusan to Chosin; An Oral History* (New York: Harcourt, Brace, Jovanovich, 1985), p. 279.

200 **"Naturally I," "She was," "Furthermore," "I was":** Thomas A. Buell, *Naval Leadership in Korea: The First Six Months* (Washington, DC: Naval Historical Center, Department of the Navy, 2002), p. 30.

201 **"WITH THE UNITED":** *New York Herald Tribune*, Sept. 18, 1950.

202 **"Hello, there":** Higgins, *News Is a Singular Thing*, p. 197.

202 **"Miss Higgins' Story":** *New York Herald Tribune*, Sept. 18, 1950.

203 **"peacemaker":** Beech, interview by Kluger, 1982.

203 **"One of us," "Homer and Maggie,":** Ibid.; Beech, *Tokyo and Points East*, pp. 172–73.

203 **"chaperoned":** Higgins, *War in Korea*, p. 150.

203 **"giving me," "Dear Maggie":** Buell, *Naval Leadership in Korea*, p. 30.

203 **"Miss Higgins":** "A Girl with a Flare for Fireworks," *Courier-Journal* (Louisville, KY), Nov. 10, 1950.

204 **"Of the special," "Homer Loves":** Esther Crane, "Reporting the War," *Stars and Stripes*, Sept. 23, 1950.

204 **"Lili Marlene," "Marguerite":** "The Press: Homer's Odyssey," *Newsweek*, Jan. 22, 1951.

205 **"It was bitter," "played it":** Letter, Carl Mydans to Kathleen Kearney Keeshen, July 3, 1980, KKKP.

205 **"In the case":** Emery, *On the Front Lines*, pp. 102–3.

205 **"In her quest":** Beech, *Tokyo and Points East*, p. 183.

CHAPTER 12: PERILS OF FAME

206 **"From somewhere deep":** Conger to Keeshen, March 4, 1982.

206 **"What does it":** Higgins, *News Is a Singular Thing*, p. 11.

207 **"Maggie wears," "The question," "to deny":** Mydans, "Girl War Correspondent."

207   **"Maggie already has become"**: Editor's note, *Life*, Oct. 2, 1950.

208   **"LIFE DISPLAY"**: Cable, George Bye to Marguerite Higgins, 1950, Box 2, Correspondence, Marguerite Higgins Papers, SCRC; Murray, "Marguerite Higgins," p. 151.

208   **"INTERESTED IN SECURING"**: Cable, Douglas Whitney to Marguerite Higgins, Sept. 30, 1950, Box 8, Correspondence, Marguerite Higgins Papers, SCRC; Murray, "Marguerite Higgins," p. 152.

208   **"insisted"**: Cable, Lew Wasserman to Marguerite Higgins, Oct. 3, 1950, Box 8, Correspondence, Marguerite Higgins Papers, SCRC; Bill Perlberg to Marguerite Higgins, Oct. 6, 1950, Box 8, Correspondence, Marguerite Higgins Papers, SCRC; Murray, "Marguerite Higgins," p. 152.

209   **"having a full-length"**: Cable, Whitelaw Reid to Marguerite Higgins, Oct. 6, 1950, Reid Family Papers, Manuscript/Mixed Material, Library of Congress, retrieved from https://lccn.loc.gov/mm82065491.

209   **"PLEASE TELL SKOURAS"**: Cable, Marguerite Higgins to Whitelaw Reid, Oct. 9, 1950, Reid Family Papers, Manuscript/Mixed Material, Library of Congress, retrieved from https://lccn.loc.gov/mm82065491; Box 9, Correspondence, New York Herald Tribune, Marguerite Higgins Papers, SCRC.

210   **"Woman Correspondent"**: Cable, Ken McCormick to Marguerite Higgins, Oct. 11, 1950, Box 3, Correspondence, Doubleday, Marguerite Higgins Papers, SCRC.

210   **"She was the queen"**: Miller to Keeshen, Feb. 23, 1982.

210   **"genius"**: Beech, *Tokyo and Points East*, p. 182.

210   **"GI's Maggie," "still photogenic"**: *Honolulu Advertiser*, Oct. 19, 1950.

211   **"I feel slightly"**: *New York Herald Tribune*, Oct. 20, 1950.

211   **"stupidity," "A number," "Perhaps"**: Helen Rogers Reid, "Remarks Introducing Higgins at Herald Tribune Forum," Oct. 25, 1950.

212   **"Unpreparedness," "he is"**: *New York Herald Tribune*, Oct. 26, 1950; *Christian Science Monitor*, Oct. 27, 1950.

213   **"Everywhere"**: Helen Rogers Reid, "Remarks Introducing Marguerite Higgins at West Side Association Dinner."

213   **"third world war"**: *New York Herald Tribune*, Nov. 1, 1950.

213   **"every weapon," "alarmist"**: Ibid., Nov. 10, 1950.

213   **"President Truman," "charming"**: Ibid., Nov. 28, 1950.

213   **"Front Page," "courage"**: Ibid., Nov. 18, 1950.

214   **"Young Women"**: Ibid., Dec. 11, 1950.

214   **"12 Smartest"**: *San Francisco Chronicle*, Jan. 2, 1951.

214   **"major general"**: *New York Daily Mirror*, Dec. 12, 1950.

215   **"daredevil angel," "She is back"**: Ibid., Dec. 22, 1950.

215   **Changjin Reservoir offensive, "Nightmare Alley"**: *New York Herald Tribune*, Dec. 6 and 8, 1951; Marguerite Higgins, "The Bloody Trail Back," *Saturday Evening Post*, Jan. 27, 1951; Higgins, *War in Korea*, pp. 173–78.

216   **"Korean Valley Forge," "faulty generalship"**: Higgins, "Bloody Trail Back."

216   **"The men were," "The chaplain," "walk out"**: Ibid; *New York Herald Tribune*, Dec. 6, 1950.

217 **"seizure of chivalry"**: Higgins, *War in Korea*, p. 195.

217 **"Just as I"**: Martin Russ, *Breakout: The Chosin Reservoir River Campaign, Korea 1950*. (New York: Fromm International, 1999), p. 398.

217 **"How Marines"**: *New York Herald Tribune*, Dec. 7, 1950.

217 **"The marines"**: Ibid., Dec. 8, 1950.

217 **"home by Christmas," "Wave and look," "If only"**: Ibid., Dec. 11, 1950.

218 **"I'm afraid," "already some"**: Marguerite Higgins and Homer Bigart, "On the Battlefront in Korea," *New York Herald Tribune*, Dec. 6, 1950.

218 **"both told better"**: "Two Faces of War," editorial, *New York Herald Tribune*, Dec. 7, 1950; Casey, *Selling the Korean War*, pp. 152–54.

218 **"calm air," "came in"**: *New York Herald Tribune*, Jan. 4 and 5, 1951.

219 **"CONGRATULATIONS"**: Cable, Whitelaw Reid to Marguerite Higgins, Dec. 26, 1950, Reid Family Papers.

219 **"refuse to work"**: "Bigart Bans Higgins," *Quick*, Jan. 12, 1951.

219 **Pulitzer Prizes awarded to women**: John Hohenberg, *The Pulitzer Prizes: A History of the Awards in Books, Drama, Music and Journalism, Based on the Private Files over Six Decades* (New York: Columbia University Press, 1974), pp. 36–37.

220 **"Marguerite Higgins"**: Editor's note, and Higgins, "Bloody Trail Back," *Saturday Evening Post*, Jan. 27, 1951.

220 **"a woman's magnificent"**: Marguerite Higgins, "Front Line Diary of Marguerite Higgins," *Woman's Home Companion*, April 1951.

220 **"one of the few"**: *New York Herald Tribune*, March 23, 1951.

220 **"In Korea"**: Reynolds, "In Korea, It Was Blood."

221 **"beautiful, able"**: Charles Poore, "Books of the Times," *New York Times*, April 12, 1951.

221 **"prisoner of his," "La Higgins," "a sufficient"**: Marquis Childs, "A Woman as Correspondent in Korea," *New York Herald Tribune*, April 15, 1951.

221 **"This Maggie's eye"**: S. L. A. Marshall, "Almost Alone at the Front," *Saturday Review of Literature*, April 21, 1951.

221 **"female Ernie Pyle"**: Doubleday newspaper advertisement, April 1951, Scrapbooks, Marguerite Higgins Papers, SCRC.

222 **"courage, integrity"**: *New York Herald Tribune*, April 30, 1951; Hohenberg, *Pulitzer Prizes*, p. 352.

222 **"entitled to special"**: Mike Pride, "The Jury Has Spoken," *Columbia Journalism Review*, Spring 2016, https://www.cjr.org/the_feature/the_jury_has_spoken.php.

222 **"demonstrated," "the only"**: "1951 Pulitzer Prize Pair," *New York Herald Tribune*, May 14, 1951.

222 **"was now a"**: "People Are Talking About," *Vogue*, June 1951.

223 **"*Messer Marco Polo*," "not unlike"**: Walter Winchell, "Walter Winchell in New York," *Washington Post*, Jan. 8, 1951, reprinted in June 1951.

223 **"walking arm-in-arm"**: Hy Gardner, Newsreel, *Chicago Tribune*, May 15, 1951.

223 **Higgins to sub for Lippmann**: *New York Herald Tribune*, June 23, 1951.

224 **"Red Scare"**: "Red Scare," History.com, https://www.history.com/topics/cold-war/red-scare.

224 **"Around Russia's Curtain":** *New York Herald Tribune*, Aug. 28, 1951.

224 **"gastronomic splurge," "If we let this":** *Washington Post*, Aug. 15, 1951; Marguerite Higgins, "Marguerite Higgins 'Round the World Diary," *Woman's Home Companion*, Nov. 1951.

225 **"fight with fervor":** *New York Herald Tribune*, Aug. 6, 1951.

225 **Tito's pledge:** Ibid., Aug. 27, 1951.

225 **Greece's fight:** Ibid., Sept. 6, 1951.

225 **"very much part":** Ibid., Aug. 30, 1951.

225 **"aura of selflessness":** Ibid., Sept. 24, 1951.

225 **"Red infiltration":** Cable, Whitelaw Reid to Marguerite Higgins, undated 1951, Reid Family Papers, Manuscript/Mixed Material, Library of Congress, retrieved from https://lccn.loc.gov/mm82065491.

225 **"playboy emperor":** *New York Herald Tribune*, Oct. 4, 1951.

226 **"Marguerite Higgins' Round":** Higgins, "Round the World Diary," Nov. and Dec. 1951, Jan. 1952.

226 **"Preview of the War," "great men":** The Editors, "Operation Eggnog," *Collier's*, Oct. 27, 1951.

226 **"in a country":** Marguerite Higgins, "Women of Russia," *Collier's*, Oct. 27, 1951.

227 **"doesn't think so," "nearly as":** "Is It a Man's Game?," *Seventeen*, Oct. 1951.

227 **"social menace," "He had":** Higgins, *News Is a Singular Thing*, pp. 243–44.

227 **Hall divorced in counterpetition:** *Washington Post*, Oct. 26, 1951.

228 **"Woman of the Year":** *New York Herald Tribune*, Dec. 15, 1951.

228 **"have everything," "In my conceit":** Higgins, *News Is a Singular Thing*, p. 245.

228 **"Whatever it was":** Ibid., p. 216.

CHAPTER 13: WINGING IT

229 **"Ride a fast plane":** Harry Evans, "Broadway Diary," *Family Circle*, April 1952.

229 **"turning out":** *Oakland Tribune*, Nov. 18, 1951.

230 **"semi-nervous breakdown":** "Maggie Higgins Must Curtail Lecture Tour," *Editor & Publisher*, Jan. 12, 1952.

230 **Cancellations/W. Colston Leigh claim:** *Santa Fe New Mexican*, Jan. 12, 1952; Marguerite Higgins, Correspondence, Dec. 1951–Feb. 1952, "Colston Leigh, Inc.," Box 18, Marguerite Higgins Papers, SCRC.

230 **"ill from overwork":** Evans, "Broadway Diary."

231 **"It seemed to me," "to be inane":** Higgins, *News Is a Singular Thing*, p. 250.

231 **"made the grade":** Karen Rothmeyer, *Winning Pulitzers: The Stories behind Some of the Best News Coverage of Our Time* (New York: Columbia University Press, 1991), p. 2.

231 **"unique phenomenon":** Higgins, *News Is a Singular Thing*, p. 213.

231 **"It is in," "with his toothbrush":** Russell F. Anderson, preface to Hartwell and Rooney, *Off the Record*, p. v.

232 **"to familiarize myself":** Marguerite Higgins, letter to an agent, March 1952, Box 2, Correspondence Misc., Marguerite Higgins Papers, SCRC.

232 **"Marguerite Higgins' Hill 346":** Advertisement for "Marguerite Higgins' Hill 346: A Report on Korea" (*Pulitzer Prize Playhouse*), *New York Times*, Feb. 26, 1952.

232 **"practicing the art," "exclusives," "gasp," "It's very":** Letter, Marguerite Higgins to Joseph Bailey of the John E. Gibbs Agency, undated circa March 1952, Box 2, Correspondence Misc., Marguerite Higgins Papers, SCRC.

233 **"To me the devilish":** Higgins, *News Is a Singular Thing*, p. 249.

233 **"Non Sibi," "She looks":** *Oakland Tribune*, April 9, 1952.

234 **"You get":** Evans, "Broadway Diary."

234 **"I certify":** Riflery target, Box 44, Miscellaneous, Marguerite Higgins Papers, SCRC.

234 **"hiding out," "whose name":** Herb Caen, "Baghdad-by-the-Bay," undated, Higgins Scrapbooks, SCRC.

234 **"After many," "I was":** Higgins, *News Is a Singular Thing*, p. 245.

235 **"Marguerite Higgins":** *New York Herald Tribune*, April 27, 1952.

235 **"I will marry":** "Milestones," *Time*, May 5, 1952.

235 **"This was not":** Higgins, *News Is a Singular Thing*, p. 245.

235 **"Since I consider":** Letter, Higgins to Helen Rogers Reid, April 23, 1952, Reid Family Papers.

236 **"aloneness," "live so narrowly," "I used to feel":** *News Is a Singular Thing*, pp. 254–55.

CHAPTER 14: BETWEEN THE LINES

238 **"Time to play":** Summers, "2,000 Bulbs."

238 **"Here I am":** Letter, Higgins to Carl Mydans, Feb. 23, 1953, Box 7, Correspondence, Carl Mydans, Marguerite Higgins Papers, SCRC.

238 **"a very easy," "range from Taft," "Bill and I":** Ibid.

239 **"I'm so organized," "We had," "screaming liberal," "causes":** Hall, interview by Keeshen, Feb. 26, 1973.

240 **"moral and material," "exclusive":** *New York Herald Tribune*, March 7, 1953.

240 **"I've been":** Letter, Carl Mydans to Marguerite Higgins, March 26, 1953, Box 7, Correspondence, Carl Mydans, Marguerite Higgins Papers, SCRC.

240 **"more or less," "could be put":** Letter, Marguerite Higgins to General Lucius D. Clay, April 1, 1953, Box 2, Correspondence, Marguerite Higgins Papers, SCRC.

241 **"I don't agree":** Letter, Lawrence D. Higgins to his daughter, April 8, 1953, Box 1, Correspondence, Family, Marguerite Higgins Papers, SCRC.

241 **"daring, restless":** *New York Herald Tribune*, March 10 and May 1, 1953.

242 **"an armistice," "a typical":** Casey, *Selling the Korean War*, p. 357.

242 **"proceed on its":** *New York Herald Tribune*, June 22, 1953.

243 **"haze of hurt":** Letter, Higgins to Howard (no last name), undated 1953, Correspondence, Marguerite Higgins Papers, SCRC.

243 **"At the time":** Higgins, *News Is a Singular Thing*, p. 246.

243 **"It was an awful," "It was":** Hall, interview by Keeshen, Feb. 26, 1973.

243 **"As Sharon died," "for I":** Marguerite Higgins, "Thoughts on the Death of a Five Day Old Child," *Good Housekeeping*, Aug. 1954.

244 **"Oh g-good," "devoured her":** Betsy Wade, ed., *Forward Positions: The War Correspondence of Homer Bigart* (Fayetteville: University of Arkansas Press, 1992), p. 224.

244 **"No way I":** Bigart, interview by Kluger; Kluger, *The Paper*, p. 448.

245 **"Friendship":** Summers, "2,000 Bulbs."

245   **"Everything she did," "She loved animals," "She loved":** Hall, interview by Keeshen, Feb. 26, 1973.

246   **"I recall," "Everyone":** Letter, Hope Ridings Miller to Kathleen Kearney Keeshen, May 10, 1982, KKKP.

247   **"Both of us":** Letter, Ruth Montgomery to Kathleen Kearney Keeshen, Jan. 13, 1975, KKKP.

247   **"America's most," "The answer":** *Meet the Press*, transcript of Dec. 13, 1953, broadcast, Box 8, "Meet the Press," Marguerite Higgins Papers, SCRC; *Meet the Press*, kinescope of Dec. 13, 1953, broadcast, Meet the Press Collection, Motion Picture and Broadcasting and Recorded Sound Division, Library of Congress, Washington, DC.

249   **"pleasant insanity":** May, *Witness to War*, p. 200.

249   **"cottages":** Letter, Marguerite Higgins to Andrew Kirkpatrick, Feb. 23, 1953, "Round Hill Development Ltd.," Box 11, Correspondence, Round Hill Developments, Marguerite Higgins Papers, SCRC.

249   **"retreat," "Not being":** Letter, Marguerite Higgins to John Pringle, undated 1954, Box 11, Round Hill Developments, Marguerite Higgins Papers, SCRC.

249   **"mighty pretty":** Letter, Bill Weeks to Marguerite Higgins, March 17, 1954, Box 9, Correspondence, New York Herald Tribune, Marguerite Higgins Papers, SCRC.

249   **"Contracts,"** *The Maggie Higgins Story*: *New York Herald Tribune*, March 22, 1954.

250   **"the tough woman," "Why not":** Letter, Marguerite Higgins to Lela E. Rogers, Jan. 12, 1954, Box 11, Correspondence, Lela Rogers, Marguerite Higgins Papers, SCRC.

CHAPTER 15: THE FINE PRINT

251   **"So well-known":** Kluger, *The Paper*, p. 515.

251   **"As if to underline":** Keyes Beech, *Not without the Americans: A Personal History* (New York: Doubleday, 1971), p. 310.

251   **"Here we go":** Beech, *Tokyo and Points East*, p. 30.

252   **"It seemed":** *New York Herald Tribune*, June 22, 1954.

252   **Dien Bien Phu, "domino" effect:** Jager, *Brothers at War*, pp. 300–303, p. 290.

253   **"village after village":** *New York Herald Tribune*, May 28, 1954.

254   **"THINK INDOCHINA":** Cable, Marguerite Higgins to Whitelaw Reid, June 19, 1954, Box 9, Correspondence, New York Herald Tribune, Marguerite Higgins Papers, SCRC.

254   **drinking, terrible fights:** Ruth Montgomery, interview by Kim Bryce Landon, Sept. 24, 1975, in "War Correspondent Marguerite Higgins: Conflict as a Career" (master's thesis, Syracuse University Graduate School of Journalism, 1975), p. 68.

254   **"If I wasn't":** Hall, interview by Keeshen, Feb. 26, 1973.

255   **"demon ambition," "paradoxical person," "a social," "What does":** Evans, "Broadway Diary."

255   **"But was it," "rough, but":** Higgins, *News Is a Singular Thing*, p. 254.

255   **"five-star bitch":** "The Iron Maiden," *Kirkus Reviews*, June 15, 1954.

255   **"In the course":** Herbert Mitgang, "Life on the Record-Star," *New York Times*, Aug. 22, 1954.

256 **"She was," "a catalyst," "drove the spikes":** Lanham, *Iron Maiden*, pp. 17, 222, 216.

256 **"She shrank":** Lisagor, interview by Keeshen, Dec. 12, 1972.

256 **"the exhilaration," "hyena":** Higgins, *News Is a Singular Thing*, p. 255.

258 **"Miss Higgins herself":** "New and Old in the Soviet Union," *New York Herald Tribune*, Dec. 11, 1954.

258 **"Russian Diary":** Marguerite Higgins, "Russian Diary," *Woman's Home Companion*, April 1955.

259 **"special spot":** Letter, Marguerite Higgins to Ogden (Brownie) Reid and Frank Taylor, May 8, 1955, Box 10, Ogden Rogers Reid Papers, Manuscripts and Archives, Yale University Library, New Haven, CT.

259 **"I let her":** Letter, Kerr to Keeshen, Nov. 30, 1982, KKKP.

259 **"competitive," "the most contentious":** Lewis Gannett, "Book Review," *New York Herald Tribune*, May 20, 1955.

259 **"burning ambition":** Tania Long, "Miss Higgins Files Her Own Story," *New York Times*, May 22, 1950.

259 **"Higgins was not," "The men":** Ben Bradlee, *A Good Life: Newspapering and Other Adventures* (New York: Simon & Schuster, 1995), p. 197.

260 **"People either liked":** Kathleen McLaughlin, interview by Kathleen Kearney Keeshen, May 29, 1982, KKKP.

260 **"Terror Still":** *New York Herald Tribune*, Dec. 11, 1955.

260 **"one of the world's":** Marguerite Higgins, "What the Top Russians Are Like," *U.S. News & World Report*, Jan. 6, 1966.

260 **"having a nodding," "Watching":** Ibid.

261 **"a Correspondent":** *New York Herald Tribune*, "Contract with Miss Higgins," Jan. 19, 1956, Box 10, Ogden Rogers Reid Papers, Manuscripts and Archives, Yale University Library, New Haven, CT; Kluger, *The Paper*, pp. 515–16.

261 **"The circumstances":** Letter, Kerr to Keeshen, Nov. 30, 1982, KKKP; Kluger, *The Paper*, pp. 515–16.

261 **"could not go on":** Robert J. Donovan, "Letter to Betty," Jan. 15, 1983, Box 4, Richard Kluger Papers, Manuscripts and Archives, Yale University Library, New Haven, CT.

262 **"paid publicity":** "Miss Higgins Dropped from Press Gallery," *Editor & Publisher*, Nov. 16, 1957.

262 **"One Billion":** "The Press: The Fine Print," *Time*, Nov. 25, 1957.

262 **"Shows you should," "sponsored":** Ibid.

262 **"If the standing," "Well, the boys":** John O'Donnell, "Capitol Stuff," *Daily News*, Nov. 15, 1957.

262 **"Tempest," "seems," "Oh God!":** "Tempest in Toothpaste," *Newsweek*, Nov. 25, 1957.

263 **"She ran":** Walter Cronkite, interview by Richard Kluger, 1982, Box 4, Richard Kluger Papers, Manuscripts and Archives, Yale University Library, New Haven, CT.

263 **"Jacqueline arrived":** Ruth Montgomery, *Hail to the Chiefs: My Life and Times with Six Presidents* (New York: Howard McCann, 1970), p. 128.

263 **"Blessed Event":** *Daily Mirror*, April 14, 1958.

264 **"If you don't":** Hall, interview by Keeshen, Feb. 26, 1973.

264 **"It was a little," "That was":** Ibid.

265 **"just another":** *New York Herald Tribune*, July 24, 1960.

265 **"He [JFK] gave":** Peter Lisagor, recorded interview by Ronald J. Grele, April 22, 1966, John F. Kennedy Library Oral History Program.

266 **"She pantingly":** Montgomery, *Hail to the Chiefs*, p. 207.

267 **"What was it?," "But Mr.":** *New York Herald Tribune*, Oct. 5, 1960; "Maggie," *Newsweek*, Jan. 17, 1966.

267 **"merely uncertainty," "I hadn't":** Letter, Marguerite Higgins to Robert M. White III, Jan. 7, 1960, Box 9, Correspondence, New York Herald Tribune, Marguerite Higgins Papers, SCRC.

CHAPTER 16: THE MAGGIE HIGGINS HOUR

268 **"In the early sixties":** Tom Wicker, *On Press: A Top Reporter's Life in, and Reflections on, American Journalism* (New York: Viking Press, 1978), p. 170.

268 **"Kennedy Sr." "He urged":** *New York Herald Tribune*, Dec. 12, 1960.

269 **"personally known to":** Internal newsletter, *New York Herald Tribune*, Dec. 16, 1960.

269 **"absolutely no":** *New York Herald Tribune*, Dec. 12, 1960.

269 **"His Brother's":** Ibid., Dec. 5, 1960.

269 **"Bobby: I left":** Letter, Higgins to Robert F. Kennedy, undated, Robert F. Kennedy, Pre-Administration Papers, Political Files, Box 14, "Higgins," JFK Library.

270 **"Your article," "looking forward":** Handwritten note, Robert F. Kennedy to Marguerite Higgins, Dec. 5, 1960, Robert F Kennedy, Pre-Administration Papers, Political Files, Box 14, "Higgins," JFK Library.

270 **"The Private":** Marguerite Higgins, "The Private World of Robert and Ethel Kennedy," *McCall's*, Feb. 1962.

270 **"RSVP," "forbidding":** Marguerite Higgins, "RSVP The White House," *McCall's*, Aug. 1962.

270 **"Jack always," "Kennedy would":** James P. O'Donnell, recorded interview by Sheldon Stern, July 16, 1981, John F. Kennedy Library Oral History Program, JFK Library.

271 **"Marguerite," "But Jack," "Look":** Ibid.

271 **"She had," "platonic," "she could":** Ibid.

271 **"Few presidents":** Steel, *Walter Lippmann*, p. 538.

271 **"For a newspaperman," "got it right":** Bradlee, *A Good Life*, p. 208.

273 **"CONGRATULATIONS":** Telegram, Marguerite Higgins to John F. Kennedy, July 16, 1960, John F. Kennedy Papers, President's Office Files, Box 541, "Higgins, Marguerite, 1960," JFK Library.

273 **"chaotic last," "I, of course":** Letter, John F. Kennedy to Marguerite Higgins, Aug. 8, 1960, John F. Kennedy Papers, President's Office Files, Box 541, "Higgins, Marguerite, 1960," JFK Library.

273 **"Summer Scandal," "to win":** *New York Herald Tribune*, Sept. 6, 1960.

273 **"Congolese Hostile," "As we":** Ibid., March 15, 1961.

274 **"fire-horse flamboyance," "Is it courage":** "Maggie in the Congo," *Newsweek*, April 3, 1961.

275 **"care and feeding"**: Donovan, interview by Richard Kluger, Nov. 10, 1981, Box 4, Richard Kluger Papers, Manuscripts and Archives, Yale University Library, New Haven, CT.

275 **"frozen out"**: "Periscoping the Press," *Newsweek*, Nov. 28, 1960.

275 **"I want peace," "If that's true," *Vostok***: Jeremy Isaacs and Taylor Downing, *Cold War: An Illustrated History, 1945–1991* (New York: Little, Brown, 1998), p. 173.

276 **"a very sober"**: Smith, *Lucius D. Clay*, p. 634.

276 **"The Next," "in Laos"**: *New York Herald Tribune*, June 19, 1961; Richard Reeves, *President Kennedy: Profile of Power* (New York: Simon & Schuster, 1993), p. 177.

277 **"Take it easy," "Permit me," "No American"**: Eleanor Lansing Dulles, *The Wall: A Tragedy in Three Acts* (Columbia: University of South Carolina Press, 1972), pp. 48–49; *Der Speigel*, Feb. 8, 1966; Norman Gelb, *The Berlin Wall* (New York: Sharpe Books, 1986), pp. 261–62; Russ Braley, *Bad News: The Foreign Policy of the New York Times* (Chicago: Regnery Gateway, 1984), pp. 111–14.

277 **"all hell," "Wake them up"**: O'Donnell, interview by Stern, July 16, 1981; Braley, *Bad News*, p. 113.

278 **"our lives," "Tyranny's days"**: *New York Herald Tribune*, Aug. 20, 1961.

278 **"The Clay mission"**: O'Donnell, interview by Stern, July 16, 1981.

279 **"Five more"**: *New York Herald Tribune*, Sept. 4, 1961.

279 **"the firebug"**: Reeves, *President Kennedy*, p. 214.

279 **"I am most"**: Letter, Marguerite Higgins to Jacqueline ("Jackie") Kennedy, Jan. 20, 1962, Box 7, Correspondence, Jackie Kennedy, Marguerite Higgins Papers, SCRC.

279 **"surprised," "Bob and I"**: Letter, Marguerite Higgins to John F. Kennedy, March 8, 1962, Papers of John F. Kennedy, Presidential Papers, President's Office Files, General Correspondence, 1962: HE-HOG, JFKOF 010–02–0074; Box 19, Correspondence, White House, Marguerite Higgins Papers, SCRC.

280 **"I resent," "Pierre"**: Letter, Marguerite Higgins to Robert F. Kennedy, March 6, 1962, Papers of John F. Kennedy, Presidential Papers, President's Office Files, General Correspondence, 1962: HE-HOG, JFKOF 010–02–0074; Box 19, Correspondence, White House, Marguerite Higgins Papers, SCRC.

280 **"a number," "You have"**: Letter, Robert F. Kennedy to Marguerite Higgins, March 16, 1962, Papers of John F. Kennedy, Presidential Papers, President's Office Files, General Correspondence, 1962: HE-HOG, JFKOF 010–02–0074; Box 19, Correspondence, White House, Marguerite Higgins Papers, SCRC.

280 **"the Golden Age"**: Peter Lisagor and Marguerite Higgins, *Overtime in Heaven: Adventures in the Foreign Service* (New York: Doubleday, 1964), pp. 2–3.

281 **"We thought"**: Letter, Marguerite Higgins to John F. Kennedy, Sept. 3, 1963, Papers of John F. Kennedy, Presidential Papers, President's Office Files, JFKOF-018–001-p0012, Folder: 1963: HI; Marguerite Higgins Papers, Box 7, Correspondence, John F. Kennedy, Marguerite Higgins Papers, SCRC.

281 **"They were having," "a little"**: Carl T. Rowan, *Breaking Barriers: A Memoir* (New York: Harper Perennial, 1991), p. 237.

281 **"a reporter's reporter"**: *Washington Post*, May 29, 1983.

281 **"very intense," "She had," "She was":** Lisagor, interview by Keeshen, Dec. 12, 1972.

282 **"unauthorized disclosure":** *New York Herald Tribune*, March 14, 1962; "Unauthorized Disclosures of Classified Information," Dec. 1, 1958–Aug. 5, 1963, Series 05, Subject: National Security and Defense/News Media, Papers of John F. Kennedy, Presidential Papers, National Security Files, JFKNSF-310-006.

282 **"It is understood":** *New York Herald Tribune*, Feb. 2, 1962.

282 **Maggie's Cuba tip:** *Time*, Jan. 14, 1966; Fred Farris, interview by Richard Kluger, 1982, Box 4, Richard Kluger Papers, Manuscripts and Archives, Yale University Library, New Haven, CT.

283 **"act of aggression":** Isaacs and Downing, *Cold War*, pp. 194–202; Reeves, *President Kennedy*, pp. 398–99, 420–21.

283 **"cause of freedom":** *New York Herald Tribune*, Nov. 5 and 26, 1962.

283 **"The New Frontier," "one battle":** Ibid., Dec. 31, 1962.

CHAPTER 17: WAR OF WORDS

285 **"A few weeks ago":** "The View from Saigon," *Time*, Sept. 20, 1963.

285 **"Could she go":** Higgins, *Our Vietnam Nightmare*, p. 1.

286 **"miracle of Asia":** Isaacs and Downing, *Cold War*, p. 208.

286 **"until we win":** *New York Herald Tribune*, Aug. 28, 1963.

287 **"a black eye," "Don't leave":** Higgins, *Our Vietnam Nightmare*, pp. 3–4.

287 **"What is needed":** Edward C. Keefer and Louis J. Smith, eds., *Foreign Relations of the United States, 1961–1963, Volume III, Vietnam, January–August 1963* (Washington, DC: Government Printing Office, 1991), Document 207: "Report by the Joint Chief of Staff's Special Assistant for Counterinsurgency and Special Activities (Krulak)."

288 **"they were softening up":** *New York Herald Tribune*, July 28, 1963.

288 **"it would be hard," "I don't *represent*," "10, 15," "What did":** *New York Herald Tribune*, Aug. 27, 1963; Higgins, *Our Vietnam Nightmare*, pp. 33–35.

289 **"Rover Boys":** Prochnau, *Once upon a Distant War*, p. 332.

289 **"one session":** David Halberstam, *The Making of a Quagmire: America and Vietnam during the Kennedy Era* (Lanham, MD: Rowman & Littlefield, 2008), p. 83.

289 **"an incompetent":** David Halberstam, *The Powers That Be* (New York: Knopf, 1979), p. 449.

289 **"the invention":** Neil Sheehan, *A Bright Shining Lie: John Paul Vann and America in Vietnam* (New York: Random House, 1988), p. 347.

290 **"Four days":** Prochnau, *Once upon a Distant War*, p. 333.

290 **"Dragon Lady," "barbecues":** Higgins, *Our Vietnam Nightmare*, pp. 59–63.

290 **"Marguerite Higgins was":** "Vietnam: A Television History; Interview with David Halberstam, 1979 [part 3 of 5]," interview by Stanley Karnow, Jan. 16, 1979, GBH Archives, http://openvault.wgbh.org/catalog/V_A0BD959F4CB841FB9145B55A5 EBBF257.

291 **"Those arrogant upstarts":** Browne, *Muddy Boots*, p. 183.

291 **"You know," "No, we are":** Peter Arnett, email to author, Nov. 12, 2022.

292 **"Five O'Clock":** Beverly Deepe Keever, *Death Zones and Darling Spies: Seven Years of Vietnam War Reporting* (Lincoln: University of Nebraska Press, 2013), p. 82.

292   **"Why can't you"**: Browne, *Muddy Boots*, p. 163.

292   **"young and inexperienced"**: Ibid., p. 155.

292   **"boorish behavior"**: Keyes Beech, "Some Observations on Vietnam," presented at a US Army War College faculty seminar on military-press relations, April 26, 1978, published as Appendix A in "Press Coverage of the Vietnam War: The Third View" (draft report) by William V. Kennedy (Carlisle Barracks, PA: Strategic Studies Institute, US Army War College, May 25, 1979).

292   **"generation gap"**: Beech, "Not without the Americans," pp. 304–5.

293   **"The embassy," "Partly that"**: Higgins, *Our Vietnam Nightmare*, pp. 125–26.

293   **"in a matter of days"**: "Saigon Summary," Speech of Hon. Thomas J. Dodd of CT, *Congressional Record*, vol. 110 (Jan. 14, 1964).

294   **"I maintain"**: *New York Herald Tribune*, Aug. 25, 1963.

294   **"VIETNAM—FACT AND FICTION," "cut through"**: Editor's note, *New York Herald Tribune*, Aug. 26, 1963.

294   **"seldom told"**: *New York Herald Tribune*, Aug. 26, 1963.

294   **"media events," "After 18 months"**: Ibid.; Higgins, *Our Vietnam Nightmare*, pp. 25–27.

294   **"majority," "perhaps fifteen"**: *New York Herald Tribune*, Aug. 26, 1963.

294   **"Catholic," "Why do American"**: Ibid., Aug. 27, 1963.

295   **"deteriorated," "opposite," "The tragic irony"**: Ibid., Aug. 26, 1963.

295   **"anything scurrilous"**: Ibid., Aug. 27, 1963.

295   **"strategic hamlet"**: Ibid., Aug. 28, 1963.

296   **"helping to compound," "Caravelle camaraderie," "But the balm"**: "View from Saigon."

296   **"egregious crusade"**: John Mecklin, *Mission in Torment* (New York: Doubleday, 1965), p. 120.

296   **"a political time," "a Marguerite"**: "View from Saigon."

297   **"INFORMATIVELY," "WHAT IS," "ON THAT," "MAGGIE COPY"**: Prochnau, *Once upon a Distant War*, pp. 397–98.

298   **"IF YOU SEND"**: "The Press: Foreign Correspondents; The Saigon Story," *Time*, Oct. 11, 1963; Sheehan, *Bright Shining Lie*, p. 349.

298   **"I'm combative"**: "Vietnam: A Television History; Interview with David Halberstam."

298   **"Anything—even"**: Higgins, *Our Vietnam Nightmare*, p. 128.

298   **"Reporters here"**: Ibid.; "The Press: Foreign Correspondents: The Saigon Story"; Higgins denied ever saying it in John Hohenberg, *Foreign Correspondence: The Great Reporters and Their Times* (Syracuse, NY: Syracuse University Press, 1965), p. 446.

298   **"typewriter strategists"**: Higgins, *Our Vietnam Nightmare*, p. 131.

299   **"People in the," "the penultimate"**: "Vietnam: A Television History; Interview with David Halberstam."

299   **"Tears were for," "Hemingway heroes"**: David Halberstam, "A Letter to My Daughter," *Boston Globe*, May 2, 1982.

299   **"My name is," "Yes," "I want to tell"**: There are many versions of the tale: Halberstam, "Letter to My Daughter"; Halberstam, "Getting the Story in Vietnam," *Commentary*, Jan. 1, 1965; Prochnau, *Once upon a Distant War*, pp. 394–95.

300 **"Well, it's not"**: Prochnau, *Once upon a Distant War*, pp. 394–95.

300 **"It was a cat-and-dog"**: Beverly Deepe, interview by the author, April 21, 2021.

300 **"I never got"**: Ibid.

300 **"sold out"**: Prochnau, *Once upon a Distant War*, p. 333.

300 **"She covered"**: Beverly Deepe, interview by the author, April 21, 2021.

300 **"Being the"**: Joyce Hoffmann, *On Their Own: Women Journalists and the American Experience in Vietnam* (Cambridge, MA: Da Capo Press, 2008), p. 127.

300 **"allegedly informed," "See last," "It seems"**: Letter, Marguerite Higgins to Robert F. Kennedy, Sept. 20, 1963, Papers of John F. Kennedy, Presidential Papers, President's Office Files, JFKOF-018–001-p0012, Folder: 1963: HI.

301 **"Unless the Viet," "Could I come"**: Letter, Marguerite Higgins to John F. Kennedy, Sept. 3, 1963, Papers of John F. Kennedy, Presidential Papers, President's Office Files, JFKOF-018–001-p0012, Folder: 1963: HI; Box 7, Correspondence, John F. Kennedy, Marguerite Higgins Papers, SCRC.

301 **"A diplomatic," "a kind of"**: *New York Herald Tribune*, Sept. 24, 1963.

301 **"get-Diem"**: Ibid., Oct. 2, 1963.

302 **"Higgins's reports"**: Braley, *Bad News*, p. 231.

302 **"last straw"**: Letter, Marguerite Higgins to John Hay "Jock" Whitney, Jan. 30, 1964, Box 19, Correspondence, John Hay "Jock" Whitney, Marguerite Higgins Papers, SCRC.

302 **"Holy Mother Church"**: "The Press," *Time*, Jan. 17, 1966.

302 **"Leaving the *Trib*"**: "Maggie's Move," *Newsweek*, Oct. 21, 1963.

303 **"Are they"**: Higgins, *Our Vietnam Nightmare*, pp. 224–25.

303 **"Congratulations," "How does," "Oh, come on"**: Ibid.

303 **"new mess"**: *Newsday*, Nov. 22, 1963.

303 **"We've had a hand," "the worst"**: Keever, *Death Zones and Darling Spies*, p. 117.

303 **"play God"**: Mecklin, *Mission in Torment*, p. 146.

303 **"It was a valiant"**: Braley, *Bad News*, p. 242.

304 **"By becoming a party"**: Kennedy, "Press Coverage of the Vietnam War," p. 25.

304 **"Who was he," "was parrot"**: Deepe, interview by the author, April 21, 2021.

305 **"Her name"**: Prochnau, *Once upon a Distant War*, p. 333.

305 **"He cared," "He was"**: Gay Talese, interview by author, Dec. 8, 2021.

305 **"I think the boys"**: George J. W. Goodman, "Our Man in Saigon," *Esquire*, Jan. 1, 1964.

306 **"It was a great storm"**: "Vietnam: A Television History; Interview with David Halberstam."

306 **"war of words"**: "Dateline, Saigon: War of Words," *Newsweek*, Oct. 7, 1963.

306 **"For the military"**: Neil Sheehan, E. W. Kenworthy, et al., *The Pentagon Papers as Published by the New York Times* (Toronto: Bantam Books, 1971).

306 **"they were all," "alibi books," "closing"**: Braley, *Bad News*, p. 258.

CHAPTER 18: A LEGEND

308 **"To underestimate"**: Prochnau, *Once upon a Distant War*, pp. 333–34.

309 **"torrent of," "infinite compassion"**: *Newsday*, Dec. 28, 1963.

310 **"Who are you?," "I could"**: Ibid., Jan. 27, 1964; *Los Angeles Times*, Jan. 11, 1964.

310   **"I got a lot"**: Rowan, *Breaking Barriers*, pp. 238–39.

310   **"Bill, let's"**: Notes on Marguerite Higgins Luncheon; *Newsday*, Jan. 27, 1964.

310   **"He was," "Johnson," "enjoyed"**: *Newsday*, Jan. 27, 1964.

311   **"Johnson has now," "more top"**: Ibid., Jan. 26, 1964.

311   **"I could almost," "nice"**: Rowan, *Breaking Barriers*, p. 240.

311   **"Irish mafia"**: James P. O'Donnell, recorded interview by Sheldon Stern, July 16, 1981, John F. Kennedy Library Oral History Program.

311   **"If I had walked"**: *Newsday*, Jan. 15, 1964.

312   **"He is back," "President Kennedy"**: Ibid.

312   **"up in the air"**: Letter, Marguerite Higgins to Robert F. Kennedy, Aug. 5, 1964, Box 6, Correspondence, Harper & Row, Marguerite Higgins Papers, SCRC.

313   **"Kennedy magic," instinctive"**: *Newsday*, Sept. 28 and Oct. 2, 1964.

313   **"close to the news"**: Letter, Marguerite Higgins to William "Bill" J. Woestendiek, Feb. 13, 1964, Box 19, Newsday, Marguerite Higgins Papers, SCRC.

313   **"Those 'assurances,'" "negotiate," "On the Spot"**: Letter, Marguerite Higgins to William "Bill" J. Woestendiek, Feb. 25, 1964, Box 19, Newsday, Marguerite Higgins Papers, SCRC.

313   **"formal farewell," "hoped that," "If Jim"**: Letter, Higgins to Whitney, Jan. 30, 1964.

314   **"I had known," "Whatever," "Well," "Maggie"**: Thomas B. Dorsey, interview by Robert Keeler, Oct. 30, 1987, Robert Keeler Papers, Stonybrook, NY; Robert E. Keeler, *Newsday: A Candid History of the Respectable Tabloid* (New York: Arbor House, 1990).

314   **"The best kept," "delivering, "historic mission"**: *Newsday*, Aug. 4, 1964.

315   **"an exclusive," "This national"**: Ray Erwin, "Marguerite Higgins Breaks Cuba Story," *Editor & Publisher*, Aug. 15, 1964.

315   **"Lady on the Spot"**: Newsday Specials Advertisement, undated, Box 19, Correspondence, Newsday, Marguerite Higgins Papers, SCRC.

315   **"Small wonder," "I gladly"**: Bernice Buresh, "Maggie, Gal Reporter," *Columbia Journalism Review*, Jan./Feb. 1984.

316   **"Ugly Americans"**: Marguerite Higgins, "Ugly Americans of Vietnam," *America*, Oct. 3, 1964.

316   **"dip into," "When you"**: Letter, Higgins to Crosby Noyes, Sept. 29, 1964, Box 11, Correspondence, Evening Star, Marguerite Higgins papers, SCRC.

316   **"reform," "The good Americans"**: Higgins, "Ugly Americans of Vietnam."

316   **"friendly to"**: Documentary transcript, National Educational Television (NET), undated 1964, Marguerite Higgins Papers, SCRC; Marguerite Higgins, "Is the United States Responsible?," *Report*, Dec. 1964.

317   **"I told you so"**: Letter, Thomas B. Dorsey to Marguerite Higgins, Sept. 23, 1964, Box 3 and 19, Correspondence, Newsday, Marguerite Higgins Papers, SCRC.

317   **"to take all necessary"**: Clarence R. Wyatt, *Paper Soldiers: The American Press and the Vietnam War* (New York: W. W. Norton, 1993), pp. 130–31.

317   **"The torpedo boats"**: *Newsday*, Aug. 10, 1964.

317   **"the great American," "The thesis"**: Letter, Marguerite Higgins to Evan Thomas, Executive Vice President, Harper & Row, Oct. 12, 1964, Box 6, Correspondence, Harper & Row, Marguerite Higgins Papers, SCRC.

318   **"twilight zone," "professional":** *Newsday*, Nov. 18, 1964.

318   **"The weapons":** Ibid., Dec. 2, 1964.

318   **"it is," "to be fought":** Ibid., Dec. 18, 1964.

319   **"She was in":** Lisagor, interview by Keeshen, Dec. 12, 1972.

319   **"the internationally-known":** *Oakland Tribune*, Nov. 28, 1964; *San Francisco Chronicle*, Nov. 29, 1964.

319   **"But I would," "I did it":** Letter, Marguerite Higgins to Tom Dorsey, Dec. 11, 1964, Box 4, Correspondence, Newsday, Marguerite Higgins Papers, SCRC.

320   **"Give me just":** Letter, Marguerite Higgins to Thomas Dorsey, Nov. 13, 1964, Box 3 and 19, Correspondence, Newsday, Marguerite Higgins Papers, SCRC.

321   **"but the joke," "untakeable":** Letter, Marguerite Higgins to Tom Dorsey, Jan. 29, 1965, Box 3 and 19, Correspondence, Newsday, Marguerite Higgins Papers, SCRC.

322   **"hardly pays":** *Ft. Lauderdale News*, March 10, 1964.

322   **"But I do like":** *Oakland Tribune*, Sept. 10, 1965.

322   **"I was typecast":** *Los Angeles Times*, Jan. 11, 1965.

322   **"What makes," "would always be":** Higgins, *News Is a Singular Thing*, p. 252.

323   **"furiously conflicting":** Higgins, *Our Vietnam Nightmare*, p. 5.

323   **"nervous and prone":** Letter, Marguerite Higgins to Evan Thomas, March 31, 1965, Box 6, Correspondence, Harper & Row, Marguerite Higgins Papers, SCRC.

323   **"a sadly unnecessary":** Letter, Marguerite Higgins to Evan Thomas, Oct. 12, 1964, Box 6, Correspondence, Harper & Row, Marguerite Higgins Papers, SCRC.

323   **"second thoughts":** Higgins, *Our Vietnam Nightmare*, pp. 214, 211.

323   **"Our Vietnamese":** Ibid., p. 314.

323   **"minority report":** Ibid., dustjacket.

323   **"Dangerous as":** Ibid., p. 314.

324   **"sensed":** Letter, Marguerite Higgins to Mrs. Marguerite Munson, Oct. 12, 1964, Box 6, Correspondence, Harper & Row, Marguerite Higgins Papers, SCRC.

324   **"It seems":** Letter, Marguerite Higgins to Evan Thomas, July 21, 1965, Box 6, Correspondence, Harper & Row, Marguerite Higgins Papers, SCRC.

324   **"blur," "national interest," I don't know":** Ibid.

324   **"more palatable":** Cable, Marguerite Higgins to Evan Thomas, July 22, 1965, Box 6, Correspondence, Harper & Row, Marguerite Higgins Papers, SCRC.

325   **"I'm utterly":** Letter, Marguerite Higgins to Thomas Dorsey, Aug. 4, 1965, Box 3 and 19, Correspondence, Newsday, Marguerite Higgins Papers, SCRC.

325   **"hassle":** Letter, Marguerite Higgins to Thomas Dorsey, Aug. 1965, Box 3 and 19, Correspondence, Newsday, Marguerite Higgins Papers, SCRC.

325   **"Beginning with WWII":** *Newsday*, Oct. 25, 1965.

326   **"You should," "Maggie," "Oh, I can't," "Look":** Thomas Dorsey, interview by Robert Keeler, Oct. 30, 1987, Robert Keeler Papers, Stonybrook, NY.

326   **"not unwilling":** Cable, Marguerite Higgins to Tom Dorsey, Oct. 5, 1965, Box 3 and 19, Correspondence, Newsday, Marguerite Higgins Papers, SCRC.

326   **"I'm afraid," "If you will":** Letter, Marguerite Higgins to Tom Dorsey, Oct. 25, 1965, Box 3 and 19, Correspondence, Newsday, Marguerite Higgins Papers, SCRC.

327   **"I wasn't":** Hall, interview by Keeshen, Feb. 26, 1973.

327   **"She could be":** Lisagor, interview by Keeshen, Dec. 12, 1972.

327   **"certain to":** Higgins, *Our Vietnam Nightmare*, dustjacket.

328   **"helping her," "She's going":** Thomas Dorsey, interview by Robert Keeler, Oct. 30, 1987, Robert Keeler Papers, Stonybrook, NY; Keeler, *Newsday: A Candid History*, p. 352.

328   **"The bravery":** *Newsday*, Nov. 10, 1965.

328   **"treat the problem":** Ibid., Dec. 31, 1965.

329   **"kill ratio":** Harold G. Moore and Joseph L. Galloway, *We Were Soldiers Once . . . and Young: Ian Drang, the Battle That Changed the War in Vietnam* (New York: Random House, 1992), p. 339.

329   **"unprecedented victory":** William M. Hammond, *Reporting Vietnam: Media and the Military at War* (Lawrence: University Press of Kansas, 1998), p. 68.

329   **"She suffered," "Yes, this is":** Thomas Dorsey, interview by Robert Keeler, Oct. 30, 1987, Robert Keeler Papers, Stonybrook, NY.

330   **"Did you think":** Letter, Ruth Montgomery to Kathleen Kearney Keeshen, Sept. 4, 1975, KKKP.

330   **"Thank you," "She was an absolutely":** Hall, interview by Keeshen, Feb. 26, 1973.

330   **"She was sick":** Lawrence O'Higgins Hall, interview by author, March 2021.

331   **"There was steel," "Marguerite Higgins":** *New York Times*, Jan. 4, 1966.

331   **"combat casualty":** M. L. Stein, *Under Fire: The Story of American War Correspondents* (New York: Julian Messner, 1968), p. 223.

332   **"She had soldier-like":** *Newsday*, Jan. 5, 1966.

332   **"For twenty years":** Parton, *Journey through a Lighted Room*, p. 204.

332   **"Maggie was a cross":** "Maggie," *Newsweek*, Jan. 17, 1966.

332   **"She made me":** Ibid.

ARCHIVES AND LIBRARIES

Dwight D. Eisenhower Presidential Library, Abilene, KS

Getty Images Archive

Harry S. Truman Presidential Library, Independence, MO

Imperial War Museum, London, UK

John F. Kennedy Presidential Library, Boston, MA

Kathleen Kearney Keeshen Papers, Private Archive

Library of Congress, Washington, DC

Lyndon B. Johnson Library, Austin, TX

National Archives and Records Administration, College Park, MD

Proquest Historical Newspapers

Robert E. Keeler Papers, Private Archive

Special Collections Research Center, Syracuse University Libraries, Syracuse, NY

Sterling Memorial Library, Yale University, New Haven, CT

United States Holocaust Memorial Museum, Washington, DC

University of Southern California Shoah Foundation, Institute
for Visual History and Education, Los Angeles, CA

SELECTED BIBLIOGRAPHY

Alsop, Joseph W., and Adam Platt. *"I've Seen the Best of It": Memoirs*. New York: W. W. Norton, 1992.

Arnett, Peter. *Live from the Battlefield: From Vietnam to Baghdad; 35 Years in the World's War Zones*. New York: Simon & Schuster, 1994.

Baehr, Harry W. Jr. *The New York Tribune since the Civil War*. New York: Dodd, Mead, 1936.

Beasley, Maurine H., and Sheila J. Gibbons. *Taking Their Place: A Documentary History of Women and Journalism*. State College, PA: Strata Publishing, 1993.

Beech, Keyes. *Tokyo and Points East*. Tokyo: Charles E. Tuttle, 1955.

———. *Not without the Americans: A Personal History*. New York: Doubleday, 1971.

Belford, Barbara. *Brilliant Bylines: A Biographical Anthology of Notable Newspaperwomen in America*. New York: Columbia University Press, 1986.

Bourke-White, Margaret. *Portrait of Myself*. New York: Simon & Schuster, 1949.

———. *They Called It "Purple Heart Valley."* New York: Simon & Schuster, 1944.

Bradlee, Ben. *A Good Life: Newspapering and Other Adventures*. New York: Simon & Schuster, 1995.

Braley, Russ. *Bad News: The Foreign Policy of the New York Times*. Chicago: Regnery Gateway, 1984.

Browne, Malcolm W. *Muddy Boots and Red Socks: A Reporter's Life*. New York: Times Books, 1993.

Buell, Thomas A. *Naval Leadership in Korea: The First Six Months*. Washington, DC: Naval Historical Center, Department of the Navy, 2002.

Casey, Steven. *Selling the Korean War: Propaganda, Politics, and Public Opinion 1950–1953*. Oxford: Oxford University Press, 2008.

Chamberlain, John. *A Life with the Printed Word*. Chicago: Regnery Gateway, 1982.

Clay, Lucius D. *Decision in Germany*. New York: Doubleday, 1950.

Dann, Sam, ed. *Dachau 29 April 1945: The Rainbow Liberation Memoirs*. Lubbock: Texas Tech University Press, 1998.

Dulles, Eleanor Lansing. *The Wall: A Tragedy in Three Acts*. Columbia: University of South Carolina Press, 1972.

Edwards, Julia. *Women of the World: The Great Foreign Correspondents*. Boston: Houghton Mifflin, 1988.

Elwood-Akers, Virginia. *Women War Correspondents in the Vietnam War, 1961–1975*. Metuchen, NJ: Scarecrow Press, 1988.

Emery, Michael. *On the Front Lines: Following America's Foreign Correspondents across the*

Twentieth Century. Washington, DC: American University Press, 1995.

Fleming, Alice M. *Reporters at War*. New York: Cowles, 1970.

Gelb, Norman. *The Berlin Wall*. New York: Sharpe Books, 1986.

Gellhorn, Martha, and Virginia Cowles. *Love Goes to Press: A Comedy in Three Acts*. Lincoln: University of Nebraska Press, 2009. First published 1995.

Goldberg, Vicki. *Margaret Bourke-White: A Biography*. Reading, MA: Addison-Wesley, 1987.

Greene, Graham. *The Quiet American*. New York: Penguin Books, 1955.

Gun, Nerin E. *The Day of the Americans*. New York: Fleet, 1966.

Halberstam, David. *The Best and the Brightest*. New York: Harper & Row, 1967.

———. *The Making of a Quagmire: America and Vietnam during the Kennedy Era*. Lanham, MD: Rowman & Littlefield, 2008.

———. *The Powers That Be*. New York: Knopf, 1979.

Hallin, Daniel C. *The "Uncensored War": The Media and Vietnam*. Berkeley: University of California Press, 1989.

Hammer, Ellen J. *A Death in November: America in Vietnam, 1963*. New York: E. P. Dutton, 1987.

Hammond, William M. *Reporting Vietnam: Media and the Military at War*. Lawrence: University Press of Kansas, 1998.

Harrington, Daniel F. *"The Air Force Can Deliver Anything!": A History of the Berlin Air Lift*. Washington, DC: USAFE Office of History, Jan. 1998.

Hartwell, Dickson, and Andy A. Rooney, eds. *Off the Record: The Best Stories of Foreign Correspondents*. New York: Doubleday, 1953.

Hawkins, Eric. *Hawkins of the Paris Herald*. New York: Simon & Schuster, 1963.

Hemingway, Mary Welsh. *How It Was*. New York: Knopf, 1976.

Higgins, Marguerite. *Jesse Benton Fremont: California Pioneer*. Boston: Houghton Mifflin, 1962.

———. *News Is a Singular Thing*. Garden City, NY: Doubleday, 1955.

———. *Our Vietnam Nightmare: The Story of U.S. Involvement in the Vietnamese Tragedy, with Thoughts on a Future Policy*. New York: Harper & Row, 1965.

———. *Red Plush and Black Bread*. Garden City, NY: Doubleday, 1955.

———. *War in Korea: The Report of a Woman Combat Correspondent*. Garden City, NY: Doubleday, 1951.

Hoffmann, Joyce. *On Their Own: Women Journalists and the American Experience in Vietnam*. Cambridge, MA: Da Capo Press, 2008.

Hohenberg, John. *Foreign Correspondence: The Great Reporters and Their Times*. Syracuse, NY: Syracuse University Press, 1965.

———. *The Pulitzer Prizes: A History of the Awards in Books, Drama, Music and Journalism, Based on the Private Files over Six Decades*. New York: Columbia University Press, 1974.

Howard, Toni. *Shriek with Pleasure*. New York: Pyramid Books, 1950.

Ilma, Viola. *The Political Virgin*. New York: Duell, Sloan and Pearce, 1958.

Isaacs, Jeremy, and Taylor Downing. *Cold War: An Illustrated History, 1945–1991*. New York: Little, Brown, 1998.

Jager, Sheila Miyoshi. *Brothers at War: The Unending Conflict in Korea.* New York: W. W. Norton, 2013.

Keeler, Robert E. *Newsday: A Candid History of the Respectable Tabloid.* New York: Arbor House, 1990.

Keever, Beverly Deepe. *Death Zones and Darling Spies: Seven Years of Vietnam War Reporting.* Lincoln: University of Nebraska Press, 2013.

Kluger, Richard. *The Paper: The Life and Death of the New York Herald Tribune.* New York: Alfred A. Knopf, 1986.

Knauth, Percy. *Germany in Defeat.* New York: Alfred A. Knopf, 1946.

Knightley, Phillip. *The First Casualty: From the Crimea to Vietnam; The War Correspondent as Hero, Propagandist, and Myth Maker.* New York: Harcourt Brace Jovanovich, 1975.

Knox, Donald. *The Korean War: Pusan to Chosin; An Oral History.* New York: Harcourt Brace Jovanovich, 1985.

Lanham, Edwin. *The Iron Maiden.* New York: Popular Library Edition, 1954.

Lawrence, Bill. *Six Presidents, Too Many Wars.* New York: Saturday Review Press, 1972.

Linden, John H. *Surrender of the Dachau Concentration Camp 29 April 45: The True Account.* Elm Grove, WI: Sycamore Press, 1997.

Lisagor, Peter, and Marguerite Higgins. *Overtime in Heaven: Adventures in the Foreign Service.* New York: Doubleday, 1964.

Lowings, Ben. *The Chancellor: George Millar; A Life.* Cowes, Isle of Wight, UK: Taniwha Press, 2021. E-book.

Malcolm, Janet. *The Journalist and the Murderer.* New York: Vintage, 1990.

Man, John. *Berlin Blockade.* New York: Ballantine Books, 1971.

Marzolf, Marion. *Up from the Footnote: A History of Women Journalists.* New York: Hastings House, 1977.

Mathews, Joseph J. *Reporting the Wars.* Minneapolis: University of Minnesota Press, 1957.

May, Antoinette. *Witness to War: A Biography of Marguerite Higgins.* New York: Beaufort Books, 1983.

McManus, John C. *Hell before Their Very Eyes: American Soldiers Liberate Concentration Camps in Germany, April 1945.* Baltimore: Johns Hopkins University Press, 2015.

Mecklin, John. *Mission in Torment.* New York: Doubleday, 1965.

Merry, Robert W. *Taking on the World: Joseph and Stewart Alsop—Guardians of the American Century.* New York: Viking, 1996.

Middleton, Drew. *Where Has Last July Gone?* New York: New York Times Book, 1973.

Millar, George. *Horned Pigeon: The Great Escape Story of World War II.* London: Cassell, 1946.

———. *Maquis.* London: William Heinemann, 1945.

———. *Road to Resistance: An Autobiography.* London: Bodley Head, 1979.

Mills, Kay. *A Place in the News: From the Women's Pages to the Front Page.* New York: Columbia University Press, 1988.

Montgomery, Ruth. *Hail to the Chiefs: My Life and Times with Six Presidents.* New York: Howard McCann, 1970.

Moore, Harold G., and Joseph L. Galloway. *We Were Soldiers Once . . . and Young: Ian Drang, the Battle That Changed the War in Vietnam.* New York: Random House, 1992.

Moorehead, Caroline. *Gellhorn: A Twentieth-Century Life*. New York: Henry Holt, 2003.

Mydans, Carl. *More Than Meets the Eye*. New York: Harper & Brothers, 1959.

O'Donnell, James. *The Bunker: The History of the Reich Chancellery Group*. Boston: Houghton Mifflin, 1978.

Oldfield, Barney. *Never a Shot in Anger*. New York: Duell, Sloan and Pierce, 1956.

Parton, Margaret. *Journey through a Lighted Room*. New York: Viking Press, 1973.

Penrose, Antony. *Lee Miller's War*. Boston: Little, Brown, 1992.

——. *The Lives of Lee Miller*. New York: Holt, Rhinehart & Winston, 1985.

Pomeroy, Charles, ed. *Foreign Correspondents in Japan: Reporting a Half Century of Upheavals; From 1945 to the Present*. Rutland, VT: Charles E. Tuttle, 1998.

Prochnau, William. *Once upon a Distant War: David Halberstam, Neil Sheehan, Peter Arnett—Young War Correspondents and Their Early Vietnam Battles*. New York: Vintage, 1995.

Reeves, Richard. *Daring Young Men: The Heroism and Triumph of the Berlin Airlift, June 1948–May 1949*. New York: Simon & Schuster, 2010.

——. *President Kennedy: Profile of Power*. New York: Simon & Schuster, 1993.

Reynolds, Quentin. *Leave It to the People*. New York: Random House, 1948.

Rollyson, Carl. *Nothing Ever Happens to the Brave: The Story of Martha Gellhorn*. New York: St. Martin's Press, 1990.

Rooney, Andy. *My War*. New York: Public Affairs, 1995.

Ross, Ishbel. *Ladies of the Press*. New York: Harper & Brothers, 1936.

Rothmeyer, Karen. *Winning Pulitzers: The Stories behind Some of the Best News Coverage of Our Time*. New York: Columbia University Press, 1991.

Rowan, Carl T. *Breaking Barriers: A Memoir*. New York: Harper Perennial, 1991.

Russ, Martin. *Breakout: The Chosin Reservoir River Campaign, Korea 1950*. New York: Fromm International, 1999.

Schilpp, Madelon Golden, and Sharon M. Murphy. *Great Women of the Press*. Carbondale: Southern Illinois University Press, 1983.

Selzer, Michael. *Deliverance Day: The Last Hours at Dachau*. Philadelphia: J. B. Lippincott, 1978.

Settel, Arthur, ed. *This Is Germany*. New York: Houghton Mifflin, 1950.

Sevareid, Eric. *Not So Wild a Dream*. New York: Alfred A. Knopf, 1947.

Sheehan, Neil. *A Bright Shining Lie: John Paul Vann and America in Vietnam*. New York: Random House, 1988.

Sheehan, Neil, E. W. Kenworthy, et al. *The Pentagon Papers as Published by the New York Times*. Toronto: Bantam Books, 1971.

Sicherman, Barbara, and Carol Hurd Green, eds. *Notable American Women: The Modern Period*. Cambridge, MA: Belknap Press of Harvard University Press, 1980.

Smith, Jean Edward. *Lucius D. Clay: An American Life*. New York: Henry Holt, 1990.

Sorel, Nancy Caldwell. *The Women Who Wrote the War*. New York: Arcade, 1999.

Steel, Ronald. *Walter Lippmann and the American Century*. Boston: Atlantic Monthly Press, 1980.

Stein, M. L. *Under Fire: The Story of American War Correspondents*. New York: Julian Messner, 1968.

Stivers, William, and Donald A. Carter. *The City Becomes a Symbol: The U.S. Army in the*

Occupation of Berlin, 1945–1948. Washington, DC: Center of Military History, United States Army, 2017.

Stoy, Tim. *Sharpen Your Bayonets: A Biography of Lieutenant General John Wilson "Iron Mike" O'Daniel, Commander, 3rd Infantry Division in World War II*. Philadelphia: Casemate, 2022.

Toland, John. *In Mortal Combat: Korea, 1950–1953*. New York: William Morrow, 1991.

Voorhees, Melvin B. *Korean Tales*. New York: Simon & Schuster, 1952.

Wade, Betsy, ed. *Forward Positions: The War Correspondence of Homer Bigart*. Fayetteville: University of Arkansas Press, 1992.

Walker, Stanley. *City Editor*. New York: Frederick A. Stokes, 1934.

Wicker, Tom. *On Press: A Top Reporter's Life in, and Reflections on, American Journalism*. New York: Viking Press, 1978.

Wyatt, Clarence R. *Paper Soldiers: The American Press and the Vietnam War*. New York: W. W. Norton, 1993.

ILLUSTRATION CREDITS

Frontispiece: Marguerite Higgins in helmet. Library of Congress.

Page 152: *Shriek with Pleasure* cover image. Courtesy of Wildside Press.

Page 332: Marguerite Higgins postage stamp. Peregrine / Alamy.

PHOTO INSERT

Marguerite Higgins and Chinese nurse. Photo taken by Lawrence Higgins. Marguerite Higgins Papers, Syracuse University, SCRC. Courtesy of Lawrence Hall.

Lawrence Higgins in uniform. Marguerite Higgins Papers, Syracuse University, SCRC. Courtesy of Lawrence Hall.

Maggie in rowboat. Photo taken by Lawrence Higgins. Marguerite Higgins Papers, Syracuse University, SCRC. Courtesy of Lawrence Hall.

Maggie at college. Photo taken by Lawrence Higgins. Marguerite Higgins Papers, Syracuse University, SCRC. Courtesy of Lawrence Hall.

Maggie poolside. Photo taken by Lawrence Higgins. Marguerite Higgins Papers, Syracuse University, SCRC. Courtesy of Lawrence Hall.

Graduation picture. Photo taken by Lawrence Higgins. Marguerite Higgins Papers, Syracuse University, SCRC. Courtesy of Lawrence Hall.

Professor Stanley Moore. Photo by *Oregon Journal*, courtesy of the Oregon Historical Society.

Marguerite Higgins of the *NYHT*. Library of Congress.

Helen Rogers Reid and sons, Ogden and Whitelaw Reid. Photo by Allyn Baum. The *New York Times* / Redux.

Surrender of the Dachau Concentration Camp, 1945: white flag. Photos taken by Raphael Algoet. #168990–168992. Archives générales du Royaume et Archives de l'État dans les Provinces/Cegesoma.

Surrender of the Dachau Concentration Camp, 1945: taking cover. Photos taken by Raphael Algoet. #168990–168992. Archives générales du Royaume et Archives de l'État dans les Provinces/Cegesoma.

Guarding the Waffen-SS troops at Dachau, April 29, 1945. United
States Holocaust Memorial Museum, courtesy of Sol Feingold.

George Reid Millar. Courtesy of National Archives UK.

Correspondent Marguerite Higgins at Nuremberg. US Army
Signal Corps, courtesy of NARA, 238-NT-567.

Reporters observe "Exercise Harvest," Germany, Sept. 1949. US
Army Signal Corps, courtesy of NARA, 111-SC-332749-1.

Marguerite Higgins in Korea 1950. Photo by Carl Mydans. Shutterstock.

Keyes Beech. US Marine Corps, courtesy of NARA, 127-MW-308.

Homer Bigart. AP.

Marguerite Higgins interviewing Gen. Douglas A. MacArthur in Korea, June
29, 1950. US Army Signal Corps, courtesy of NARA, 111-SC-342846.

The Korea correspondents. Shutterstock.

Marguerite Higgins asleep in a slit trench, Oryong, Aug. 1950. US Army
Signal Corps, courtesy of NARA, 111-ADC-8169-1, Source: AFCF
(A-2512 & 2513), FILM: ARCH & APC MP 519'ea Silent.

The Rover Boys, Vietnam correspondents. AP.

Marguerite Higgins and General William E. Hall
honeymoon. Photo by Clarence Hamm. AP.

Maggie with baby Lawrence. Photo taken by William Hall. Marguerite
Higgins Papers, SCRC, courtesy of Lawrence Hall.

Maggie leaving on book tour. Photo taken by William Hall. Marguerite
Higgins Papers, SCRC, courtesy of Lawrence Hall.

INDEX

Page numbers beginning with 337 refer to notes.